ARTHUR HERTZBERG

THE
JEWS
IN
AMERICA

Four Centuries of an

Uneasy Encounter:

A History

Simon and Schuster

New York   London   Toronto   Sydney   Tokyo

Simon and Schuster
Simon & Schuster Building
Rockefeller Center
1230 Avenue of the Americas
New York, New York 10020

Copyright © 1989 by Arthur Hertzberg
SIMON AND SCHUSTER and colophon are registered trade-
marks of Simon & Schuster, Inc.
Designed by Levavi & Levavi
Manufactured in the United States of America

1 3 5 7 9 10 8 6 4 2

Library of Congress Cataloging in Publication Data

Hertzberg, Arthur.
    The Jews in America : four centuries of an uneasy
encounter : a history / Arthur Hertzberg.
        p.   cm.
        1. Jews—United States—History.   2. United
States—Ethnic relations.   I. Title.
    E184.J5H566   1989
    973'.04924—dc20   89-36191
                                                       CIP

ISBN 0-671-62709-0

We gratefully acknowledge permission to reprint the following:
"To America," by H. Leyvik. Taken from *American Yiddish
Poetry: A Bilingual Anthology,* edited by Benjamin and Bar-
bara Harshav, the University of California Press. Copyright © 1986 The Regents of the University of California.
Used by permission.

"Israel and American Jewry," by Arthur Hertzberg. Reprinted from *Commentary,* August 1967, by permission; all
rights reserved.

Acknowledgments

The most pleasant task of all in writing a book is to remember and thank the many people who have helped. The greatest debt of all, I owe to my father, Harav Zvi Elimelech Herzberg, who was leader of the Chasidic community in Baltimore until his death in 1971. He said many times that American Jews were drawn overwhelmingly from one class of the Jews of Europe, the poor. Testing this remark against the evidence that I collected in research, I concluded that he had understood American Jewish experience better than almost anyone else of the last generation.

Until his untimely death in the fall of 1988, my greatest companion was Shmuel Ettinger, professor at the Hebrew University and the central figure in Jewish historical studies in Israel. In many hours of discussion in Jerusalem or Englewood, New Jersey, we often disagreed, but always agreeably. The Hebrew edition of this book will be dedicated to the memory of this great scholar and beloved friend. Much of this book was first drafted in 1982 in Jerusalem at the Institute of Advanced Studies of the Hebrew University, where I spent most of the year as Fellow. That environment reflected the generosity of spirit and high intellectual standards of the director, Professor Aryeh Dvoretsky. Henry Graff, friend and colleague in the History Department of Columbia University since 1961, helped greatly and generously with puting the specifics of the American Jewish experience in the context of American history as a whole. My colleagues and friends in the Middle East Institute at Columbia, Professors Richard Bulliet, Lisa Anderson, and Gregory Gause, have sustained me in my work.

Since the spring of 1985, I have spent most of the academic year at Dartmouth College in the Department of Religion. The chairmen under whom I have served, Ronald Green and Robert Oden, and all my colleagues in the department, have

7

ACKNOWLEDGMENTS

helped me to think my way through aspects of this text. Sandra Curtis, the academic assistant of the department, has been extraordinarily supportive. Timothy Duggan and Bernard Gert, of the Philosophy Department at Dartmouth, have been generous with their time and their counsel. On literary matters, the novelist, Alan Lelchuk, has let me impose on his knowledge and his time. Deans Hans Penner and Dwight Lahr, Associate Deans Richard Sheldon and Gregory Prince, and the executive officers Foster Blough and Robert Griesemer have provided student assistants and other forms of support. David McLaughlin and James O. Freedman, his successor as president of Dartmouth, have done everything within their power to help me; I am deeply grateful for their friendship.

This book could not have been written from the study of documents alone. I am indebted to the congregations for what I learned in more than four decades as a rabbi, ten years in Nashville, Tennessee, at the West End Synagogue, and the next twenty-nine years in Englewood, New Jersey, at Temple Emanu-El. Much of what I know about organized Jewish life I learned by being involved since my teens, and especially in the 1970s when I served as president of the American Jewish Congress, and, concurrently, as a member of the executive of the World Zionist Organization.

Many younger people helped at various stages in the research of this book. Thanks are due to Noam Marans, who worked hard with me on the question of who came to America, and Mark Friedman, who helped devotedly and intelligently on the final chapters and the "Notes on Sources." Several of my students at Dartmouth labored at producing the manuscript. Special thanks are given to Edward Nelson, Jevin Eagle, Jamie Heller, Gary Katz, Andrew Klein, and Michele Dogin. In earlier stages of the work I was helped by a number of my students at Columbia: Rena Hozore, Jay Lefkowith, Mark Segall, Steven Farber, Noah Schonfield, and Andrew Hyman. In June 1989, in Paris, Francoise Pistre volunteered to help me rewrite the last chapter, and Nancy Shore helped especially with the "Notes on Sources." William Ober, physician, historian, and friend of many years, read proof with exacting care. My greatest debt of all is to two people who worked with me through the years in Englewood, Reby Evans and Carol Ivanovski. Their devotion was extraordinary. I am deeply grateful.

Books are nurtured by other books, often very obscure ones. Scholars depend on two lifelines. One is the goodwill of librarians, and those who work in the libraries of Dartmouth, Columbia, the Jewish Theological Seminary of America, and the Hebrew University have been helpful, indulgent, and unfailingly sympathetic. The other lifeline is the support of people who care about ideas. This book exists in large part because of their generosity. I am grateful to Edgar Bronfman, to Joseph and Arlene Taub, and to Harry Starr and William Frost of the Littauer Foundation for their friendship, and for the spirited discussions with each of them which helped me formulate some of the thinking in this book.

Don Cutler has been friend and confidant through a long campaign. In the last two years, as this book was finished and rewritten, Alice Mayhew and her associate David Shipley, at Simon and Schuster, have contributed, as great editors do, to making an author do better than he set out to do. I would also like to thank Mary Solak for her fine copy editing.

The one who has given most to this book is my wife, Phyllis. She has collaborated in every sentence, and she has borne with grace all the personal deprivations that are inevitable when "a work in progress" is inside the tent. This book is dedicated to her, to our daughters, their husbands, and our first grandchild.

Arthur Hertzberg

For Phyllis,
Linda and David,
Susan and Stephen,
and Rachel,
and the other grandchildren, d.v., yet to come
that the tradition may continue

ללמד וללמד לשמר ולעשת

Contents

CONTENTS

Introduction

In 1782 St. John de Crèvecoeur, a minor French nobleman who had come to New York to farm, described America as the land of "the poor of Europe who are settled here." American history is the tale of the society that the poor, unrestrained by the "classes," created in the new land. American Jewish history is also the story of the poor: the Jewish poor of Europe, of their unique success in America, and of the new Jewishness that they fashioned in the place that they called, by turns, the "golden land" and "America, the thief," in which the dreams of many came to naught.

The Jewish community, like the rest of America, was never a random sample of all of European Jewry. Poverty and anti-Semitism pushed mostly the poor out of Europe. The better off and the better educated could, until the Nazi era, stay put and survive even in difficult times. This assertion about the class origins of Jewish migration is central to this book. Two striking facts make the point.

First, in 1906, the year when some two-hundred-thousand Jews, more than ever before or since, came to the United States, only fifty listed themselves as professionals (at that time, between five and ten percent of the Jews in the various countries of Eastern Europe, including Czarist Russia, were in the professions). The intellectual and religious traditions of American Jewry thus have shallow roots.

Second, there was in almost all the immigrants to America a conscious anti-European streak. This was especially true among the immigrant Jews who felt betrayed by the societies, the governments,

13

the rabbis, and the rich Jewish leaders who had cast them out, or, at the very least, had failed to find room for them. Such immigrants were not predisposed to construct in North America a replica of their unhappy European past. They would not allow the very people who had betrayed them in Europe to exercise authority in America. The immigrants wanted to give to their Jewishness the aroma of the religious tradition and of folk memory, but on the condition that they could decide on what they wanted to keep and remember. Their Jewishness was essentially ethnic culture.

It is a major contention of this book that this American Jewishness reached its zenith in the 1960s and the years immediately thereafter— but that this era is now over. Most American Jews are now three or even four generations removed from their immigrant origins. They are now living in a society which is more open to Jews than any before in the long history of the Diaspora; immigrant memories and ingrained fears of anti-Semitism are fading.

Why is America suddenly so open? Historians continue to argue about anti-Semitism in America. Some think it was of little account before the Civil War, but no one doubts that from the 1860s to the 1950s the prejudice was serious. It is, therefore, too convenient to maintain that America is different because it had no medieval past— no structure of systematic exclusion of Jews. Though France had a very medieval past, which included elaborate anti-Jewish legislation, the French Revolution gave Jews, and everyone else, equal citizenship. But America, by the nature of its society, was different. In France, and almost everywhere else in Europe, the state represented a majority culture which demanded that minorities assimilate. Such demands were made in America as well, even though an expanding economy needed workers from everywhere. The Puritans wanted no aliens in their Commonwealth; some of the founders of the Republic wanted to impose conformity to republican virtue; in the 1890s aristocrats and nativists joined in the fight to protect the predominance in America of the descendants of the oldest settlers.

The United States was not by its nature more virtuous than Europe. America supported slavery and, for almost a century after the Civil War, condoned Jim Crow laws. America imported Chinese coolies to help build the railroads and then refused to allow them to stay, interned Japanese Americans in 1942, and kept Catholics and Jews on the fringes of society.

INTRODUCTION

Those who fought to limit mass migration to the United States won their battle only in 1924, too late to save the dominant role in America for descendants of the older settlers. Though Jews were only about eight percent of the newcomers to the United States between 1880 and 1924, Henry Adams, the New England Brahmin, was not entirely wrong in his fulminations that the open door to America was giving Jews the chance to challenge his class. Of all the battles that American Jews fought for themselves and their brethren abroad, this was the most fateful. The victories before 1924 were the seed of a radical and permanent change in the nature of America; the defeat, which barred hundreds of thousands more from coming to America, was a preamble to the Holocaust, and even to the creation of the State of Israel.

John F. Kennedy was elected president by the excluded minorities: Catholics, blacks, Jews, and blue-collar workers, who represented various ethnic groups. The descendants of the older America voted against him. Kennedy's election was as profound a turning in American history as the end of the frontier had been in the 1890s. Even so liberal and humane a spirit as Reinhold Niebuhr, the most famous Protestant thinker of the day, asserted in 1960 that the presidency was not entirely a secular office; it represented the spirit of America, and the dominant element in the American spirit was Protestant Christianity.

The recent history of anti-Semitism in America is particularly revealing. Jews had fought for centuries for their total equality in America, and they had failed. Despite the war with the Nazis, the murder of six million Jews in Europe, and America's postwar affluence, anti-Semitism did not lessen in the late 1940s—it actually increased. Only in the 1960s did anti-semitism begin to fade. Two decades later, by the mid-1980s, Jews had become an important element in almost all of America's elite.

Very early in the story of Jews in America, those who wanted to exclude them had kept saying that admitting Jews meant opening the doors to such outlandish people as Turks and Muslims. The objectors were correct. Jews succeeded only when America became an untidy jumble of ethnic identities, ideological factions, and economic interests. The fight of Jews for total equality could not be won in confrontation with a solid majority; the victory could occur only when power was widely dispersed among many, very different "factions."

INTRODUCTION

It is not an accident that the reputation of James Madison has risen in recent years. In *Federalist Paper Number Ten* Madison, defending the proposed new Constitution of the United States in 1788, described a loosely textured society of factions. He insisted that the thirteen colonies, by then independent states, were marked by numerous divisions, in religious opinion, region, and economic class. He did not imagine for a moment that any of these identities or associations would be made to conform to each other. He argued for "representative government" because he thought those elected to office would be men who would stand beyond any particular interest and would adjudicate among them for the public good. Madison denied that any particular American virtue inhered in the culture or values of any of the "factions."

Madison's vision of the Constitution fits the new American society. The "factions" are now numerous, and none will concede to any other group the right to question its Americanism. Jews have been among the major architects of this new society. They were critical to the election of Kennedy in 1960, and their support of Israel in June 1967, before and during the Six-Day War, was an unabashed expression of Jewish solidarity in an America in which Jews had never talked up quite so boldly in their own interest. In their new boldness, Jews had really become "just like everybody else." They fought for their interests and made alliances with other groups. The difference from the past was clear and striking. In the 1860s, Judah P. Benjamin, who served as secretary of state of the Confederacy, was constantly attacked as a Jew. In the 1970s Henry Kissinger, national security adviser and secretary of state in the Nixon and Ford administrations, was a figure of controversy, but not as a Jew.

In the course of nearly four centuries, American Jews have realized their emancipation. Only in America, of all their settlements among the Gentiles, do Jews have significant power. But is this untidy American society viable? What can the "factions," including the Jews, do to ensure stability? What, for that matter, are the Jews to do with themselves? In a supremely open society, they can no longer define themselves by fear and exclusion. The era of ethnicity is ending and the question is now open: How will American Jews affirm their Jewishness? To imagine this future, we must first search the past.

1.

New Amsterdam:

The Last Stop

I

No one knows when the first Jew arrived in North America. That question cannot be answered. "New Christians," Jews who had converted to Christianity under force, were among the first Spaniards to come to Mexico. They arrived with the conquistador, Hernando Cortes, in 1519. By 1521 there were so many "New Christians" in Mexico that the Spanish closed the territory to all those who could not show four generations of Catholic ancestors. Immediately, false documents which described such ancestors were sold on the black market in Spain and Portugal. Soon it was widely rumored that in Mexico there were more "New Christians" of Jewish origin than Catholics. The Inquisition was formally established in Mexico City, as an independent tribunal of the Holy Office, in 1571, but the extirpation of heresy had begun earlier. The Church discovered a "Judaizer" in 1528; he was soon burned as a heretic in the first auto-da-fé in America.

There were probably some Judaizers among the Spaniards who crossed the Rio Grande a few years later into what is now the south-western United States. A friar or two among the founders of the first Christian missions in the American Southwest were rumored to be "Marranos," that is, crypto-Jews, who practiced Judaism in secret, but these Marranos were isolated individuals.

Many of those who were persecuted as Judaizers in Spain and Portugal, and later, in Mexico, were not guilty. They had already abandoned the Judaism from which they sprang. The "New Christians" who came to America were from the middle class or even the nobility; they did not come to find bread, but, rather, to escape persecution. They had been falsely made into "Jews" by enemies jealous of their positions in government and society. Some, those who did practice Judaism in secret, were actually guilty of the "crime" of which they were charged. In 1599 Luis de Carvajal was burned at the stake in Mexico City, and he remained a defiant, believing Jew to the very end: "This is the path to the glory of Paradise. . . . I would give away a thousand [lives], if I had them, for the faith of each of His holy commandments." Half a century later Tomás Treviño de Sobremonte was the host of a secret synagogue which met in his home in Mexico City. He was condemned to the auto-da-fé, but not only because he Judaized. He knew, as he said to the Inquisitors, that economic jealousies had played a role: "I have been of service to the residents of the cities where I have lived since I came to this country, because I have supplied them with goods at lower prices than the other traders, my motto being small profits and quick returns."

The situation on the Atlantic coast of North America was different. The scattering of individual Jews who arrived in the 1600s were not fleeing the threat of being burned at the stake; they were looking for the chance to make a living. In the seventeenth century, even in the most tolerant European lands, Jews were still restricted to peddling and moneylending and to a few trades. On the new frontier a Jew, if he did not trumpet his Jewishness, might be left alone to do anything to which he might turn his hand. Antiquarians have found rumors, some of which represent probable facts, that there were settlers of Jewish origin among the founders or near founders of most of the thirteen colonies. These individuals could not have been very devoted to their Jewishness, for they knew in advance of their coming that there would be no way for them to practice Judaism on the frontier. Without exception, these stray Jews soon disappeared into the majority community, mostly by intermarriage. The reecho of their presence in America is to be found in the history of some of the oldest American families. One reads or hears stories (some families tell them with pride and others whisper at them as a deep secret) that a Jewish peddler passed through some early outpost on the frontier and that he remained to marry a daughter of the house. Such happenings have, of course, not been limited to the encounter between Jews and Gentiles. The ongoing assimilation of individuals— few or many—into the majority is part of all immigrant history, but the prime subject of minority history is the community which affirms its identity. For the Jews, that history began in North America in 1654.

In early September of that year twenty-three Jewish refugees— four couples, two widows, and thirteen children—landed in New Amsterdam. Their original destination had been the islands of the Caribbean, but when their ship, *Ste. Catherine,* had made port in Jamaica and in Cuba, the Spanish had not allowed them to remain. By the time their ship reached harbor in North America, the twenty-three Jews on board had run out of money. Only their furniture remained, and it could not be sold for enough to pay the exorbitant fare the captain demanded. The very moment that the gangplank was down, the captain went to the local court to sue his passengers. He may have thought that the authorities in this farthest outpost of the Dutch West India Company would pay the bill for these Dutch Jews. At very least, he was informing the governor of New Amsterdam, Peter Stuyvesant, in the strongest terms that he would take these refugees no farther. A group of Jews had thus arrived on American shores for whom New Amsterdam was not the port of choice, but their last hope. Peter Stuyvesant was confronted with a problem that he did not want: twenty-three Jews were too numerous to ignore; they would not disappear quickly as individuals among the thousand souls who then inhabited New Amsterdam. If they remained, Jews as a community would have their first outpost in North America.

The twenty-three on board the *Ste. Catherine* were running from Recife (it was called Pernambuco in those days), Brazil, the easternmost point of South America, which the Dutch had conquered from the Portuguese in 1630 and had held until it was surrendered back to the Portuguese in January 1654. Jews had come from Europe to Recife in large numbers. According to their own minute book, in

1645 there were 1,450 Jewish souls in Recife. There they had founded a large, European-style community, the first in the New World. There was a synagogue in Recife and two schools. More significantly, in 1641 Isaac Aboab da Fonseca arrived to be their rabbi, bringing along Moses Raphael Aguilar as his deputy. Orthodox religious authority of the classic kind thus existed in Recife. Isaac Aboab wrote a hymn in Hebrew (published) and a volume on theology (unpublished) during his tenure in Recife; these were, of course, the first such works to be produced in the New World. Earlier, Aboab had been a teacher in Amsterdam in the yeshivah, the school of Talmudic studies, where the young philosopher Baruch de Spinoza had been his student. When Aboab returned to Amsterdam, in 1654, he was added to the rabbinate of the community and joined in excommunicating Spinoza for the heresy of denying the divine origin of the Bible. The Jewish community of Recife had, thus, been a place where the inherited Jewish religious values had reigned. It had been a European Jewish community, a little Jewish Amsterdam, which had been transplanted with all its institutions to the Americas.

After Recife fell, its Jews scattered. The pattern of their dispersal was not new. In the last years of Dutch rule, the economy of embattled Recife was disintegrating. It was the port for the export of sugar from the plantations in the backcountry, and this territory was increasingly reconquered by the Portuguese. A majority of the Jews had gone home to Holland to rejoin the established Jewish community from which they had come. When Recife surrendered, there were still 650 Jews in town. Some, especially a few plantation owners of great wealth, chose to remain under the Portuguese in order to protect their property. Inevitably, they had to become Christians, but a number remained crypto-Jews. The twenty-three refugees who came to New Amsterdam could make neither choice. They were affirming Jews with no intention of becoming Marranos, and they were too poor to have any hope of reestablishing themselves in Holland. Their sole alternative was to push themselves into a place where they were not wanted.

The governor of New Amsterdam, Peter Stuyvesant, did not like Jews. Though he did use such terms as "Christ killers" or "Christ rejecters," as he fought against letting them stay in town, his quarrel with them was primarily economic. The animosity had started in Curaçao, on the northern shore of South America, where Stuyvesant had served as the principal agent of the Dutch West India Company, before his headquarters was moved to New Amsterdam. The company needed farmers. Grain had to be sent to the American colonies from Holland, because the get-rich-quick types who were going out to these far places on the edge of civilization had no patience for clearing the land and plowing the soil. The gold of El Dorado beckoned, or, at very least, the hope of making a quick fortune by trading with the Indians. The authorities in Amsterdam had allowed themselves to be persuaded by Jo'ao de Illan, a Jew who had been born as a Christian in Portugal, to establish a Jewish farming colony of some sixty families in Curaçao. The Dutch West India Company was grateful for this promise of help. De Illan received a large grant of land—but he did not farm. He preferred to raise horses and smuggle them to Spanish possessions in the Caribbean and even to New England (thus, incidentally, establishing the first commercial contact between the Puritans and the Jews). Peter Stuyvesant was furious. The Dutch West India Company was upset by his reports, but it did not chase de Illan off the land. He had friends among the company's powerful Jewish stockholders, and the company did not want to annoy these interests. Stuyvesant had thus lost his first battle with Jews.

He was to lose again in New Amsterdam. To be sure, in an earlier instance, in the summer of 1654, when two Jews, Solomon Pietersen and Jacob Barsimson, arrived from Holland with some capital and with passports giving them full permission to land and to trade in the colony, their Jewishness was not an issue to Stuyvesant. But the twenty-three on the *Ste. Catherine* presented a far different problem. Two weeks after they landed, Stuyvesant heard the complaint from the local merchants and from the Church that "the Jews who had arrived would nearly all like to remain here." Stuyvesant decided to chase them out. Using the usual formulas of religious invective—he called the Jews "repugnant," "deceitful," and "enemies and blasphemers of Christ"—Stuyvesant recommended to his directors that "Owing to their present indigence they [the Jews] might become a charge in the coming winter, we have for the benefit of this weak and newly-developing place, and the land in general, deemed it useful to require them in a friendly way to depart."

To be sure, Stuyvesant and his allies were not believers in religious toleration, for this idea had barely appeared in the middle of the seventeenth century. In the 1650s decent men still knew what the truth was, especially in religion, but Stuyvesant had not decided to expel the Jews because he detested rejecters of Christ. The governor of New Amsterdam was an employee of the Dutch West India Company, and the purpose of this firm was not to foster Christianity among the Indians; it existed to make money for its stockholders— and the company was not doing very well. It had made a real profit only once, in 1629, when its ships cornered and pillaged the "silver fleet," the Spanish galleons carrying that year's silver yield from the mines of Peru to Spain. This onetime act of piracy had paid handsomely, but the mundane business of the trading outposts in the Western Hemisphere was barely breaking even, in the best years. New Amsterdam was losing money: Curaçao and Suriname were showing small profits; Recife had just fallen. If the Dutch burghers who had put their money in the West India Company were to see a return, they needed the investment of new capital. It made good sense, then, to oblige the rich Jews of Amsterdam. And so, in the winter of 1654–55, Peter Stuyvesant's bosses in Amsterdam were reluctant to uphold their representative in a squalid little quarrel in their outpost at the mouth of the Hudson. The leaders of the Dutch West India Company had no patience with the local merchants, who were arguing that the advent of these Jews would hurt the profits of the company; this contention seemed hollow to the directors in Amsterdam. The local merchants in the colony were, indeed, supposed to operate for the benefit of the company, but, without exception, they had for years been trading for their own account and stealing from the owners. Peter Stuyvesant himself was, in fact, as guilty as the rest, and the company knew it.

When Stuyvesant's letter arrived in Amsterdam, the Jewish investors in the West India Company were consulted. Their response was frank and pointed: "There are many of the nation [i.e., Jews] who have lost their possessions at Pernambuco [Recife]. They have arrived from there in great poverty, and part of them have been dispersed here and there. Your petitioners had to expend large sums of money for their necessaries of life, and through lack of opportunity all cannot remain here to live." There was free farmland in New Amsterdam. This outpost imported grain from Holland, and it was crying out for hands to work the fields. Why not get the right for poor Jews to stay there by pushing them into becoming farmers, or, at least, by suggesting that they might do so? In this same memorandum the Jewish leaders wrote: "Yonder land is extensive and spacious . . . The Company has by a general resolution consented that those who wish to populate the Colony shall enjoy certain districts of land gratis. Why should now certain subjects of this State not be allowed to travel thither and live there?"

But the directors in Amsterdam of the West India Company did not believe the suggestion that the men among these twenty-three Jews, who had not been very successful at trade in Recife, were now eager to farm in the semiwilderness. The officers of the company also knew that at that very time Jo'ao de Illan was failing, willfully, in the project which they had blessed, to create a Jewish farming settlement in Curaçao. The decision by the West India Company was given in a letter they wrote to Stuyvesant on April 25, 1655: "These people may travel and trade in New Netherland and live and remain there, provided the poor among them shall not become a burden to the Company or to the community, but be supported by their own nation." They added, repeating arguments that had been made in the Jewish brief, that this had to be done out of consideration for the losses of Jews in Brazil and "because of the large amount of capital which they still have invested in the shares of this Company."

In this letter the authorities informed Stuyvesant that they had given passports to five Jews of means, several of whom had just arrived in Amsterdam from Recife. The West India Company had opened New Amsterdam to Jews. Poor Jews were already in place. Five rich families were now being sent out from Amsterdam to add to the trade of New Amsterdam and, incidentally, "to take care of their own poor."

Despite all this, the local interests refused to give in. They did not like Jews, and they did not want more competitors in a place where trade was languishing. Every kind of harassment was tried. The Council in New Amsterdam made difficulties about a cemetery for Jews, and it tried to stop private worship in individual homes. In such bigotry the Calvinists in New Amsterdam were not singling out the Jews, for they were doing the same, or worse, to dissenting Protestants and, of course, to Catholics. Stuyvesant made the connection in one of his letters to the company: "Giving them [the Jews] liberty, we cannot refuse the Lutherans and Papists." Consequently, on March 13, 1656, the authorities in Holland confirmed that Jewish worship would be forbidden in New Amsterdam, even in private, so "that the wolves may be warded off from the tender lamb of Christ." The Jewish leaders in Amsterdam, of course, intervened, citing the obvious precedent that there were open synagogues in Amsterdam itself. The order was reversed. The directors of the company soon wrote to Stuyvesant that Jews might "exercise in all quietness their religion within their houses, for which end they must without doubt endeavor to build their houses close together in a convenient place on one or the other side of New Amsterdam—at their choice—as they have done here."

The houses that these Jews built or, more probably, rented in New Amsterdam were exactly the same as all the other houses in town, with one marked exception, the food in their kitchen. The twenty-three in New Amsterdam were almost certainly the first Jews in America to observe the rituals of kosher cuisine. It was usual practice in those days that heads of families learned how to slaughter fowl according to the prescribed rituals. Despite the clear intention of the order by the company, that Jews establish themselves in an enclave of their own, they scattered among the Gentiles on several streets. Still, these were within a short walk of one another. Jews had to be able to gather for prayer, and on the Sabbath and on festivals, travel by any conveyance, even by horseback, was forbidden by religious law. The Jews who came to New Amsterdam had not been constrained to establish a ghetto, but where they lived was the first Jewish neighborhood in America.

The wrangle about the freedom of religion had, in essence, been an irrelevance. Jews had come to New Amsterdam to trade. If they succeeded in remaining, they would one way or another conduct their own worship services. Stuyvesant knew it, even as he fought against "their abominable religion." The real question was economic; how much pressure could Jews mount in Amsterdam to counter the continued stonewalling of all the local interests against them? Stuyvesant had ruefully become a realist. He knew that the Jews would prevail. In the very letter in which he thanked his superiors for prohibiting the public exercise of Jewish religion in his town, he added, "What they may be able to obtain from your honors, time will tell."

Stuyvesant's problem was not even with the West India Company alone. In the 1650s the Dutch Republic was more nervous about its commercial future than it had been for decades. The Dutch had invented the doctrine of mercantilism, the notion that the state existed not to save souls but to increase wealth. For such purpose, Jews or Turks—all who brought money and commercial connections—were welcome. Spanish and Portuguese "New Christians" had begun arriving in Holland before 1600, and they were allowed to drop their Christian disguise and to live as Jews. Some had been admitted to the Amsterdam mercantile exchange at its very beginning in 1611; the Jews were seated in a good place, together with the sugar refiners and the securities dealers. The next year, there were ten "Jew brokers" among the three hundred sworn members of the exchange. A few years later, in 1618, the French envoy in Holland wrote to Paris about "the cleverness, commercial energy, and communal solidarity of the Jews." They kept in touch with other Jews all over the world, even with secret communities in England and France, so that "the Jews in Amsterdam are the best informed about foreign commerce and news of all people in the world"; therefore, "they are needed by the city."

The Jewish leaders in Amsterdam thus knew that they had the power to cajole or even to intimidate the West India Company— but these rich Jews were also afraid. Even in Amsterdam, the most liberal of European cities, no one knew how many poor Jews would be tolerated by the civic authorities. The Jewish population of Amsterdam had been growing through the century with little problem, but the 1650s were a turbulent time. The leaders of the Jewish community had to conduct frequent fund-raising campaigns to pay for the relief of their poor, who kept drifting into the community from all over Europe. Such a collection was again made in the summer of 1654, to help those who had fled from Recife. It is an interesting detail that Baruch de Spinoza, who was then still a member of the Jewish community, is recorded as dutifully giving five florins to this drive on September 13, 1654. In the next year the pressures increased. The Jews in Eastern Europe were being slaughtered by the Ukrainians in a series of murders that had begun in 1648. A shipload of refugees escaped through the Baltic Sea, but the Jews of Amsterdam were afraid to let them stay. There was always room in mercantilist Amsterdam for Jewish capitalists, but the elders of the city were becoming restless at the sight of poor Jews who kept insinuating themselves into the city. They were trying to make a living as peddlers and as petty traders in competition with the local retailers. These tensions made Amsterdam's rich Jews nervous. They reflected this discomfort in their letter to the West India Company: "through lack of opportunity all cannot remain here to live." They were far too nervous to want their twenty-three wandering compatriots back. It was better that these refugees from Recife remain in a distant colony.

American Jewish history thus began with no ringing debates about religious freedom or about the rights of individuals. The twenty-three remained in New Amsterdam, and began the first avowed Jewish community in North America, because money talked. The Dutch West India Company needed the Jews, even as many restrictions against Jewish trade persisted in Amsterdam itself, and religious prejudices based on Calvinism remained strong there. On the frontier in the New World, the company was much more open and obliging—and yet there was continuing struggle in the colony about the rights of Jews and especially about the open practice of Judaism.

II

The five wealthy merchants who arrived in New Amsterdam in 1655 belonged to the international network of Jewish men of affairs who descended from the "aristocratic" Jews of Spain and Portugal, the Sephardim. They carried a big stick; they could threaten to move elsewhere, taking their money and commerce with them. As befitted their power and station, these five families immediately demanded the right to own houses in New Amsterdam. David Ferara and Salvador Dandrada fought this issue out with the local authorities. It took them only a few months to win, but they never exercised this right. They had come to New Amsterdam to try out the place as a base for large commercial enterprises, and they would not commit themselves to remain until they saw the possibility of success. Even after winning the quarrel over owning houses, these Jews were still harassed with a minor, troubling restriction; they were denied the right to employ Christian servants. This annoyance reflected a larger policy. Having been forced to accept Jews in New Amsterdam, Peter Stuyvesant continued to try to hem them in with all the restrictions that still existed on the books in Amsterdam. In Amsterdam, Jews could engage in large enterprises, in wholesale commerce of all kinds, but not in retail trade, for it competed with local merchants. This prohibition was passed, but it was simply ignored in New Amsterdam.

The crucial quarrel was about the fur and tobacco trade, the colony's most lucrative pursuits. The rich Jews who had come in 1655 wanted to enter this business; they kept moving upriver, and angering their competitors. Albany (then called Fort Orange) was the major trading post to the north. Jews were soon there, competing with those who had been trading with the Indians. In September of 1655 the Dutch moved south and captured the Swedish colonies on the Delaware River (it was then called the South River). Three of the Jewish merchants immediately shipped goods there, but Stuyvesant and the Council of New Netherland would not let them do business. In late November, an exchange between the Council and these merchants—Abraham de Lucena, Salvador Dandrada, and Jacob Cohen—resulted in a temporary compromise. The Jewish shippers were permitted "to send one or two persons to the South River in order to dispose of the same [i.e., the goods shipped], which being done, they are to return hither." The inevitable appeal to Holland brought back a decision in March 1656 that Jews had the right to trade on the Delaware. They were soon back on the river, exchanging cloth and liquor for furs and tobacco. David Ferara even traded for tobacco in the English colony of Maryland.

By April 1657, the battle of the five merchant families for economic rights had succeeded. Four of them—all except David Ferara, who seems then to have been away trading for tobacco in Maryland—joined in a petition to Stuyvesant and the Council in which they asked for the right to be enrolled as burghers of New Amsterdam. Notably, they did not ask for the "great burgher right," which carried with it full political equality, to which the Jews did not aspire. They wanted the right to engage in retail trade, which could be exercised by possessors of the "small burgher right." The petitioners argued that they, too, paid taxes, and that they were entitled to "the same freedom as other inhabitants of New Netherland enjoy." This time the authorities did not respond with delaying tactics. Perhaps the local interests now needed these Jews, for they were among the largest taxpayers. More probably, the colony as a whole was becoming less and less governable. That spring, English settlers on Long Island rebelled against Dutch rule in the "Flushing Remonstrance," in which they protested the persecution of Quakers and pleaded for toleration of all settlers without regard to their religion; the remonstrants specifically included the Jews among those to be permitted in the colony. Stuyvesant, the son and son-in-law of Calvinist ministers, could not persist in religious oppression; Stuyvesant, the surreptitious partner of a number of local merchants, could no longer protect these interests.

Neither the Jews nor the company were, however, permanently wedded to New Amsterdam. For the company it soon became clear that this was the least interesting of its remaining possessions. Great and immediate profits were likelier in the Caribbean, in the sugar trade. Dandrada, Ferara, and the rest had come to New Amsterdam to get much richer quickly, and this was not happening. They began to leave, most probably to go back to Holland. By the time the English fleet came, during the Dutch-English War, not a single one of these Sephardi hidalgos was left in town. The Scroll of the Law, which they had brought with them from Amsterdam when they arrived in 1655, had been returned to the mother congregation in 1663. Most of the twenty-three who had come on the Ste. Catherine had also taken off for other places. Of the two who had "met the ship," one, Solomon Pietersen, had converted to the Dutch Reformed Church and had become a notary public, a position one could acquire only by taking the oath "on the true faith of a Christian." The other, Jacob Barsimson, had simply disappeared; he was perhaps the husband of a lady who was recorded in 1680 in Barbados as a widow.

Only one Jew who had been visible in Dutch New Amsterdam, Asser Levy, was prominent in English New York. He was one of the refounders of the Jewish community in the 1670s. Levy was different from those who left as the Dutch colony was failing. They were Sephardim, bearers of the Jewish culture that had been created in Spain and Portugal before the total expulsions of Jews in 1492 and 1497; he was an Ashkenazi, that is, he came from the Yiddish-speaking communities of Central and Eastern Europe, which the Sephardim regarded as lower caste. The Sephardi hidalgos belonged to a network of international traders; Levy was a self-made businessman, who had arrived poor among the twenty-three who landed in 1654. In fact, the first battle that he personally fought with the local authorities was caused by his poverty. In that era, standing guard was not anywhere regarded as an honor, or a mark of political equality. On the contrary, well-off people, even those on the frontier, bought out from military duty.

The Jewish attitudes to such duty were different. In Europe Jews had rarely been asked or allowed to bear arms, because they were excluded from society. This had broken down in the New World. When Recife was besieged, Jews had fought beside the rest. One ex-Marrano who had helped defend Recife had been executed after its fall, as a traitor to Portugal. In New Amsterdam the five Sephardi entrepreneurs paid a tax in lieu of military service in the "trainbands" (the local home guard) without giving the matter a second thought, but Asser Levy and Jacob Barsimson could not afford even the measly sum of sixty-five stivers. On November 5, 1655, they petitioned "to keep guard with other burghers, or be free from the tax which others of their nation pay, as they must earn their living by manual labor." Levy and Barsimson were refused, and they were told that they could leave the colony if they wished. Levy kept pushing, and within two years he had won the right to serve in the militia. For that matter, it was Levy, and not the Sephardim, who had initiated the battle for "small burgher rights"; he needed the right to petty retail trade more than they, and he intended to stay in New Amsterdam.

The commerce of the well-to-do Sephardim had not gone well; they were already contemplating leaving New Amsterdam, and so they had remained in rented quarters. In 1661, Levy became the first Jew to own a house in New Amsterdam, or anywhere in North America. In seven years he had become a middleman, selling finished goods imported from Amsterdam and trading even in Fort Orange (Albany). He was perhaps involved directly in the fur trade; more probably, he sold supplies to the traders. When the British were on the attack in 1664, Levy was taxed a hundred guilders as his share of the fund for strengthening the fortifications. This was as much money as each of the five rich Sephardim had been assessed in taxes on their arrival in 1655. Levy had become well-to-do. In the course of his first ten years in the colony, despite resistance from unfriendly Dutch authorities, he had spread out in many directions. He had become a representative of Dutch merchants in New Amsterdam and a moneylender. He even sold liquor. In 1661 he was given license to be a butcher. Levy did not open a slaughterhouse until 1678 after the Dutch left. He had a Christian partner in this business; it is of some interest that this abattoir was located on the very site of present-day Wall Street.

Levy was also spreading out in public life. Since 1657 he had been marching with the militia. It is likely that Levy was excused from his duties in the militia on Sabbaths and Jewish holidays, for such exceptions continued to be made in colonial New York, and elsewhere in the English colonies, until the American Revolution. In 1671, under the British, he sat on a jury, the very first Jew in America to be allowed to hold such office. One of the cases that was tried that term involved his old enemy, Peter Stuyvesant, who had remained in New York after the surrender. Levy seems to have been completely fair, because Stuyvesant won the case. Levy lent money that year to the Lutherans to help them build a church. That same year, a Jewish peddler was given a reduced fine by a court in New England as "a token of their respect to . . . Mr. Assur [sic] Levy."

Levy had to be an aggressive person who fought for his rights. New Amsterdam was a rough town. A visitor reported that eighteen languages were spoken in this outpost of only a thousand souls, that all the streets were mud ruts, and that every third building was a grogshop. It was definitely not safe to walk around at night. Such an environment inevitably bred disputes. Jews were no different from all the rest of the inhabitants. There is record of a suit that Levy brought against a butcher who had accused him of associating with thieves. Mrs. Abraham de Lucena called someone a rogue; he responded by calling her a whore. This quarrel was patched up in court with mutual apologies. An even more interesting case never came to trial. Elias Silva was accused of having "carnal relations" with the Negro slave of another man. He was arrested, but there is no record of any action by the court.

So long as the community existed under Dutch rule, Levy was part of it, but what happened to his Jewish piety in 1663, when almost all of the other Jews were gone? In the spring of 1664, did Levy bake his own unleavened bread, the matzoth, for Passover? Did he keep the room in which the now departed community had said its prayers, as his private, personal synagogue? When no other Jews were looking, did he perhaps work on the Sabbath—or did he insist on being odd, even when he and his family were the only Jews in town? Asser Levy had to redecide everything in his Jewish life that the inherited tradition had decided for all of his ancestors. It is clear from Levy's will that he remained to the very end an affirming Jew. According to the official inventory, his estate included pistols, a gun and two swords—but also a Sabbath light, goblets which were undoubtedly used for saying the Friday night blessing over the wine, and a spice box which was used for the ceremony marking the end of the Sabbath.

Levy's religious problems were not new. They had been experienced for centuries by isolated European Jews who made their living by peddling from wagons, without any fixed habitation. His chance to get rich in less than ten years was much more "American." Levy had risen and prospered because New Amsterdam, and almost all of the other North American colonies, had been created without any pretense of a religious purpose. They were economic entities, which needed population, and thus they were essentially hospitable to Jews, or to anyone else who wanted to work and make something of himself. Those who had money, and expected large immediate returns, like the five Sephardi families who had come in 1655, had other places to go, even if they were Jews. For the rising poor, like Asser Levy, New Amsterdam had put fewer obstacles in their way than any other place in the world—and so it was to remain in New York for generations to come.

2.

Puritans and Jews:

Truth vs Error

I

Asser Levy was fortunate that he lived in New York, to which people had come to make money, and not in Boston, which was founded as a godly commonwealth. In the middle of the seventeenth century these ungodly views prevailed in Amsterdam, and therefore in New Amsterdam, but Boston was dedicated to making God's kingdom on earth. The Puritans were obsessed by the Jewish Bible—but they were not hospitable to Jews, or to Judaism. They had left Europe, which was their "Egypt," the place of their enslavement, and had gone out into the American wilderness on a messianic journey, to found the New Jerusalem. In the famous sermon on the *Arbella,* the ship which had brought the second group of Puritans to Massachusetts Bay in 1630, John Winthrop had compared the passengers on board his ship both to Noah's Ark and to the dry bones in the vision of Ezekiel. These were to be the ancestors of a new mankind, after Europe was destroyed for its sins. Soon, Samuel Wakeman, one of the New England divines at the heyday of Puritanism, preached an election day sermon in which he asserted that "Jerusalem was, New England is; they were, you are God's own, God's covenant people; put but New England's name instead of Jerusalem."

The Puritans were convinced that they were the true Jews, the ultimate and total heirs of the promises that God had made in the Hebrew Bible. The errors of the biological Jews had to be excluded.

Essays without number have been written to argue that the Puritan theocracy, which was so self-consciously modeled on biblical Judaism, created a pro-Jewish core to the American intellectual and political tradition. This reading is wrong. Because the Puritans knew that they had the truth, they were intolerant of all other believers. One of the founders of New England, Nathaniel Ward, wrote in 1645 that anyone who "is willing to tolerate any religion . . . besides his own . . . either doubts his own or is not sincere in it." An even more important figure, John Cotton, had denied, emphatically, that "God did ever ordain [democracy] as a fit government for either church or a commonwealth." Edward Winslow, who had been governor of New Plymouth, was even more emphatic in a letter that he wrote to his friend, John Winthrop, the former governor of Massachusetts Bay. Winslow said that he "utterly abhored" universal tolerance, for that "would make us odious to all Christian commonweales . . . to allow and maintaine full and free tollerance of religion to all men . . . Turke, Jew, Papist . . . or any other." A generation later, in 1681, another divine, Samuel Willard, looked back on the Puritan beginnings of Massachusetts and flatly asserted that the first to come were "professed enemies of toleration." No other version of Christianity could be tolerated. This Puritan intolerance is remembered to this day primarily because witches were hanged in Salem, to protect the faithful from those who were consorting with the devil. It has been more than half forgotten that Quakers were being hanged in Boston, because Christians who were not Puritans were "vipers in the garden of the Lord."

Jews, however, had never been Christian. Even at the height of Puritan power in New England, they were never in danger of their lives. Yet, they were never welcome. The first test of the attitude of the Puritans toward Jews in their midst came in 1649. Solomon Franco arrived from Holland, in charge of goods consigned to the major general of the Boston militia, Edward Gibbons. Franco may have jumped ship or he may have been left behind. It is not known

33

whether he wanted to remain in Boston, but the local authorities gave him no choice. He was a Jew who had no intention of converting to Christianity in its Puritan version. On May 3, 1649, they decreed to "allow the said Solomon Franco six shillings per week out of the Treasury for ten weeks, for subsistence, till he can get his passage into Holland," and they commanded him to leave before the ten weeks of grace ran out. In 1675, when Rowland Gideon, one of the first Jews to do business in Boston, had to appear before a court, he had known that he was an alien, for he begged the court to be kind by acting as "fathers of this scattered nation." But Gideon did have a text to quote at these Puritans; he reminded them of the biblical injunction that "God commands our fathers that the same law should be for the strangers and sorjouners as for the Israelites." Gideon won the suit, but he did not remain in Boston.

On the other hand, at the very beginning of their settlement in North America, some Puritans had allowed a family of Jewish extraction to remain in their midst. In 1621, Moses Simonson and family, reputed to be "from the Jewish settlement in Amsterdam," landed in Plymouth harbor one year after the *Mayflower*. They had no trouble remaining because the Simonsons had probably already turned Christian in Holland before joining the Pilgrims, or, at very least, they converted in Plymouth. One of their daughters is known to have married a grandson of Miles Standish and John Alden.

Thus, at the very beginning of their settlements in New England, the Pilgrims had let a convert remain in Plymouth, and the Massachusetts Bay Colony had chased professing Jews out of Boston. Three generations after the beginning of these colonies, Samuel Willard summarized Puritan attitudes in a sermon that he preached in 1700: the Jews were a "scorn and reproach to the world"; it was best to keep them out, for only "the happy day of their conversion could improve their condition." This was standard Christian doctrine, but there was a particular twist—and a unique intensity—to this attitude. The conversion of the Jews was necessary, and not primarily for their own good, or to avoid the infection of society through their presence as Jews. Every Jew who converted to Puritanism assured the Puritans that they were right: they were the true Israel. There was an even more pressing reason for converting the Jews: the end of days was coming, and one could not wait patiently for the Jews to see the light; had it not been foretold that Jesus would appear again, but only if the obdurate Jews acknowledged him as Savior?

The Puritans were faced with a quandary. The Second Coming could not happen unless most Jews were converted, but the bulk of this obdurate people would remain in Europe, unavailable to the light of Puritan truth. Fortunately, for the Puritans, the answer to this problem lay in America's sizable Indian population. Some of the founding fathers of New England concluded that the Indians should be Jews. And it was therefore "proven" through a "discovery" made by a rabbi (what greater expert!) that this was so. The man who made this discovery was Manasseh Ben Israel of Amsterdam. An able, though not outstanding, scholar of the Talmud and a Kabbalist who wanted to help effect "the end of days," a Latinist, a man whose friend Rembrandt made an etching of him, Manasseh was unusual even in Amsterdam, the most open society of the day. When he suggested that the Indians of the Western Hemisphere were descendants of the Lost Ten Tribes of Israel, this "finding" speedily reached New England.

Manasseh Ben Israel did not, of course, invent the idea. This myth had begun a century earlier in South America, when the Spanish and Portuguese were conquering the continent. But in 1649 Manasseh revived the story with a very clear purpose of his own. During the convulsions of the late 1640s in England, as Charles I was being tried and beheaded and Oliver Cromwell was coming to power, Manasseh began to think that he could persuade the new rulers of the British Isles that the time had come to allow the Jews to return to the land from which they had been banished by Edward I in 1290. By claiming that the Indians were Jews, Manasseh's first line of argument was to appeal to the Puritan hope for the "end of days." In a pamphlet entitled *The Hope of Israel,* Manasseh maintained that the messianic era was about to begin. The Jews would, first, have to spread out to the four corners of the earth; therefore, they had to be allowed into England immediately. As for America, the farthest corner of the world, Manasseh asserted that the Indians were Jews. He told a strange story: Antonio de Montezinos, who was also known as Aaron Levi, had come to Amsterdam in September 1644 and had testified before its rabbinic court that he had met Indians in Ecuador who were Jews. Montezinos said that he had taken a long and adventurous journey to a riverbank, on the other side of which a goodly throng of Indians assembled in his honor (they would not let Montezinos cross over). They gave ample evidence of being Jewish by reciting the "Here O Israel" in Hebrew.

It is questionable that Manasseh and his colleagues in Amsterdam believed this story. If they did, it makes no sense that they kept such good tidings secret for five whole years. Manasseh Ben Israel seems to have put the tale told by Montezinos out of his mind until 1649. That year, strange tales seemed more likely, because revolutionaries in England were shocking Europe in 1649 by daring to execute their lawful king, Charles I. In any event, Manasseh found this story useful in his effort to persuade Christian believers in England to readmit the Jews. Several of them did accept this tale with great enthusiasm; they spread it abroad, even before Manasseh's pamphlet was printed in 1650. It was through these enthusiasts that the story traveled almost immediately to New England, where it had an interesting life of its own. Manasseh seems to have first told the story in Amsterdam to an English Puritan, John Durie, who was chaplain to Mary, princess of Orange. Durie repeated it to a friend in London, Thomas Thorowgood, who was involved in supporting John Eliot, the first and most famous Puritan missionary. Thorowgood instantly imagined that the Indians whom Eliot was trying to convert were the same as those whom Montezinos had encountered, and so he published a pamphlet under the sensational title of *Jews in America*. A few months later John Durie published a pamphlet of his own in which he fully supported Thorowgood's views on the Indians in North America. In order to make his point totally convincing, he told the Montezinos story as he had received it from Manasseh Ben Israel.

The only person who seems to have kept his head, at least for a while, was John Eliot, the missionary and apostle to the Indians in New England. Eliot had begun his mission in 1646; a year later, in 1647, he wrote the first printed account of the Indians whom he was trying to convert. This was a sober production in which Eliot guessed that the Indians of North America were most probably "Tartars passing out of Asia into America." There was not the slightest suggestion of any possible Jewish origin. Eliot even included a down-to-earth forecast that not many Indians were likely to convert at any time soon, for mass conversion of those who had not yet accepted

Christianity was likely to happen only when "the Jews come in." It was only after Thorowgood, his chief financial supporter in England, had made the suggestion that these Indians were Jews, that Eliot allowed himself to be half-persuaded that this might be true. Eliot then argued, without much conviction, that he "saw some ground to conceive that some of the Ten Tribes might be scattered even thus far." It is nearly certain that Eliot said this to humor Thorowgood. Eliot was always broke; he needed the money that Thorowgood was collecting in England.

Roger Williams, the radical theologian who most troubled the early Puritans, seems to have believed the notion that the Indians were of Jewish origin, and so did a number of more orthodox Puritan divines. But the idea was abandoned, as the Puritans got to know the Indians better. What did remain at the center of Puritan concern was messianic speculation, which had been at its height in the 1640s and 1650s when the myth of the Jewish origin of the Indians had been floated. The spiritual leaders of New England remained particularly attentive to any rumor of messianic expectations, and especially when such hopes appeared among the Jews. In the 1660s there was a major convulsion in world Jewry. Shabtai Zvi, a Kabbalist from Smyrna, proclaimed himself the messiah. He appeared immediately after the mass murder of Jews in the Ukraine from 1648 into the mid-1650s, and at a time when the Inquisition was persecuting crypto-Jews in Spain and Portugal and their possessions with unabating vigor. Jews wanted a miracle, and so most of world Jewry believed him. In many places sober people sold their goods and awaited the new age in which they would return to Zion. These strange events were widely noticed, everywhere, and even in New England. As early as 1669 Increase Mather, the second generation of the most important Puritan divines, had preached sermons in which he had maintained that "some great revolution of affairs" is widely expected, "not only by Protestants but also by Papists, Jews, Turks, Mohammedans and other idolators." Both the Turks and the pope were about to fall, leaving the field clear for the true Christianity of the Protestants; they would lead the way toward the Second Coming. Jews would join with the Gentiles in one universal society. The Jews would return to Judea "to repossess their own land." In a preface to these sermons by Mather, another Puritan divine, John Davenport, wrote that

Mather was maintaining something "reasonable," because there were constant reports from various places in the world that "the Israelites were upon their journey towards Jerusalem," and that they were being carried in great multitudes in that direction by miraculous means "to the admiration and astonishment of all who had heard it." Davenport added that the Jews had written to "others of their nation in Europe and America to encourage and invite them to hasten to them." No communications from the followers of Shabtai Zvi to Jews in America have yet been found, but it is conceivable that such letters were sent. By 1669, the date forecast for the restoration of the Jews (the year 1666) had passed, and the "messiah" himself had converted to Islam, but the messianic convulsion had not yet ended.

A more immediate encounter with contemporary Jewish reality by a Puritan leader occurred in 1689, when William Sewell of Boston was in London as a representative of the Massachusetts Bay Company to try to renegotiate the terms of the royal charter that had been forced on the Puritans five years earlier. Sewell took occasion to see the synagogue and cemetery of the Sephardim. His account of his visit to the cemetery was quite fair. Sewell was interested in the Jewish burial practices; as he left, he told the keeper that he wished that they might meet in heaven. This was a most tolerant encounter, but theological ideas about converting the Jews were not foreign even to the worldly William Sewell. Two years earlier Sewell had recorded hearing a sermon by Samuel Lee, a preacher from Bristol, Massachusetts, who was also visiting in London, in which Lee had asserted that the end of days was near, the conversion of the Jews was imminent, and that "the Jews were called and would inhabit Judea and Old Jerusalem."

Thus, in the great days of Puritanism in New England a consensus had been reached about Jews. Even the most tolerant Roger Williams remained deeply committed to converting them. He insisted that he "did profess a spiritual war against Judaism and the Turks." What separated him from the rest was his belief that Jews, along with all other dissenting faiths, could best be persuaded of the truth of Puritan Christianity only at close range, if they were allowed into the civil society. In one of his pamphlets Williams denounced the Christian world for persecuting the Jews, "for whose hard measure the nations and England have yet a score to pay." When Williams was banished from Massachusetts for heresy, he established a commonwealth in

Rhode Island on the principles of complete civic equality. This settlement was the first to allow the Jewish community to be established in New England, in Newport.

II

The Puritan founders of the Massachusetts Bay Colony had arrived in 1630 with a charter which gave them unparalleled power. They were not governed from England; they governed themselves. Since their purpose was the creation of a godly community, the church and the state were essentially one. This endeavor began to founder after half a century. In 1684, Charles II withdrew the original charter, and he thus weakened Puritan control over Massachusetts. When his successor, James II, came to the throne in the next year, he soon instructed the royal governor to permit "liberty of conscience in matters of religion to all persons." This decree was issued for the benefit of Anglicans and Catholics, but, in effect, it also included the very few Jews who were then to be found anywhere in New England. Nonetheless, despite these defeats in London, the Puritans continued, in the last days of the seventeenth century, to hope for God's final victory in New England. The greatest of all their scholars, Cotton Mather, took to wearing a skullcap in his study and to calling himself a rabbi. Mather was no eccentric on the fringes of New England. True, he was moody and imperious. He was twice denied the post which he wanted all his life, the presidency of Harvard College, but even his enemies acknowledged that Mather was the moral leader of Boston and the greatest scholar in North America. He also bore the right names. His grandfathers, John Cotton and Richard Mather, had been leading figures among the Puritan divines who had put their stamp on the Massachusetts Bay Colony.

At the moment at which Mather donned the skullcap, probably in 1696, and took to calling himself "rabbi," he was completing his most important book, the *Magnalia Christi Americana,* a huge account of the founding of the Massachusetts Bay Colony. In this book Mather defined and summed up the meaning of the Puritan venture into the American wilderness. In this account, he "invented" New England as a redemptive society. Mather retold Puritan history in biblical, mythic accents. In Mather's tale, the generation of his grand-

parents had left the slavery of Europe not simply to escape persecution. They had come on a messianic journey to bring about the
Second Coming of Christ. John Winthrop, the founding governor
of Massachusetts, was the new Moses; the essential meaning of his
enterprise was to establish the new Zion. Among the Puritans, some
thought that the "City on the Hill" was a refuge for a saving remnant,
which would remain as God's kingdom on earth after Europe and
the rest of the sinful world were destroyed in the conflagration of
Armageddon. Others held that the Puritan theocracy was redemptive.

All the opinions among the Puritans agreed that they, and not the
Jews, were the chosen people. In the late 1690s when Cotton Mather
was finishing the *Magnalia Christi,* he was also writing a textbook
for the conversion of the Jews. It was a set of "proofs" from their
own Bible, using verses from the Old Testament alone, to establish
the incontrovertible truth of Christianity. Mather hoped that this
book would, in the first instance, convert the Frazon brothers, who
were the only avowed Jews then trading in Boston. Mather was
disappointed, for the Frazons remained Jews. When one of them died
a few years later, his body was transported to the Jewish cemetery
in Newport, Rhode Island. Mather had failed with the Frazons, but
he was encouraged by the news that his book brought a Jew in South
Carolina to conversion. Mather must have patted his skullcap with
approval—and in renewed hope—when the news came from South
Carolina, but there were no more such encouraging stories. The Jews
ignored Mather's book.

The question of the Jews had occupied Mather from the very
beginning of his spiritual journey. At twenty-one, he went through
the crisis that all Puritans were supposed to experience, that of struggle with his "lusts" in order to become spiritually reborn, and thus
to offer "proof" of having joined the "elect," that is, those who had
been chosen by God to be His people. Mather wrote about this in
his diary. The rhetoric is biblical: he had resolved to "circumcise all
lusts of the flesh." Mather had found a place in his spiritual world
for the biblical commandment of circumcision, but it no longer
meant, as the "literalist Jews would have it," something mundane
and even vile. At twenty-one, Mather had found a way of giving
the commandment a Puritan interpretation: he would be "active in
the execution of all these evil inclinations as the Jews were in the

execution of my dearest Redeemer." Thirteen years later, as he was completing the *Magnalia Christi,* Mather had another experience of inner illumination. This divine light assured him of his own central role in the world. He wrote in his diary that he would not be the one who bears witness "unto the Lord for no less than all the nations and kingdoms." He was now both a rabbi and a prophet; he was donning the skullcap to define a program by which the kingdom of Christ would be realized. At the top of the list, Mather assigned himself the task of the "conversion of the Jewish nation." Mather then turned to such minor matters as the fate of France and of the British dominions, and the well-being of his own province, all of which had to fit into the divine scheme.

Mather kept hoping for the ultimate triumph of Puritanism, but it did not come. He had to live with his disappointments, and not only about the Jews. His father, Increase Mather, had already been troubled half a century earlier, while some of the founding fathers of Puritanism were still alive, by the growing tendency of men of affairs to put their own interests first, thereby changing New England from "a religious to a worldly interest." When Increase Mather spoke, around 1650, New England had already grown to a population of perhaps thirty thousand, and most of those who had come were not, like the earliest founders, godly people. Nonetheless, the elect, those few who were admitted to membership in the Puritan congregations, continued to govern the Massachusetts Bay Colony as a theocracy for half a century until the original charter was revoked.

The response in New England to this fundamental change, which took civil rule away from the Puritans and put it in the hands of a royal governor, was a religious revival called the New Piety. The Puritans consciously turned inward, away from public affairs, which they could no longer dominate. Cotton Mather became a leading exponent of this New Piety. He even began to believe, in the last decade of his life, that prophecy had begun again. Cotton Mather gave up on the notion that there would be large-scale conversion of the Jews, or that this was a necessary part of the drama of the end of days. He consoled himself by holding all the harder to the hope that the end of days was at hand, that Christ would soon rise again— and the elect, the chosen, would be given the glory they deserved.

Despite this change of mind, Cotton Mather rejoiced in any convert. In Mather's last years there was one such case in Boston. Judah

Monis, a Jew from Italy who was probably originally from Algiers, had arrived in Boston from New York in 1720. Two years later Monis converted to Christianity before a large crowd in College Hall at Harvard. He was soon appointed to teach Hebrew there, and he was the author of the first grammar of that language, and the first book which used Hebrew type, to be published in America. Mather was not the clergyman who officiated at Monis's conversion, but he was deeply moved by this event. In 1724 Mather observed in his diary that he ought to go and talk to Monis about passages in the Old Testament which were unclear to Mather, but which Monis might understand better, for "a Jew rarely comes over to us that he brings treasures with him." Monis had indeed brought "treasures" for Puritan believers. At his public baptism, he published "three discourses written by Mr. Monis himself, the Truth, the Whole Truth and, Nothing but the Truth." Monis even delivered one of these "discourses" as a speech at this great occasion. What he had to say uplifted the elite of Boston. This learned Jew defended Christianity, and especially the Doctrine of the Trinity, on the basis of "the Old Testament with the Authority of the Cabalistical Rabbies, Ancient and Modern." Christianity thus stood confirmed in Boston, out of the mouth of a Jew who even sometimes claimed to have been a rabbi.

Monis seems to have been sincere in his conversion, even though Cotton Mather's father, Increase, was guardedly dubious in the introduction that he wrote to the printed version of Monis's *Three Discourses*. Increase Mather's doubts were disproved by Monis's later life. When he retired from Harvard in 1760, after thirty-eight years of teaching, Monis went to live with relatives of his late wife (they had married after Monis's conversion) in Worcester County, Massachusetts. Monis was a leading figure in the local church, and he even presented the congregation with two silver communion cups, which might possibly have been the kiddush cups that he had used in his earlier, Jewish life. In his will Monis left money for the relief of poor widows of Massachusetts clergymen. The fund still exists and is administered by the American Unitarian Association which Monis's church joined some time after his death. In any event, on the day of Monis's conversion, Cotton Mather had reason to remember that he had written a book more than twenty years before to prove Christianity from the Jewish Bible, the Old Testament.

Mather left College Hall that day in the sure and certain faith that the Second Coming was near, and that the few Jews in the colonies would join Monis before long and would thus help bring about the "end of days."

But these hopes were vain. When Monis converted in 1722, organized Jewish communities were functioning in New York and in Charleston, South Carolina. Decade by decade other Jewish communities were being established in port towns all along the seaboard, as far south as Georgia. Nearer at hand, in the middle of the century, the Jewish community in Newport, Rhode Island, which had existed in the 1680s and had evaporated after 1700 for unknown reasons, was refounded in the 1750s by a group of Jewish sea traders and merchants. In the course of the eighteenth century, Jewish merchants did settle in Boston and in other places in New England, but they had no more rights than Anglicans, Quakers, and Baptists, who continued to be taxed for the support of the Congregational Church, and, even after these taxes were abolished in 1727–28, these Christian minorities were still harassed. But, in 1740 the British Parliament passed the Plantation Act which allowed all the immigrants of the colonies, except Catholics but including Jews, to be naturalized. The Puritans had to bow to this law. Individuals were allowed to trade in New England, and sometimes even admired, but they were nonetheless held at arm's length. The older attitudes, that Judaism was a false religion and that Jews could be accepted in society only if they converted, remained firm, even though the Puritans were losing ground in New England to secular, commercial interests.

Ezra Stiles was the Puritan divine (he later lost much of his orthodoxy) who was the most involved with Jews. He had come to Newport in 1755 as a Congregational minister, and remained there for twenty-three years, until he became president of Yale College in 1778. There were then some fifteen Jewish families in this port city, and several were important in the sea trade and in the civic community. Stiles became very interested in their synagogue. In 1767 he began to study Hebrew under the guidance of Isaac Touro, who was the religious functionary of the congregation. Newport's Jews were the hosts to a succession of rabbinic visitors from abroad, who came to collect alms for the Holy Land. The most striking figure among these emissaries was Isaac Carigal. Stiles went far out of his way to become friends with this rabbi, and a portrait of Carigal, painted for

Stiles, still exists. Carigal is depicted with piercing eyes and a long, thin, black beard, dressed in Oriental clothing. The relations between Stiles and Carigal were so friendly that there were exchanges of letters, in Hebrew, after Carigal left Newport for Barbados in 1774.

Stiles admired the public-spiritedness of some of the leading figures in the Newport Jewish community, and yet, when he first encountered these Jews, he wrote in his diary in 1762 that the dispersal of the Jews was a dire punishment which they merited for having rejected the Lord, and that it was inconceivable that a community of Jews could exist permanently in America. Stiles wrote this before he began to study Hebrew seriously or had met Carigal, but, even as he came to know the Jews of Newport better, he never changed his mind. In 1781, during the American Revolution, Stiles gave a speech to inaugurate a new academic year at Yale in which he insisted that the Jews did not understand their own Bible correctly. They were wrong to deny that the Old Testament taught the basic Christian doctrine of a "suffering Messiah." Hillel, the greatest figure of rabbinic Judaism, had misled the Jews. He had willfully corrupted biblical teaching in the years immediately before the appearance of Jesus.

The Puritans had begun, in the seventeenth century, by excluding all other Christians from their city of God. By the end of the eighteenth century, when the Republic was being founded, they had moved to accepting other Protestants—but not Catholics—as part of their America. The attitude toward Jews was ambivalent. Catholics and even other Protestants had nothing to teach Puritans. Jews, however, might help them understand the Hebrew Bible. Still, one had to be on guard against the Jews' cleverness and perversity. Judah Monis had not been liked, even though he was valued as a Hebraist. The students at Harvard complained that he was a bad teacher and, more pointedly, that he demanded too much money as payment for his grammar book, which was the required text in his class. A copy of the grammar that was owned by one of Monis's students still survives. This student amended the title page so that it no longer read "composed and accurately corrected by Judah Monis, M.A." The student wrote, instead, "confuted and accurately corrupted by Judah Monis, Maker of Asses." And Stiles, who prided himself on writing letters to Rabbi Carigal in Hebrew (it was very bad Hebrew), wrote continually in his diary that the rabbi was a rabbi and thus the representative of bad doctrine. Jews, no matter how intriguing they might be as individuals, remained outsiders. They could become part of America only if they ceased being Jewish.

A great question had been joined in colonial times: Was America to become the land of Asser Levy—a land of equal opportunity for any immigrant—or was it to be the land of the Puritans—a society which demanded conformity?

3.

Colonial Jews:

Almost Free

I

The Jews who came to colonial America were specks of dust, individuals picked up by some wind in Europe and blown across the Atlantic. Jewish poverty was increasing during the eighteenth century. Hordes of Jewish vagabonds were walking from town to town all over Europe looking for handouts; Jewish petty traders, the backbone of European Jewry, were increasingly in trouble throughout Europe. But only a very few Jews came to America. Many more might have come but the New World was remote and the journey dangerous. More important, the mass of those in trouble could not imagine living outside the established traditional Jewish community. They knew that it would be hard to be a Jew on the edge of the wilderness. Thus, those who crossed the Atlantic represented the few among European Jews who were least bound by tradition.

Colonial Jews were not very different from colonial Christians. The Americans, these "new men," were an unruly lot, even in religion. On the frontier all religion was remade by laymen. In colonial times both the Episcopalians and the Roman Catholics had no bishops in the colonies; these new settlements were treated as missionary territories. After the Revolution, in 1784, Samuel Seabury, the Episcopalian priest in New York, found his way to Scotland, after the authorities in London had put him off for many months; he was consecrated in Aberdeen as the first Episcopalian bishop in the United States. Six years later John Carroll was raised in London to be the first Roman Catholic bishop of a newly established diocese in Baltimore.

During the next half-century both these centrally organized churches established their network of authority throughout the United States, but the bishops of both churches were often defied. Under American conditions individual congregations were in law, from colonial times, independent bodies. Their properties were owned by individual trustees, and the laity chose their clergy. In Virginia, the most "English" of the colonies, the pattern was established very early; the clergy were the hired men of the congregation. This distemper with authority did not abate after bishops appeared in the United States. The Episcopalian bishops in America would never acquire the power of their English counterparts. The congregations remained the owners of the church buildings; they were never transferred to a central authority. Among the Roman Catholics the battles became especially bitter. Some congregations preferred to remain independent so that they could elect their own priests, even though they were excommunicated as schismatics.

Even in New England, where Puritanism was dominant, there was more disorder than uniformity. The very heart of Puritanism was the assertion that religious authority flowed from the individual congregation. It alone could consecrate a minister as its spiritual leader. It was an archheresy for a Puritan minister to be ordained by bishops of the Church of England or by Presbyterian elders. The flight of the founding fathers of the Massachusetts Bay Colony into the wilderness had represented a profound and very self-conscious act of breaking with Europe. The Puritans came to the New World to establish there a purer Christianity, to free the true faith of the corruption that had disfigured it in the old country. Puritanism was a shaping influence on all the other expressions of religion in early America. It did not succeed in teaching the lesson of Calvinist obedience to the awesome will of God, but all the sects learned from the Puritans what they wanted to hear, that no human authority stood above them.

In colonial America, the synagogues were like the churches; they were free associations. Individuals could choose to ignore the synagogue or to use it for whatever Jewish purposes they might wish. Many abandoned their Jewishness in North America during the seventeenth and eighteenth centuries. Where such individuals were prominent, their Jewish origins are widely remembered, very often to the discomfiture of their descendants. The Monsantos in New Orleans are an example of such immigrants. Upon arrival in America, this family was involved in the slave trade in New Orleans. They intermarried early and their Jewishness soon ceased to matter to them or to those around them. There were also some formal conversions to Christianity by adult Jews. Ezra Stiles told in his diary of meeting two Jews from London who had become Christians in Europe. In 1728, the pastor Henry Caner baptized Mordecai Marks in Fairfield, Connecticut; it is possible that Marks agreed to this step because he was about to marry a Christian. Michael Hayes, of a well-known New York family, joined the Baptist Church in Philadelphia around 1770. He was perhaps angry with his father for having cut him out of his will; the reason that the father gave was because of his "disobedience and general conduct." It is impossible to estimate the numbers of those Jews who left the Jewish community in colonial and early republican times, or to measure their influence on American life. The proportion was high, perhaps one in four of all the Jewish immigrants.

The Jews who cared established institutions which seemed to be exact copies of those that they had left behind in Europe. They had no other models. They therefore created synagogues in which the ritual was Orthodox, along with cemeteries, facilities for the slaughter of animals for food according to the kosher ritual, and mikvaot (ritual baths). The lay leaders of the earliest colonial synagogues behaved like their peers in Europe; they tried to enforce obedience to the ancient ways by all their members—but they failed, for, unlike the authorities of the Jewish communities in the European ghettos, the Americans had not the power to coerce. In the 1760s, New York's only synagogue fined members of the congregation who did not attend Sabbath services, but this practice was abandoned within twenty years because it was unenforceable. The earliest statutes had ruled that no one who was intermarried could be buried on the grounds of the synagogue's cemetery. Such offenders were eventually allowed to rest with other Jews, though the congregation stood fast on the rule that non-Jewish members of the family could not be accorded that privilege. Jewish shops in New York were closed on the Sabbath in the last half of the eighteenth century, but some Jews began to break ranks and open their stores on the holy day.

Even earlier, in the 1740s, Lutheran Pastor Henry Melchior Mühlenberg asserted that the Jews in Philadelphia were "practicing atheists." This was no doubt an overstatement, but we do know that several decades later, in the revolutionary era, the congregation in Philadelphia was troubled by members of the synagogue who desecrated the Sabbath. It was even more troublesome that some known Jews were entirely indifferent. According to a statement in a draft constitution of the synagogue, in the 1770s, sanctions were recommended against "people in the community who do not want to make any contribution and separate themselves from the group and do not want help to support the community."

The population of avowed Jews was some 250 in the year 1700 and perhaps 2,000 at the time of the Revolution. By the middle of the century, synagogues existed in five cities; in Charleston, New York, and Philadelphia, Jews numbered in the several hundreds. In these three centers, the communities were large enough and rich enough to invite a rabbi to be their religious leader, but they did not. This was a matter of choice. Many a poorer and smaller town in contemporary Europe was then supporting a fully structured Jewish community, with a rabbi at its head. It is not true that rabbis were hard to persuade to come to the New World. In the years of the American Revolution there were rabbis in Suriname, Curaçao, and Jamaica. In Jamaica, the learned rabbi of Kingston, Isaac Córdoba, was busy writing a defense of the Bible against the godlessness of the greatest paladin of the Enlightenment, Voltaire. The rabbi feared the inroads of Voltaire's thinking on the young of his congregation. His volume was first published anonymously in Jamaica in 1788 but there were soon two editions in the United States, in Philadelphia in 1791 and in Richmond in 1804.

The dangers to the faith seem to have been at least as serious among the Jews of the United States as among those of Jamaica. Otherwise, what need was there of two printings of Córdoba's book in the

United States? The work was actually read by American-educated children of immigrants to colonial America; it is listed among the goods in several estates. Nonetheless, despite the presence of some troubled, questioning younger people, the authorities of the various synagogues felt no need to persuade a rabbi such as Córdoba to come to New York or Philadelphia. The Jews in the American colonies employed only functionaries, such as cantors and ritual slaughterers. A resident rabbi or two might have insisted on exercising authority over the laity and on cultivating the study of the sacred texts.

This estimate of American Jews in the last half of the eighteenth century, that they did not care about Jewish learning, is confirmed by two stories from Rhode Island. The Jewish community of Newport was at the height of its prestige in the 1770s. Led by Aaron Lopez, the leading Jewish shipowner in America, these were among the most acculturated and elegant Jewish merchants. They thought of themselves, and were regarded by others, as belonging to the Jewish hidalgos of North America—and they were not lacking in generosity. After Lopez died by drowning, he was praised by a newspaper in Newport for representing "the most amiable perfections and cardinal virtues that can adorn the human soul." Ezra Stiles wrote: "His beneficence to his family connections, to his [Jewish] nation and to all the world is almost without parallel." Lopez supported numerous widows and orphans, and so did the rest of the Newport community. But these charitable men were indifferent to an offer that was made in the early 1770s by the founders of Rhode Island College, the ancestor of the present Brown University. The college opened its doors to Jewish students, and it extended an invitation to Jews to "have a tutor of their own religion." The founders of the college went even further; they would be glad to establish a chair in "Hebrew and Oriental languages" if Jews would contribute the money. The Jewish merchants declined. They were raising their children to succeed in business, not to go to college or to become Hebrew scholars.

Lopez and his friends were not totally indifferent to Jewish learning; they simply believed its proper place was in Europe or the Holy Land. The subject of Jewish learning was raised almost inevitably by Rabbi Isaac Carigal during his visit to Newport in 1773. Carigal had come to America to collect money for the academy of rabbinic studies (yeshivah) in the holy city, Hebron. The state occasion of

Carigal's visit was a sermon that he gave for the Shevuot (Pentecost) Festival. Carigal pleaded for "the frequentation of sacred colleges and synagogues where we daily hear the word of the Lord." He went on to insist that study of the Bible and of the rabbinic literature which flowed from it were the surest antidote to sin; it was the source of all the Jewish virtues. His listeners were moved by this plea. Carigal was sent on his way with a handsome donation for Hebron, but no school of Jewish studies was established in Newport. On the contrary, the leaders of this community were then spending their evenings playing cards together in a social club they had established; it was a cardinal rule of this establishment that the business of the synagogue should never be discussed. After Carigal's visit, as before, the sons of the merchants in Newport and elsewhere in the colonies were given sufficient instruction to celebrate their bar mitzvahs and to participate in the ritual of the synagogue, but only a handful of native-born Jews in all of colonial America were ever taught enough of the tradition to be able to conduct the service of the synagogue.

A letter from Haym Salomon, a man of business who maintained close relations with the leaders of the Continental Congress, confirms this picture of the inner life of early Jews in very graphic terms. He wrote in 1783 from Philadelphia, one of the three most established Jewish communities of colonial times, that "there is very little *Yiddishkeit* [Jewishness] here." This is all the more striking since Haym Salomon himself was hardly a paragon of Jewish piety. Haym Salomon himself seems to have known just enough Hebrew to read the prayer book mechanically, and to dictate letters in bad Yiddish, but beyond that he had no Jewish education. He had no doubt that America was not the place for learned Jews. In the last days of the Revolution, he passed a message back to his father in Europe: "Should any of my brothers' children have a good head to learn Hebrew, I would contribute towards his being instructed." The implication was clear that such a nephew should stay in Europe, and not come to America. Salomon told an uncle that Jewish learning meant nothing in America, and that it was better that this uncle not come to join him in Philadelphia. Another correspondent from Philadelphia wrote to relatives in Amsterdam two years later that "most of the sons of this province are not devoted to Torah and do not understand our tongue." An unsigned letter exists from the days of the Revolution in which a Jew announced that he was going back to Europe because America was no place for a man of piety; religion was weak and only money was well respected. Such discouragements would be written back home to Europe from all the future waves of immigration. They would act, as they did in the eighteenth century, to reduce severely the number of learned Jews who came to America.

Lopez and Salomon reflected the flatness of two functioning Jewish communities, Newport and Philadelphia. Elsewhere, on the frontier, where Jews were but a small, unorganized handful, or, even more difficult, lived as isolated individuals, the religious problems were far worse. Some immigrants wrote pained letters in Yiddish back to their families in Poland, in which the writers spoke of the Sabbath as a memory and of their inability to keep the dietary laws. Male children were often circumcised several at a time when a circuit-riding mohel appeared. But the picture was not all negative, even in outlying places. In 1754, a number of Jews from Philadelphia were engaged in land purchase and speculation in Lancaster, Pennsylvania; a congregation was formed there in 1776, and a synagogue was built in 1789. In Newport and New York, preserved kosher meat (salted beef) was imported on a regular basis from Jamaica, where it was prepared under the auspices of the local rabbinate. Great care was taken to make sure that these preserves arrived suitably labeled. Early in the nineteenth century this traffic was reversed; kosher meat was exported from New York to the islands.

Non-Jewish observers and travelers were struck by the hard struggle of some Jews to cling to their religion and by the complete indifference to the tradition of others. They reported on Jews who went to great lengths not to eat pork and to observe the Jewish Holy Days, but they told of others who did eat pork and who worked on the Sabbath. A Swedish scientist, Peter Kalm, observed as early as 1748 that "many of them (especially the young) when travelling did not make the least difficulty about eating this or any other meat." On the other hand, one can cite Hart Jacobs, who asked the authorities in Philadelphia in January 1776 to be exempt "from doing military duty on the city watch on Friday nights, which is part of his Sabbath." This wish was granted, provided the citizen performed "his full tour of duty on other nights." Aaron Lopez kept his business closed on the Sabbath and he refused to see anyone on business affairs, even at home, on any of the Jewish Holy Days. Occasionally, as in the case of two Jewish bankers, pious Jews let their businesses be run for them on the Sabbath by a trusted Christian employee.

Inevitably, technical problems in the Jewish religion arose which were beyond the competence of the local people. Marriages could be performed according to Jewish ritual by semilearned laymen, but conversions and religious divorces were more technical matters, requiring rabbinic learning and specific skills. Such learning was rarely to be found in America before the 1840s. Conversions to Judaism were often defective in form. One such case involved the second wife of Abraham Alexander, who was the cantor of Beth Elohim in Charleston, South Carolina, until he resigned in 1784. That same year he was married to a Huguenot lady. She lived as a faithful and observant Jew all her life, and yet she was denied burial in the Jewish cemetery because her conversion had not been carried out according to the prescription of Jewish ceremonial law.

And yet, American Jewry of colonial times was not totally Philistine and bereft of knowledge of the tradition. Several learned laymen did turn up, possibly because they were fleeing creditors in Europe. One such figure was Jonas Phillips, who arrived in Charleston, in 1756, at the age of twenty, as an indentured servant. After three years of such servitude, Phillips moved to Albany, where he opened a store, but the business that he hoped to do with the British garrison, which was then fighting the French and Indian War, was not sufficient to keep him from bankruptcy. Jonas Phillips soon moved to New York. He was employed for four years, in the 1760s, by the local congregation as the *shohet,* the ritual slaughterer of animals for kosher meat. To perform this task required some learning in Jewish religious law, which Phillips had evidently proved to the rabbis who had granted him qualification in Europe. He wrote rabbinic Hebrew well enough so that he could correspond with the rabbis in London. Manuel Josephson, of German birth, was probably even more of a scholar. Josephson made his living as a merchant in New York, but he was often consulted on matters of Jewish law. He wrote excellent rabbinic Hebrew, and he owned the best library of rabbinic texts in colonial America. It is clear from his will that he did not believe that there was a future in America for knowledge of the rabbinic texts. He specified that his volumes in Western languages be sold at auction, but that his books in Hebrew be packed up and sent back to Europe.

Rabbi Córdoba's refutation of Voltaire was the only original work by a Jew on Judaism that was published in early America, and this book had not been written in the United States. Nonetheless, colonial Jews did produce the first translation of the prayer book into English. The first volume appeared anonymously in 1761 in New York; it contained the evening service for the High Holy Days. Five years later, a much larger volume appeared; it included all of the Sabbath prayers and all of the High Holy Day liturgies. The name of the translator, Isaac Pinto, was given on the title page. Pinto was probably also the anonymous translator of the earlier volume. In the introduction to the second book, Pinto wrote that translation of the liturgy in English was required, because Hebrew is "imperfectly understood by many" and "by some, not at all." Pinto's translations were accurate, reflecting substantial knowledge of biblical and rabbinic Hebrew.

II

By mid-eighteenth century a few Jewish families had already lived in North America for two and some for even three or four generations. The most prominent were several branches of the Franks family. They had come to New York and Philadelphia from England as merchants and army purveyors. Everyone knew them to be Jews, but, even though some of its members belonged to synagogues, the Franks clan was already in the process of evaporating from the Jewish community. David Franks, who lived in Philadelphia, was the most prominent of them all. He remained part of the family business, and he seemed to have maintained good personal relations with his relatives, but he married a Gentile and all his children were baptized at birth. David Franks himself had been born and educated in New York City. His father, Jacob Franks, was president of the Jewish congregation for seven terms, and he was a man of some learning in rabbinic texts. David's bar mitzvah was, of course, celebrated in the synagogue. After David's father died, he observed the traditional period of mourning, and he even continued for a while to contribute to the synagogue in New York, but he never joined the congregation in Philadelphia, where he lived. David Franks owned one of the most elegant homes in Philadelphia; he was one of the few men of business there who had his own carriage. He remained in touch with Jews because he did business with them, especially with members of his own family, but he did not move socially in Jewish circles. David Franks was too elegant for that; he found his friends among the descendants of William Penn, who had founded the colony, and the rest of that circle. And yet, David Franks remained a Jew. To the end of his life he insisted on swearing oaths not "on the true faith of the Christian" but with his hand resting on the Hebrew Bible.

David Franks was not the only American Jew who remained Jewish despite intermarriage, and despite the social distance that he kept from other Jews. Unlike Franks, his cousin, Benjamin Levy, was even married to a Jew, but the family drifted out of the Jewish community. Levy did so well socially in Philadelphia that he was among the elite who were invited to contribute to the Pennsylvania Hospital, and he was among the signers, in 1767, of a formal address to welcome Lieutenant Governor John Penn. Benjamin Levy and his family moved to Baltimore. When his wife, Rachel, died, she was buried there in an Episcopalian cemetery. It is likely that this was decided by her children, who had intermarried and become Christians.

By the end of the colonial era, the handful of Jews on the Eastern Seaboard of North America had already defined three types. Some were like the second and third generation of the Franks family; they were rapidly assimilating, because success and social acceptance were their dominant concern. Others, a minority, followed after Jonas Phillips, who fought very hard for the preservation of Orthodox Judaism in the New World. The majority were assimilating into Gentile America, while maintaining considerable Jewish feeling. Haym Salomon represents this mainstream of early American Jews. He was the largest contributor to the Mikveh Israel Congregation in Philadelphia, but he was hardly its most pious member. Like so many Jews in the generations that were to follow, he paid his respects to the Lord by coming occasionally to services and by writing the synagogue generous checks.

Colonial America was different from Europe. In Europe in those days, assimilation usually meant the assumption of a new identity through religious conversion, or remaining Orthodox. A third option had begun to appear in Europe in those days: a few had ceased believing in the Orthodox tradition, and yet they chose to stay within the Jewish community. Such men were very busy inventing new definitions of Judaism to justify their changes in belief and practice. In the 1770s and 1780s, the philosopher Moses Mendelssohn and a whole circle of friends and disciples in Berlin were trying to define how one could be both a man of the world and a Jew. In America, there was no contemporary echo of the writings of Moses Mendelssohn. Partial or very nearly total nonobservance of the commandments of the religious tradition became the norm very early without any attempt at an intellectual defense. In America, those who wanted to leave Judaism did not need to convert or to explain themselves to themselves. If they wished, they could live on the border, as some did, between leaving and remaining. American Judaism was becoming in practice almost as many "Judaisms" as there were individuals. A new version of a Jewish persona was defined in America as early as the eighteenth century: it was an individual who lived like everyone else, and yet "felt Jewish."

In eighteenth-century America such Jewishness did not last beyond a generation or two. There is little doubt that before 1800 less than half of the grandchildren of the early Jewish settlers remained Jews. We know from precise genealogical tables that one-third of the grandchildren of those who remained Jews in the time of the Revolution had left the community by 1840. The rate of assimilation had decreased, no doubt because by then there were already more Jews in the United States, at least three times as many as the two thousand of the 1780s. There was thus a greater possibility of marrying within the fold. In generations to come, the rate of assimilation of the grandchildren of immigrants would remain fixed at one-third. "German Jews" and "Russian Jews" would, in turn, define their Jewishness in America in the same terms as the handful of colonial Jews: to be a Jew meant to "feel Jewish," rather than to be learned or pious.

III

Biblical Jews were ever present in the minds of the Puritans, but there were almost no living Jews in Massachusetts or elsewhere in New England except in the port city of Newport, Rhode Island. The existing Jews were in the middle and the southern colonies, from

New York to Georgia and South Carolina. Jews were discussed and sometimes they were harassed, but the tensions were of marginal importance. True, Jews had no political equality in any of the colonies before the Revolution; officials had to swear their oaths "on the true faith of a Christian," or by affirming their belief in the divinity of both the Old and the New Testaments. The situation varied from colony to colony. The charter for South Carolina, written by the philosopher John Locke, allowed any seven people to assemble and to constitute a church, including "Jews, heathens and other disenters." Maryland, on the other hand, even though founded by Catholics, had specified in its charter that only Christians would be allowed to live in the colony, even though stray Jews who came to trade or even to settle were not overtly molested.

Nowhere, not even in the most tolerant places, did Jews have secure rights to vote in elections for representatives to colonial legislatures. Jews did vote in New York in 1737 in a bitterly contested election, but their votes were thrown out. The argument against them was that Jews had no such rights in England, and that they remained guilty of the Crucifixion. In Rhode Island in 1762 the lower house of the legislature held that Jews did not have the right to hold office or to vote in elections. Nonetheless, Jews seem to have voted in local elections in several of the colonies, because nobody bothered to stop them. Peter Kalm had remarked as early as 1748 that "Jews enjoyed all the privileges common to other inhabitants." What they lacked in equality seemed insignificant or irrelevant to a foreign observer.

The vital issue for Jews in the eighteenth century was economic rights. Here, the Jews in the American colonies were, both in law and in practice, free and equal at least half a century before this was true even in England itself. Despite some laws on the books, the rights that Jews had fought out very early in New Amsterdam, to trade in local commerce like all other burghers, were never seriously contested either there or in any other colony. Their right to engage in sea trade was denied by the English, as part of their ongoing attempt under the Navigation Act of 1660 to limit the import and export trade of all English colonies to English ships, which were manned by Englishmen. Individual Jews managed to win exceptions to this rule. Rabba Couti, a Jewish burgher from New York, won a case in 1672 before the Council for Trade and Plantations, which held that he was not an alien. The Navigation Act of 1696, as originally drafted, would have excluded from international trade anyone who was not a native of one of the colonies, or born in England. This provision was dropped under pressure from Jews and Huguenots in London, who appeared on behalf of their brethren in the American colonies. The Jewish petition argued that Jews were the enemies of the Inquisition, and that they regarded the land which gave them refuge as "their native country." These problems ended when the Naturalization Act of 1740 was passed; it allowed all Protestants, Jews, and Quakers to be naturalized in the English colonies. After that, the difficulties that Jews had were not different from those of all other American sea traders. The pattern had thus been set a generation before the Revolution: in America, as nowhere else, Jews could make their living without constraint, as they pleased.

Nonetheless, many of the Jews who came to the colonies in North America did not remain. They did not do as well in the New Land as they had hoped. We know of a Jewish merchant community of some twenty families in Newport in the 1680s, but this community was not the ancestor of the famous and more important one which existed in the middle of the next century. In a number of cemeteries in the Caribbean—in Barbados, Jamaica, Curaçao, Suriname, and St. Eustatius—there are gravestones of people who lived a good part of their active lives in the American colonies, and even in the nascent Republic, and then went elsewhere. Some left in search of a more Jewish life, but most were looking for a better living.

As early as colonial times, the economic profile of the Jew was radically different from that of the rest of the country. In earliest America, more than four out of five people made their livings working the land, but not the Jews. They were the only denomination which consisted, in its large majority, of city people. The country needed middlemen and artisans, and those were the skills that Jews had acquired in Europe where for many centuries very few had been permitted to farm. In the next two centuries Jews would enter many new occupations, but the identification of Jews with the cities, and with the urban economy and culture, has remained fixed as a fact of American and of American Jewish life.

Attempts would be made in the future, some of them successful, to limit Jewish immigration to America, but there was never any serious discussion by non-Jews (as there was often in Europe in the eighteenth century and thereafter) that Jews ought to be restratified economically by sending them off to "healthy" occupations on the land. This dream, or fantasy, would be harbored by some Jewish immigrants to America toward the end of the nineteenth century and the beginning of the twentieth, but it never penetrated the consciousness of American anti-Semites (perhaps, in part, because these Jew haters were often themselves farmers, and they had no desire to have Jews in the farm across the road).

In the North American colonies Jews were totally absent from the one heavy industry of those days, the making of iron. They were of no consequence in the trade of grain and tobacco, the two most important agricultural exports of the era. These products were raised on farms and plantations in Maryland and Virginia, where there were hardly any Jews. Jews did figure very early, even before 1800, as middlemen in the sale of copper, but they were not principals in the few small mines that were being worked in the eastern United States. On the eve of the Revolution, most Jews were artisans or petty merchants. Only a very few were well-off, and even they did not have the capital with which to launch themselves toward the highest reaches of the American economy. There were only two marked exceptions to the rule that colonial and early American Jews were artisans or middlemen. There were some farmers in Georgia. Aaron Lopez manufactured candles in Newport from the spermaceti of whales; this was the only economic endeavor in which in the eighteenth century Jews were important, producing about thirty percent of the total output. Jewish financiers were of little consequence, because North America was then no great financial center. The Franks family of army purveyors (this pursuit involved advancing large credit to military authorities) had branches in New York, Philadelphia, and Montreal at various times, but the center of the enterprise was in London.

There was some anti-Semitism, even in the colonies which were hospitable to Jews. Even in supposedly tolerant Charleston, South Carolina, a Jewish funeral procession was attacked in May 1743, probably because of some economic quarrel between the family of the deceased and Gentile competitors. In almost every quarrel between Jew and Gentile, somebody managed to throw in the slur that the Jews had crucified the Lord, and that they were therefore untrustworthy, even in business. At the very beginnings of Jewish settlement in America, the Reverend John Megapolensis had asked the authorities in New Amsterdam to expel them, not only because he hated their religion, but because the Jews had no other God "than the unrighteous Mammon, and no other aim than to get possession of Christian property, and to win all other merchants by drawing all trade towards themselves." Right before the Revolution, in 1770, Ezra Stiles confided to his diary without a breath of doubt that in London, Jews headed a spy operation in the colonies on behalf of the government and that all their agents were local Jews. On the other hand, colonial Jewish businessmen were often complimented for their honor and uprightness. On the whole, the language about Jews was no more hostile—indeed, less so—than the rhetoric that was often directed against Catholics.

Almost everyone who mentioned the Jews in colonial America suggested or at least implied that they ought to convert to Christianity, but there were no missions to the Jews anywhere. American society was, then, in the process of becoming. A colony might exclude people it did not like, but those who were admitted were by and large not troubled in the exercise of their religion. Colonial society was too fragmented and untidy for persecution to work. The persecuted could, like Roger Williams, move into the wilderness and start their own settlement, or they could avoid places like Boston and do business in places like the more tolerant Philadelphia. Contrary to the later, nativist myth, the population of colonial America was not overwhelmingly Protestant, of English origins. Some forty percent of the earliest Americans came from all over Europe, and they belonged to an enormous variety of religious sects, such as Quakers, Mennonites, and Seventh-Day Adventists. In this complex early America, Jewish religious rites were not entirely strange or unique.

Sometimes the sects even helped each other. Jews made the first "interfaith" gesture as early as 1711, when seven contributed to the building of Trinity Church in New York. After the middle of the eighteenth century, Jews and Christians had worked together in organizing several Masonic lodges. When the new synagogue building in Newport was dedicated in 1763, the governor of the colony and other civic dignitaries were present. The symbolic high point of this Jewish-Christian amity was probably the sermon that Rabbi Carigal delivered in that synagogue in the spring of 1773. The congregation, that day, included the governor of Rhode Island, judges and other civic officials, and, of course, Ezra Stiles. The sermon was given in Spanish, but it was soon translated into English and offered for sale to the general community. Carigal impressed his audience, according to Stiles's diary, with his elocution, and even more with his garments: "a fur cap, scarlet robe, green silk damask vest, and a chintz under-vest—girt with a sash or Turkish girdle—beside the alb [prayer shawl] with tzitzith [ritual fringes]."

Before and after this great occasion, Carigal had engaged in many conversations which involved comparisons of Jewish and Christian theological doctrines. His Christian interlocutors, led by Stiles, did not accept Carigal's Jewish views, but they had great respect for his learning and intelligence. Carigal proved that Jews could be more than successful merchants: they had ties to the Holy Land, and they belonged to a tradition of learning—like the Puritans. Carigal's visit gave Newport's Jews vicarious dignity. The honor and the money that the Jews of Newport gave to Carigal, in all his Oriental Jewish splendor, acted to make the community into a "normal" American denomination.

But Jews were the only settlers in the colonies who were not Christian. They were therefore, inevitably, the most exotic. At the state occasion at which Carigal had preached, the governor had come out of respect for the importance of the Jewish merchants of New-port, and Stiles attended because he was fascinated by the Oriental Jewish sage who preached the sermon, but the governor stood at the head of a colony which had refused to naturalize Lopez (he had had to appeal to Massachusetts, of all places), and Stiles kept confiding to his diary that he admired Lopez and Carigal, but he wanted them to turn Christian. There is no written record of what Lopez and Carigal thought that day, but they must have marveled at the pres-ence of the Christian dignitaries, even as they knew that the visitors to the synagogue were half hiding some ambivalences about Jews. Lopez had been born a Marrano in Portugal, and he and his wife had fled to America in 1752 in fear of the Inquisition. Carigal came from Hebron, where Jews were *dhimmi,* a tolerated, sometimes per-secuted, minority of inferior status. Lopez and Carigal knew that even in America Christians did not regard Jews as their equal—and yet, America was different.

4.

Revolutionaries—and Some Tories

The American Republic would have been founded exactly as it was if there had not been a single Jew in the thirteen colonies. There were simply too few of them for their efforts to make a serious difference during the Revolution. True, the great majority of the two thousand Jews who dwelt in America were Whigs, supporters of the revolt. Even by the most unsentimental estimate, they did contribute far more to the American cause than anyone could have expected from so small a community. Almost a hundred Jews have been identified as soldiers in the revolutionary armies. The first patriot to lose his life in Georgia was Francis Salvador. In July 1776, he accompanied William Tennent, a Presbyterian evangelist, to North Carolina to try to persuade some Tories to join the Revolution. On August 1, Salvador was ambushed and shot and scalped by Tories and their Indian allies. In Charleston, South Carolina, almost every adult male Jew served in the military. Captain Lushington's company, which was half Jewish, became known as the "Jew Company." One of its braver soldiers, Jacob I. Cohen, some years after the war, was the owner of land in Kentucky, and he hired Daniel Boone to survey his property. There was one area of military action in which Jews took a notable part. About six percent of the American privateers, the warships that were outfitted and sent to sea by individual owners or companies, were financed by Jews, with Aaron Lopez of Newport in the lead.

The contribution of Jews for the conduct of the war was even greater among the civilians. Mordecai Sheftall, the leader of the Jewish community in Savannah, was also a central figure among the rebels in Georgia. When the British occupied Savannah in December 1778, Sheftall was jailed on a prison ship. The British governor of Georgia, James Wright, was so enraged at the Jewish Whigs that he wanted to bar those who had fled from ever returning to the colony. He wrote home to London that "These people, my Lord, were found to a man to be violent rebels and pursecuters [sic] of the King's loyal subjects." One hundred men bearing arms, even with an outsized proportion of heroes, were not the hinge of the Revolution—but Jews played a more than honorable role in achieving independence.

Jews also helped to keep the Continental Congress from going bankrupt. The most important figure in this tale was Haym Salomon, who had arrived in New York in 1772 and had opened a business as merchant on commission, securities dealer, and ship broker. Salomon joined the rebels very early. In August 1778, he was arrested by the British in New York on suspicion of espionage and sabotage, and he was sentenced to death. He escaped prison and turned up in Philadelphia later that month, opening a brokerage house there. Soon Salomon was lending money to the Continental Congress. In the last days of the war, after his friend, Robert Morris, became superintendent of finance, Salomon advanced the American government over two hundred thousand dollars in hard currency to help provision the armies. What he got in security was paper which was never redeemed. Salomon died bankrupt in New York in 1785, and his family, despite half a century of effort, never succeeded in collecting the debt.

Most of the Jews were partisans of the Revolution, but a pronounced minority were Loyalists. Jewish artisans and small merchants almost all rallied to the cause of the rebels. The Jewish Tories were mostly shipowners who were involved in the direct import of finished goods from England. There were, indeed, more Jewish Loyalists than the first, "patriotic" historians of colonial Jewry wanted to find. The Hart family were Tories. They rivaled Aaron Lopez among the Jewish merchants and international traders in Newport, Rhode Island. On July 1, 1780, the Assembly of Rhode Island formally deprived three members of the family of their rights and property. Soon thereafter, Isaac Hart was brutally murdered because of his support of the British. Nevertheless, some of the international Jewish traders were partisans of the Revolution. Isaac Lopez, of Newport, was the most prominent. He had long flaunted the British by dealing directly with the islands in the Caribbean. Lopez was even praised by local authorities in Rhode Island for his attainments as a smuggler, and he continued during the Revolution to run ships which evaded the blockade by the British navy.

Jewish opinion was split in New York, as well. In 1776, when the British occupied the city, a "loyal address" was presented to General Sir William Howe; among its signers were fifteen Jews. A number of Jewish partisans of the Revolution did flee to Philadelphia, along with their cantor, Gershom Mendes Seixas; he was the first Jew who was born and trained in America to become the religious leader of a congregation. The Jewish Tories of New York did not, however, remain without a clergyman. Isaac Touro, the cantor of the congregation in Newport, Rhode Island, left that city when the rebels were in control, and found his way to New York. In 1783, when peace was made, Touro left for Jamaica, where he could live under the British crown. He soon died and his family, including his son Judah, who was later to become famous as a philanthropist, returned to the United States.

Jews were also divided in Philadelphia. Haym Salomon fled to New York to escape British occupation, but David Franks did not. The Franks family changed sides a few times. They were, by turn, purveyors to the army, whether Patriot or British. When General Sir William Howe occupied Philadelphia in 1778, Rebecca Franks, a celebrated beauty and charmer, the daughter of David Franks, was the belle of the ball in the social circle of British officers. In 1782, she married one of Howe's officers, Lieutenant Colonel Henry Johnson. After the war, Rebecca went to England with her husband. Colonel Johnson was eventually made a baronet; the Johnsons ended their days in Ross Castle in Ireland.

The Patriot majority of American Jews, represented by Haym

Salomon of Philadelphia, Aaron Lopez of Newport, and Mordecai
Sheftall of Savannah, were not crucial to the American Revolution.
Their importance to Jewish and American history lies not in what
they did, but simply because they were there. The decisions by the
Constitutional Convention to create absolute equality in the United
States among all kinds of believers and nonbelievers was made in
awareness that there were Jews in America, and in the expressed
intention that they, too, should benefit from the new Constitution.

This document defined the rights of citizens in the federal government, but the individual states lagged behind. By law, Jews did
not have full rights in any of the colonies, and the situation did not
change all at once during and after the Revolution. By 1777, only
one state, New York, had given complete political equality to men
of all faiths, or none. In 1790, Virginia, Georgia, South Carolina,
and Pennsylvania followed suit. It took many decades for the last
obstacles to be removed from all of the state constitutions. Some of
these documents retained the provision that oaths for public office
had to be taken on the "true faith of a Christian," but the federal
Constitution was evermore the dominant political arrangement. The
vestiges of exclusion in colonial times eventually faded from all the
state constitutions. The last to fall was New Hampshire, which
waited until 1868 to delete a Christian oath as a requirement for
office.

When the Constitutional Convention assembled in Philadelphia in
1787, there were some fears that Jews might be limited by the national
government to the rights that they already had in the colonies, and
that they would thus be excluded from voting and from holding
office. Jonas Phillips addressed a petition to the assembled delegates.
He begged them not to require officeholders to be sworn in on "the
true faith of a Christian." Phillips was particularly worried about the
deliberation at the Constitutional Convention, because the Jews had
lost a battle in the state assembly of Pennsylvania eleven years earlier.
In December 1783, a group which included Haym Salomon and
Gershom Mendes Seixas had petitioned in protest against the state
constitution which required that members of the assembly had to
"acknowledge the Scriptures of the Old and New Testament to be
given by divine inspiration." This declaration effectively excluded
Jews from office. The writers of the petition called this act "a stigma
upon their nation and their religion." It is revealing and important

that the writers of the petition more than gently threatened the authorities in Pennsylvania. They themselves had no great passion for public office, but, so they argued, maintaining such exclusions would harm Pennsylvania: Jews in Europe or elsewhere who might want to come to America might prefer to go to places like New York "where there is no such like restraint laid upon the nation and religion of the Jews." This protest by Jews in Philadelphia was the very first time in American history that Jews demanded equality, citing their services as patriots as the undeniable argument. This petition was ignored, but the religious test was removed six years later, when a new state constitution was written.

Phillips's petition to the Constitutional Convention was unnecessary, though he could not have known it, because the deliberations of that body were taking place in total secrecy. Two weeks before he wrote, the Constitutional Convention had passed, on August 20, the sixth article of the new national Constitution: no religious test would be required of officeholders. Two years later, the First Amendment to the Constitution strengthened this foundation of the new American Republic by decreeing the separation of church and state. In federal law, Jews, the smallest of all recognizable minorities, now had totally unrestricted freedom and equality in the United States.

II

Like everyone else in America in the era of the Revolution, Jews, of course, knew that they were living in the midst of great events, and yet they reacted as Jews: they were not quite ready to believe their good fortune. Even after they had read the new Constitution, they needed reassurance that their place in America was secure.

Popular anti-Semitism had always existed. The uneducated and unreflective mass of the immigrants to the New Land, of whatever origin, had brought with them the age-old stereotypes that Jews were alien and bad. The more specific charge, that Jews did harm to the economy, was very seldom made in colonial America, but it was hurled during the Revolution. When the British invaded Georgia in 1778, a number of the Jews in Savannah sent their families to Charleston for safety, while they remained to fight. A letter in the

Charlestown Gazette on December 1, 1778, accused the Jews of disloyalty. The anonymous writer charged that the Jews, "after taking every advantage in trade the times admitted of in the state of Georgia, as soon as it was attacked by an enemy, fled here for asylum for their ill-got wealth, dastardly turning their backs on the country, which gave them bread and protection." Equally anonymously, "a real American and true-hearted Israelite" answered the next day that the attack was a lie because only women and children had been evacuated, while all the men had remained for their patriotic duty.

The economic charge against Jews was made once again in Philadelphia in 1784. Miers Fisher, a former Tory, returned to Philadelphia at the end of the war and tried to obtain a charter to open a bank. He argued that his bank would serve the public by reducing the rate of interest; the citizens of Pennsylvania would thus be protected against the usury of the Jews. An anonymous "Jew Broker" (he was probably Haym Salomon) answered in the press. The writer was outraged that Fisher had defamed the Jews of Philadelphia. How dare he say such things against people who had been "second to none" in their "patriotism" and their "attachment" to the American cause. Salomon did suggest that there might have been a few Jews who had behaved badly in business, but were the many to be punished for the sins of the few? How could Miers Fisher suggest that Jews as a whole behaved less well than all other Americans, when the truth was that they were to be found among the best patriots of all?

The first direct attack on Jews, after the declaration of the United States, was made in the early 1790s. Jews seem to have been criticized (we do not know by whom) for their supposed clannishness. Dr. David Nassy, who was in medical practice in Philadelphia in the 1790s, seems to have been the first polemicist in America to defend Jews against the charge of clannishness. He listed a number of Jews in Philadelphia who were "lawfully married to Christian women, who go to their own churches, the men going to their synagogues, and who, when together, frequent the best society." Such Jews could not be accused of self-segregation, so Dr. Nassy argued. Nassy was evidently not an opponent of assimilation.

A more serious incident took place in 1800. A leading figure in the Philadelphia Jewish community, Benjamin Nones, was attacked in the *Gazette of the United States,* a publication of the Federalist party, for being a Jew and a Republican (i.e., a supporter of what is today the Democratic party). Nones did not flinch. He affirmed his loyalty to the revolutions in the United States, in France, and in Holland, because these were the only regimes which had yet given equality to Jews. Nones's answer to the *Gazette* was a passionate expression of Jewish anger at centuries of persecution:

I am a Jew. I glory in belonging to that persuasion, which even in its opponents, whether Christian, or Mahomedan, allow to be of divine origin—of that persuasion on which Christianity itself was originally founded and must ultimately rest—which has preserved its faith secure and undefiled, for near three thousand years—whose votaries have never murdered each other in religious wars, or cherished the theological hatred so general, so unextinguishable among those who revile them. . . .

But I am a Jew. I am so—and so were Abraham, and Isaac, and Moses and the prophets, and so too were Christ and his apostles. I feel no disgrace in ranking with such society, however it may be subject to the illiberal buffoonery of such men as your correspondents. . . .

I am a *Republican!* . . . Among the nations of Europe we are inhabitants everywhere—but Citizens of nowhere *unless in Republics. Here, in France, and in the Batavian Republic alone, we are treated as men and as brethren. In republics we have rights,* in monarchies we live but to experience *wrongs.* . . .

How then can a Jew but be a Republican? In America particularly. Unfeeling & ungrateful would he be, if he were callous to the glorious and benevolent cause of the difference between his situation in this land of freedom, and among the proud and privileged law-givers of Europe.

Thus, in the earliest days of the United States, society was largely open to Jews, but some ambivalence about them did persist. Their enemies, who were fortunately not many, insisted the Jews were obnoxious. Jews answered that they had as much right to be in America as anyone else. The "Jew Broker" had even defended their right to have a few unlovely characters among them; Jews had earned such total equality by their superior services to America. Dr. Nassy had answered critics by assuring America that Jews were becoming just like everybody else, and by more than hinting that they would soon blend totally into the majority through intermarriage. Benjamin Nones gloried in being both a political liberal, an enemy of privilege everywhere, and a totally devoted Jew. All these types would recur in future generations.

III

At the time of the American Revolution the vast majority of the Jews of Europe lived in Poland, a country that was being divided and redivided by the emperor of Austria, the king of Prussia, and the czar of Russia. Despite their troubles, the Jewish masses in Poland were as inert in the 1770s and 1780s as the rest of the population. Some heard rumors of the revolt in America, but what they heard left them puzzled. Rebellion against the state had not been an option for Jews for sixteen centuries, after the last revolt against Rome had been crushed in Judea in the year 135. In the Diaspora, even under very bad conditions, Jews had always tried to make accommodations with authority; they had not imagined the possibility that they might be among the armed rebels, who were helping to make a new political order that would include them as equals.

Western and Central Europe were much more aware of the American Revolution. Because the war that the Americans and the English were fighting in America affected the balance of power in Europe, Frederick the Great of Prussia was a close observer of the events in America. France, hoping the American revolt would weaken Great Britain, was much more involved. The financial subsidies provided by France and its direct military intervention on behalf of the rebels were critical to the survival of Washington's forces and to the eventual success of the Revolution. Even so, there was remarkably little echo of the American Revolution and of the founding of the Republic among the Jews of France and Germany. What was said—and what was not said—prefigured the reactions future generations of European Jews would have to America.

The Jews of France were almost totally uninvolved in the American Revolution. In 1782, after the British defeated the French fleet under de Grasse in the Caribbean, an appeal was made in Bordeaux to purchase another ship. The vessel cost 1.5 million livres. The amount was quickly raised among the grand bourgeois of the city; Jews contributed a little more than 60,000 livres to this subscription. This was an act of loyalty to the policy of France; it did not represent any special identification of the Jews of Bordeaux with the Americans. Indeed, the first and only serious discussion in French by a Jew of the revolt in America had been negative. Isaac de Pinto, the first Jew to be a figure of some consequence in French letters, had published a pamphlet in 1776 denouncing the American rebels. He had argued that it was to the interest of the major powers to guarantee peace and order in the world; therefore they should join in obstructing the independence of the American colonies. The Americans were leading to "the overthrow of order and true liberty . . . it is the temper of Oliver Cromwell." Great Britain was not simply enforcing a tax on tea, so Pinto argued; it was defending the basic principles of political order and legitimacy.

Pinto's reaction to the American Revolution was not as strange as it seems. He was a man of the Enlightenment who wanted to think of himself as belonging to the European intelligentsia. In 1762, he had written a famous open letter to Voltaire, in which he had argued against Voltaire's contempt for the Jews. Pinto pleaded for equality at least for the Sephardim; they had become Westernized men of affairs and they were thus different from all other Jews. Pinto did include some Ashkenazim: "The rich among them are devoted to learning, elegance, and manners to the same degree as the other peoples of Europe, from whom they differ only in religion." Pinto more than hinted that his candidates for acceptance in society had ceased believing in the Jewish religion, but they would not leave the fold "because of the delicacy of their emotions," and because they had "the greatness of soul" to continue to be identified with "a religion which is proscribed and held in contempt."

Years before the American and French revolutions, Pinto used the language of the Enlightenment to redefine the age-old position of the Jewish upper class. They wanted no political overturns. Pinto presented his "clients," the "enlightened Jews," as already belonging to the economic and intellectual world of the high bourgeois of Europe. Pinto painted the Jewish men of business as the most clear-headed among the partisans of mercantilist economic interests. Such

Jews deserved permanent admission to the club of the powerful.

Reacting to the beginnings of the American Revolution, Isaac de Pinto had thus become the archetype of modern Jewish political conservatism. He was soon imitated even in America. After the Republic was established, Jews were among the first to put the spirit of rebellion behind them. As groups fought each other in those early years of the United States, Jews tried to be as inconspicuous as possible in public. They reserved their otherness for the intimacy of the synagogue. In politics they pronounced themselves to be the best and most devoted upholders of order in America. A few were so eager to identify with established America that they were even to be found among the earliest nativists.

Pinto, writing in French, had not written for Jews; he had addressed himself to the learned world. Among Jews, only a small minority, to be found among the Sephardim of Bordeaux and Bayonne, could read him in French. The bulk of the Jews in France, some thirty thousand, lived in the border region between France and Germany in the two provinces of Alsace and Lorraine. Their lives had remained unchanged for centuries. Except for a few rich army purveyors and horse traders, most made poor livings by lending small sums to the peasants or selling them goods on credit. In 1777–78 the peasants were incited against the Jews. This unrest in eastern France brought the discussion of "the Jewish question" to a head. The enemies of Jews had been saying for decades, even in the language of the Enlightenment, that the misery of the Jews was their own fault: supposedly, they preferred the unlovely, "Jewish" occupations of petty moneylending or peddling. Therefore, society had no choice but to defend itself by walling off the Jews in a separate enclave. Reformist opinion held that the Jews had no preference for these pursuits; they had been condemned to such degradation because most Jews had not been allowed to do anything else. In this fateful debate, the favorable situation of American Jewry played an important role.

The first pleading for the Jews was published by Christian Wilhelm Dohm in 1781. The work, entitled *Concerning the Political Reform of the Jews,* appeared first in German and the next year in French. Dohm was an official of the court of Frederick the Great, the king of Prussia, where the events in America were closely watched. Moses Mendelssohn, who was the first Jew to acquire a reputation in German

71

literature and thought, had asked Dohm to write in defense of the Jews. The money to pay Dohm for his trouble came from the leader of the Jews in eastern France, Cerf Berr. In his book, Dohm maintained that the Jews would give up moneylending and peddling, if the state and majority society would only let them. As convincing proof that this could happen, Dohm cited the Jews in America. They were engaged in productive occupations. They were so grateful to the societies which had given them freedom that they now supported the Revolution against Great Britain. If these Jews in North America were capable of such transformation of themselves, so were all other Jews who were still living in misery in Europe.

There were other reverberations in Germany of the unique good fortune of the handful of American Jews. In 1783, as the peace treaty between the rebellious colonies and the mother country was being signed, an anonymous Jew wrote a letter in German to the president of the Continental Congress. The author asked for a definition of the conditions under which a group of families, perhaps as many as two thousand, would be allowed "to settle into the desert in America and convert it into a fertile land." The writer described the misery of the Jews of Germany in the darkest colors. He knew that reformers like Dohm wanted to help the Jews, but the anonymous petitioner doubted that such efforts would do any good. Europe was not going to change for the better. America was the place where Jews could start over again. Nothing came of this letter, but the suggestion that European Jews might establish an enclave of their own in America had been made for the first time.

But America was far away and strange; it set no immediate precedent for Europe, where monarchs still reigned everywhere, except in Switzerland. All Europe knew by 1789 that Jews, too, had been included as equal citizens by the Constitution of the United States, but this was no precedent for the Jews in France. On the eve of the French Revolution they prepared requests *(cahiers)* for the Estates General, which Louis XVI convoked in 1789. In these documents, the Jews asked for the right to trade and to be artisans "on a plane of equality with the rest of His Majesty's subjects," but not for any change in their political status. In the debates in France about Jews between 1789 and 1791, their unparalleled status in America was barely mentioned, but it did not have to be. The new American

Republic of virtue and equality was the immediate model for the French revolutionaries.

The American Revolution was a much gentler and more modest affair than the one in France, but it can be argued that the events in America were ultimately more important for the history of mankind. The American Revolution was certainly more important for Jews. The emancipation of the Jews in France was granted grudgingly, between 1790 and 1791. Other countries in Western and Central Europe granted Jews political equality in the course of the nineteenth century, but everywhere after a bitter fight. When these laws were blown away by Adolf Hitler, few resisted. The results of the American Revolution have lasted.

Despite the attacks on Jews in the age of the Revolution and of the founding of the Republic, they had many more friends than enemies—and the Constitution was profoundly in their favor. But the Jews themselves were not quite sure what the new Republic represented for them. Was it a total transformation of their history in exile? Or was the American Revolution a sign of profound stirrings in heaven itself that the end of days and the restoration of the Jews to Zion were near? And the Christians were not at all sure what they wanted the Jews to become in the new America.

5.

James Madison's America

I

During the era of the Revolution and of the founding of the Republic, there was almost no debate about Jews, but the views of the Enlightenment in Europe, and of the heirs to the Puritan tradition in America, and of the Whigs who wrote the Constitution were all stated, if only by inference.

Thomas Paine, the most radical intellectual among the makers of the American Revolution, transplanted to America the open bitter criticism of the Bible that was current among the "enlightened" of Europe. One of the first essays that he wrote in America, a few weeks after he arrived in 1774, was an attack on the enslavement of the Negroes. Some of those who defended this practice had said that slavery had been permitted to the Jews in the Bible. Paine replied that "the example of the Jews, in many things, may not be imitated by us"; he went on to quote passages from the Bible in which Jews had been ordered utterly to destroy several nations. On the other hand, in his most famous pamphlet, *Common Sense,* Paine quoted biblical history as authority for attacking the principle of monarchy.

The prophet Samuel had been opposed to establishing a monarchy, as contrary to the will of God. "In the early ages of the world, according to scripture chronology, there were no kings; the consequence of which was, there were no wars."

But Paine's basic teaching was undisguised contempt for the Bible. He wrote *The Age of Reason* in 1793, after he had left America for France. This tract, which was widely read in the Republic Paine had helped found, centered around the notion that

> Whenever we read the obscene stories, the voluptuous debaucheries, the cruel and torturous executions, the unrelenting vindictiveness, with which more than half the Bible is filled, it would be more consistent that we called it the word of a demon, than the Word of God. It is history of wickedness, that has served to corrupt and brutalize mankind; and, for my own part, I sincerely detest it, as I detest everything that is cruel.

Paine was as contemptuous of Christianity as he was of Judaism:

> But when, according to the Christian Trinitarian scheme, one part of God is represented by a dying man, and another part, called the Holy Ghost, by a flying pigeon, it is impossible that belief can attach itself to such wild conceits.

There was, however, a half-explicit difference between Paine's attacks on Christianity and his distemper with Judaism. For Paine, Christianity was a false religion which ought to be abandoned. Those who would free themselves of such superstitions would then be able to move on to the God of Reason. Judaism was the religion of the Jews; as was self-evident, the Jews of that time were the biological descendants of those of ancient times. His calling Moses "that chief assassin and imposter" was more than an attack on the religion of the Jews; it was a slur on their character. This was all the clearer in *The Age of Reason,* where Paine maintained that the ancient heathens "were a just and moral people, and not addicted, like the Jews, to cruelty and revenge." This "ancient Gentile world," according to Paine, respected virtue and distanced itself from vice; they had been defamed by "the Jews, whose practice has been to calumniate and blacken the character of all other nations."

In *The Age of Reason,* Paine injected into America a distinction between Christians and Jews that had been made by Voltaire: Christians were Gentiles who needed to unlearn the religion that some sectarian Jews had once foisted on them; the Gentiles would then return to their roots in ancient, pagan philosophy. Jews, however, needed to be cured of their very character—and who knows whether such a character is curable. Paine himself never asked this question explicitly, but those who read him had to conclude that practicing Jews were a danger to enlightened society, and that only those who would assimilate completely might be acceptable.

This "enlightened" idea, that Jews should assimilate into the majority, was acceptable to believing Christians, the very Americans who were the most outraged by Paine's attack on the Bible. In their view, the new American society was to be a Protestant commonwealth. The most interesting exponent of this vision was Ezra Stiles. Even as he expressed the new patriotism, Stiles remained an heir of the Puritans. He kept repeating that the Jews were perverse outsiders. As we have seen, Stiles had inaugurated a new academic year at Yale in September 1781 by insisting, as he had before, that the Jews did not understand their own Bible correctly. Those who were still devoted to rabbinic Judaism might be equal citizens, but their religion was an affront to the truth. Stiles did not expect the Jews, or the Catholics, for that matter, to become Calvinist Christians, but he did identify America with Protestantism. The new American society was, for Stiles, the realization of the dream that the Puritans had had of founding a new Zion in the wilderness. Writing about America during the Revolution and immediately thereafter, Stiles asserted that the founding of America was the climax of human history; the new Republic was to be the example, and salvation, for all of humanity. America as a whole had now replaced the theocratic Massachusetts Bay Colony which had been founded by the Puritans as "the City on the Hill." Those who chose to come to the United States would become part of this new glory. Stiles implied strongly that the alien who came in any other spirit had better stay home, for what he brought with him was out of keeping with the meaning of America. The Americans were the new "chosen people," and their history was the realization of sacred drama.

Stiles was not tenderhearted about those who did not fit into the new order. Like his Puritan forebears, he knew that some people had to be excluded, or held as second-class citizens, lest they contaminate the New Jerusalem. He was fierce enough in his last years to become not only a partisan of the French Revolution but also a defender of regicide, of the execution of kings by revolutionaries. Such acts were necessary in order to make an end of the old order and to usher in the new. Stiles died too soon, in May 1795, to have the time to take full account of the French Revolution. His fervent appreciation of the new, republican America, therefore, remained the capstone of his spiritual career. He expressed it in the sermon that he gave in Connecticut on election day in 1783. He foresaw an America that would extend its population all over the continent and that would be the center of international trade. Stiles was certain that a representative democracy, where the government was not imposed from above by a monarch, would guarantee the happiness of all its citizens. In such a democracy the people would elect leaders of stature and merit, and they would have the chance periodically to reverse any errors that they might have made. This glorious new American society would extend liberty of religion to all Protestant denominations. Jews, and Catholics, would exist largely on sufferance until they assimilated and disappeared. Stiles, the Hebraist and the friend of the Jews of Newport, and of its rabbinic visitors, defined an Anglo-Saxon, Protestant republic.

One deep truth was reflected by the dissimilar visions of Paine and Stiles: the American Revolution was a break with the past; it was a fresh beginning. The victory of a bunch of colonial irregulars against the might of the British Empire was improbable and near miraculous. The sound of the music that the British band had played at Yorktown, Virginia, in 1781 reechoed among the revolutionaries. Lord Cornwallis, the most experienced British general, had surrendered in a formal ceremony to the tune of the song, "When the world turned upside down." The three million inhabitants of the new state in North America, who had withstood the might of Great Britain and astonished the world by establishing a republic, were the obvious candidate for the role of that perfected society which the thinkers of the Enlightenment, or the patriotic Christians, were imagining. The American settlement was relatively new, no more than 150 years old in the 1780s, and its inhabitants, by the very fact of their emigration to the New World, had come to America to make a fresh beginning. But the dreamers of a new America did not speak with one voice.

Most opinion agreed that society needed to be made better, but, in their majority, Americans were willing to wait for the blessings of liberty to transform the unworthy into true citizens, and to leave the worthy untroubled. The only test was obedience to the political arrangement of the new Constitution.

The visions of Tom Paine and Ezra Stiles were not enshrined in the Constitution. On the contrary, the defense of untidiness was the basic and undoubtable meaning of the American Constitution. The motto on the Great Seal of the United States, *novus ordo saeclorum* (a new order of the ages) did not mean, despite Tom Paine and Ezra Stiles and those who thought like them, that the United States was being defined as a redemptive society. The authors of *The Federalist Papers,* and especially James Madison, were absolutely clear that they meant the contrary: the American Constitution spelled out a form of government which would enable many utterly dissimilar "factions" to be themselves; that many such "factions" and "interests" existed in the United States was the guarantee that a political majority could not be formed to suppress any minority. Thus, the new American Constitution was not a program for creating a harmonious society of the like-minded. On the contrary, social disharmony, the continuing warfare between many, often dissimilar subgroups, was the surest guarantee of liberty.

James Madison was the most eloquent, and the clearest-headed exponent of this definition of the new United States. Madison was consistent and absolutely clear in making the distinction between loyalty to the new political arrangements and pressure toward conformity of any kind. In 1776 and again in 1785 he fought very hard to forbid the establishment of religion in Virginia. Because there were few Jews or Catholics in the state, this action meant that the Episcopal Church was being put on a plane of equality with all other denominations. In 1789 Madison was the principal author of the First Amendment of the Constitution in which it was decreed that the Congress could make no law establishing any religion or prohibiting its "free exercise." Here, Madison still seems to have been thinking mostly about equality among the Protestant sects. He wrote that he wanted "to disestablish individual Protestant churches in the several colonies (such as the Episcopalians in Virginia and the Congregationalists in Massachusetts and Connecticut) and to keep peace among them."

The separation of church and state in America had much wider meaning; it made faith, any faith, into a private, personal matter. It gave equality to all believers and unbelievers. But it was still possible to imagine that all other behavior, both public and private, could, and perhaps should, be governed by a new culture of republican virtue. In a very few years, that attitude would become the explicit doctrine of those who made the French Revolution. They guillotined people for lack of *civisme* (civic virtue), for not belonging to the new revolutionary culture. Jews were told explicitly, in the debates at the very beginning of the French Revolution, that they would be granted equality only if they gave up their Jewish specificness.

In *The Federalist Papers,* Madison made it unmistakably clear that no such conformity was demanded of anyone by the American Constitution:

If a majority be united by a common interest, the rights of the minority will be insecure. There are but two methods of providing against this evil: the one by creating a will in the community independent of the majority—this is, of the society itself; the other, by comprehending in the society so many separate descriptions of citizens as will render an unjust combination of a majority of the whole very improbable, if not impracticable. The first method prevails in all governments possessing an hereditary or self-appointed authority. This, at best, is but a precarious security; because a power independent of the society might as well espouse the unjust views of the major, as the rightful interests of the minor party, and may possibly be turned against both parties. The second method will be exemplified in the federal republic of the United States. Whilst all authority in it will be derived from and dependent on the society, the society itself will be broken into so many parts, interests, and classes of citizens, that the rights of individuals, or of the minority, will be in little danger from interested combinations of the majority. In a free government the security for civil rights must be the same as that for religious rights. It consists in the one case in the multiplicity of interests, and in the other in the multiplicity of sects.

This was no casual utterance in *Federalist Paper,* Number 51. Madison knew exactly what he was saying, for he had referred in an earlier essay (Number 39) to the political teachings of Montesquieu. As Madison understood him, Montesquieu had taught the importance of the confederation of small groups: in such a political structure, there would be so many interests that no majority could be mustered to oppress a minority. Madison knew that the various minorities were not necessarily pure and virtuous. On the contrary, they "are united and actuated by some common impulse of passion, or of interest, adverse to the rights of other citizens or to the permanent or aggregate interests of the community." But one dare not remove faction, either by destroying liberty or by "giving to every citizen the same opinions, the same passions and the same interests." In *Federalist Paper,* Number 10, Madison, after defining the problem, insisted that human nature is various in all its parts, and that "the protection of these faculties is the first object of government."

Madison never entertained the thought that the various "factions" that he was discussing would resemble one another. His America was not going to be some tidy arrangement of ethnic subgroups, or of religious sects, or of economic interests. The word "faction," as he used it, meant the turbulence of all kinds of groups, which cohered for often totally dissimilar purposes:

> A religious sect may degenerate into a political faction in a part of the Confederacy; but the variety of sects dispersed over the entire face of it must secure the national councils against any danger from that source. A rage for paper money, for an abolition of debts, for an equal division of property or for any other improper or wicked project, will be less apt to pervade the whole body of the Union than a particular member of it; in the same proportion as such a malady is more likely to taint a particular county or district, than an entire State.

Madison was thus listing all of the special interests that came to his mind, for they were present in his America. It was still possible to imagine, as even he did sometimes in his later years, that such complexity needed to be countered by some devotion to national unity, but Madison always returned to defining national unity as the devotion to all the political institutions which had been created by the Constitution. Madison's writing in *The Federalist Papers* presumed without question that the various "factions" in America existed because each had some power; they did not survive on each other's goodwill.

It was, of course, possible, then and later, not to want any more "factions" in America, but this was not what Madison taught. He defined America as a place to which people had come—and obviously more would come in the future—to associate in any way that they wished. The only restriction was that they could not band together to destroy the Constitution. New groups would matter in America to the degree to which they succeeded, under that Constitution, in acquiring the power which flowed from their achievements.

In its first encounter with Jews, the new government of the United States spoke not in the accents of Paine or Stiles, but in those of Madison. In 1790, the six congregations which then existed in the United States decided to write a letter of congratulation to George Washington on his inauguration as the first President. As was to happen again and again in the next two centuries, all of the Jewish bodies could not agree to act together. In the end, four of the congregations wrote one letter and the other two, the synagogues in Richmond, Virginia, and Newport, Rhode Island, wrote separately, but in the same spirit. The rhetoric of these letters is instructive. These congregations did not describe themselves as Jews or as Israelites; they used the phrase "children of the stock of Abraham," no doubt to suggest that they belonged to the same tradition as the Christians, who often called themselves descendants of Abraham. Those who drafted those letters wanted to sound as little separatist as possible. The operative plea, in the words of the Jews of Newport, was to ask of the new President that his government give "to bigotry no sanction, to persecution no assistance." Washington echoed the sentiment in his response, in which he affirmed that "the children of the stock of Abraham" were indeed equal within the new Republic, in which "all possess alike liberty of conscience and immunities of citizenship."

Unlike some of his most important colleagues in the making of the Revolution, Washington was not a reflective man. There is no evidence that he ever thought about the relation of Jews to society in any theoretical way. He did know that there had been some dramatic scenes of Jewish-Christian amity and cooperation in those earliest years of the Republic. Gershom Mendes Seixas, the cantor of the congregation in New York, had participated in Washington's inaugural in November 1789. Some months earlier, so Benjamin Rush reported, "the rabbi of the Jews, locked in the arms of the ministers of the gospel, was a most delightful sight" at Philadelphia's great parade to celebrate the acceptance by Pennsylvania of the United States Constitution. There had even been a kosher table at that mammoth party. The year before, in 1788, the Jews of Philadelphia had turned to Gentiles for help in building their synagogue. Benjamin Franklin was among the contributors. None of this was entirely new, for, as we have seen, such interfaith occasions had occurred in colonial days. Washington was responding in the spirit of this tradition and of the recent interfaith events. He was, in fact, saying to the Jews exactly what he was declaring to the Catholics in those very days. George Washington wrote to the New Church in Baltimore: "In the enlightened age and in this land of equal liberty . . . a man's religious tenance [sic] will not . . . deprive him of the right of attaining and holding the highest Offices that are known to the United States."

II

Jews responded to the founding of the Republic in several ways. Their participation in the Revolution as equals had predisposed some to enter public office, even before Washington had made it clear to both Jews and Catholics that they had the right, and even the duty, to participate in the staffing and management of the new government.

Toward the end of the Revolutionary War, David Salisbury Franks was sent abroad twice as courier of diplomatic documents. In 1784, he was appointed vice-consul in Marseilles, and the next year he went to Morocco as part of an American delegation which negotiated a treaty to end piracy directed against American vessels. Franks was thus the first Jew to be appointed to a post in the diplomatic service of the United States. A young Jew, Simon M. Levy, was a member of the first class to graduate from West Point in 1802. In the early decades of the nineteenth century, two grandsons of Jonas Phillips, Mordecai Manuel Noah and Uriah Phillips Levy, became prominent in American life, Noah as politician and writer and Levy as naval officer. Both Noah and Phillips were attacked by anti-Semites; their enemies said that as Jews they were unworthy of offices of trust in the public service. But Franks, Levy, Phillips, and Noah were the first avowing Jews to hold office in government.

The immediate religious response to the American Revolution reflected older ideas about the "exile of the Jews," but here, too, there was a shift in response to the new age. The man who thought most about these issues was Gershom Mendes Seixas. He wasAmerican-born, and more fully integrated into New York society than any Jewish clergyman was ever to be until the twentieth century. Seixas was for many years a trustee of King's College (which later became Columbia University). The sermon that he preached in his synagogue in New York on November 26, 1789, as part of the day of thanksgiving and prayer to celebrate the ratification of the Constitution, is particularly interesting and instructive. Seixas took pains to emphasize that the children of Israel still needed to return to their earliest estate, when they dwelt in their own land which God had promised to their ancestors. He would "cause us to be again established under our own government, as we were formerly." Seixas was grateful that "we are, through Divine goodness, made equal partakers of the benefits of the government . . . with the rest of the inhabitants"; nonetheless, he did not allow himself or his listeners to forget that "still we cannot but view ourselves as captives in comparison to what we were formerly, and what we expect to be hereafter when the outcasts of Israel shall be gathered."

Seixas returned to the messianic theme in a sermon that he preached in his synagogue nine years later, on May 9, 1798. He asserted that "the depravity and corrupt state of human nature that prevails almost throughout the world" assured him that "the glorious period of redemption is near at hand" and that God would soon be "again collecting the scattered remnant of Israel and establishing them according to His Divine promise."

There had been earlier echoes within the small American Jewish community of the hope for the Redemption. Ezra Stiles reported in his diary that the Jews in New York had expected the Messiah to come in 1768. There was another prediction that the miraculous year was to be 1783; this speculation was reported by both Stiles and Gershom Mendes Seixas. A vague story exists that someone came to New York in 1788 and told its Jews of "proofs" of the continued existence of the Lost Ten Tribes of Israel. In 1795 a ship captain docked in New York and told of a Jewish community in Pien-ching, now K'ai-feng, China. The leaders of the synagogue hastened to write a letter in Hebrew to these far-off brethren. They inquired whether the Jews of China were descended from those who had been exiled after the destruction of the Second Temple, or whether they were remnants of the Ten Tribes who had been scattered in Asia after the destruction of the First Temple. No answer was ever received to this missive, perhaps because by then the remnants of Chinese Jewry knew little Hebrew. However, in the very act of sending it, the leaders of the synagogue in New York signified that they continued to believe in the messianic redemption of the Jews and in their ingathering from the exile.

By 1807, in response to Napoleon's calling together a "Sanhedrin" in Paris to get the Jews to adjust their religion to the new circumstances of political equality in his empire, Seixas had become more guarded and ambivalent. He no longer was certain, in a sermon that he preached on January 11, 1807, that God "means to accomplish our re-establishment . . . as a nation in our former territory." Seixas thought that at the very least Jews would be "a particular society" in the Gentile world, equal in rights to all other religious groups. Nonetheless, he remained enough of a messianic mystic to cling to the belief that the Jewish people in exile could now expect that "the third time is nearly and rapidly approaching when we shall be established forever."

These messianic dreams of Gershom Mendes Seixas seemed to be repeating, in American English, the kind of visions that he had learned from pious books in Hebrew. Raphael Mahler, the contemporary Israeli scholar who has studied these sermons and writings, has pronounced Seixas a proto-Zionist, the first in the United States. This is not so. American Zionism has never thought that the Jews of America themselves were or should be on their way to the Holy Land. From Zionism's beginnings in the late 1880s, Zionists in America have imagined that they, secure in the land of liberty, would help their less fortunate brethren in Europe establish the Jewish homeland. As a "Zionist," Seixas belongs not among modern, activist nationalists, but rather among Orthodox Jewish believers in the Messiah, who would come to restore the Jews to ancient glory. But there was an "American" element in his messianic sermons. Some of the Protestant preachers agreed in those years with Ezra Stiles that the new United States was itself the redemptive society. Christian revivalists saw the creation of the Republic as a strange and wonderful event, which gave them hope that the Second Coming was at hand. Seixas was saying to his congregants that the "end of days" was near, but that it would happen as the Jews, and not as Christians, had predicted. Messianic times were on the way but they would not begin with the Second Coming of Christ.

The pronouncements by Seixas were heard in the synagogue, but there is no reason to believe that his congregants paid sermons much attention. Even if they did, the notion that the Messiah might come had no practical effect on what they were doing with their lives. In the here and now, the Jews of New York and Philadelphia, and of all of the other places in which Jews lived, were establishing themselves in business. Some were even becoming part of high society. They were settling in to live in America, like everyone else, as equal citizens.

The news of the freedom for Jews in America made an increasing difference in Europe. In 1819 an American Christian, W. D. Robinson, published a pamphlet in which he urged Jews to form a company to buy land in the upper reaches of what is now Mississippi and Missouri, to resettle some of the poor Jews of Europe. Such suggestions remained schemes on paper only. European Jews were city and village people. Excluded from the land by feudalism, many Jews lived in the villages and bought and sold cattle and grain, but they had not farmed in Europe for many centuries. There was no reason to come to the United States to do what they did not know. But, even though Robinson's pamphlet as such had little echo in Europe, it reflected an atmosphere of acceptance of Jews as Jews in the early United States. They were being invited to the New World and not told that they were unwelcome. This was heartening knowledge to European Jews—and soon there was a reaction.

After the fall of Napoleon in 1815, the rights that the French Revolution had extended to Jews remained secure only in France and in Holland. In Germany, this freedom was reversed, and medieval anti-Jewish restrictions were reintroduced. The young Jews who had taken advantage of their emancipation under French rule in the Rhineland were now trapped. One such, Karl Marx's father Heinrich, saved his career as a lawyer by converting to Christianity in 1817. Others of that generation remained in the fold and fought for the emancipation of the Jews. Several such intellectuals organized a society in Berlin to raise the respect for Judaism and thus to help persuade the state to grant Jews equality, but they were not very hopeful of success. These men looked over their shoulders to America. In 1822, one year after the society had been founded, they wrote to Mordecai Manuel Noah, asking him to become associated with their body and to be their link with the United States. The three signers of the letter (Eduard Gans, Leopold Zunz, and M. Moser) did not conceal their objective from Noah. They wrote "the better part of European Jewry are looking with eager countenance of hope to the United States of North America." They dreamed of immigration because they wanted "to exchange the miseries of their native soil for public freedom," and they invited Noah and his friends to "establish a perpetual correspondence with us about the means of transplanting a vast portion of European Jews to the United States." Nothing came of this effort. There is no record of a response by Noah, who was probably less than enthusiastic about the scheme. Large migration was not yet possible, at very least because sailing ships were still the only mode of crossing the Atlantic.

III

In the United States, the discussion about Jews continued, even as their equality under the Constitution was never questioned by anyone. Social critics of various kinds continued to suggest that Jews still needed to reform themselves to some degree.

John Adams, the second president of the United States, had been influenced by the Enlightenment, even as he distanced himself from the most extreme "enlightened" views about Jews. He was well read in the works of Lord Bolingbroke and Voltaire, who were the sources of Tom Paine's distemper with the Bible, but Adams rejected the charge made by all three of these thinkers that the Bible had been a negative moral influence. In 1809, Adams wrote that "the Hebrews have done more to civilize men than any other nation." Without the Jews, so Adams asserted, mankind would not have "a doctrine of the Supreme, Intelligent, Wise and Almighty Sovereign of the universe, which I believe to be the essential principle of morality and consequently of all civilization." While John Adams did not pretend that he loved the Jews, he insisted that one had to try, even though "it is very hard work to love most of them." Adams even believed in the restoration of the Jews to their own land, to Judea. His reason was the hope that such an event "would soon wear away some of the asperities and peculiarities of their character, possibly in time [for them] to become liberal Unitarian Christians." In 1818, Adams, responding to a letter from Mordecai Manuel Noah, was totally positive. He voiced the hope that Jews might be "admitted to all privileges of citizenship in every country of the world." It was the duty and glory of the United States to take the lead in making an end of "every narrow idea in religion, government, and commerce."

Noah sent this same letter to several others among the still-surviving Founding Fathers of the United States. He included, for each of them, a copy of his discourses on the consecration of the new synagogue building on Mill Street in New York. James Madison responded that freedom of religion and opinion belonged equally to everyone, but not, interestingly enough, because this freedom was, of itself, an absolute value. Madison saw this basic rule of the American Constitution as "the best human provision for bringing all either into the same way of thinking or into that mutual charity which is the only proper substitute." Madison would not have been more comfortable with the first option, that of assimilating all America into one opinion. On the contrary, he had always believed in untidiness, in the right of various identities to be themselves in America. In his own personal behavior, Madison had not acted as an ideologue, who was so firmly persuaded of his principles that they admitted no exceptions. Despite his passion for the separation of church and state, Madison had, as a leader in the House of Representatives, created the office of chaplain and he had hired a Protestant divine. As president, Madison had appointed Noah in 1813 to be American consul in Tunis, but Madison had allowed his secretary of state, James Monroe, to withdraw the appointment in the next year on the avowed ground that Noah's Jewishness was a liability in dealing with the local rulers. Madison's practice was, in this case, worse than his theory in *The Federalist Papers*.

Thomas Jefferson, too, harbored some ambivalence about Jews. He responded to Noah's letter by asserting that Jews have "a particular need, evidently greater than that of any others, to pay more careful attention to education." They should labor to achieve equality in science, that is, in secular learning, so that "they will become equal objects of respect and favor." Jefferson was thus expressing the view of the mainstream of the Enlightenment, that all men could attain equal place in society, but the "entrance fee" was that they should

87

adopt the ways and the outlook of the "enlightened." Jefferson apparently did not consider that a Yiddish-speaking Jew who knew the Talmud was equal in usefulness to society with a classically trained thinker like himself.

The most forceful expression of early American ambivalence toward Jews is to be found in the writings of Hannah Adams. A descendant of Henry Adams of Braintree, Massachusetts, and thus a distant cousin of John Adams, Adams published in 1812 a volume on the history of the Jews which was based in part on the work of the Abbé Henri Grégoire, a leader during the French Revolution in the battle for the emancipation of the Jews. In addition to her literary and personal connections with Grégoire (who thought that kindness, and not persecution, was the best approach to converting the Jews), Hannah Adams was also associated with the earliest efforts of the London-based Society for the Promotion of Christianity among the Jews in America. In her history, Hannah Adams wrote that the suffering of the Jews was due to their rejection of Christ. She did, however, note that during the Christian Middle Ages, "while Christendom was involved in darkness and ignorance," the Jews had learned from the Muslims to be in the forefront of learning. In her continuing quarrel with the Jewish religion, Hannah Adams judged Jewish rituals as too rigid. She accused Jews of continuing to regard themselves as "the chosen people, superior to all others," and she asserted that they still "look down on all nations." Hannah Adams did not make any political suggestions. She certainly accepted the equality of the Jews under the American Constitution, but she believed, like Ezra Stiles a generation earlier, that American freedom was simply an opportunity for Jews to be converted to an enlightened Christianity.

There was, however, one new note in Hannah Adams's work. She was aware that the solvents of the Enlightenment had worked on a number of Jews, and that many had "imbibed the principles of infidelity and no longer believed in the divine inspiration of the Bible and the coming of the Messiah." For Hannah Adams, this development was entirely negative; nonbelieving Jews were not candidates for conversion. Indeed, she feared that Jewish faithlessness increased the danger of such "infidelity" in Christian circles. The first hint was thus expressed in America by an enlightened Christian that the secularization of the Jews might be a subversion of American culture.

Another form of ambivalence about Jews appeared in the most important journal of early national days, the *Niles' Weekly Register,* which was edited in its greatest days by Hezekiah Niles. Niles fought hard for total equality everywhere in America, including such states as Maryland, which continued to exclude Jews from public office, but Niles, too, thought that Jews were different. He said several times in his journal that "Jews are consumers, not producers." Perhaps the best definition of the early republican attitude toward the Jews is to be found in several of Niles's comments in 1820. He asserted that while "this is the most preferrable country for the Jews, they will not cultivate the earth nor work at mechanical trades, preferring to live by their wit in dealing and acting as if they had a home nowhere." Nonetheless, Niles asserted that "all this has nothing to do with their rights of men." It is not clear whether Niles was being critical of the potential immigrants from Europe, or whether he included also the already-assimilated Jewish residents of the United States. Perhaps he did not know himself.

American Jewry, then and later, has remained nervous about this lack of clarity. Jews have kept insisting that they have become a "normal" American group, even though they have remained city people in a country in which farmers and ranchers are the mythic Americans, and non-Christians in a country of many religious sects. The basic mold was set early: while the Jews were accepted as a part of America under the Constitution, everyone knew that they were different. In the earliest days of American history, Gentiles and even Jews pretended less often than in some later times that they thought that Jews were "just like everybody else." A certain unique nervousness began early in the relationship between this minority and the rest of the country. It would remain.

6.

Patriots in the New Nation

In the early nineteenth century, most American Jews were native-born. This changed in the 1830s, when the "German Jews" began to arrive, for they came in such numbers that they soon constituted a majority of the Jews in America. During the next century, successive waves of immigration ensured that every census until 1940 would continue to show a majority of foreign-born. The critical difference between the community these days and the one that existed in the early years of the Republic is size: there were perhaps six thousand Jewish souls in the United States in the 1820s; in the 1940s, and after, there were over five million. Nonetheless, the early, small community acted in ways which seem remarkably contemporary.

In those early days, Jews had little trouble in entering the American economy. The country was growing. Despite losses to commerce which were caused by the War of 1812, and the economic panic of 1819, the first three decades of the nineteenth century were heady days. This was the era of the Louisiana Purchase of 1803, when the United States more than doubled in size, and of the creation of new towns and cities on the frontier in the West, beyond the Appalachian Mountains. New York, Philadelphia, and almost all the other port cities were growing; they had become cities with a past, with established societies and institutions. Jews were part of this growing economy, both on the frontier and in the major cities. No American Jew then possessed a great fortune on par with the Astors in America or, among Jews, the Rothschilds in Europe, but American Jews were almost all part of the urban middle class.

After 1800, Jews, for the most part, had remained in their accustomed pursuits as merchants and middlemen. Most were and remained moderately well-off storekeepers. Some, such as the parents of Judah Benjamin, the future secretary of state of the Confederacy, did not do well (his mother kept a fruit shop), but they were helped by relatives. Others found their way into the very center of the social and economic establishment. In New York, Daniel Peixotto was a physician of high professional reputation and social acceptability. John Moss, a Jew who came to Philadelphia from England in 1796, had quickly integrated into the economic oligarchy of the city; he sat on the boards of the Lehigh Coal and Navigation Company and of the Commercial Bank of Pennsylvania. Despite the persistence of some anti-Semitism, the social position of some Jews was strong. In Philadelphia, the Gratz family, which had become a clan of leading merchants, remained socially acceptable even though Simon and Hyman Gratz went bankrupt in 1826. A daughter of the house, Rebecca Gratz, conducted a salon attended by many of the best American writers. Through her friend Washington Irving, Rebecca Gratz was sufficiently well-known in Europe so that it was reputed that Sir Walter Scott had modeled Rebecca, the Jewish heroine of his novel, *Ivanhoe,* after her.

Rebecca Gratz was devoted to Jewish causes, and especially to teaching young people about their religion in classes that she organized on Sundays, but the Jewishness of most was evaporating. A contemporary Jewish observer, Jacob Lyons of Savannah, Georgia, wrote in 1820 that "a synagogue, as it exists in the present organization, will not be found in the United States fifty years hence." This was not a wild guess. By 1837, when the descendants of colonial Jewry were into their third generation, the rate of intermarriage was one in three. The old synagogues remained, but individual members rarely came to worship services. The congregations were burial societies. A shrinking minority was still Orthodox, but the majority was passive and largely indifferent. A few did care enough to want to make changes. This happened for the first time in America in Charleston, South Carolina, in the mid-1820s. The Beth Elohim Congregation in that city was, then, still undeviatingly Orthodox. In fact, in the synagogue's new constitution which was promulgated in 1820, it had even been decreed that those who were "publicly violating the Sabbath or other sacred days shall be deprived of every privilege of the synagogue." The reigning Orthodoxy was, however, that of the older generation.

In 1824 perhaps two-fifths of the entire community, over forty adults, petitioned the synagogue for a revision of the rituals. These members asked that some of the prayers, all of which were said in Hebrew, be repeated in English. They wanted to remove "everything superfluous" from the service, and to add a sermon to the Sabbath service. When these requests were ignored, Isaac Harby, a young and not very successful journalist and playwright, took the lead in forming a Reformed Society of Israelites. On November 21, 1825, this body was formally organized; within a year it had fifty members, almost half of all the families who had previously belonged to Beth Elohim. The reformers established their own Sabbath service, almost entirely in English, and they worshiped with uncovered heads. But Harby and his friends were breaking with Orthodox beliefs even more than with Orthodox rituals. These younger Jews in Charleston belonged to a time and place in America when it was possible for Thomas Cooper, then president of South Carolina College, and a major figure in town, to deny to successive senior classes "the authenticity of the Pentateuch"—and to pronounce Holy Writ to be a tissue of errors.

These views were reflected in the prayer book of the Reformed Society of Israelites. It was based on the assertion that only the moral law, not the ritual prescriptions, was divinely revealed. The editors of this volume added that they were acting "for themselves and for their children and for all those who think the period has arrived when the Jew should break in pieces the sceptre of Rabbinical power." The messianic hope for the return of the Holy Land was never mentioned in the new prayer book, except very obliquely in the marriage service. The ten articles of faith which were put at the front of the volume were a Deistic document addressed to all mankind; the Jews and the Jewish religion, as such, did not figure.

The society of religious reformers in Charleston did not last long. It began to fall apart soon after Isaac Harby left for New York in 1828 in search of his fortune as a writer and teacher (he died there within the year). By May 2, 1833, the society was formally disbanded, and the moneys that had been collected toward building its own synagogue were returned. The stirrings that this group represented were not even important, as precedent, in the bitter battle that was to begin two decades later over transforming the parent congregation, Beth Elohim, into the first Reform synagogue in America. By then, that synagogue was largely in the hands of newer immigrants. Nonetheless, Isaac Harby is a significant figure in the history of Jews in America. He was the very first Jew in America who made his career as a writer. Harby had nothing original to say, either in his essays or his plays, but he did reflect the intellectual and religious outlook that dominated, then, among cultivated young men and women—and he was bold enough to refashion Judaism to be "American."

Mordecai Manuel Noah was much more picturesque, gutsier, and more successful than Isaac Harby. At least formally he remained an Orthodox Jew, even though he observed the rituals of the tradition in a most eclectic way. Noah was a curious mix. Upwardly mobile, a patriotic American and self-dramatizing, Noah tried to act heroically on the stages of both American and Jewish history. He was a disciple of Jonas Phillips, his maternal grandfather who had raised him in Philadelphia, and of Gershom Mendes Seixas, to whose New York synagogue Noah belonged. Noah was born in 1785. His father was a bankrupt who seems to have faded out of the family. He grew up in the home of his grandfather. He was apprenticed to learn the trade of gilding and carving, but he spent all of his spare time reading in the Philadelphia public library. In 1808, Noah was one of the founders of the Democratic Young Men in Philadelphia, who advocated Madison's candidacy for president. He had begun to write even before he took a hand in politics, for a play of his was put on the boards while he was still in his teens. In 1809 Noah moved to Charleston, South Carolina, to edit the *City Gazette*. The paper supported the reelection of James Madison as president. Madison was under attack from his opponent, Governor DeWitt Clinton of New

York, for having entered the War of 1812 with Great Britain. Noah defended Madison. After the election, which Madison had won with the help of South Carolina's electoral votes, Noah traveled to Washington to ask for political reward. As we know, the President appointed him American consul in Tunis, a post for which Noah had been campaigning since 1811.

On his return from Tunis, Noah moved to New York and established himself as a journalist, playwright, and political figure. His uncle, Naphtali Phillips, published a newspaper in New York, the *National Advocate,* and Noah became its editor in 1817. This paper supported the Democratic party, which meant Tammany Hall. This organization, which had begun in politics in 1789 as a group of middle-class opponents of the Federalists, had become coextensive with the Democratic party in New York. In fact, in the very year in which Noah assumed the editorship of the *National Advocate,* Tammany was both strengthened and changed by Irish immigrants who forced their way into the organization. Until the *National Advocate* was sold in 1824, Noah was near the very center of Tammany politics. He derived political advantage from this connection. In 1821, Noah was given an interim appointment to the office of high sheriff of New York by a Tammany-controlled Council of Appointments. When he ran for election the next year, it was alleged by his enemies that one of the tasks of the sheriff was to supervise hangings, and that it was against Christian sentiment for a Jew to be an instrument in the execution of true believers. These were anti-Semitic remarks, but the attacks on Noah as a Jew were no more vicious, and perhaps even less so, than the calumnies which were the usual rhetoric of politics in those days. Worse things were being said then by Protestants and by Catholics about each other.

Noah broke with Tammany in 1825, when he supported its enemy, DeWitt Clinton, for governor. The next year he established a newspaper of his own, the *New York Enquirer,* in opposition to Tammany Hall. In 1829, Andrew Jackson, whom he had supported for president, named Noah "surveyor and inspector of the New York Port." This was a substantial piece of patronage: Noah's salary was $5,000 a year, plus fees for various services, and he was able to continue editing the *Enquirer.* Twelve years later, in 1841, Noah was made a judge of the Court of Sessions. Without ever reaching high office, Noah had a middling career in politics. He might have done better had he not been a Jew, but that is unlikely. Journalism has seldom been the launching pad for major political careers in America.

As a Jew, Noah had apparently paid attention to the sermons of Seixas. In 1825, he staged and acted the principal role in the most theatrical event of the first two centuries of American Jewish history. As a supposed preamble to the ultimate ingathering of all the exiles to the Holy Land, Noah made himself the center of an effort to found a self-governing Jewish entity in the United States. Noah issued a proclamation to announce that he had helped purchase a tract of land on Grand Island in the Niagara River, which he renamed Ararat. This place was to be an ark of refuge for all the Jews of the world. Noah styled himself "high sheriff of the Jews," among other magniloquent titles, and he even presumed to instruct the leaders of the Jewish communities in Europe (who had no advance knowledge of what Noah was doing) to make regular collections in support of his enterprise and to report to him on their activities. Noah proclaimed that in God's name "do I revive, renew, and re-establish the government of the Jewish nation, under the auspices and protection of the Constitution and laws of the United States of America." This refuge was to be a "temporary home" for the Jews. In Ararat, "an asylum is prepared and hereby offered to them [the Jews] where they can enjoy that peace, comfort, and happiness which have been denied them through the intolerance and misgovernment of former ages." Noah even knew of the seventeenth-century notion that the Indians were the remnants of the Ten Tribes; he proposed in Ararat to begin the effort to reunite these American aborigines with their long-lost Jewish brethren.

The inauguration of Ararat took place in the early fall of 1825 in a ceremony in St. Paul's Episcopal Church in Buffalo, New York. Noah himself marched in between two rows of brightly uniformed local militia. An enormous crowd gathered to behold this spectacle, but these were almost all curious Gentiles. A leading American paper, *The Weekly Register,* mocked Noah as a land speculator who had invested in land on the island and now wanted to get rich quick by selling parcels to Jewish settlers. A Jewish journal in Vienna refused to take such theater seriously, especially since the gaudy inauguration had taken place in a church. Noah's colorful first act had no continuation; no one bought land, and no spade was ever turned in Ararat. All that remains of Ararat today is the memory of its founder's bombast, and, remarkably enough, the cornerstone that he dedicated that day, which turned up some years ago and now rests in the museum of Buffalo's Historical Society.

Ararat failed, but Noah had conceived it as a stopgap on the way to the ultimate, classic Jewish dream of the ingathering of the exiles. He returned to this theme, on which his minister Seixas had preached a quarter of a century earlier, in a speech which he gave in New York in 1837. Noah stated the traditional view that it was forbidden to try to compute the exact date of the Restoration. Nonetheless, he asserted that "faith does not rest wholly on miracles" and that "the Jewish people must now do something for themselves" to prepare for the Restoration. He proposed that a sum of twelve to thirteen million dollars, "a sum of no consideration to the Jews," be found with which to buy Syria (it then included Palestine) from the pasha of Egypt.

The restoration of the Jews to the Holy Land was the "last cause" of Noah's life. Noah even tried to enlist Christian support. In 1845 he spoke before two large and distinguished audiences in New York, which included the Roman Catholic bishop of the city and several leading Protestant ministers. Noah argued that the return of the Jews to the Holy Land was a necessary preamble in Christian theology to the miracle of the "end of days," and, therefore, it was to the Christian interest to help the Jews regain Zion. This approach was angrily rejected by Jewish critics both in New York and in London. They thundered that Noah was dangerously clever in trying to use those Christians, who wanted to convert the Jews, as his allies in an effort to reestablish a Jewish kingdom in Judea. In fact, Jewish opinion in Europe was dominated in those days by the drive for equal citizenship. A suggestion of reestablishing the Jews in Zion, especially if made to Christians, was feared, because it opened the door to the argument that Jews were aliens who should be sent back to Palestine. Noah had essentially agreed with these enemies of the Jews in Europe. He had accepted the idea that Jews remained alien in all of these lands, and that, except for America, their only hope was to return to Zion.

In this speech, Noah rose to his most eloquent climax in praising the United States as "the only country which has given [Jews] civil and religious rights equal to that of all other sects." The United States had therefore "been selected and pointedly distinguished in prophecy as *the* nation, which at the proper time, shall present to the Lord his chosen and trodden-down people and pave the way for their restoration to Zion." Noah did not expect the Jews of America to go to Palestine ("we may repose where we are free and happy"), but he was sure that almost all the rest of the Jews in the world, who are "bowed to the earth by oppression," would gladly leave their places of bondage and reestablish themselves as "a nation, a people, a sect."

Noah was a superpatriot and even a nativist. As early as 1817, he had urged Columbia College to appoint only Americans to teaching positions; he did not want to permit "the minds of our children to be warped by foreign prejudices." It is perhaps not an accident that Noah acted out the role of belonging to the older America, and even to the elite which set norms for college education, in the very year in which the Irish first fought their way onto the political scene by breaching Tammany Hall. Noah's attitude toward immigrants was that it took at least a generation for them to become passably American, and this could happen only through great educational effort. His attitude toward the Irish did not become more accepting after he broke with Tammany Hall, in which they were an increasing power. In 1835, he was an avowed supporter of the newly formed Native American party, the forerunner of the Know-Nothings of the next two decades. But Noah could not try to exclude the Irish and other immigrants without having to face the question of the Jews. As late as the 1830s, Noah was clearly not eager to welcome uncouth foreign Jews to New York or Philadelphia, because Jews like himself might find their own integration into America called into question. He preferred that they go to Ararat on the American frontier or directly to Palestine. Occasionally, he suggested that Jewish immigrants were a better element, easier to integrate into America than any of the other new arrivals. Inevitably, and correctly, Noah was attacked for these views by James Gordon Bennett, the leading figure among New York editors and journalists, who wondered how someone who belonged to a tribe that "had been aliens and renegades throughout the world" would dare foster the principle of social exclusion.

But Noah moved with the times. At the end of his life Noah allied himself with the Central European Jews who had begun to arrive in some numbers in his last years. He needed these newcomers, because

his own contemporaries and their children had become largely un-
interested in their Jewishness. Noah found his Jewish continuity in
the immigrants.

Noah was universally regarded as the premier public figure among
American Jews of that day. He made a career both in politics and as
the leading spokesman of American Jews—and his self-assumed role
as leader of the Jews made him more newsworthy and important
than his modest successes in politics. Noah was often ridiculed by
his enemies as a publicity seeker and sensationalist, but that was a
very American thing to be. In those very days, P. T. Barnum began
his career, in 1835, by parading an aged lady around the country as
supposedly 161 years old and the nurse of George Washington. Revivalists were traveling from town to town making national repu-
tations by use of exaggerated rhetoric. Among the more educated,
attending lectures was the prime form of entertainment, and lecturers
increased the demand for their services by being colorful. It was,
therefore, not unusual that the most striking figure among the Jews,
who were still regarded as an exotic minority, might be a bit of a
mountebank.

The supreme example of American Jewish success was Judah
Touro, the son of Isaac Touro, who had been the cantor in Newport,
Rhode Island, before the Revolution. Touro, in life, was a much
more sedate and drab figure than Noah. In 1801, at the age of twenty-
six, Judah Touro left New England for New Orleans. Though he
never became one of the major powers in the business world of New
Orleans, he did accumulate a substantial fortune. For most of his life
Touro had little to do with the attempts to found a Jewish community. In New Orleans, though, he did provide the money with
which to purchase an Episcopal Church building for a synagogue.
Touro died in 1854. Touro, who seems never to have worshiped
together with his fellow Jews in New Orleans, continued to contribute to the upkeep of the grounds of his father's old synagogue.
That congregation had vanished in the early 1800s, leaving behind
only a building and a cemetery. At Touro's death, his body was
brought from New Orleans and interred in Newport. Touro then
became famous. In his will, he had given away the largest amount
of money, many hundreds of thousands of dollars, that anyone in
America had yet donated to charity. His benefactions included non-
Jewish and Jewish causes in New Orleans. He left money for Jewish

institutions in seventeen cities throughout the United States, and for the relief of the poor in the Holy Land. Touro's will had enormous resonance throughout the Jewish world. Those who were thinking about coming to the United States in the 1850s imagined that they might ultimately find their fortune in some town or city, as Touro had found his in New Orleans.

Touro's life, death, and apotheosis into charity were an appropriate epitaph for colonial and early republican Jewry. Touro's Jewishness belonged to the past. He remembered the synagogue in Newport, in which he had been the son of the poorest Jew in town, the cantor. When he became rich, his benefactions extended to Jews and Gentiles alike, as had the benefactions of Aaron Lopez, the richest member of the synagogue in Newport in the 1770s and 1780s, when Touro was a child. But there was a generational difference between Touro and Lopez. The earlier figure lived within a functioning Jewish community; Touro kept very personal memories of his childhood, and he returned to his family in death, but Touro spent his active years with little connection to his Jewishness. Such biographies would recur again and again among future generations of American Jews. For that matter, the careers of Isaac Harby and Mordecai Manuel Noah would also be reinvented, when future waves of Jewish immigration to the United States reached their second and third generation. Adjustments to America would evoke and reevoke the desire of Harby to fashion Judaism into a "respectable" American denomination. Public figures would arise again and again in generations to come to repeat Noah's attempt to range the Jews within the American elite.

All of these figures—Harby, Noah, and Touro—essentially accepted the notion that there was an American society which set norms of conduct, and that they would find ways of being accepted into this society. They wanted to be liked and included. The striking exception in that generation was Uriah Phillips Levy, first cousin of Mordecai Manuel Noah. Levy had the most "American" of all careers, for he was a professional navy officer. Levy had run away to sea in 1802 at the age of ten. He rose in fifteen years through the ranks to be commissioned in March 1817 as lieutenant in the navy. He spent the next forty some years in and out of the navy. He was court-martialed six times. Some of the woes he brought upon himself by a volatile temperament, but most of his problems were caused by his opposition to the dominant orthodoxies of the service. Levy was opposed on principle to the practice of punishing seamen by flogging, and he violated the code of the naval establishment by going to Congress. The officer corps never forgave him. Levy remained defiant. He was kept as an outsider, and he was often accused of derelictions of duty. In 1857, he was finally vindicated of all charges against him and given command of the USS *Macedonian,* of the Mediterranean Squadron. Later that year, he was made commodore of the squadron, and held that rank for some months before he was ordered home in May of 1860. Even in this exalted rank, Levy remembered his religious obligations. He spent the Day of Atonement that fall with the Italian Rothschilds. When he sailed home, he brought along a wagonload of earth from the Holy Land to New York, and he was thanked by the Spanish-Portuguese congregation to which he belonged, for such earth was used in funeral rituals to pillow the heads of the dead.

From the very beginning of his navy career, in 1812, Levy was doubly in trouble. He had arrived in the service not as a midshipman, through the Naval Academy, but from the ranks, by being given a warrant as a sailing master—and he was a Jew. On both counts he repeatedly had difficulty with officers in the wardrooms of the ships on which he sailed. The eminent American historian, George Bancroft, had been secretary of the navy in 1845–46, and he had refused to give him a command. Bancroft testified in the proceedings in November and December of 1857, in which Levy was vindicated and recalled to active duty, that he "never doubted Captain Levy's competence," but that he kept him out of the service in large part because of "a strong prejudice in the service against Capt. Levy, which seemed to me, in a considerable part attributable to his being of the Jewish persuasion." Bancroft added that he held the same liberal views as the President and the Senate, who had given him the rank of captain, but that, as secretary of the navy, he had to take account of "the need for harmonious cooperation which is essential to the highest effectiveness."

Levy pursued his cause vigorously in the proceedings in late 1857. Dozens upon dozens of American figures of the highest reputation spoke up for him, including thirteen officers who were still on active duty in the navy, and six others who had been previously connected with the service. Against Levy there stood the insistence of some of

his old enemies that charges which had once been dismissed or regarded as minor should still be invoked as proof of his incompetence.
Levy himself knew that he was being attacked as a Jew. Testifying
in his own behalf, he warned American Christians against "the persecution of the Jew":

> And think not, if you once enter on this career, that it can be
> limited to the Jew. What is my case today, if you yield to this
> injustice, may tomorrow be that of the Roman Catholic or the
> Unitarian; the Presbyterian or the Methodist; the Episcopalian or
> the Baptist. There is but one safeguard; that is to be found in an
> honest, whole hearted, inflexible support of the wise, the just, the
> impartial guarantee of the Constitution.

Levy's travail prefigured exactly the much more important battle
two generations later, in 1916, over the confirmation of Louis Dembitz Brandeis to the Supreme Court. Then, too, the issue was that
Brandeis was regarded as an outsider by the American legal establishment and that he was a Jew. Then, too, the American aristocracy
split between the nativists and those who defined America as a society
that was open to all talent that was lawfully employed.

Levy won in 1857, because he appealed to the America of the
Founding Fathers. He invoked them, not merely because it served
his cause, but as one who was deeply devoted to their memory. Levy
had bought Jefferson's home, Monticello, in 1836, and he kept it as
a kind of private shrine to the memory of the author of the Declaration of Independence. From the very beginning of his career to its
end, Levy had refused to accept the notion that he had to make
himself agreeable to his peers in the navy. The American tradition
which he revered, and from which he claimed protection, was not
the goodwill of society but the laws of the Constitution.

7.

The German Jews
Arrive

I

Western and Central Europe were convulsed in 1848 by revolutions against the reigning monarchs. Most of these insurrections failed, and those who made them, if they were fortunate enough to remain alive and out of jail, fled to safer places. Some of these political refugees came to the United States, where the most prominent among them, such as Louis Kossuth, the leader of the revolt in Hungary, were feted and lionized. These rebels were heroes who reminded Americans of the great age of their own country, sixty or seventy years before. It was an honor at the time for an immigrant to claim to be a "Forty-eighter"; their supposed numbers inevitably grew in later memory, when families were adorning their history with an honorific past.

A few decades after their arrival, the "German Jews" were cultivating the myth that large numbers among them had been revolutionaries in Europe, but the claim had no basis in reality. The most assiduous antiquarian research has turned up fewer than twenty names of Jewish immigrants to the United States who had anything to do with the liberal revolutions. The typical migrant of those days came from the family of a Bavarian cattle-dealer or peddler. He was usually a younger son who could find nothing to do in an impoverished region which was becoming overpopulated. Moreover, in the middle years of the nineteenth century, the better-off European Jews were not leaving the small towns and villages in which they had lived for generations to emigrate to America. Enterprising people with some little capital at their disposal could move closer to home, to Berlin, Prague, or Vienna, to make their fortunes. As before, in colonial times, the Jews who left for North America in the middle of the nineteenth century were the poorest, and the least educated.

It was equally mythic that these "German Jews" were all from Germany. Many came from other places in Central Europe such as Bohemia and Moravia: some came from Posen, the easternmost province of Prussia, which had been Polish until the late eighteenth century. And yet, even though America was enormously attractive in the years before the Civil War—it was the country of cheap land and new cities—it did not evoke mass migration from all over Jewish Europe. There was little emigration from Prussia because the Industrial Revolution had already begun there, and the economy was making room for a growing population. Anti-Semitism had never really abated in the towns and villages of Alsace and Lorraine, where the bulk of the Jewish population of France lived, but these Jews did not migrate in any numbers to the United States; many went, instead, to Paris. The largest Jewish population was, of course, in Russia, but in the middle of the nineteenth century, most Jews still lived there in a traditional society. The thought of emigrating and breaking ties with the community simply did not occur to them. Transportation was still primitive, and America seemed far away.

Perhaps half of all the immigrants were from Bavaria. This migration from Bavaria was a special case. It began in the 1830s and 1840s because economic doors were closed to a specific part of the Jewish community, the younger children of the petty traders and cattle dealers, the pursuits which were permitted to Jews in that region. The villages in Bavaria continued to do what they had done for centuries: they would not allow a Jew to establish a new family unless a "place" was made for him through the death or removal of someone else. Younger sons of local families who wanted to marry thus had to leave. They could not go to the cities of Bavaria. These were stagnant, for Bavaria had not even begun to experience any stirrings toward manufacture and industry. Emigration was thus the obvious choice—and in the 1840s transportation from Central Europe was ever easier and cheaper, as the railroads were built and the steamships began their regular, competing services on the North Atlantic.

These Jewish immigrants were as poor as the millions of Gentiles from Germany and Ireland, who were then coming to America, but the Jews were different. They were better prepared in advance to rise quickly in America. Many of the German Gentiles and the majority of the Irish were farmers. The Jews were peddlers and middlemen. The Germans and the Irish were mostly illiterate; even the poorest of the Jewish men could usually read, for they had been taught to read the Hebrew prayer book. Such literacy could—and was—transferred to German, and soon to English. Consequently, many of the Jews were ahead, on arrival, in the race for success in the New Land.

It was a time for success. America was booming and there was need for more population. The country was following its "manifest destiny," to extend American rule and settlement all the way to the Pacific. In the 1830s, when the first great surge of immigration began, some six hundred thousand people came to the United States. In the next decade the number was one and a half million, and in the one thereafter, the last before the Civil War, the immigration almost doubled to nearly three million. America was changing during those years from an almost entirely agricultural society to one in which almost half of all the citizens lived in cities. The figures are startling: in 1820, four out of five Americans made their livings on farms; by 1860 this number was down to a bit more than half. New cities were being founded, and almost all the older ones were growing rapidly, as trading posts and manufacturing centers. A market was being created in America itself to exchange what the farmers produced for what the cities manufactured. Never again in American history were middlemen to be so much in demand. The Jews who were then arriving from Central Europe brought with them long experience in buying and selling. There would never again be the opportunity for the majority of a wave of Jewish migrants to get rich in their own lifetimes.

Many began by selling from pushcarts, and soon from stores, in the already existing major cities. As early as the 1830s, Jews were selling old clothes on Chatham Street on the Lower East Side of New York. This was a lucrative business because, until the Civil War, selling old clothes was a more important trade in America than making new garments. Buyers and sellers bargained; inevitably, the buyers often resented the price they were persuaded to pay. As early as 1833, a British traveler described Chatham Street as a place which was inhabited mostly by "the Tribe of Judah," as anyone could see who went to shop there, because of "their long beards, which reached to the bottom of their waists." These merchants were not the children or grandchildren of Judah Lopez or of Haym Salomon, for the Jews who were present in America in colonial times had taken off their beards years before. Fifteen years later the neighborhood was already entirely Jewish, or so a contemporary visitor from the South maintained: "a Yankee (cute as they are) shopkeeper in Chatham Street could not exist." Later still, in 1853, Cornelius Matthews, a dramatist and journalist, wrote a sharp, ironic account of Chatham Street. He asserted that in ancient times, when Manhattan belonged to the Indians, the street had been one of their warpaths. It remained so even in these supposedly civilized times: "The old Redmen scalped their enemies; the Chatham clothes-men skinned theirs." It should be remembered that these were "German Jews," many of whom would forget how they had begun in America and would be maintaining several decades later that only "Russian Jews" were capable of sharp business practices. By the late 1840s, this area of Jewish shops in New York extended to the major streets which were to be the heart of the Jewish Lower East Side for the next hundred years: Houston, Division, Grand, and the Bowery. There are vivid accounts of comparable "Lower East Sides" in those days in Baltimore, Cincinnati, and Philadelphia. In Baltimore, several blocks of Lombard Street were then a market for dry goods and old clothes, but its specialties were such items as prayer shawls and kosher food of all varieties.

There were, of course, some tragedies and failures. On May 7, 1849, the *New York Sun* carried a story that "the body of a German named Marcus Cohen was found on Friday last. On account of pecuniary embarrassment he terminated his existence." There were other business failures, which did not end so tragically—but most of the immigrants succeeded. In Easton, Pennsylvania, twenty-four Jews out of seventy in town were peddlers in 1850, but the numbers kept dropping year by year. The pattern is the same in Richmond, Virginia, in Syracuse, New York, and in a host of other communities in the eastern half of the country. It was different in Minnesota and in the western states in general, including California. Those Jews who came there in the years before the Civil War had often already done their stint as peddlers in the East. They usually came to the place of their second settlement with enough capital to become merchants immediately on arrival. It is significant that in the Gold Rush of 1849, as towns and trading posts sprang up everywhere in the Far West, there were Jewish storekeepers in every one of them, but there were very few Jews among the prospectors for gold. Such prospectors might get rich quickly in one fantastic strike, but storekeepers were fairly sure of a stable living, and more. Even in these unusual conditions, most Jews stuck to what they knew. Trade was an almost certain avenue to wealth.

In this great, first tide of immigration, there were some 100,000 Jews; between 1820 and 1860, their numbers in the United States increased from perhaps 6,000 to 150,000. On the eve of the Civil War, Jews were no longer a handful scattered in the port cities on the Eastern Seaboard. They were to be found everywhere, in dozens upon dozens of American towns and cities. The normal pattern of the Jewish immigrant to America was to peddle for a few years and then to settle down and open a store. He also tended to send for other members of his family, and even for a wife, from back home. Thus, various nascent Jewish communities in midwestern or southern towns soon represented interrelated families with ties to the same places in Germany. Most of these immigrants became, in less than twenty years, substantial merchants on the main streets of dozens of cities.

A few Jewish capitalists came to the United States before the Civil War; they were men such as Philipp and Gustav Speyer from Frankfurt and Adolph Ladenburg from Mannheim. These were members of established banking families, and they went immediately into the trade in the United States. Oddly enough, despite an early start, these never became the most important Jewish firms, though Ladenburg, Thalmann and Co. was prominent in the financing of American railroads. The overwhelming majority of the great Jewish fortunes were amassed by more recent immigrants who began very poor. Marcus Goldman, the founder of Goldman, Sachs and Co., the famous and still extant Wall Street firm, arrived in Philadelphia in 1848 where he peddled for two years; he then opened a men's clothing store in which he made his basic capital. Around 1850, Abraham Kuhn and Solomon Loeb, founders of Kuhn, Loeb & Co., were partners in general commerce in Lafayette, Indiana, before they moved to Cincinnati, to open a general store. Henry Lehman arrived in 1844 and peddled in Alabama. Within a year he opened a store in Montgomery and, together with his brothers Emanuel and Mayer, went into cotton brokerage. Perhaps the most striking success story of those days was that of Joseph Seligman, who arrived in 1837 and worked for a year in a store in Mauch Chunk (now Jim Thorpe), Pennsylvania. He then peddled among the backcountry farmers with a pack on his back. By 1841, together with three of his brothers, he had opened a store in Selma, Alabama, which they also used as a base for peddling. A few years later they already owned a number of such stores in small towns in the South. In 1846 they broadened their horizon and established a dry goods importing house in New York; four years later, two of the brothers were to be found in San Francisco, selling clothing to the many who were coming west in the Gold Rush. By the time the Civil War began, the Seligmans were established in New York as a financial firm. They were the very first Jewish immigrants to make the leap from merchant to financier. The Seligmans became really wealthy only during and after the Civil War. Before 1861, the Jewish peddlers who became merchants had become well-off, but they were not yet rich enough to be envied.

II

Jews were too few to become the prime target of American nativism. This was reserved for the Irish and the Germans. In the four decades between 1820 and the Civil War, 1.7 million Irish and 1.3 million Germans arrived in the United States. Almost all the Irish were Catholic, and so were the majority of the Germans. American nativism began to take notice of these migrations very early, after the War of 1812, when the first trickle started to arrive. The Irish were supposedly bringing the pope and his minions, the priests and bishops who were then appearing in America in substantial numbers, to burrow under and to destroy the purportedly clean, simple, and decent values that American Protestantism had taught. One of the journalists who promoted the notion that the Irish "could not understand or appreciate the excellence of this [the American] form of government" was Mordecai Manuel Noah. The German immigrants were attacked because they had the enraging notion that their culture was superior to what was to be found in America. Obviously right-thinking Americans could not stand for such ideas. In 1854, the Native American party, the "Know-Nothings," became a full-fledged national movement. In the next year it renamed itself the American party. This nativism barely mentioned the Jews. There were a few stray Jews among its members, including one named Lewis Levin, who was married to a Catholic. Indeed, Lewis was elected to Congress for three successive terms (1845–51) as the candidate of the American party.

The Jewish immigrants, at least those who lived in the northeastern cities, were mostly Democrats. This was the party of Andrew Jackson, of the "new men," of the outsiders who were making something of themselves on the frontier, and, for that matter, in the cities. They could not find a home among the Whigs, the party which retained much more of the flavor and the prejudices of the older America. Jews held political office in remarkable numbers. For half a century, Emanuel Hart was a power in New York's Tammany Hall. Hart became the leader of the Jewish forces in the Democratic party in New York after Noah broke with Tammany in the mid-1820s. He was even chairman of the Central Committee for some years. Hart won election to one term in Congress. In Philadelphia, Henry Phillips was elected to Congress in 1856 as a Democrat. In the South, the Jews were, with few exceptions, proslavery Democrats. In Richmond, Gustavus Meyers was the only Jewish member of the city council for almost thirty years (1827–55). Henry Hyans was elected lieutenant governor in Louisiana in 1856. Most of these figures (like Senators Judah P. Benjamin and David Yulee) were from the older Jewish settlement, but there were also local officeholders who were generally newer immigrants.

But the Jews of those years were not all racing for a place in the existing political machines. Some took risks. When the new Republican party was organized in the 1850s, with opposition to slavery as its central plank, there was a high proportion of Jews among its founders. In Chicago, four of the five founders of a German-language wing of the Republicans were Jews. Jewish leaders of the party were especially important in the West, the region from which Lincoln came. These included an old friend of Lincoln's, Abraham Jonas of Quincy, Illinois, and newer ones such as Henry Greenbaum, a Democratic alderman from Chicago who, in 1855, changed parties to support Lincoln. Perhaps the most striking Jewish Republican was Louisville's Lewis N. Dembitz. In 1860 Dembitz made one of the three speeches nominating Lincoln at the Republican Convention. Dembitz was the uncle of Louis Brandeis, a future justice of the Supreme Court. In Philadelphia, Rabbi Sabato Morais, the minister (i.e., the cantor and preacher) of the Sephardi congregation, defied his lay leadership and helped organize the Republican party in Pennsylvania. Morais was Orthodox, and his faith, as he understood it, commanded him to be an abolitionist. Almost all of these Jews in politics were newcomers, and some of them were very recent arrivals, but that was not unusual at a time when the political institutions, especially those on the frontier, had been formed just a few years earlier.

III

On three occasions before the Civil War, American Jews took public action in "foreign affairs." The first was in 1840. In February of that year a Capuchin monk, Father Tomas, and his Muslim servant had disappeared in Damascus. The French consul, Ratti-Menon, encouraged the local officials to charge that Jews had murdered them in order to use their blood for the baking of matzoth. This libel had recurred frequently since the Middle Ages in Christian Europe; it had now made its first appearance in the Middle East. A number of Jews, children among them, were jailed. Some died under torture. The Jewish communities in France and England took action as soon as they heard of this outrage. The protest meeting held in London in July 1840 came to the attention of President Martin Van Buren. Van Buren wrote immediately, through his consular agent in Damascus, to the Egyptian authorities to express "surprise and pain that in this advanced age such unnatural practices should be ascribed to any portion of the religious world." Still unprompted, Van Buren sent a comparable message to the American minister in Turkey.

For their part, the Jews protested not only in the old established communities such as Charleston, Savannah, Richmond, and Philadelphia, but also in the new community of Cincinnati. The most interesting meeting was held in New York on August 19, 1840, in Congregation B'nai Jeshurun, the first Ashkenazi congregation in the city. Its creation had predated the large-scale migrations of the Jews from Germany, for it had been founded in 1825 by some of the first arrivals from England and the Continent. The meeting was to be held there, and not in the more aristocratic and "American" surroundings of the Sephardi congregation, Shearith Israel, because most of its leaders wanted to avoid "foreign entanglements." But the most striking public figure among the Sephardim, Mordecai Manuel Noah, delivered the speech of the occasion. It represented, at the very dawn of Jewish "foreign policy" in America, a summary of its future content. Noah denied that American Jews, who were "exempt from such outrages," have the right to ignore the problems of other Jews. On the contrary, they have the obligation, "in proportion to the great blessings that we enjoy," to defend less fortunate Jews, and to help with money and public support. The reasons that he gave were history, religion, and, above all, group feeling. Though scattered all over the world, "we are still one people, bound by the same religious ties, worshipping the same God, governed by the same sacred awe, and bound together by the same destiny. The cause of one is the cause of all." That was the view of the majority of American Jews. The fearful older settlers were outvoted by some in their own ranks, together with the bulk of the newer immigrants.

On this first occasion when American Jews acted on behalf of their brethren abroad, pressure in Washington had not been necessary, because President Van Buren had intervened on his own, but his example was not followed by his immediate successors. In the 1850s the United States, under two administrations, negotiated a commercial treaty with Switzerland. Almost all the cantons in the Swiss Confederation then excluded Jews from residence; the United States had agreed that they would have the right not to grant visas to Jews who were American citizens. A delegation went to see President James Buchanan, but he refused to renegotiate the agreement. In 1858, American Jewry was even more seriously angered by the tragic case of Edgardo Mortara. This six-year-old Italian Jewish child was seized by papal police in Bologna and taken from his parents because the maid in the Mortara household said that she had secretly baptized him. The Church therefore insisted that in canon law Edgardo Mortara was irretrievably Catholic. Despite an international outcry, there was no retreat. Edgardo Mortara was hidden and educated in a Catholic institution; he eventually became a priest. American Jews asked Washington to intercede, but such help was refused. The secretary of state wrote that "it is the settled policy of the United States to abstain from all intervention in the internal affairs of another country." The Mortara case did add to tensions in the United States between Jews and Irish, for the Catholics in America supported the pope. This confrontation probably helped move some Jews into the Republican party on the eve of the fateful election of 1860. An angry Jewish journalist commented on Buchanan's action by saying that Van Buren had been willing to intervene in 1840, because Muslims had no votes in the United States; Buchanan had done nothing in 1858, because Catholics made a difference in an American election.

Before 1840, American Jews had never intervened on behalf of their brethren abroad. There had been a few such efforts earlier in Europe, but the Jews in America had been too remote and unimportant to be asked to join. Now, in the middle years of the nineteenth century, the situation was different. European Jewish leaders in Europe, led by Sir Moses Montefiore who was helped by the Rothschilds, asked the Americans to join in protests against assaults on the rights of Jews in Russia or the Near East. In America these efforts brought together, for the first time, the native and the immigrant communities. In these actions, American Jews had taken a step beyond worrying about their immediate families, and more distant relatives, whom they had left behind in the old country. Those who joined together to help endangered Jews in Damascus or Bologna, or to rap the knuckles of the Swiss, were acting not for cousins but for strangers.

American Jews had adopted the misery of other Jews as their cause. This caring was their principle of unity. American Jews were not one society, for the older settlers regarded the newcomers as uncouth and embarrassing. Religion was not a unifying force, because the new immigrants were generally unwelcome in the existing congregations, and they were, themselves, more comfortable in synagogues of their own creation. Old settlers and immigrants could unite only in good works on behalf of other Jews.

In the middle of the nineteenth century, American Jews, in their large majority, made another fateful decision. They entered the arena of American politics to help their brethren all over the world, and they were willing to face whatever problems in America such actions might cause them. In the 1850s, it was already of some discomfort to be refused help by two presidents.

By 1861 Jews had been arriving in America for two and a half centuries. Like almost all other immigrants, they had been coming to succeed, and many had been willing to travel as light as possible on the way to that success by abandoning much or even all of their religious and cultural distinctiveness. Direct help and political effort on behalf of other Jews had become the common denominator of being Jewish in America as early as the 1840s and 1850s. This would remain the dominant "theology" of American Jews for the next century or so, even to present days.

8.

Worshiping America

I

In the 1840s and 1850s, American Jews of all persuasions agreed on "foreign affairs," but such concerns were not at
the center of their Jewish agenda. The American Jewish community
was still too small and too poor to make a difference in the politics
of world Jewry. More important, America itself was still a minor
player on the international stage. World politics were dominated then
by England and France. Sir Moses Montefiore, from England, and
Adolphe Crémieux, the foremost Jew in politics in France, were the
delegation who went to Damascus in 1841 and saved the Jews who
were still alive in jail. Montefiore and Crémieux succeeded because
they were backed by governments which were then the dominant
powers in the Middle East.

The tens of thousands of immigrants to the United States in those
years had, first, to find ways of surviving in a strange country. Like
all other new arrivals, their first support was each other. From New
York to California, the Jewish immigrants of the 1840s and 1850s
banded together in two hundred new synagogues—but this repre-

sented no religious revival. These congregations did, of course, provide religious services, but their prime function was to make immigrant Jews less lonely. There was no "great awakening" of piety, of commitment to ritual and tradition. Such observances had more than half-evaporated among the older settlers, and they were lessening rapidly among the new immigrants. A pious minority did exist, and many others belonged to the synagogues, even if they seldom attended. But numerous immigrant Jews chose not to belong. The religious institutions and the functionaries that the caring minority sustained did act to make the rest more comfortable. In San Francisco, the male children of Jews who were not associated with the nascent synagogue were circumcised as early as 1849; bodies of individuals who had not been known as Jews until their death were sometimes brought in from mining camps to be buried on consecrated ground. There were many such stories everywhere in those turbulent years.

The most common sentiment was family feeling, the sense of belonging as Jews to each other. The new immigrants sustained each other not only by meeting together in the synagogues, they founded numerous clubs and self-help societies. In such organizations, believers, semibelievers, and nonbelievers could all gather together— to affirm their togetherness. "Service organizations," which lasted and gained in power and importance in the next several decades, were founded in America in the 1840s and 1850s. These were associations of individuals and not confederations of synagogues. From their beginnings these bodies were created with no religious program; they were an extended family. The immigrant Jews were part of a very American pattern. Alexis de Tocqueville, the French visitor who wrote *Democracy in America,* his classic account of what the United States was like around 1830, was amazed by the energy that Americans put into "joining." Self-help organizations, of people who were comfortable with each other, became even more important in the next several decades. All the new immigrants, and especially those who came without families, needed such companionship. The typical Jewish immigrant to America in those days was most often a young man who came alone. Many Jews tried very hard, as soon as they knew some English, to join existing American organizations. For a short while, they succeeded. Since colonial times, a handful of Jews had belonged to the Masons. The Masonic lodges remained open to the larger numbers who applied in the 1840s and 1850s, but this did not last. There was soon a "ghetto" among the Masons. "Jewish" lodges were organized, and some "mixed" lodges became Jewish by the attrition of their Gentile membership.

But American society was not as open as the Jewish immigrants hoped. There was social anti-Semitism, as Mordecai Manuel Noah and Uriah Phillips Levy, of the older settlers, could have told them. Immigrant Jews were told very early that they were not wanted, and that they had no option but to organize their own social and self-help organizations. A dozen young men applied in 1843 to the Odd Fellows Lodge, but they were refused membership. These young Jewish immigrants then met together and organized a comparable body of their own, the Independent Order of B'nai B'rith. In the preamble to their constitution the founders proposed to do everything from "uniting Israelites in the work of promoting their highest causes and those of humanity," to visiting the sick and providing for widows and orphans. The emphasis on "humanity," by the founders of B'nai B'rith, was a way of saying that they, the Jews who had been forced into an organization of their own, were truer representatives of the cause of a united mankind than the Gentiles of the Odd Fellows, who had excluded them. This assertion would recur over and over again for the next century or so, as the quintessential response by Jews to anti-Semitism.

Like the Odd Fellows and the Masons, B'nai B'rith began as a "secret order" with all the paraphernalia of such a body: passwords and bombastic secret rituals. The new organization grew very rapidly. By 1851 its membership in New York City alone was seven hundred; there was comparable growth in other centers of Jewish population. It soon spread throughout the country. By 1860, three imitating organizations had been created. These "orders," as they all were called, served as extended families, and as such they had important self-help purposes. The dues and fees bought some personal insurance. B'nai B'rith, for example, gave a widow thirty dollars to help pay for her husband's funeral, along with some continuing payments to her and to her children until they reached thirteen. In an age when government relief did not exist, and when the Jewish rich were too few to help, such insurance was critical.

By 1849, there were already some fifty Jewish organizations—charitable, social, and fraternal—in New York, and their combined membership was far greater than that of the synagogues. Henry Jonas, one of the founders of B'nai B'rith, wrote in 1852: "These associations address themselves to the demoralized condition and low intellectual status of the Jews." What this remark meant in context was that B'nai B'rith worked hard to Americanize its members, to help them forget their humble origins in Europe, and to feel themselves to be as good as any other American. This was an immediate and important need. It was far more urgent than the need to say daily prayers, or keeping kosher, which had become more and more difficult within the turmoil of lives which were being spent peddling on the road or keeping stores open for fifteen hours a day. The synagogues thus became places in which to celebrate the major festivals and the rites of passages, such as bar mitzvahs, confirmations, marriages, and deaths. The "societies" were becoming the major home of organized Jewish life.

In mid-nineteenth-century America social barriers were not yet as high as they were to become later in the century, but it was clear, even in the 1840s and 1850s, that a Jew was regarded as different. It was noted over and over again, by friends as well as critics, that Jewish merchants drove themselves harder than anyone else, and that they seemed to do well more quickly. The Gentile majority knew very little about Jewish beliefs and practices, but everyone knew that all Jews denied the basic teaching of all the other religions in America, faith in Jesus. This issue was often painful, especially in the smaller towns of the Middle West and South. Christian revivalists came to these towns again and again to preach the Gospel. Almost invariably, they confronted and tried to convert the owner of the general store who was often the only Jew in town. The Jews usually refused to be converted, but inevitably, the pressure of Christianity on their lives was very heavy. Their children were attending schools where they were usually the only dissenters from the Protestantism which pervaded the atmosphere. There were prayers in the morning, stories about Jesus in history lessons during the day, and hymns, at very least during the Christmas season.

When the newcomers became numerous enough to form a community, in towns such as Nashville, Tennessee, or Grand Rapids, Michigan, the synagogue which they established was at first a carbon copy of those that they had left behind in the town or village from which they had come. Some Jewish laymen, perhaps even most, clung to these forms, and not merely or even primarily out of piety. The Orthodox synagogue was a reminder, on the frontier, of the home of their childhood. But these Jews had come to that frontier to be different than they had been in Europe. Their children were growing up in an American world. Even more than their parents, this younger generation needed a synagogue which was not "foreign."

Everywhere, the religious institutions themselves were rapidly being adjusted to the American scene. With one exception, Temple Emanu-El in New York, every synagogue that these newcomers established had begun as Orthodox. In roughly twenty years the vast majority had been transformed into "Reformed" congregations. Almost everywhere sexes were no longer separated; there were organs, and prayers in German, and soon in English. As was to be expected, these changes were deplored by the Orthodox, who were ever weaker and more on the defensive, but the dominant tide in mid-century favored the "moderate reformers," who were creating a "respectable" American Judaism. The tone was set by laymen who were refurbishing their synagogues so that they would be acceptable to the Gentile majority. These changes were made by laymen on no authority except their own—not rabbis, but rather storekeepers in Memphis and clothing manufacturers in Rochester, New York, and their peers all over Jewish America. These are the principal ancestors of the most "American" version of Judaism: that Jewish religion—and everything else that Jews believe or do—must not act to keep Jews apart in America; Judaism and the Jewish community must be reshaped and used as instruments of the success of Jews in American life. There was no ideological content to these reforms. The immigrant reformers were not Deists, like Isaac Harby in Charleston in the 1820s. They were tinkering with synagogue ritual and with their religious practices for pragmatic reasons—to become "American" as rapidly as possible.

Who were these laymen? The minutes and other documents of the nascent congregations of the 1840s and 1850s were not recorded by educated men. The most interesting of these texts is the account book of a messenger who came to America in 1849 to collect money for support of Jews in the Holy Land. The givers entered their contributions in their own hand; thus the institution to which they were donating had a way of checking up on their emissary's accounts without being totally dependent on his honesty. Some of the well-known figures of that period, including Mordecai Manuel Noah, were among the donors. The most interesting signatures were from Syracuse and Utica, in upstate New York. These modest contributors signed their names in Hebrew and in Yiddish, and several even added a few lines of text, to describe their origins. A few appear to have been men of some Jewish learning, but the educated (they were most likely to be stray individuals from Eastern Europe) were exceptions. Most of the immigrants of the 1840s and 1850s knew no language except Yiddish, as it was still spoken then among German Jews, and street German.

Despite rebuffs from Gentiles, and feeling most at home with each other, these immigrants wanted to become part of the larger society. They had left Central Europe at a time when the battles for equality for Jews were being fought, but they had not yet been won anywhere east of France. America was different. Here Jews were equal, in law, upon arrival, and they refused to believe that social exclusion of Jews, to the degree to which it existed in the New Land, was anything more than a vestige of outworn attitudes. In America, so they thought, anti-Semitism was in process of vanishing. This optimism was the faith of the "German Jews" from their immigrant beginnings.

The Gentiles whom they approached first were the German immigrants, with whom they shared a language. This union with Germans was sought because it could happen "only in America." Jews were still being excluded from all such bodies back home in Germany. Friendship between German-speaking Jews and Gentiles did exist, but only for a while, in such centers of German immigration as New York, Cincinnati, and Milwaukee. In New York, the Arion Glee Club had Jewish members among its founders. By the late 1860s, however, the club had barred Jews and even added anti-Semitic songs to its repertoire. In the earliest years after their arrival in the United States, Jews were a majority in the audiences of the German theater in New York. Many of the Germans did not like it. Theodore Griesinger, writing from Stuttgart in 1856 about his stay in America, talked sarcastically about the newly rich Jewish wives who showed off their finery by "bend[ing] over the railing of the first gallery." This involvement in German culture was essentially a brief phase. For a generation these immigrants still spoke German with each other, and for a decade or two it was the language of the sermons in their synagogues. There was even among some a conscious identification with the glories of German *Kultur,* which was then claiming to be the most important intellectual tradition of the Western world.

Almost without exception, however, these immigrants wanted to become American as quickly as possible. B'nai B'rith began in German, but it moved to English by 1855. The minute book of Temple Emanu-El, which was on the way to becoming the leading congregation of the "German Jews" in New York, changed languages, from German to English, as early as 1856.

II

The leader and the symbolic figure of this generation was Isaac Mayer Wise. His life is the central story of the "German Jews" in America, from their arrival until the immigrant generation was totally gone around 1900, the year of Wise's death. Wise was not much different from the flock he led. At the zenith of his career, he was very proud of his intimate social intercourse with the laity. He ate and drank with them gladly, though he did draw the line at playing cards with his parishioners. These Jews had come to America to succeed, and to leave their lower-class status in Europe behind. They did not want to be encumbered by memory and by guilt—and neither did Wise. Wise held to this view self-consciously, with remarkable consistency, throughout his long and often stormy life. He was thinking such "American" thoughts even before he left Bohemia for the United States.

In the mid-1840s, Isaac Mayer Wise was religious functionary and schoolmaster in Radnitz, a small town in Bohemia. He was not very learned in the Talmud, and there is even some doubt to this day whether he had actually ever been ordained. He took some courses at the Prague University, but he received no degree. Nonetheless, he took to calling himself "Rabbi" immediately after his arrival in the United States, and he added "Doctor" some years later. America offered ambitious men like him the chance to be big fish in a new and growing pond. In 1846, when Wise came off the sailing boat, together with his wife and a two-year-old daughter, after a harrowing journey of sixty-three days, there was no one in New York to challenge his definition of himself as a Jewish spiritual leader. Wise hated the old-school lay leaders, the *parnassim,* who continued to direct the Jewish communities in Europe with their accustomed autocracy. He thanked God that "in America, there were no petty tyrants, like the chief rabbis of England and Germany," to rule over less well-placed Jewish clerics. Wise had come to the New Land to leave these older authorities behind.

Wise arrived with only two dollars in his pocket. The journey of the Wise family from dockside to the Lower East Side was not without incident. A porter of German origin tried to overcharge him. When Wise refused to pay, the porter reviled him as a dirty Jew. But, despite such incidents, in America even anti-Semitism was different. Jews were still exotics, at least in the recently founded cities of the Middle West. In 1817, when the first Jew had arrived in Cincinnati, a farm woman who heard the news journeyed two days in a horse and wagon to see the horns and tail which a Jew was supposed to possess—but she came to Cincinnati much more out of curiosity than out of unkindness. On the advancing frontier Jews were excluded from nothing in the economy which they really wanted. The remaining discomforts of being Jews in a Gentile society were little in comparison to the European anti-Semitism which they had left behind.

Wise's character was vigorous, and pugnacious. He picked some fights which brought immediate discomfort to his laity. His admiring biographers have, therefore, praised him as a leader who fashioned American Reform Judaism according to his will. This estimate of Wise does not survive critical examination. The battles that he chose to fight were all related to his one consuming passion, to make the Jews absolutely at home as equals in America. In 1854 he sued in Ohio (he was by then the rabbi of the Plum Street Temple in Cincinnati) against prayers and Bible reading in the public schools. In this issue he was joined by the Roman Catholics in the state. When Wise lost the suit in the Supreme Court, the laymen of his congregation complained that the bringing of this action endangered them, because it aroused anti-Semitism—but such arguments were tactical. These laymen wanted the result of Wise's actions, an American public life that was religiously neutral, but they did not want to bear the pain of the fight.

In the 1850s, Jews were far better off than Catholics. Some Jews thought that they would be accepted by the Protestant majority if they kept their heads down, for the Catholics were then the prime object of exclusion. This was undoubtedly in the mind of some of those who were angry with Wise, when he joined the Catholics in going to court against prayers in American public schools. Wise was the first Jewish leader to create such an alliance. This was an important choice. Jews were on the border between being considered exotics and being tolerated. Catholics were severely embattled; there were several murderous riots against them in the 1850s in New York. In 1854 Wise made a decision: he would not accept toleration at the cost of living under the pressure of Protestantism which pervaded public life. He insisted that the majority had to be forced to accept the notion, even if only grudgingly, that the sensibilities of Jews, and of Catholics, should not be offended in America.

Wise was particularly sensitive to Christian teachings which blamed Jews for the Crucifixion. Over and over again, he protested Thanksgiving proclamations which contained Christian references. Wise challenged every slur on Jews, and he advocated the boycott of anti-Semites. He fought very hard against Christian missionaries who were trying to convert the Jews. He joined in all the interventions in Washington against foreign governments which discriminated against Jews. This is the record of a man who was often ahead of his flock—but Wise was running ahead in the direction in which his congregants wanted to go. He was doing battle for the deepest desires of his contemporaries. They wanted to be at home in an America in which the dominant Protestantism would have no special status.

Wise was even more the representative figure of his generation as religious reformer. He was never ideologically consistent. At various times, he accepted and then rejected the religious authority of the Talmud and other rabbinic writings; he maintained that he subscribed to the divine origin of the Bible, without being particularly obedient to its culinary injunctions. Like the laity, his central objective was to rearrange Judaism to be at home in America. In the late 1840s, near the beginning of his years in the United States, Wise began to work toward defining a *Minhag America,* a liturgy and set of practices which would belong uniquely to the New World. The older Judaism in which he and the other immigrants had been raised was full of the sorrow of being Jewish in an unfriendly world. Here in America, so Wise insisted, the time had come for Judaism without tears.

But as religious leader, Wise here, too, sometimes ran ahead of his flock, especially in the early years, but he was pulling them in the direction in which the majority wanted to go. Wise ran into trouble in his very first pulpit in Albany, New York. He had come there in 1846 to be the rabbi of the existing congregation, which was then still Orthodox. It split in the next year, because the bulk of the laity would not accept Wise's program of religious reform. There was even a fistfight on the pulpit on the Day of Atonement, in 1849, between the newly arrived Rabbi Wise and the president of the congregation. A minority followed Wise, but the Reform congregation which they created was not religiously radical enough for him; it did not provide him with a platform for his ambitions. He gladly accepted election in 1854 as the spiritual leader of a congregation in Cincinnati that had been founded twelve years earlier by Jews from Central Europe. Its building was situated in what was becoming an undesirable neighborhood, and so a new building was begun in 1863. This was to become Wise's cathedral.

On August 24, 1865, the B'nai Yeshurun Congregation dedicated this splendid structure. Since there was no tradition of synagogue architecture, for few such buildings had survived destruction in Europe through the centuries, a style had to be invented. The new building in Cincinnati was decidedly Moorish, but its towers were shaped like pomegranates rather than minarets, and there was a great and imposing dome. In his dedicatory address, Isaac Mayer Wise announced with pride that he had named the new house of worship a temple, and not a synagogue, because divine service would be held there in the spirit of "gladness and not in perpetual mourning, as in the synagogue." Some months earlier, in preparation for this event, Wise had published an account of the first years of the congregation. He had introduced a choir to accompany the service, and a new prayer book, *Minhag America,* "the American rite," which he had edited. This was the one tangible result of his labors for the last fifteen years to create an American-Jewish code of ritual practice. The essential theology of this new prayer book was that "doctrines inconsistent with reason are no longer tenable." The Jews were politically equal in the United States and were on the way to such equality, so Wise believed, all over the world. Therefore, they have a home and "cannot feel homesick." Jews no longer "wish to return to Palestine, nor do we pray for the coming of the Messiah." One can almost feel Wise pulling himself erect to full height as he wrote the climactic sentence: "We are American citizens and Israelites by religion."

His congregants more than shared in this glorying in America. On the day of dedication, Wise pronounced that "Judaism welcomes the light of day, and decks itself with becoming pride." In Cincinnati in those days, this was very true. On the Sunday before the dedication, $90,000 was raised to help pay the remaining cost of the building. Whatever else the congregation owed was realized by the sale of pews; the first two were bought for $4,600 each. These amounts represent at least ten times the present value of the dollar; very large amounts of money, in real value, were thus being given by men who had been peddlers less than twenty years before.

Wise gloried in exchanging pulpits with the fashionable Protestant ministers whose churches were literally across the street from his Plum Street Temple, but Wise knew that the major protection of the equality of Jews in America came not from such goodwill but from the Constitution. In 1854, he had decided not to be quiet but to join with the much more hated Catholics to try to push the Protestant majority away from dominance in civic life. This was Wise's most shining hour.

III

In the 1850s most people in America hoped that the issue of slavery could be avoided; so did most Jews. In the Southern states Jews almost unanimously supported the proslavery interests. In the Midwest and in the border states, Jewish wholesale houses had many customers in the South. These merchants knew that slavery was a moral issue, but they hoped it would be resolved "gradually." And yet, some voices were raised powerfully against slavery.

The issue came to a head in the winter of 1860, as the Civil War was breaking out. As was to be expected, the Jewish clergy in the South, without exception, endorsed the Confederacy. These preachers, most of whom were quite recent immigrants from Germany, summoned up great passion in their defense of states' rights. They repeated the conventional Southern platitudes of that day, that the black race was incapable of taking care of itself, that slavery was a way of discharging the responsibility of whites toward their childlike inferiors, and (to quote J. M. Michelbacher of Richmond) that the North was inciting the slaves "to assassinate and slay men, women, and children." So loyal were some of these Southern rabbis to the Confederacy that one of them, Benjamin Gutheim of New Orleans, went into exile in 1863, after the Union troops had conquered the city, rather than take an oath of allegiance to the Union.

In 1860, the most important Jewish intervention in the public debates was by Morris Raphall of New York, the best-known Orthodox American rabbi. Raphall had recently been the first Jewish clergyman to act as chaplain of the day in Congress. Raphall preached and printed a sermon in which he maintained that Judaism did not forbid slavery, though he carefully added that he was speaking only of the days of the Bible. Why had he chosen that moment for such a supposedly scholarly exercise? Raphall wanted to preserve the Union, and he seems to have thought that slavery, deplorable though it was, had best be allowed to wither. It is at least conceivable that Raphall, who had come to New York from Manchester, England, had some concern for the cotton interests in the South, which were providing the mills of Manchester with the raw material for their production of textiles. This sermon was widely, and correctly, understood as support for the South. Raphall's sermon raised a storm. The antislavery forces hastened to print the English translation of a doctoral dissertation that had been written in Germany by Rabbi Leo Merzbacher. He had come to the United States to a still Orthodox congregation in Philadelphia and later went to the "Reformed" pulpit of Temple Emanu-El in New York. In his dissertation, Merzbacher had established that Jewish slavery had been well-nigh abolished in ancient times by Talmudic legislation. The clear implication of his work was that slavery in the United States was morally unacceptable.

Isaac Mayer Wise had been an antiabolitionist before the war. After it broke out, he was a moderate loyalist. Some years later, he managed to "remember" that he had been a great and passionate proponent of Lincoln. The truth is that as late as 1863 he had been a

Democrat and a frequent critic of the war. Indeed, he was ready to run in that year as a "Copperhead" (i.e., antiwar) Democrat candidate for senator from Ohio, but his congregation vetoed this plan. What Wise was actually doing, as the Civil War broke out, was straddling the fence. He joined the debate over Raphall's sermon. Wise did not like Raphall; he had an old score to settle with him from 1849, when they first debated each other in Charleston. Wise's ringing declaration, then, that he did not believe in either the resurrection of the dead, or in a personal messiah, had caused him trouble in his congregation in Albany. Wise therefore relished disagreeing with Raphall on slavery. Wise argued in his journal, *The Israelite,* that Moses had been opposed to slavery, and that he had legislated on this issue in order to make "the acquisition and retention of bondsmen contrary to their will" an impossibility.

Having mocked Raphall's scholarship, Wise then proceeded, quite astonishingly, to reverse himself. As he contemplated the contemporary South, Wise said that "we are not prepared, nobody is, to maintain that it is absolutely unjust to purchase savages, or rather their labor, place them under the protection of the law, and secure them the benefit of civilized society and their sustenance for their labor." One suspects that such sentiments did not make him enemies in 1860 in his congregation, which included many merchants in the Southern trade. In Baltimore, the Orthodox rabbi, Bernard Illowy, agreed totally with Raphall. He invoked the Bible to insist that "these are irrefutable proofs that we have no right to exercise violence . . . against institutions, even if religious feelings and philanthropic sentiments bid us disapprove of them." These reverend gentlemen were not indifferent to human suffering. Wise wanted peace between North and South because there were Jews on both sides of the conflict. Most of the congregations which accepted his leadership were, in fact, in the South. Jewish organizations such as B'nai B'rith, which had chapters by 1861 in both the North and the South, simply avoided taking any public position. These laymen, and Rabbis Wise, Illowy, and Raphall, were behaving no differently than a number of Protestant leaders who were "Copperheads" because they were trying to protect the unity of their communities. This was not Wise's shining hour.

The only truly devastating criticism of Raphall was written by the best lay Jewish scholar of those days, Michael Heilperin, a Polish Jewish intellectual who had taken part in the Hungarian revolution of 1848. Heilperin had made a career in America as an editor in a magazine of general circulation, but he retained connection with the Jewish community. He responded to Raphall's sermon by calling it a "divine sanction of falsehood and barbarism." Heilperin pronounced himself to be "outraged by the religious words of the rabbi."

Two rabbis did take substantial personal risks in joining Heilperin. In Philadelphia, Sabato Morais, the spiritual leader of Mikveh Israel Congregation, which had been founded in colonial times, was an uncompromising abolitionist. These views were resented by many in the congregation; he survived in this pulpit only because Moses Aaron Dropsie, the richest individual in the synagogue, defended him. In Baltimore, David Einhorn, the rabbi of the "Reformed" Har Sinai Congregation, had much more trouble. Baltimore was more Southern than Northern: the state of Maryland almost seceded on the eve of the Civil War. Abraham Lincoln had to be sneaked through Baltimore in the dead of night on his way to Washington for his inauguration. By denouncing slavery in the most vigorous terms, Einhorn upset the Jews, many of whom were in trade with the South, and angered the Gentiles. His life was not safe. He had to leave Baltimore in 1861 and find himself another pulpit. On the eve of the Civil War the issue of slavery had thus cut across denominational lines in American Jewry. Morais was Orthodox, and Einhorn was the most radical "reformer" of all American rabbis. They agreed on very little, except that both found slavery morally repugnant; both were certain that Jews could not avoid the greatest moral issue before America.

IV

Wise never completely won the leadership of American Jewry, not even at the height of his influence in mid-century. The Orthodox were, of course, opposed to him. A few representatives of the "old school," the first transplants to the United States from the European yeshivoth, the Talmud academies of the Old World, had already come to America. They were simply heartsick at what they saw. Abraham Rice was the first rabbi who had been trained in a yeshivah to settle in the United States. He came to Baltimore in 1840, where he lived unhappily ever after. Before his eyes, and in utter disregard of his pleading, the Baltimore Hebrew Congregation began to institute "reforms," such as the use of an organ to accompany the Sabbath service, the abolition of the separation of sexes at prayer, and even a revision of the Orthodox prayer book, the text of which had been sacrosanct for many centuries. Rice's face, in the only portrait of him that remains, is wan and sad. His eyes seem to be looking across the Atlantic to the vibrant academy of Talmudic learning in Pressburg (Bratislava), in Slovakia, where he had studied under Moses Schreiber, one of the great rabbinic authorities of that generation. Rice resigned his position as rabbi in 1849. He wrote in utter despair to a friend in Germany: "I dwell in darkness without a teacher or companion. . . . The religious life in this land is on the lowest level; most people eat forbidden food and desecrate the Sabbath in public. . . . Under these circumstances my mind is perplexed and I wonder whether it is even permissible for a Jew to live in this land." For the next thirteen years Abraham Rice, ill and broken, tried to support himself and his family by keeping a store. When he died in 1862, his colleague, Bernard Illowy, preached the eulogy in the blackest accents: "We must acknowledge to our own shame that since the downfall of the Jewish monarchy there has been no age and no country in which the Israelites were more degenerated and more indifferent towards their religion than in our own age and in our country."

These outcries reflected a decline in Jewish piety which seemed almost inevitable. In 1853, Leo Merzbacher, then the rabbi of Rodeph Shalom Congregation in Philadelphia, wrote that "in reality, there is no one here who has not changed greatly in the observance of ancient regulations." Nonetheless, these new immigrants had begun by founding their congregations as exact replicas of those they had left behind in Europe. The first congregation in Chicago, which was named in Hebrew "Congregation of the Men of the West," was established in 1846 on so Orthodox a basis that its members scrupulously observed the Sabbath by keeping their businesses closed. Before the Civil War, the overwhelming majority of the newly formed congregations had on the surface moved but a little away from the principles and practices on which they had been founded. I. J. Benjamin, a European Jewish scholar who traveled through the

United States in the 1850s, gave a very optimistic report of Judaism in America. He saw the situation as "full of hope" and as advancing toward an "exalted and prosperous future." He found, then, more than two hundred Orthodox congregations, and only eight Reform ones. The situation was to be exactly reversed in twenty years. In 1880, the United States census reported that there were some two hundred Reform congregations and only six Orthodox ones.

And yet, Reform never triumphed completely in America. Wise was opposed throughout his career by an American "enlightened" Orthodoxy. Isaac Leeser was the spokesman for this view. Leeser had even fewer pretensions than Wise to Jewish learning. He had come to Richmond, Virginia, from his native Prussia in 1824, at the age of eighteen. Leeser claimed no rabbinic degree, and he actually spent his first five years in the United States working in his uncle's general store. In 1829, he became the minister (i.e., the cantor and preacher) of the Spanish-Portuguese synagogue in Philadelphia, and he remained in that city until his death in 1868. Leeser was a moderate who wanted American Jews to adopt a dignified, English-speaking, "Western" form of the Orthodox Jewish faith. In religion, he tried to cooperate with the reformers, so long as they did not go very far in breaking with tradition. As communal leader, he worked harder than anyone else to create national Jewish associations which would allow for some religious diversity. As scholar, he produced, among other works, the first translation of the Bible into English done by an American Jew (1845).

Leeser was not a man of forceful character; he was a thoroughly decent person who seemed easy to push around—and yet he, and the far more pugnacious David Einhorn, kept Wise from taking over all of American Jewry. They did not allow him to create his cherished *Minhag America,* the American religious rite—with himself as the high rabbi, of course. Both Leeser and Einhorn would not countenance the idea that American Jews were a new religious phenomenon. American Jews were living under unprecedented conditions, but that did not make them a new tribe in world Jewry. For both Leeser and Einhorn, the Jewish religion remained a worldwide phenomenon. All Jews, everywhere, were part of the same religious people.

The battle between Orthodoxy and Reform first came to a head in America on a national level in 1855. Isaac Mayer Wise called a conference of rabbis in Cleveland. He proposed to define American

Judaism and to organize a central religious body. Wise wanted this meeting to succeed, that is, to include everybody in American Jewry. He took the lead in pronouncing the Bible to be divine, and in specifying that Scripture was to be "expounded and practiced according to the comments of the Talmud." Wise himself did not believe this declaration, for he had already frequently denied the authority over modern Jews of biblical and Talmudic commandments. Leeser soon left the meeting, because he could not trust a body led by Wise to be even mildly Orthodox. Einhorn, who was not there, attacked the meeting from the religious left. In the next year, in 1856, Einhorn published a Reform prayer book of his own, entitled *Olat Tamid* ("a perpetual offering"), with a translation into German, which was far more radical in its theology and practice than Wise's "American Rite." For his part, Leeser kept a weekly journal, *The Occident and American Jewish Advocate,* alive from 1843 to the end of his life in 1868. Despite enormous difficulties, Leeser persisted in publishing this weekly, in which he continued to challenge "reform." Near the end of his life, in 1867, Leeser founded Maimonides College, the first seminary to train rabbis to be established in America. The effort soon collapsed, but Leeser had at least flown the flag of moderate traditionalism against Wise's well-known hope to establish a rabbinic seminary of his own, to train rabbis for his "American" Judaism.

In the middle years of the nineteenth century, Wise was the acknowledged religious leader of the Jews in the Midwest and the South, but Leeser and Einhorn had some followers even there. They were much stronger on the Eastern Seaboard, which was nearer to Europe than Wise's bastions west of the Appalachians.

In 1860, fighting over slavery, Einhorn, Heilperin, and Morais, who disagreed about many things, had together asserted that being Jewish meant that one had moral responsibility for the pain of the friendless. Einhorn, Heilperin, Morais, and Leeser kept asserting, in their various ways, that being Jewish meant belonging to an ancient, worldwide, tradition, which Jews had no right to reform into American respectability. Leeser died in 1868, but the others lived on into the next era. Einhorn died in 1879, living long enough to exercise a major influence on the ideological self-definition of Reform Judaism in America. Morais and Heilperin were alive when the newest wave of immigrants, the East Europeans, began to come in large numbers in the 1880s. Heilperin was at pains to encourage the Jewish scholars and Hebraists among them. Morais took the lead in 1887 in founding a traditionalist (i.e., anti-Reform) rabbinic school, the Jewish Theological Seminary of America. These men were only a few, but they did not allow American Jewry to be swept away entirely by the doctrine of adjustment to America in the name of success.

9.

Getting Rich Quick

In 1860 thousands of Jews were still peddling, but more thousands had settled down to keep store in cities and towns in both the North and the South. One of the distribution networks for the South radiated from Baltimore, a city on the border which was then a seaport equal in importance to New York. Cincinnati was another major commercial center; it looked down the Ohio River to the entire middle South. In both these cities important Jewish communities had already formed; they traded with Jewish merchants in the smaller towns. It was not easy to get goods from one place to another. Despite the thirty thousand miles of railroad track that were laid by 1860, an integrated system of transportation did not yet exist. Most of these lines were small and local, and their gauges were often mismatched so that railroad cars could not be moved from one line to another. Nonetheless, goods were distributed, and profits, often large ones, were made by middlemen, especially in the agricultural South.

The story of the economic rise of Jews during and after the Civil

War cannot be told without some attention to the question of smuggling across the military lines between the Union and the Confederacy. Smuggling was a well-established, even major, economic enterprise during the four years of the war. There were many scandals on the Union side involving people in very high places. By its very clandestine nature, there are no reliable estimates of the significance of smuggling in the economic history of the Civil War. Jews were involved. In 1862, their participation in smuggling led to the issuance of an order by Ulysses S. Grant, then commander in the Department of the Tennessee, in which he unfairly named Jews as the worst offenders and then expelled them from all the territory under his jurisdiction. This Order Number 11 is the one overtly anti-Jewish decree in all of American military history. The question of the role of the Jews in smuggling has, therefore, become clouded by apologetics, then, and to this day. The story needs to be retold without the prior presumption that Jews were always saints without blemish.

The tale is briefly told: Grant was then in command of the Department of the Tennessee, having conquered the state from the Confederacy. During the war, smuggling across the battle lines was more often than not tacitly condoned by both governments. That was how the North got some of the cotton it needed, and the South got some coffee and some manufactured goods. The trade was widespread, and it even involved army officers who offered protection in return for payoffs. At the end of 1862, General Grant's command had lost patience with the amount of smuggling in the area. An order was issued which was directed by name against the Jews. They were "hereby expelled from the Department within twenty-four hours of the receipt of this order." As soon as this document was published, it caused a storm. Jewish delegations began to organize to protest to President Lincoln. However, before the formal protests could be made, an individual, Cesar Kaskel from Paducah, Kentucky, who was a friend and supporter of Lincoln, simply went to Washington and made the President aware of the order. It was promptly revoked. By the time the formal delegations arrived, they simply thanked the President for what he had done. Most unfortunately, a resolution to revoke the order had meanwhile been introduced in Congress, and it lost in both Houses. Congress was willing to believe that the Jews were indeed unusually prominent among the smugglers and speculators.

Though a military order directed specifically at Jews and not, in more general terms, at all those engaged in smuggling, was indefensible, the question does have to be asked: Did Jews play a role of special prominence in the smuggling trade? The records of trials by civil and military courts for these crimes show that Jews amounted at most to some six percent among all of those who were convicted for economic offenses of any kind. There is no reason to believe that Jews were specially singled out for prosecution. But these figures are suspect, as perhaps too low, on the evidence of what various rabbis were saying at the time. A few months before General Grant's Order Number 11, Rabbi Jacob Peres wrote from Memphis to Isaac Leeser, that more than twenty Jews had been in prison in Memphis for smuggling. The rabbi called such activity a "profanation of the name of God." His colleague in Memphis, Rabbi Simon Tuska, was equally upset with the practices of Jewish traders from the North who had followed the Union Army. Leeser himself responded to the order in an article in which he deplored "the crowd of needy adventurers who travel, or glide through the highways and byways of the land in quest of gain, often we fear unlawful." Leeser added that some of these adventurers pretended to be good Jews when they were not. David Einhorn insisted the Jews were no worse than others, but that it was the duty of the Jews to uproot such crimes which brought disgrace to the whole Jewish community. The most interesting point in Einhorn's passionate sermon was his remark that "little rogues are brought to punishment, whereas big ones are allowed to escape." The rabbis of that time seem to have felt that Jews were "overrepresented" in smuggling, but that they were not the major figures in this trade.

There is reason to believe that some of the staff officers who composed Order Number 11, which Grant signed, were involved in protecting large-scale smuggling endeavors by Gentiles. During that period an order was issued in Memphis declaring fifteen clothing firms off-limits for various infractions, while allowing only two to continue to furnish uniforms to the troops. It was not accidental that all fifteen of the firms were Jewish-owned, and that the two which were declared acceptable were not. It takes no great stretch of imagination to conclude that those who tried to create this monopoly, by military order, stood to benefit from the action. Jews were certainly not the only smugglers and illegal traders, but only apologetic fervor would insist that they were unimportant. They seemed to have been comparatively petty smugglers; they were, therefore, not the best protected among these illegal traders. Nonetheless, it is beyond doubt that some Jewish fortunes and many more Gentile ones have roots in profits that were made in smuggling during the Civil War.

Jews were singled out in Grant's Order Number 11 because anti-Semitism, which had been almost nonexistent in the United States, had been aroused by the turmoil of the war. The financier August Belmont was widely attacked in the Northern press as a "Jew-banker" who was a crypto-supporter of the South. The charges were totally false, on two counts. Belmont was hardly a Jew because he had effectively left the Jewish community long before the Civil War. In 1837, when he arrived in New York as representative of the Rothschild banking interests, he was known as a Jew, but he soon abandoned his Jewish identity. Belmont found his way to the top of American society, marrying the daughter of a national hero, Commodore Matthew Perry. It was even less true that Belmont was a secret supporter of the South. Though Belmont was a leading Democrat, the chairman of the national committee of the party, and therefore leader of the political opposition to Lincoln, he was totally committed to the cause of the Union. He even organized and equipped, at his own expense, the first regiment of soldiers who were German-born. But these facts did not deter the anti-Semites.

Belmont's loyalty and the active patriotism of the overwhelming majority of Northern Jews did not stop the press across the country from repeating the charge that Jews dominated the speculation in gold and that they were "engaged in destroying the national credit in running up the price of gold." The *New York Dispatch* said that on the corner of William Street and Exchange Place one saw only the "descendants of Shylock." The Jewish journals in New York countered by asking those who made such remarks to walk through the gold exchange and count Jews. Obviously, those anti-Semitic outbursts were false, as a minority of the newspapers knew and said, but they were part of the "evidence," together with Order Number 11, for the restatement in America of a classic anti-Semitic theme: the Jews are doing too well; therefore all those who are doing too well in business or finance are Jews.

Grant's order was revoked because of the constitutional guarantees

against singling out any group, and because of the towering personality of Abraham Lincoln. But overt anti-Semitism of the economic
variety, which had made its debut in the New World in Peter Stuyvesant's New Amsterdam, had now reappeared in America to trouble
a much larger community.

There was some vocal anti-Semitism in the Confederacy during
the war years. Here, too, the prime targets were two Jews who, like
Belmont, had abandoned their Jewishness. Judah P. Benjamin and
David Yulee, two former United States senators, were under constant attack as being untrustworthy because they were Jews. Benjamin was under the worse fire, because he was the closest friend
and adviser of Jefferson Davis, the president of the Confederacy. It
was convenient to attack Davis through him, and to attack Benjamin
as a Jew. After the defeat, Benjamin was the only major leader of
the Confederacy who went into exile rather than make his peace with
the Union; he ended his life as a barrister in London. Despite Benjamin's obvious passion for the Southern cause, several of his critics
in the Confederate Congress even introduced a resolution, which
Davis ignored, in which they asked for the resignation of Secretary
of State Benjamin, as an act which would be "subservient to the
public interests."

Economic anti-Semitism was less pronounced in the South than
in the North. The blockade of the Confederacy by Union ships meant
that very little was getting through from Europe or from the Caribbean. As prices went out of reach, the people who were buying
from middlemen became even angrier. The slurs on unpatriotic merchants included snide remarks about Jews. Jews, however, were not
major targets of this anger—the blockade-runners had the worst
reputation for price gouging, and there were almost no Jews among
them.

The more serious anti-Semitism was in the North, and not only
for economic reasons. The charge that Jews were slackers, that they
avoided army service, appeared for the first time in American history.
In 1863, the Irish went on a rampage in New York against the
proposal to impose a military draft. This would have made them
fight for the Union, a cause they regarded as a Protestant one. The
Irish rioted in Jewish neighborhoods, as well, and they looted Jewish
stores. The outcry was that Jewish middlemen were taking unfair

advantage as they sold scarce consumer goods. This was class anger. The Irish in New York were poor, mostly laborers, while the Jews had already risen into the middle class. Such tension between the two groups would continue for many decades.

There was a more pervasive canard that Jews were not pulling their weight in the army. This particular anti-Semitic charge, that Jews had not fought in the Civil War, was to be repeated quite often to the very end of the century, as the generation which had been young in the 1860s came to maturity and took over the leadership of America. What lent substance to the charge was the fact that in the Civil War it was possible to avoid the army. In the North, payment of three hundred dollars bought an exemption; in the South, one could get out of military service by providing a substitute. In both regions people who were well-off were much more likely to avoid the army than poor people, and many immigrant Jews could already afford to buy their way out of service. The charge of slacking was not true, but it persisted, and it was not answered adequately until it arose again in the 1890s. In 1891, Simon Wolf, a Washington lawyer who had been the American Jewish lobbyist and representative in the capital for a number of decades, felt it necessary to collect the evidence for Jewish participation in the Civil War. He published a book entitled *The American Jew as Soldier, Patriot and Citizen,* in which he listed eight thousand men who had served in the Union and Confederate armies, and the list was obviously incomplete. The task of "antidefamation," of "proving" in the face of hostile attack that Jews were "good Americans," did not begin with Wolf's book. A century earlier, Haym Salomon had made the same argument when he had replied to an attack on Jews: he proclaimed that the Jews had served beyond their numbers in the armies of the Revolution.

In the immediate years after the Civil War, most Jews remained in retail trade. The business directories of the cities are instructive. Between 1865 and 1875 the number of Jewish business firms in Baltimore more than doubled. In Cincinnati there were three times as many Jewish businesses in 1880 as there had been in 1860; in those two decades the number had multiplied by four in Cleveland. The increases in New York, Philadelphia, Chicago, Milwaukee, and St. Louis were of a similar order. We have no way of knowing how well-off the owners of these firms were, but it is obvious that new businesses are not established if older ones are doing badly. In the economic depression of 1879, some fifty-two thousand American businesses failed, but there seemed to have been very few Jews among them. By 1880, about half of the Jewish business firms in the country were in clothing and allied occupations, both in manufacturing and in retail sales. Three-quarters of all the clothing businesses of all kinds were controlled by Jews. They owned an even higher proportion of the department stores that were then being opened on the "main street" of almost every city in the country. There were, of course, unsuccessful Jews who remained artisans or employees. These were to be found in the larger cities where two-thirds of the Jews in the labor force worked for other people. On the other hand, by the 1870s nine out of ten Jews in the smaller towns were self-employed businessmen.

The several Jewish firms which were established on Wall Street in the 1860s were being attacked by American anti-Semites who insisted that Jews dominated the stock market, but in actual fact none was at the front rank until near the turn of the century. Even as late as 1880, only two percent of the gainfully employed Jews were in finance, and almost all of these were employees and not principals.

Despite General Grant's Order Number 11 (which he deeply regretted for the rest of his life), anti-Semitism in America did not inflict substantial damage during and after the Civil War. Essentially Jews were not in competition with other economic interests. The strength of the "German Jews" was that they had created an enclave of their own in the American economy; they had concentrated in a few middlemen occupations which they dominated. In the mind of America, by the 1870s and 1880s, there was a "Jewish economy" of clothing manufacturers, storekeepers, department-store owners, and some financiers. This concentration in a very few pursuits acted to define Jews as different. The families which owned the major clothing firms, department stores, and financial houses were heavily interrelated. In a highly competitive world only members of the family could be trusted. Thus, the "German Jews" had repeated in America an age-old pattern of the ghetto. In the medieval ghetto in Europe, Jews had been forced into a very few pursuits, and they were a trading network in which everyone knew everyone else. In America, Jews largely remained in these pursuits in the first two generations after their arrival in the 1840s and 1850s, and they remained an extended family, from New York to San Francisco.

Social anti-Semitism reinforced this separateness. In 1869, there was a famous incident when Joseph Seligman, then a leading banker in America, arrived in his own railroad car at Saratoga Springs, New York, to spend a vacation in what was then the summer capital of the socially aspiring new rich. The owner of the hotel in which Seligman wanted to stay refused to have Jews on the premises. Such exclusion of Jews was to remain very common for at least the next half-century in American resorts of all classes. All over urban America, in those years, when well-to-do Jews moved into posh neighborhoods, the Gentiles soon moved out; they left the Jewish new rich in what amounted to a gilded ghetto. Thus, the "German Jews" cohered as a group, in part by exclusion. Their Gentile peers in business might have lunch with them, but they stoutly refused to introduce these Jews to their wives. The newly rich Jews had no choice but to create social institutions which were parallel to those of the Gentile upper middle class. When they were immigrants and poor peddlers, these Jews had imagined that they would be accepted by "society" when they came to wealth. The newly rich "German Jews" discovered in the 1870s and 1880s, during America's Gilded Age, that this was not so. The Gentiles who had just come to money were themselves fighting to enter "society," and they were even less hospitable to the Jews than the older aristocrats. A seal was thus set on a peculiarly American formulation of what makes a Jewish community: clannishness by Jews and exclusion by Gentiles, reinforcing each other. The affirmation of Judaism played a much lesser role. In the new circumstances of wealth, the situation of these Jews was no different than it had been in the 1840s, in poverty, when the Odd Fellows had rejected them and forced them to found B'nai B'rith.

But, even as Jews were being annoyed by social exclusion, the national government was remarkably hospitable. Within months after Joseph Seligman had been insulted in Saratoga Springs, General Grant, the new President of the United States, offered him a seat in his cabinet, which Seligman refused because he did not want to leave his business as banker. Had Seligman accepted, he would have been the first Jew to serve in so high an office in the federal government. The most prominent "German Jew" of his time, Joseph Seligman,

was repeating the experience of Uriah Phillips Levy, of the older
settlement, a decade earlier: he was an American not because society
was willing to forgive him for being a Jew, but because the Constitution guaranteed equality.

In the decades after the Civil War the "German Jews" built elaborate temples in every major and middle-sized city in America. Like
Isaac Mayer Wise and his laymen in Cincinnati, their peers everywhere wanted to announce, and to claim, their status among the
American upper middle class. The great occasions of the life cycle,
such as marriage and death, were celebrated in these buildings. The
major Jewish festivals were occasions for large gatherings. But their
social clubs were at least as elaborate and even more central to their
lives. The network of Jewish social organizations which, as we have
seen, had been started in the 1840s and 1850s, grew in members and
in the quality of their amenities. In Philadelphia, for example, a group
of "German Jews" had founded the Mercantile Club in 1853. It
contained among its members such figures as Marcus Goldman and
Charles Bloomingdale, the progenitor of the Bloomingdale's department store clan. In the first years of the club's existence, it moved
to several ever-posher rented quarters. Finally, in 1880, the club
occupied "a handsome and well-furnished house" of its own. In
Atlanta, the Concordia Club, which was founded in 1877, had an
elegant building which was much admired and commented upon.
In Rochester, New York, several clubs were created in those years.
They were finally united into a grand and elegant place which was
"well-considered by the general community." In 1881, this club was
disbanded and a new club called the Eureka was founded. The club
members bought a mansion and refitted it at great expense. By 1893
the property of this club was worth the then princely sum of a
hundred thousand dollars. In San Francisco in the 1870s, the wealth
of ten of the leading members of its Reform congregation was estimated at the combined total of forty-five million dollars. When
Isaac Mayer Wise visited the city in 1877, he was, of course, taken
to the mansion of the Concordia Club (this was a favorite name for
such establishments in various cities), which he described as "an
elegant place."

Within these clubs an intense social life was lived, balls were held,
and marriages were arranged. These clubs even attempted to suggest
that they were the arbiters of taste and elegance for the entire com-

munity. Such claims ran into difficulty with Gentile critics, who regarded such a notion as a presumption on the part of any nouveaux riches, and certainly on the part of Jews. So, in San Francisco a Mr. Greenway, of the Jewish elite, declared that there were only four hundred persons in town who were fit to go into good society. He was mocked in a newspaper as representing the "parvenu advertising society" trying to hand down "a new set of commandments to take the place of the old, reliable ten that Moses broke."

Those who had arrived at the economic status which enabled them to live within the society of the clubs obviously did not have working wives. On the contrary in this Gilded Age, well-to-do women were overdressed and affected airs, thus establishing, as the contemporary sociologist Thorstein Veblen soon observed, that people of wealth engaged in "conspicuous consumption" and "conspicuous display." Rich men were announcing their success through what they could give their women to wear, and by freeing them from work. Some of these wives took frequent trips back to the old country, to Germany, to display their wealth. They did not always succeed in being accepted in what they thought was their new dignity. The older, more structured European society was not easily impressed, even by success in America.

For all the glitter and success of this German Jewish immigration, some of the immigrants remained poor, and problematic. The charitable organizations which had been created in the 1840s and 1850s existed for self-help for the newly arrived. In their extension and growth after 1865 these organizations acquired the character of the rich taking care less of their own poor than, more and more, of the East Europeans. In Rochester, New York, for example, a group of men and women met in October of 1877 to form a Jewish orphan asylum. Two years later this endeavor was consolidated with comparable bodies in Syracuse and Buffalo. These were not self-help agencies, as B'nai B'rith and its competitors had been in the immigrant days of the 1840s and 1850s. The widows and the orphans of the "German Jews" usually had rich relatives who took them in. The new social agencies which were created in the 1870s, and thereafter, expressed the concern of the "German Jews" for the newest immigrants, the very "Russian Jews" whom they regarded as socially and culturally inferior. Most of these orphans were of East European origin, for by the 1870s there were substantial numbers of Jews from Russia and Austria-Hungary in these upstate communities.

After the Civil War, the Jews of Syracuse organized both a society for visiting the sick and a much more elaborate one for taking care of the poor, and especially for burying the dead of poor families who could not afford funerals. In New York, a great network of such charitable bodies kept growing in the post–Civil War period. In 1867 Edmond Pelz, a German who had visited the United States, published a book in Hamburg about New York; he complained that the German Gentiles had been attempting to establish a hospital but had managed to raise only thirty thousand dollars, one-tenth of the sum that was needed, while the Jews had already built their hospital long before. (Mount Sinai Hospital had been established by the oldest American Jews, the Sephardim, in 1855; it was rebuilt at great expense and renamed in 1869 by the "German Jews.")

In the 1870s and 1880s, the "German Jews" built Jewish hospitals and established a variety of social service organizations in all the major cities of the United States. Creating these agencies cost large amounts of money, but the affluent "German Jews" were generous. They were imitating the behavior of generations of Jewish rich, that it was the responsibility of those who had money to take care of their poor brethren. So it had been in America, at least most of the time; the first Jewish settlement in New Amsterdam had taken care of its own poor; Haym Salomon had praised his own generation for doing the same. Always, from the beginning, there had been another reason: such charities were necessary as self-protection for the Jewish rich. The Jewish poor had to be kept from becoming a problem to America as a whole. By the 1870s, even before the migration from Eastern Europe became massive, the growing number of socially dependent cases was creating a threat of anti-Semitism. In such arguments there was a large element of the thesis that was becoming ever more widespread among the "German Jews," that all would be well in America, and that anti-Semitism simply would not have appeared, had the mass migration from Eastern Europe not arrived.

This assertion could not be further from the truth. On the contrary, when the great immigration of "Russian Jews" was at its height in the 1890s, Populist anti-Semitism attacked the Jews on Wall Street, and not this mass which was then largely laboring in sweatshops.

The farmers in the Midwest and the South had no quarrel with industrial labor in the East. They were at war with those who determined interest rates and the value of money. To the degree to which they unfairly centered their attack on Jews, who were, as we have seen, not really important on Wall Street, they were attacking not the newest arrivals, but the successful Jews who had been in America for a generation or so.

But this was not how the "German Jews" perceived their situation. They did feel threatened; in their view these new arrivals were underscoring the foreignness of Jews in America. Their very first concern was thus to try to limit immigration, but, if not, at least to "Americanize" the new immigrants as quickly as possible. On the surface this meant to teach them English and Western manners, but much more than that was soon attempted. The German Jewish rich wanted to disperse these Jewish masses around the country and not have them crowd into several of the major cities, and especially not into New York. They wanted also to effect economic restratification, that is, for the East European Jews to engage in a whole host of occupations other than commerce, to which they were all aspiring. There was particular emphasis on the need to farm, and much money and effort were expended in promoting such settlements. This criticism of Jewish economic abnormality was never directed by "German Jews" at themselves, for they had no doubt that they ought to remain near their businesses. They wanted these new arrivals to furnish them with the rest of the economic pyramid of farmers and workers, in "healthy" occupations spread all over the country, which would allow their German Jewish patrons to be the two or three percent at the top. The Americanization of the immigrants would validate the older settlers as representatives of a "normal" Jewish economy, existing side by side with the economy of the country as a whole.

The older settlers thus accepted responsibility for the new migration, in part in order to protect themselves, but the concern of the "German Jews" for the newly arrived Yiddish-speaking masses was not entirely self-serving. There was much compassion for, and even identification with, these poor "coreligionists," as the new immigrants were then called in the circles of "our crowd." And yet both the involvement in the newest arrivals and the recoil from them reflected the fears and needs of the "German Jews" in those days.

To gain acceptance for themselves in America was the central issue of their agenda; it colored everything that they felt and did.

II

The desire of the "German Jews" for equality in America continued to involve them in the fight against the notion that America was a Protestant, Christian country. On this issue, the very Jews who wanted society to accept them as nice, inoffensive people were increasingly eager to do battle. During the Civil War, there might have been some reason for Jews to want to avoid raising any seemingly divisive issue, but a notable and largely unsuccessful battle was waged over religious discrimination against Jews in the military. Congressional legislation had provided that for a clergyman to be appointed a chaplain in the military establishment, he needed to be a minister of some Christian denomination. Jewish representation did succeed in removing this qualification from the law, but no rabbi was admitted to the army. Several Jews, not all of them ordained rabbis, did serve on the fringes of the chaplaincy, especially in hospitals, but nowhere, not even in one or two largely Jewish companies from northeastern cities, was there a Jewish chaplain in the field.

In the 1860s, Jews continued the fight that Isaac Mayer Wise had begun a decade earlier against the notion that America was a "Christian country." Jews opposed the Sunday blue laws, which prohibited keeping businesses open on the Lord's Day, but usually to no avail. Christian prayers and Bible reading in the public schools remained a perennial issue, and here, too, the Jewish counterattack met with only qualified success. Having failed in the 1850s, Isaac Mayer Wise did succeed in having such readings eliminated from the schools of Cincinnati, where the number of Jews among the students was quite substantial. The case was appealed and reappealed by both sides, until the Supreme Court of Ohio finally held that such Bible reading was an infringement on the separation of church and state. In 1869, Wise explained why he was willing to confront Christian opinion: "We want secular schools or nothing else, nor has any state a shadow of a right to support any other." In another connection Wise had said: "We stand or fall with the liberal phalanx of this country, come what may." Wise had wrapped himself in the Constitution. In a religiously neutral America, Reform Judaism, the religion of the successful middle class, would be one of the many American religious denominations, and it would be fully equal to all of them.

But these Jews wanted, desperately, to be liked. During their first twenty years in America, the German-Jewish immigrants had made relatively minor changes in their synagogue ritual. It was in the era immediately after the Civil War that the reformers in the United States became the most radically untraditional sect in all of world Jewry. The new rich formally jettisoned almost all of the Jewish rituals. In Europe at that time, religious reform had become less radical as the years went by, both because the inherited tradition still largely dominated the organized Jewish community and because the dominant forms of Christianity in Europe were Catholic, Orthodox, or highly structured Protestant. In Europe, except for the temple in Hamburg, there was never a single synagogue anywhere in which worship was conducted bareheaded. By the 1870s, this was becoming the majority form of American Reform congregations. These synagogues almost all abolished the dietary laws and removed head coverings from the men at prayer; some even observed the Sabbath on Sunday. Most of the laity was, of course, given comfort by a Judaism which had dispensed with all of the ritual restrictions on Jewish conduct and had thus encouraged individual Jews to mix freely with their Gentile neighbors. Such temples, with their impeccable decorum and their churchiness, could act as calling cards for those who had now become rich enough to move to Fifth Avenue in New York and to its equivalent all over America. The Christian patterns which these temples chose to follow were the same as those affected then by many of the descendants of the old Puritan elite. Their churches had all begun as Congregationalist, holding fast to Calvinist theology, but many of them had turned Unitarian or Universalist in the nineteenth century.

Everywhere, the Jewish temples cultivated formal interfaith activities. Such theologically liberal Protestant churches were the ones which were most immediately available for relations with Jews. For example, as early as 1870, Berith Kodesh, Rochester's Reform congregation, was host to a lecture given by Newton Mann, the minister of the First Unitarian Church. Three years later this clergyman was invited to preach from the pulpit. In 1874, Berith Kodesh, together with both the Unitarian and the Universalist churches in town, gave a joint Thanksgiving service. This was a great occasion for the Reform Jews of Rochester, and it continued annually until nearly the turn of the century. The event grew by the accession in the 1890s of the Plymouth Congregational Church. The trustees of that institution were so pleased that they congratulated their minister, William T. Brown, who had also been exchanging pulpits with the rabbi, for this display of "the tolerant and enlightened spirit which is the chief glory of our country." Unfortunately for this seemingly idyllic scene, the Reverend Mr. Brown became increasingly radical in his social and political views. The clothing industry, which was the major employer in Rochester, was in turmoil because a boycott had been declared by the American Federation of Labor against the manufacturers, who were Jews, and who were the leaders of the Berith Kodesh Congregation. Mr. Brown's flock stood by him in his identification with the cause of labor, but the trustees of Berith Kodesh considered him to be "subversive of existing social organization." They instructed their rabbi, Dr. Max Landsberg, not to join in any religious services together with the Reverend Mr. Brown. This action took place in 1901. It is useful to cite it here, in a discussion of a somewhat earlier time, to make the point that interfaith activity was not an end in itself, for spiritual reasons, for these German Jews. It was, rather, a way of drawing closer to their Gentile peers. When interfaith sometimes clashed actively with class interest, it was economic interest that usually prevailed—but, as we shall soon see, it was not always so.

In the 1870s Isaac Mayer Wise finally succeeded in realizing his dream to create the forms of national Jewish religious organization. His model was the major Protestant denominations, which met regularly in national and church conferences and in clerical associations. Such bodies existed even among those denominations which were not hierarchical, such as the Congregationalists, where the central body had not the power to legislate ritual forms or conformity of belief for individual congregations. All these Christian denominations had long before established seminaries to train their own clergy; they had ceased being dependent on Europe. This example had become especially important to the American Reform synagogues, because rabbis of European origin then occupied all of the pulpits. Most such men remained foreign; many never became truly comfortable in English. Some took theology "too seriously." There were those among them who believed in the "un-American," old-fashioned idea that rabbis had authority over their congregations. Such a notion was harbored, as we have seen, not only by Orthodox figures such as Sabato Morais but even by an ultrareformer, such as David Einhorn, who was far more religiously radical than Isaac Mayer Wise. In the 1870s, the American synagogues of the comfortably rich could thus be persuaded that they needed a new generation of rabbis, American-born and trained, who would minister to them rather than attempt to command them. The earlier stirrings before the Civil War toward creating national synagogue and rabbinic organizations and a rabbinic seminary in America had failed. They were opposed or ignored because they were understood as attempts to impose older Jewish discipline in the New Land. Now, after the Civil War, a generation who had come to wealth and power was willing to pay for such bodies, because it did not fear them.

The first organization that Isaac Mayer Wise put together was the Union of American Hebrew Congregations, which he created in Cincinnati in 1873. The twenty-eight synagogues which came to the meeting were those of the South and the West. There was no one from the East at this founding conference, but within two years the eastern congregations of Reform persuasion joined the union. The conference that Wise had called in 1855 in Cleveland, to found a national body of all the synagogues in America, had failed because most of the congregations were then in the uneasy opening stages of turning reformed. He succeeded in 1873, because Reform then dominated the scene. The central task of this new body was to create a seminary for the training of young Jews, to give them, in Wise's formulation, an "enlightened education" in the Jewish religion, to prepare them for the rabbinate. The Hebrew Union College was opened in 1875, in the building of Wise's temple in Cincinnati, and so Cincinnati had laid claim to being the religious center of American Jewry. Some years later, in 1889, the organizational structure of Reform Judaism in America was completed by the creation of the Central Conference of American Rabbis.

The word "reform" was not mentioned in the names that were devised for these three bodies. The rhetoric meant to suggest that they represented not a part, or a faction, but all of American Judaism. Almost all of the two hundred congregations which were rich enough to own buildings were identified with the Union of American Hebrew Congregations, but Wise and his colleagues knew very well that there were, by the 1870s, a growing number of Orthodox synagogues with buildings of their own, and many Orthodox prayer conventicles, in every city of the country. A few were older congregations, which had remained Orthodox despite the trend to Reform. Most were being created by Yiddish-speaking Jews from Russia and Austria-Hungary, who had begun to arrive in some numbers in the 1870s. The creators of the self-styled "Union of American Hebrew Congregations," "Hebrew Union College," and "Central Conference of American Rabbis" were consciously asserting that the "Polish forms of the Jewish religion" were marginal and alien in America. At the very least, the Reform Jews suggested that they were aristocratically distant from such backward people—as the older Jewish settlers, who claimed to be Sephardim, had suggested in the 1840s when the "German Jews" had first arrived.

And yet Wise and his supporters began to fail in the 1870s, at the very height of their success, and not merely because Jews from Eastern Europe were beginning to arrive and create their own way of Jewish life and Jewish worship. Within the "reformed" camp itself, major figures existed who rejected harping on Americanization and on social acceptance as the central themes of Jewish religious life. These opponents of Wise controlled the meeting which took place in Pittsburgh in 1885, at which the official platform of Reform Judaism was formulated. The central figure in this endeavor was Kaufmann Kohler, who was then the rabbi of one of the reformed congregations in New York. Wise and Kohler detested each other. Kohler, the son-in-law of Wise's old enemy, David Einhorn, was also a substantial scholar and theologian, whose learning made Wise feel inferior. Kohler invited a number of Reform rabbis to Pittsburgh in November 1885 to consult together and to adopt a joint statement of their views. Wise had little choice but to attend. He accepted the eight-point program for Reform Judaism that was written there, though he would have preferred a less challenging statement.

The more radical, ideologically-minded people who wrote the Pittsburgh platform were dealing with a problem other than the social acceptance of Jews. They faced squarely the basic theological question: What was left of "Mosaic legislation," after these reformers had announced that "they accept as binding only the moral laws of Judaism" and that they reject all the ceremonies that "are not adapted to the views and habits of modern civilization"? In the light of these assertions, why cling to Judaism? Those who framed the Pittsburgh Platform answered that Judaism needed to continue to exist as a prime agent in the bringing about of universal morality. This was the "mission of Israel." The authors of this document added that "the spirit of the broad humanity of our age is our ally in the fulfillment of our mission." The question still remained: What was the content of that "mission"? These rabbis answered in the eighth, and concluding, section of the Pittsburgh Platform: "We deem it our duty to participate in the great task of modern times, to solve on the basis of justice and righteousness the problems presented by the contrast and evils of the present organization of society." Judaism in America had thus been defined as the "conscience of the rich," as a call to the Jewish rich to concern themselves with the poor.

In one of its meanings, the doctrine of the Pittsburgh Platform was a very bold bid indeed for the complete social acceptance of Jews in America. Isaac Mayer Wise had been contenting himself all his life with the dream of leading respectable rich Jews to be welcomed by respectable rich Christians, to their class. Those who framed the Pittsburgh Platform went far beyond Wise even in their social aspirations. In the 1880s, the most advanced Protestant theology in America was the "Social Gospel"; Christianity was then being translated into concern for all those who were suffering in this world. Through the Pittsburgh Platform, Reform Judaism had asserted that the Jews were now ready to join with other well-to-do Americans in worrying about the poor. The "German Jews" had announced, unilaterally, that they no longer thought of themselves as being on approval in any sense in America. They were not a problem even to themselves, so they said; they had now declared themselves to being among the problem solvers. In effect, social anti-Semitism was ignored. It was assessed to be marginal, on the way to disappearing in the new world of enlightened humanity.

Most of those who have commented on the Pittsburgh Platform have remembered its anti-Zionism, its firm declaration that Jews did not regard themselves as a nation in exile—but this assertion was hardly new and original. It was simply a restatement of what reformers had already said at the synods in Germany in the 1840s. Such views then dominated among the Jewish bourgeoisie everywhere, in Central and Western Europe and, of course, in America.

What was really new in the Pittsburgh Platform was the assertion that Jews as a religious group had an obligation to take risks for the creation of a more just society. It was no accident at all that the principal author of this document, Kaufmann Kohler, had married into the family of David Einhorn, the flaming abolitionist of 1860. Einhorn had been a minority then, in part because the "German Jews" still felt themselves to be too weak and foreign to do battle for social justice in America. In 1885, a quarter of a century later, these very Jews were now affluent and powerful, and some of them felt impelled by conscience to fight for all the poor, as Uriah Phillips Levy had fought, a generation earlier, to stop the flogging of sailors.

Statements about social justice were being made occasionally by Jewish religious reformers in the Old World in those years. In an ever more anti-Semitic, and more ideological, Europe such statements were not much more than verbiage. Those Jews in Europe who were taking risks for the cause of a more just society were not in the Reform synagogues; they were, instead, in the movements which were trying to make political revolutions. There were few liberal rabbis in Europe among these revolutionaries. America was different. Here there was room, even in the midst of social anti-Semitism, for some of the Jewish well-to-do from the temples, and especially for some of their rabbis, to join the cause of social reform. The most immediate result of the Pittsburgh Platform was that a generation of Reform rabbis soon arose who took its call for social action seriously. The young Stephen S. Wise (he was not related to Isaac Mayer Wise) began his public career as rabbi in Portland, Oregon, in 1900, where he fought successfully for a law limiting child labor. Judah Leon Magnes went to the length of being a pacifist in the First World War. Both had stormy careers from their beginnings, but both were legitimate leaders in Reform Judaism because the Pittsburgh Platform had justified intervention on behalf of the poor.

Some rabbis made themselves unpopular with their overwhelmingly capitalist congregants by supporting the organization of labor unions. As the East Europeans kept arriving in their tens and hundreds of thousands, several Reform rabbis joined to help found the Jewish Agricultural Society, which created farming settlements for immigrants. The young Henrietta Szold, daughter of a Reform rabbi in Baltimore, took to teaching newcomers the English language and American ways. Even more remote figures who felt most threatened by the new arrivals, such as the aging Isaac Mayer Wise, could not stand aside and pretend that they were uninvolved or unmoved. In the 1890s, Wise spoke for the Reform effort to help the new immigrants.

Felix Adler and Lillian Wald were perhaps even more interesting examples of these social concerns, precisely because both Adler and Wald were by choice on the fringes of the Jewish community. Felix Adler, the son and chosen successor of Samuel Adler, the rabbi of Temple Emanu-El in New York, really believed the universalist ideas of Reform Judaism. He took these values to demand that he abandon all traces of ethnic Jewishness. In the 1870s, Adler left the organized Jewish community and founded the Ethical Culture movement, to express a high-minded concern for all the underprivileged. Adler took with him some of the younger elements within Reform Judaism in New York. He founded a body that was in theory free of ethnic loyalty, even though the Society for Ethical Culture consisted overwhelmingly of Jews. Nevertheless, despite this break, Adler continued to harbor marked components of Jewish feeling. He had a deep and abiding concern for the miseries of the Jewish masses who were arriving from Eastern Europe. Adler was once even accused by a Rochester Jewish newspaper of suggesting that the Jews vote as a bloc in national elections, in order to further their interests. The charge was basically true. Adler did give such advice to the Jews on the Lower East Side of New York in several elections; he urged them to vote their interests as poor people.

Lillian Wald came from a rich German Jewish family in Rochester. She could, therefore, have spent her life in the comfortable society of "our crowd," but she decided to become a nurse. Wald worked among the immigrants of New York's Lower East Side. In 1895, she founded the Henry Street Settlement, to provide health, educational, and recreational services to those who were living in tenements. As the years went by, Wald fought for every cause of social reform in her day, including, especially, the support of trade unionism. Like Rabbi Judah Leon Magnes, she opposed the entry of the United States into the First World War; Wald remained a pacifist during the conflict. The "Social Gospel" was Lillian Wald's faith. She was a believer in the universal brotherhood of man, and, despite her involvement with the Lower East Side, she was no partisan of "the things that make men different."

Adler and Wald were not willing to affirm that they had a special commitment to the Jewish people; as each worried about Jews, they insisted that they were acting on the stage of American society as a whole. The majority of their contemporaries remained within Judaism. For some, their Jewish ties represented inertia, or, as has been said above, they were based on family feeling. For others, it was a deep commitment to be in the forefront, as Jews, of the battles for social justice in all the world, and especially in American society. There were laymen, and not only rabbis, among the second generation of the "German Jews" who believed that Jews had a "mission," that they had been set apart by God Himself to take risks for justice. Joel Elias Springarn, the founder of the National Association for the Advancement of Colored People, was one among many such people.

These Jews of the second generation were not content simply to disappear, or to pretend to themselves that they were disappearing, among the successful in America. These reformed Jewish idealists wanted to be different, and to make a difference, as Jews. They answered anti-Semitism by trying to remake America. They knew in their bones that they had special responsibilities because they were Jews. These men and women were not "adjusting" to the existing America, and, least of all, to the life of their own enclave of rich, respectable Jews. The classic doctrine of Jewish theology, "chosenness" had reappeared among them, in America, in the guise of their special vocation to fight for social justice.

10.

The Russian Jews
Arrive

I

In the half century after the end of the Civil War,
no less than thirty-five million people came to America. This was,
by far, the largest wave of immigration in American history. These
masses came to the United States because Europe was becoming
overpopulated, especially with the poor. Modern medicine had cut
the death rate of infants, but the birthrate still remained high. The
problem was especially acute in southern Italy and in Czarist Russia.
The Industrial Revolution had barely come to these countries. There
were too few new jobs to provide work for the ever-larger numbers
of the poor. This was the "push" factor: the lack of hope in Europe
was making mass migration necessary. The "pull" factor was the
attraction of America: the still-existing frontier offered land for those
who wanted to farm, and the industrialization of America was creating millions of jobs in the cities. "Pull" was so important that any
falling off in the American economy resulted within a year in a
slackening of immigration from Europe.

More than two million of these newcomers were Jews. These

masses represented at least fifteen percent of all of European Jewry and nearly eight percent of all the immigrants to America. This migration, so it has often been argued, was caused by a third factor that was specific to Jews, the flight from anti-Semitic violence. In fact, pogroms (physical attacks on Jews) played a minor role as a cause of the emigration of Jews from Eastern Europe. The dominant cause of mass migration was poverty. Almost all middle-class Jews managed to find ways of reestablishing themselves elsewhere in Russia; it was the peddlers and the tailors who left for America. America gave the "Russian Jews" the chance to rise from the class in which they originated, but it is much better to imagine that one's grandparents were already part of the "better people" in Russia, and that America was the haven of refuge from anti-Semitism. This myth suggests by implication that those who arrived were the bearers of a high intellectual and cultural tradition. The truth is starker, and more heroic. The Jews from Russia arrived in the United States penniless and largely uneducated even in Judaism; they rose, in less than two generations, to the very apex of American life.

Immediately after the pogroms of 1881–82, in which hundreds of Jews were killed or injured all over Czarist Russia, there was some flight to America, but the numbers did not increase radically until late in the decade. Even as czarist persecution of Jews was increasing in those years, especially through the expulsion of many thousands of Jews from Russia's villages and towns, more Jews moved to the cities in Russia than fled abroad. Those who had some money, or family connections, tended to remain. The poorest left for America. It is striking that there had been no pogroms in Austria-Hungary or Romania, and yet a larger proportion of the Jewish population of these countries emigrated westward in the late nineteenth century than came from Czarist Russia. In the Austro-Hungarian Empire, Franz Joseph I protected Jews against violence; in Romania, anti-Semitic outbreaks were checked to some degree by the guarantees of equality for all that Romania had given in 1879, when it was granted independence in the Treaty of Berlin. Anti-Semitism did indeed limit the economic possibilities for Jews in all three countries, but the middle class found ways of surviving. It was the poor who were most affected by the lack of opportunity; they were the people who emigrated.

The Jews who arrived in the United States before the First World

War were, thus, not a random sample of all East European Jewry; they were the masses without the classes. The evidence for this assertion is overwhelming. It is to be found in literature of the era, in the languages that Jews wrote, and in the many contemporary statistical studies of East European Jews, both in Europe and later in America. There was, indeed, a long tradition, of at least a century and a half, of rabbinic and intellectual distaste for the New World. It was most pronounced during the very years of the largest Jewish mass migration to the United States. This European literature has not been read in any connected fashion, until now, by students of American Jewish history. There has, perhaps, been a certain unwillingness to confront this tradition of contempt for America. The reading of such literature suggests that the "better people" were kept from coming to the United States. The truth is that few of the "better people" wanted to come to America. Contemporary essays and later memoirs support this thesis; it is proved beyond doubt by the immigration statistics of those years.

A few modern Hebrew poets and a novelist or two had been cast up on American shores in the years when hundreds of thousands were on the move. Most of them were teaching in Jewish afternoon schools, which supplemented the public schools with some instruction of religion and Hebrew as a language. Almost without exception the theme of these writers was their personal alienation in Jewish America, which they depicted as uncouth, money-mad, and destructive to the spirit. Israel Efros, one of the Hebrew writers of that generation, expressed this distance, and this sorrow, in a striking epic poem entitled *The Wigwams Are Silent*. Efros published the poem in 1932, but it was written earlier, and reflected the mood of his first experiences in the United States as a young immigrant in the first years of the century. On the surface this was a poem about Indians, the noble savages, the purity of whose culture had been destroyed by American greed. But, on another level, the author was his own "Indian," an East European Jewish intellectual, caught among his contemporaries whose souls were being destroyed, so he thought, in the sweatshops. It did not matter whether they succeeded in business or whether they failed to rise into the beginnings of affluence. The result in spiritual impoverishment, so Efros and all the other Hebraists insisted, was the same. The shtetl, idealized by nostalgia, had been the home of Jewish purity, the "wigwam" which was now increasingly silent because it had been abandoned by those who had come to America. Eventually a number of the Hebrew writers in the United States found their way to the renascent Jewish settlement in the Land of Israel. Few of those who remained in "exile" ever really made peace with America.

The most important Jewish writer to come to America was Sholem Aleichem (pen name for Sholem Rabinovitz), who came to New York for the first time in 1906. He hoped to stay, but he could not bear the place (he shared the dominant view of European Jewish intellectuals that American Jews were raw and uncouth), and he returned to Russia after a few months. When the First World War broke out, Sholem Aleichem had no choice but to gather his family and leave for New York. In these last two years of his life he tried to adjust to America, but he remained a fish out of water. His last major work, *Mottel Peise, the Cantor's Son,* was a tale about a young man who came to America impoverished, but from a family of some learning and of European Jewish middle-class values. Sholem Aleichem died in 1916 before the second, "American" part of the novel (it was running in installments in one of the Yiddish dailies) could be finished, but the clear message of the tale was that America was not a comfortable place for the likes of Mottel Peise.

Like almost every immigrant, Mottel Peise, on arrival, went looking for *landsleite,* that is, other immigrants from the same hometown in the old country. The Lower East Side of New York was then brimming with many hundreds of such associations. There *greene* ("greens"), that is, newly arrived immigrants, met people they had known who were *gelle* ("yellows"), who had been in America for some time and could offer the "greens" guidance. Mottel Peise followed the pattern; he went to find his "extended family" from back home, but he discovered that it was a world turned upside down. The earliest arrivals from his shtetl had been, back home, the most ignorant and socially unacceptable. They were now the leaders of the association of his compatriots. A learned man, a ritual slaughterer back home, had been reduced to helplessness and total poverty. He lived off the occasional good graces of the masters of the association.

The most famous of Sholem Aleichem's characters, Tevye, had dreamed in Europe, in a line that has been given international currency in the musical *Fiddler on the Roof,* of what he would do "if I were a rich man." His most immediate fantasy was that, as a rich man, he would sit at the east wall of the synagogue, in the most honorific place; the rabbi would then listen to him, rather than to those to whom he usually paid attention. Mottel Peise, the cantor's son, found that Tevye's dream had been realized on the Lower East Side. There, unlearned people of the lower classes in Europe were sitting at an eastern wall in a synagogue of their own devising. They were appointing religious functionaries who would listen to them. In America, among his fellow townsmen Mottel Peise was not the cantor's son. In New York, so those who had come earlier insisted, such a self-image was irrelevant, and even obnoxious. In America a man was judged only by how successfully he made his way in the New World. "Better people" like Mottel Peise, or his creator, Sholem Aleichem, had to accept this truth. They could not impose the older order of respect on the immigrant masses.

A significant number of Jewish literary and intellectual figures did arrive in the United States between 1905 (the year when the First Russian Revolution was suppressed) and 1914, but, in their majority, like Sholem Aleichem, they recoiled from the immigrant masses which had arrived earlier. This was inevitable, not least because the learned Jews of Europe had helped create the very reality which now made them heartsick. The European rabbis had always, even before the 1880s, been especially harsh in forbidding their class to go to the New Land. In 1826 the rabbis of London had refused to recognize conversions to Judaism performed in America. The despondent accounts of the earliest American rabbis acted to confirm the view in Europe that America was no place for a learned and pious Jew.

Equally pained descriptions were sent back home from America in the 1880s and thereafter. Among the many reporters the most interesting was, perhaps, Zvi Falk Widawer. A scholar and Hebraist who came to America in the hopes of settling in the New Land, Widawer traveled to most of the major cities in the country, but he felt so totally alien in the United States that he soon went back home to Russia. Widawer summed up his assessment of American Jewry in a striking paragraph. Writing from San Francisco for a Hebrew journal published in Russia, Widawer asserted that "the Jews who live in this land did not endure long journeys and untold hardships in order to slake their thirst for the word of God and to busy themselves in the Torah in a free and untroubled place. Jews came here only to achieve the purpose which occupied their entire attention in the land of their birth. That purpose *was* money." A few years later, in 1889, an unsigned reportage to an Orthodox journal published in Galicia, the southern part of Poland which then belonged to the Austro-Hungarian Empire, echoed this opinion. The correspondent wrote from New York that "there is no faith and no knowledge of the Lord among most of our brethren who dwell in this land." He added that "the younger generation has inherited nothing from their parents except what they need to make their way in the world; every spiritual teaching is foreign to them." He then went on to plead with his readers to remain in their native land rather than come to the new country of "lies and vain dreams, which promise gain only to those who transgress the laws of the faith." Such accounts were coming back to Europe, then, from many sources. They inevitably acted to "prove" that the rabbis who opposed immigration to America had been right.

In 1893 the most distinguished moralist among the rabbis of Europe, Israel Meir Ha-Kohen, who was universally known by the title of his most important book, *Hafetz Haim* ("the seeker of life"), went beyond exhortation; he ruled against the mass migration to America. He knew that this emigration could no longer be stopped, but he pleaded with those who would heed the views of rabbis to prefer persecution in Russia to economic success in the United States. What was new in the pronouncement of the *Hafetz Haim* was an injunction that those who must go to far-off lands beyond the sea should at least leave their children behind, and they should return to Eastern Europe after making their fortune. In another passage, written in the same year, the *Hafetz Haim* ruled: "A man must move away from any place which causes turning away from the way of the Lord, even if he knows for certain that he will have great economic success there." This authority insisted that even those who know that they will retain their piety should not go to such far-off lands; the Lord's punishment upon such an uncaring population will not distinguish between the pious and unfaithful. The *Hafetz Haim* had heard that there were destructive tornadoes, floods, and temperatures of sixty degrees (centigrade) in these lands beyond the sea. Such natural disasters represented the wrath of the Lord.

These opinions became so fixed that they would remain firm among the major leaders of European Orthodoxy even in the interwar period, as the situation of European Jewry was radically worsening for all Jews, of all socioeconomic classes. In Poland, Hungary, and Romania, Jews were, then, under unrelenting attack, and there was often physical violence, but the rabbis did not urge immigration. On the contrary, the most prominent figures stood firm in urging the faithful to avoid America. Writing in the 1920s and 1930s, in his book *Divrei Torah* ("the Words of the Bible") Elazar Shapira, the rebbe (Chasidic leader) of Munkacs, insisted that there were three gates to hell: the faithlessness of some elements in European Jewry, the absolute commitment to money in America, and the secularist Zionism rampant in Jerusalem. The worst of all the options for a pious Jew was to go to the United States, for there even repentance was not possible.

To be fair, such absolute negation of America was not the only opinion among rabbinic leaders. Chaim Halberstam, the rebbe of Zanz in southern Poland, who died in 1876, is recorded as saying that the days of *galut America* ("the American exile") have now begun, but (so he "knew" as kabbalist) that this is the last "exile," after which the Messiah would come. His younger contemporary, Joshua of Belz (who died in 1894), was ambivalent about America. There is an oral tradition that was recounted by his grandson, Aaron, the fourth rebbe, that when some refugees from the pogroms in Russia arrived in Belz in 1881, Joshua advised them to go to the Holy Land and not to America. Later, many communities in the United States asked Joshua to visit, or even to stay, but he would not. There is even a story, not otherwise confirmed, that a delegation of two men came from the United States to invite him to come to the New Land for a one-year trial period, because of the grave danger to the souls of American Jews. Joshua deliberated and then answered a few days later: the world is full of evil spirits; in Europe many generations of the pious have exorcised such spirits and purified the atmosphere, but in America no one has yet done this. He could not, therefore, leave for America, but he advised the delegation to go to Lithuania, where the rabbinic leaders were less sensitive in the matter of evil spirits. The delegation went to Lithuania, so the tale goes, and persuaded Rabbi Jacob Joseph to come to New York as chief rabbi. The two delegates also went to the Chasidic leader, Ezekiel of Shinova, who was on the verge of agreeing to a visit to the United States but was dissuaded by Joshua of Belz. Ezekiel wanted the two of them to go together to "fix" America. Joshua preferred to do this by reciting one of the Psalms each day, in prayer for America's Jews.

Joshua of Belz and Ezekiel of Shinova were confused about America. They were torn between their certainty that it was the domain of evil spirits and their concern for the Jews who had gone and were going there. But, as the tide of emigration grew ever higher, even the rabbis could no longer simply write off the Jews of America, especially since some of the accounts from America had, indeed, given reason to believe that all was not hopeless. In 1887 Moshe Weinberger wrote the first book-length account in Hebrew on *Jews and Judaism in New York*. In large part his description was negative. He claimed there was no Jewish education, religious observance was very low, and peddling a disastrous occupation. He also wrote that the American reformers were too powerful, and that the Orthodox rabbis and other clergy were irresponsible and for sale. For Weinberger, there were, however, bright spots. There were neighborhoods in New York where everything was closed on the Sabbath and where more *sukkot* (outdoor booths) had been built to celebrate that festival than had been erected by the same people in anti-Semitic Russia.

Even Abraham Cahan, the editor of the *Jewish Daily Forward* and, as such, the leading voice of Jewish socialist secularism in America, gave testimony to the existence of Orthodox observance among the majority of the immigrants. Looking back upon the 1880s in the memoirs that he wrote forty years later, Cahan recounted that the majority of the Jewish workers, whom the labor unions were trying to organize, were Sabbath observers. Indeed, in his first post as editor of a Yiddish newspaper, even before he came to the *Forward,* Cahan wrote a much-admired column under the title "The Proletarian Preacher." In that role, Cahan derived socialist lessons from the portion of the Torah (the Five Books of Moses) which was the biblical lesson of that week in the synagogue. According to Cahan, Moses was the original example of a strike organizer: did he not lead the Jews to refuse to meet the piecework quota set by the pharaoh? The majority of the immigrants were not ideologues and they tried, upon arrival, to maintain many of the accustomed ways. Cahan could lead them to the labor unions only by using the rhetoric of religion.

To be sure, during those years the anarchists were organizing antireligious festivals on Yom Kippur—and a striking amount of other forms of ideological antireligion did exist. In the struggle to make a living, tens of thousands of these conventionally pious workers and petty bourgeois from Eastern Europe did work on the Sabbath, but they did so reluctantly, and with pain. Those who were joyfully abandoning the older ways in the name of socialism or anarchism were a minority. In the immigrant days, most of the homes on the Lower East Side continued to keep kosher.

Thus, the majority of immigrant Jews and their children, who were neither completely Orthodox nor ideologically secularists, could no longer be defined by the standards of the inherited Jewish law. But how could one simply write off so many hundreds of thousands as bad Jews? A change in outlook was signaled by Rabbi David Zvi Hoffman, the leading rabbinic authority in Central Europe. Hoffman was willing to accept as valid a writ of religious divorce that was written in America, even though it was likely that the witnesses to this document were unacceptable as participants in a proceeding in Orthodox religious law, because they did not observe the Sabbath. In Hoffman's opinion, those who desecrated the Sabbath in America were not heretics who had rejected the authority of the tradition. On the contrary, they were trapped in negative conditions, "like children made captive by non-Jews." Therefore, they were acceptable witnesses in a religious proceeding. America was a sad fact for which allowances had to be made.

Even as most of the immigrant Orthodox rabbis in America continued to lament their fate, some rabbinic countervoices began to be heard. The most prominent and forthright was Chaim Hirshenson, who served as a rabbi in Hoboken and Union City, New Jersey, in the 1920s. Hirshenson had been born in the Holy Land and was descended from a very distinguished family of rabbinic scholars. And he himself was a sufficiently learned Talmudist to be accepted as an equal by the leading Orthodox authorities in Europe and Palestine. But Hirshenson did not regard the American Jewish community as beyond the Jewish pale. Despite his awareness of mass defection from Jewish observance, Hirshenson hailed the American Jews for their "holy passion" for helping to rebuild the Land of Israel. On several matters he tried to find reasons for lightening the burden of Jewish law, so that the many in America who did not observe these rituals would not be guilty of defying tradition. Hirshenson, while using Orthodox rhetoric, was doing for the "Russian Jews" what Isaac Mayer Wise had done two generations earlier for the "German Jews."

Hirshenson was describing what the Jews of America had made of their Judaism—deeds of charity, concern for Jews abroad, and especially those in Palestine, and selective observance of the rituals of the tradition—and finding this to be pleasing in the eyes of the Lord. God might make other demands of the communities of Europe or the Holy Land—so Hirshenson suggested—but He was willing to accept and even to be pleased with what He found among the Jews in America. Hirshenson responded with passion to one of his bitterest critics, a rabbi from Buffalo who repeated every one of the standard Orthodox charges against American Jewish life. In a sharp exchange of letters, Hirshenson asked his critic why he persisted in remaining in Buffalo: "Why don't you leave this land, in which you evidently remain for a mess of pottage, and go to the Land of Israel?" Hirshenson added that America should be judged with charity, because this was the community through which the bulk of the Jews in Europe and in Palestine were rescued during the years of trouble of the First World War and thereafter.

Even the protective and forgiving Hirshenson did not maintain that American Jews, except for a very small minority, were, by the older standards, learned or pious. The statistical accounts of those who arrived in the United States prove that only the poor, and the not very learned, came. This was clear as early as 1905, in the very midst of the mass migration. In that year, Isaac M. Rubinow wrote an essay entitled *The Russian Jew in the United States,* in which he stated that "it is evident that business and professional classes make up only a small percentage of the Russian Jewish population of New York City—much smaller, indeed, than that of the German Jews. The vast majority of the Russians are on a much lower economic level. They belong to the masses, as against the classes. The cause will be easily understood if we remember that the average Russian Jewish immigrant brought the magnificent capital of eight dollars into this country, while the average non-Jewish immigrant was the happy possessor of double that fortune." In a recent review (in 1975) of the immigrant statistics, Simon Kuznets, an economic historian, remarked that among the immigrants from Russia after 1897 and from Austria in 1900, "the commerce and professional groups are underrepresented." In both countries more than thirty percent of the Jews made their living from commerce, and five to seven percent were in the professions. Among the immigrants only five percent listed themselves as business people and only one and a third percent were professionals.

To be sure, many petty traders in Europe told the authorities at Ellis Island that they were laborers. These immigrants presumed that "laborers" were less likely to be excluded on arrival in the port of New York. The lowest economic group to come to America may thus have included more petty bourgeois than Kuznets or Rubinow asserted, but it is beyond doubt that the elite was definitely under-represented in the mass migration. The most revealing and incontrovertible figure in Kuznets' statistics concerns professionals. A doctor or a rabbi in Europe was hardly likely to claim to being a laborer; professional occupations were both honorific and in demand in America. More important still, the years after the failure of the First Russian Revolution in 1905 was the period when intellectuals and professionals from Eastern Europe did begin to arrive in some numbers. Even then, these elite elements were few in number. On average about six percent of the Jews of Eastern Europe were in the professions; even after 1905 less than one percent of the newcomers were professionals.

American Jewish history is thus, demonstrably, the tale of the transplantation to America of one part of European Jewry, the least educated. Some of these immigrants soon turned into dress manufacturers or movie moguls, and some of their children and grandchildren became writers and professors, while remembering that the literacy of most of their parents had not extended beyond reading the *Jewish Daily Forward*. Few remembered even in passing that they had not been exposed to the classic texts of Judaism, which, through the centuries, had been written in Hebrew. The folk culture of the Jewish poor was what the descendants of the immigrants accepted as Jewishness—and rebelled against.

II

Like the rest of American immigrant history, the painful and heroic saga of American Jewry is class history—but with a fateful and fundamental difference. The move of Jews to America was not only a flight from poverty; for many it was an act of rebellion or at least of defiance. The Irish and the Italians also arrived poor, but they were not angry with the Church. They soon brought over their priests and bishops, whom they venerated in America even more than they had back home. Jews, in contrast, could not wait to free themselves of the authority of their rabbis.

The angers did not begin in America. For two generations deep and unparalleled hatred had been growing among the Jewish poor in Czarist Russia against the Jewish elite. This was caused by a tragedy which took place in the middle of the nineteenth century, when the leaders of the Jewish community sold out the children of the poor in order to protect their own. In 1827, the czar decreed that young Jewish men of eighteen (much younger children were often taken) would be forced into the army for at least twenty-five years. None were stationed near their homes, for the clear intention of the czar was to convert their young people to Christianity. Each Jewish community was assigned a quota of how many such children it had to provide. It was all too human for members of the communal elite to protect their own children and to send the children of the poor. Since the quota had to be met, even as mothers and fathers hid their children, the authorities of the Jewish communities employed *chappers* ("grabbers"), people who roamed the streets and grabbed any teenage boy they could find to give him to the Russian military.

Before this episode ended in 1856, at least forty thousand—and by some estimates nearly one hundred thousand—Jewish children had been forced into this slavery. Many of these recruits were the uncles of those who, twenty years later, were to leave for America. Such immigrants had been raised on heartrending tales of communal leaders who refused to relent and return children who had been seized by the *chappers*. They had sung bitter folk songs about the selfishness of the rich and of the alliance of many (though not of all) of the rabbis with the powerful. Here is an early, inelegant translation in America of one such song:

> The streets are flooded with tears,
> Our hearts are torn by fears.
> Alas!—how great is our dismay;
> Will never dawn a brighter day?
>
> Tots from school they tear away
> And dress them up in soldier's gray.

And our leaders, and our rabbis
Do naught but deepen the abyss.

Rich Mr. Rockover has seven sons,
Not a one a uniform dons;
But poor widow Leah has an only child,
And they hunt him down as if he were wild.

It is right to draft the hard-working masses;
Shoemakers or tailors—they're only asses!
But the children of the idle rich
Must carry on, without a hitch.

America was the place where those who had been most deeply
wounded could go to escape the authority which had betrayed them.

The battle of the poor against the rich was being waged in Eastern
Europe throughout the nineteenth century over the issue of how the
Jewish community was to be financed, and this battle was transferred
as early as the 1880s to the United States. When attempts were made
to establish European-style chief rabbinates in New York and in
Chicago, these efforts foundered almost immediately over the issue
of who was to supervise the supply of kosher meat. Everywhere in
Russia this was done under the control of the official Jewish community, which derived large parts of its income from a tax levied
on each kosher chicken, or on each pound of meat that was sold in
the supervised butcher shops. In the United States the supplying of
kosher meat was a matter for "free enterprise." Individual producers
each hired a rabbi, or often someone without credentials who claimed
rabbinic authority, to certify that their provisions were kosher. In
both New York and Chicago the attempt to end this liberty, bordering on license, met with bitter opposition by most of the meat
suppliers and by the rabbis who worked for and with them. The
battles became so venomous that in New York the spirit and health
of Rabbi Jacob Joseph, who had been called in 1888 by five congregations to be "chief rabbi," was broken. In Chicago in the first years
of the twentieth century, an even greater rabbinic figure, Jacob David
Willowski, left the city, and the office of "chief rabbi." After eighteen
months he returned to Europe in bitter disgust. In both cities the
anti–chief-rabbi forces won the day, because they tapped deep sources
of resentment against authority. The placards which festooned both

cities were full of hatred for those who had paid their way in Europe by "sucking the blood of the poor" and who were now trying to come to America to repeat the pattern.

A different Jewish culture arose among the lower class, Yiddish-speaking, immigrant Jews of the United States than was to be found among their contemporaries in Europe. By 1900 there were major Jewish settlements in Vienna, Warsaw, and Odessa, with populations of roughly two hundred thousand each. These cities were centers of intellectual and cultural ferment. Before and after the turn of the century, a bewildering variety of modern Jewish movements, both political and cultural, were arising or reaching their height. Zionism, as ideology, was created mostly in Vienna and Odessa; Warsaw, Lodz, and Vilno were the principal homes of the several varieties of Jewish socialism: Odessa and Warsaw were the main centers of modern literature in Hebrew and Yiddish. Branches of all the contemporary movements in Europe existed among the immigrants to America, but none derived its major energies from its members in the New World. The vast majority of the newcomers were looking not for ideologies, secular or religious, but for rest from hard work. The East European Jewish ghettos in the United States in those years were very different from their counterparts in Europe. They provided mass audiences for the Yiddish theater, especially for the performances on Friday night and Saturday matinee. Virtuoso cantors entertained in the synagogues on Sabbath morning. Yiddish newspapers fought circulation wars by publishing the most lurid and tear-jerking serialized novels. Here are some of the titles from the 1890s: *The Kidnapped Child, or the Hangman of Berlin; Among Cannibals; The White Slaver; Innocent in the Lunatic Asylum; Crime of Passion, or the Intrigues of a London Lunatic Asylum; Suffering in Innocence;* and *The Vampire.* The author of these particular works was Isaac Rabinowitz, a Hebrew poet who had come to the United States in 1893; he had no choice but to eke out a miserable living working sixteen hours a day at such writing.

In the last decade before the First World War and during the war years themselves, New York did become the home for some of the important ideologues of Zionism and socialism, and for some of the most distinguished writers in Yiddish. The young David Ben-Gurion, who was the first prime minister of Israel, was in New York during the First World War. He had fled from Palestine, where he was under the suspicion of the Turks, who had guessed correctly that he was no supporter of their continued rule in the Holy Land. Ben-Gurion was then, as always, imperious and utterly devoted to his one consuming passion, the creation of a Jewish state. In New York he did participate in the immediate work of local Zionist groups which were sympathetic to his political views, but it never occurred to him for an instant that New York might become his home. While in New York, he courted and married a nurse, Paula Munweis, in 1917. Characteristically, he bolted from City Hall immediately after the wedding ceremony to speak at a Zionist meeting. Ben-Gurion's chief preoccupation in those years was with organizing Jewish volunteers to fight in the Middle East for the Allied cause. When such a body was organized, he enlisted and found himself in Egypt in August of 1918. At the end of the war, Ben-Gurion returned, of course, to Palestine.

During those years two of the preeminent ideologues of socialist Zionism, Nachman Syrkin and Ber Borochov, were in New York. In 1888, Syrkin was a Russian émigré in Germany. Ten years later he was the first to propose the possibility of a marriage between Zionist nationalism and socialist internationalism. After a few years in Russia, Syrkin emigrated to the United States in 1906. In New York he wrote much in Yiddish, and he changed his mind and his politics often enough to upset his most devoted disciples. Syrkin kept dreaming, most of the time and especially in his last years, of a socialist Zion, which would be a "light to the world," but he never went to Palestine. Syrkin died in New York in 1924. Ber Borochov spent the war years in New York as a refugee from Czarist Russia, where he was wanted by the police. Borochov was a more radical and revolutionary ideologue and politician than Syrkin. He was one of a handful of important young Marxists who found a way in the early 1900s to harmonize revolutionary socialism with nationalism and, in his case, with Jewish nationalism in its Zionist forms. Borochov's true homeland was the laboring Jewish masses in Russia. When the revolution came in 1917, he hurried back. He died in Kiev a few months later of pneumonia.

Overall, the Jews had the lowest rate of reemigration from the United States of any group that came in the era of mass migration. Those who did return were people with ideological reasons for not remaining, like Widawer, or Rabbi Willowski, or Ben-Gurion, or

Leon Trotsky (who spent some months in New York). Small as the rate of Jewish reemigration was, those who left represented an outsized proportion of the religious and secular Jewish intelligentsia who had come to America. Those intellectuals who remained were, quite often, bent and fashioned by the Jewish masses for their purposes. As we have seen, Rabbi Hirshenson forgave the masses for their lack of interest in Jewish learning and praised them for their charitable hearts and their passion for the defense of world Jewry. A comparable process transformed B. C. Vladeck, who arrived in the United States in 1908. A revolutionary who had labored for armed insurrection against the czar and who believed in class struggle, Vladeck, under American conditions, where, unlike Russia, the government could be called to account at the polls or in courts of law, quickly became much more moderate. In New York he soon realized that capitalism was there to stay. Very few of the immigrants, even as they sighed in the sweatshops, thought that they would be better off if they devoted themselves to tearing the system down. On the contrary, these workers—even those who remained workers all their lives— thought of themselves as temporary proletarians. They all wanted to become capitalists, if only by buying a candy store, as quickly as possible, and they did not raise their children to be proletarians. Vladeck, the labor leader, followed after his followers; he was transformed in America from a revolutionary socialist into a social reformist.

Vladeck also changed his views as a Jew. He arrived in New York a convinced anti-Zionist. Within a decade the *Jewish Daily Forward,* which he managed, was participating in relief efforts for the Jews of Palestine, and it was encouraging political activities to support Jewish claims on the land of the ancestors. The mass of the immigrants, even many who professed to be socialists and internationalists, were emotionally committed to every expression of Jewish creativity, and particularly to the renascent settlement in Palestine—and Vladeck went with them.

This rapid transformation of a revolutionary socialist and anti-Zionist is enormously revealing. What Vladeck encountered in America among the immigrant masses was their lasting concern for Jews all over the world. In order to lead these masses, Vladeck had to surrender any theoretical ideology which separated him from these sentiments. To be effective in New York, he had to accept American capitalism, and he bowed with ever greater warmth toward the Zionist communes, the kibbutzim, in the Galilee and the labor unions in Tel Aviv and Haifa. Vladeck and Hirshenson were both talking about the same phenomenon, immigrant American Jewry as it had defined its Jewish consciousness, in its own way—but what was this self-definition?

III

At least on the surface, the folk religion of the immigrant Jewish masses from Eastern Europe was an amalgam of group feeling, some religious observance, and the cumulative anger of the poor at the European Jewish elite. This description could have been applied a half-century earlier to the "German Jews." They, too, had arrived as immigrants with group feeling for each other; they had brought with them large elements of Orthodox Jewish religion and they harbored envy, and even some anger, at the more successful Jews back home. Nonetheless, there were critical differences between these two waves of immigration.

The "German Jews" had felt displaced, but they had not hated their country of origin. On the contrary, the "German Jews" had regarded their identification with Germany as so much a mark of honor that many were pro-German through the early years of the First World War, until the United States entered the conflict. Among the East Europeans who came late in the nineteenth century, the immigrants from Austria-Hungary were not angry with Emperor Franz Joseph I; on the contrary, they admired and even loved him as the friend and protector of the Jews. But these Jews from Franz Joseph's empire were a minority of perhaps one-tenth of the immigrants. The large majority of the newcomers came from Russia and Romania, and they had no attachment to their former homes. So long as the czar ruled Russia, everyone who left for America remained worried every day about the well-being and even the safety of his relatives. As these immigrants looked back to the lands of their birth, they hoped every day that the governments of Russia and Romania would fall.

The "German Jews" had never been so intensely troubled by the fate of their relatives in Europe. The Jews of Central Europe were still not free and equal in the middle years of the nineteenth century, but they were in no immediate danger. By 1870 Jews had been granted equal rights by a newly united Germany; the last discriminations against them had been removed by the Austro-Hungarian Empire three years earlier. The "German Jews" in America had had nothing to do with bringing about these decrees of equality; these actions were the results of the domestic political processes in Europe. It was less and less possible for modern, capitalist states to grant everyone equality and still discriminate, by law, against the Jews. In those liberal years, the Jews in Germany and in Austria-Hungary were on the rise. Some were getting rich and many were entering the professions. "German Jews" in America had come from these countries, and so they had no immediate involvement in Jewish misery. The problem of Jews meant the sufferings of a different tribe, of those in Eastern Europe.

The hundreds of thousands who came from Eastern Europe were much more immediately involved, every day, with the relatives whom they had left behind. The system of anti-Jewish legislation remained in place until the czar was overthrown by the democratic revolution in February 1917. There were pogroms and other outrages throughout the years before the czar fell, and there was vast suffering in the border wars which raged murderously for several years after the Russian Revolution in October 1917. From the day of their arrival in the United States, these immigrants followed the events back home with pain and passionate involvement. Some among them found ways of supporting reformist or revolutionary parties in Russia; most banded together in *landsmanshaften,* societies of expatriates from the same town or region, to help the Jewish communities from which they came. For the Jews from Eastern Europe the woes of European Jewry were thus very personal. One might lose religious faith on the way to America or soon after arrival, and thus abandon the Jewish God—but abandoning one's family, which was in endless danger, was an unforgivable act of betrayal.

The "German Jews" had had the opportunity, so long as they could ignore anti-Semitism in America, or look upon it as marginal and vanishing, to imagine that they were becoming Americans of the Jewish persuasion who harbored some social conscience about the problems of the Jews in remote Russia. The immigrants from Eastern Europe never had the luxury of such detachment. From their beginnings in America, they were a disunited, brawling group. They disagreed vehemently about politics, religion, sexual mores, but all the immigrants were closely connected with the Jews whom they left behind. This caring was the emotion that all shared. It was their common bond. The immigrants from Eastern Europe became a community as they wept over the millions of Jews who remained behind, or as they tried to help them. As we shall see, they and the "German Jews" formally joined in this effort in 1915, when they pooled their resources for relief of those in the war zones. These concerns united most Jews then, as they had once before in the 1840s and 1850s, when Mordecai Manuel Noah had led many of the older settlers into uniting with the immigrants of that era, the "German Jews" who had just arrived, in trying to help those who were being persecuted in Europe and in Syria.

There were other differences between the new and the earlier waves of immigration. The "German Jews" were always more at home with Gentiles than the East Europeans. In Europe, the "German Jewish" immigrants had still spoken some combination of West European Yiddish and the dialect of their region. The language in their mouth was not High German, but they spoke very nearly the same language as the German Gentile majority among whom they lived. Gentile farmers and Jewish cattle-dealers were not vastly different in culture. The differences between Jews and Gentiles in the villages of Bavaria in the 1830s were mostly to be found in religion. Even in America, these were the premises on which the distance of "German Jews" from non-Jews was based. What the "German Jews" did not bring with them was a fixation on the culture of their Jewish in-group as superior to that of the Gentiles. On the contrary, these "German Jews" regarded themselves as "better" because they thought they represented the virtues of Germany in America.

The East Europeans had a radically different mind-set about their relationship to the non-Jewish culture from which they came. They had been living in Russia in the towns where the mob might explode into anti-Jewish violence, or in the countryside as artisans among largely illiterate peasants. The folk memory of the "German Jews" deplored the peasants as being capable of *rishus,* that is, of Jew hating, but there were no other criticisms. The folk tales of the Eastern Europeans kept emphasizing the prevalence of drunkenness and irresponsibility among the peasants, and the superiority of Jewish family life and of Jewish culture. To be a Jew meant to preserve this supposed edge.

The Yiddish-speaking immigrants were not only different from the "German Jews" who had come earlier; they were also different from the other immigrant groups of that era of mass migration. They were the most intensely involved of all in maintaining their separateness in America. Almost all the immigrants, of whatever origin, regretted the loss of their "island within," of the ethnic and family ties which had sustained them in Europe. There were some variations: the Irish and the Italians were much more devoted to maintaining their ethnic identity than were most of the other groups. But the Irish and the Italians knew that the values of the Irish or Italian countryside, transplanted to America, were obstacles to reaching the highest levels of American life. In order to rise in America, Irish and Italian immigrants knew they had to unlearn the mind-set that had been bred into them by their past. To the degree to which they clung to the older mentality, these immigrants remained vegetable farmers and blue-collar workers, garbagemen and policemen, into the second generation. The immigrant Jews of those days had a different attitude. They knew that they had to learn American manners, and that the observances of the Jewish religion, and especially of the Sabbath, were obstacles to success. (In the 1920s the children of the immigrants were studied by Louis Wirth, who wrote a famous book, *Children of the Ghetto,* and by other sociologists; those who had remained completely Orthodox in their devotion to Jewish religion were less successful than those who had given up at least some of the religious regimen.) And yet, Jews continued to believe, into the second generation and beyond, that "Jewish values," the specific heritage that the immigrants had brought with them from Eastern Europe, had to be preserved. Their Jewishness—the "Jewish head"—was the critical element in their success in America. This "Jewish head" was the heritage of siege mentality, of centuries of being an embattled bastion in a hostile "exile," and of having only one tool for survival, the use of one's wits. Even in a much less hostile America, Jews believed that they could advance only if their "Jewish" virtues provided them with the energies to excel.

This attitude did not prevail among all the immigrant Jews, and certainly not among all of their children. Some felt confined by the Jewish world in which they had been raised; it was too at odds with the New World they wanted to enter. Among the children of the immigrants, such writers as Mary Antin and Henry Roth, at least by implication (and they were far from alone), spoke for this attitude. Mary Antin had herself been born in Poland; she came to the United States, to Boston, in her early teens. At a time when intermarriage was very unusual, she fell in love with a Gentile, one of her teachers at Columbia University, and married him. Soon, in 1912, an autobiographical novel appeared entitled *The Promised Land*. Mary Antin accepted assimilation; she insisted that to become part of America Jews had to get rid of every trace of their European past. Henry Roth was more ambivalent than Mary Antin. His novel *Call It Sleep* described immigrant life on New York's Lower East Side right before the First World War, when that ghetto was at its most vibrant and most congested. Roth depicted that society, as seen through the eyes of a child, in all its dirt and intensity. The world outside, beyond its boundaries, is at once threatening and enticing. The children, who are the major protagonists of Roth's novel, are mostly on their way out of the culture and the pieties of the immigrant ghetto. They want to embrace other, more "American," sensibilities. Though there is more than a hint in Roth's novel that this turning away causes a sense of loss and guilt, it also offers a more powerful sense of liberation, of moving from physical and spiritual congestion to the open space of America.

A vast literature has been written to describe the immigrant "Lower East Side," in New York and its equivalents in all the other large cities to which Jews came in the years before 1914. On the surface, the culture and practices of the Jewish small towns in Eastern Europe were transplanted unchanged to these American ghettos—but this was not so. The critical difference was America itself. Those who lived the culture of the "Lower East Side" had not come to the United States to establish such centers of ethnic intensity; they had come to succeed and to move away. A small, intense minority was committed, for less than a generation, to several varieties of socialism. This was the only doctrine which proposed the immigrant ghetto as a major base for effecting radical change of American society as a whole, but even in its heyday, in the second decade of the twentieth century, when the socialists won some victories at the polls in the Lower East Side of New York, socialism never approached being the dominant force among the immigrants. For most of its inhabitants, the "Lower East Side" was never more than a temporary dwelling of convenience.

It is even more true that the immigrant ghetto was not created as a bastion of Judaism. The inherited values of the Jewish religion had, indeed, been brought along to America. Their abandonment, in part or total, did trouble the majority of the immigrants and most of their children, but this was the pain of losing one's past much more than any assertion about the present or the future. This clash between the older values and "America" is the central theme of the most famous of the immigrant novels, Abraham Cahan's *The Rise of David Levinsky*. In Cahan's tale, Levinsky, a young Talmudic scholar, comes to the United States. There, he abandons the older ways and achieves worldly success. But, by the end of his life, Levinsky is in despair. Belonging neither to the world into which he had been born nor to any contemporary ideal, he is lost. Finally, he turns to the socialism of the workers in his factory. They, at least, had values for which they were fighting, and a sense of community. Levinsky was still too "Jewish" to believe that success is enough.

Antin, Cahan, and Roth all defined the same alternatives for the newly arrived Jews: assimilation into conventional American life or life in a separate immigrant Jewish world. Antin and Roth knew only that one or the other choice had to be made, but Cahan proposed a different answer. Cahan suggested that Levinsky would have been better off if he had used his energies to further the cause of socialism. In Cahan's description, Levinsky knew that those of his contemporaries who had organized labor unions were crusaders in the battle for social justice. Levinsky was aware that their particular fervor for social justice owed something to their Jewishness. Jews were not poorer than all the other immigrants, but they had had unique, age-old experience in doing battle with the hostile authorities, with resisting the powerful who controlled society. This energy could be used to help make a new America.

The bulk of the immigrant generation, and of their children, accepted none of the alternatives that the novelists offered. They were not busy abandoning their Jewishness, like Mary Antin, or becoming socialists, as Cahan suggested. They organized numerous synagogues, first in the immigrant ghettos and soon in Harlem in New York City, the "second settlement" where the more affluent moved a decade or two after their arrival. Hundreds upon hundreds of self-help organizations, cemetery associations, and "friendly societies" were established. As early as the 1880s, the Catskills began to become the summer home for the Jews of New York, though some of the more affluent and better educated among the East Europeans went to the Poconos, in Pennsylvania. Most of these Jews could do nothing else but invest their energies in creating a discrete American Jewish community of their own. These East Europeans did not want to vanish into some undifferentiated majority.

Most knew that they could not assimilate, even if they wanted to. They might try, like David Levinsky, to ape the clothes, the cigars, and the manners of the Christian business friends with whom he lunched at the Waldorf, but Levinsky knew that he remained an outsider. The Gentile majority did not forgive him for his Jewish origins, even as they beheld an individual who had worked to forget the memories of his youth and to learn to behave like any other successful American businessman. The non-Jews, especially the old-line Protestants, were no longer as religious as they used to be, but they knew that they were Christian, at least in relation to Jews. Unlike Mary Antin, who believed that the non-Jews were ready to assimilate the Jews, most immigrant Jews knew that even at their most assimilated they would remain "amateur Gentiles." This barrier did not necessarily force Jews to define their Jewishness in ways comparable to those by which Christians defined their Christianity. Christians tended to think of themselves as belonging to a religion; the mass of immigrant Jews spoke of being part of the Jewish people. Still, Jews and Christians agreed on one fundamental assertion: a person was either one or the other, either a Jew or a Gentile. The Jew/Gentile barrier was erected jointly, by anti-Semitism among the Gentiles and by group feeling among the Jews.

The immigrants from Eastern Europe had known in advance that New York was not the New Jerusalem. Very few of them had any illusion about their own future. They knew that they were likely to struggle and to remain poor for the rest of their lives. They themselves would never see the promised land, for they would never get beyond the ghetto and the sweatshops. But their children would enter America. The immigrant generation lived *far die kinder,* for the children. The young were supposed to enter businesses and professions which were closed to the children of the poor Jews in Eastern

Europe. A significant minority among the children of the immigrants became physicists, like Isidore Rabi, or novelists, like Saul Bellow, but their immigrant parents did not understand them. The opportunity for education in America meant, in the minds of parents, that the children could rise from the pushcarts and the clothing factories to working in offices. They would be doctors or lawyers or men of business.

The immigrants knew in advance that distaste for Jews had not disappeared in the New World. The Yiddish papers in Europe told many stories of discrimination. Despite Emma Lazarus's poem on the base of the Statue of Liberty, inviting the tired, huddled masses of the world to America, the immigrants harbored no fantasy that welcoming committees of the Gentile majority would be waiting in New York harbor to enfold them in loving arms. East European Jews knew that American Gentiles were not virulent Jew haters, like many of their enemies in Russia and Romania, but Gentiles remained Gentiles, everywhere. Sometimes they were less hostile and, on some happy days, they might even be friendly, but the Gentile majority remained everywhere and, at best, largely unaccepting of Jews. This was the mind-set of the immigrants, as they sang, even in America, folk songs about the differences between Jews and Gentiles.

The happiest knowledge of the immigrants about America was that here, unlike Czarist Russia, the law was not their enemy. Almost immediately after landing, immigrants did two things: they went to find a job, and they enrolled in Americanization classes. Everyone, without exception, wanted to become a citizen. This required passing an examination to prove that the newcomer understood the Constitution of the United States. When citizenship was granted, the ritual required the candidate to swear allegiance to the Constitution and, of course, to foreswear all other political loyalties. The new citizen now had rights equal to everyone else's, but the ritual had not admitted him to American society. On the way home from the ceremony which made him an American, he would still pass signs in shop windows, advertising for sales help, saying "no Jews wanted," or he would read the somewhat politer formula "Christians only" in the want ads of the newspaper that he would buy in the subway on the way home.

The "German Jews" had been few, and they had defined themselves in an open, expanding America and, to a very great degree, on its frontier. It was easy for them to think of themselves as different from other Americans only in religion. The "Russian Jews" came to the cities, when America needed hands for the factories, and they came in large masses. These Jews, and their children, would have far more trouble finding their way into America.

11.

"This Is Our Country"

I

In the mid-nineteenth century, American anti-Semitism had been mildly endemic, but it was not immediately threatening to American Jews. Religious antipathy continued to exist, but Jews had been accustomed for centuries to slighting remarks from Christians. Social barriers had increased after the Civil War, but they were of little consequence. Jews might be kept out of resorts and clubs, and old canards about their supposed sharp practices might be repeated, but few believed that Jewish businessmen were really different from Gentiles. The "German Jews" had succeeded in persuading themselves, and most Americans, that, even at their supposed worst, the few Jewish Wall Street bankers were no more obnoxious or un-American than such plungers and speculators of the Gilded Age as Jay Gould and Diamond Jim Brady.

Only with the advent of the "Russian Jews" did serious anti-Semitism appear in the United States. The main target of the Jew haters were the foreign, Yiddish-speaking immigrants. The "German

Jews" wanted to believe that the attacks were not directed toward them at all; they were suffering only because they were "coreligionists" of the benighted "Russian Jews." This was not true. The attacks were not limited to "Russian Jews." The "German Jews" were under direct fire; they were accused, frontally, of lacking legitimacy in America. They were told that they had no right to the wealth and the place in America that they had earned so quickly.

In December 1891, Henry Rogers, a well-known essayist and journalist, published a letter in a leading magazine, in which he attacked the record of Jews during the Civil War: "I had served in the field about eighteen months before being permanently disabled in action, and was quite familiar with several regiments; was then transferred to two different recruiting stations, but I cannot remember meeting one Jew in uniform, or hearing of any Jewish soldier."

This charge had to be answered. Jews had to prove that they had done their share, or even more, as citizens. In immediate response to Rogers's broadside, the "German Jews" became devotees of the study of American Jewish history. In December 1892, the American Jewish Historical Society published its first quarterly. The central personalities in this endeavor were men such as Cyrus Adler, Simon Wolf, and Max Kohler, all American-born children of immigrants from Central Europe. These men had no relationship to the Jews who had come to the colonies, but that did not deter them from writing with special relish, and in great antiquarian detail, about Spanish-Portuguese Jews in colonial America. Every soldier who served in the Revolution was described at length. It was established that there had been perhaps fifty Jewish-American Revolutionary soldiers (further research has since found fifty more), and that this number was far higher, in proportion, than that of any other group in the American population. Simon Wolf, as we have seen, the semi-official Jewish lobbyist in Washington at the turn of the century, summed up this argument for the rights of Jews in a book entitled *The American Jew as Soldier and Patriot* (1895). Wolf compiled long lists of Jews who had been in uniform in the various wars in the United States, and he took particular pride in those who had died for the country. Jewish blood, too, had helped water the tree of liberty. There had been Jews at Valley Forge and Yorktown, and at Gettysburg and Appomattox. Gentiles had no right to question the legitimate place of Jews in an America which they had helped create and defend.

Without quite saying so, the successful "German Jews" of the 1890s were laying claim to colonial Jewry; they were making ancestors out of Haym Salomon; of Gershom Mendes Seixas, the Jewish clergyman in New York in the time of the Revolution and the early years of the Republic; of Aaron Lopez, the sea trader from Newport, Rhode Island, and all the Jewish soldiers of the Revolution. This was exaggerated. There had been some intermarriage between the descendants of the older settlers and the immigrants from Central Europe who came in the mid-nineteenth century, but this biological continuity was of little consequence. The "German Jews" had essentially founded a new American Jewish community, but this Jewish claim to older legitimacy in America was in keeping with the spirit of the times. The Irish, the Italians, and a whole host of other minorities were then founding "historical societies" to argue that men and women of their kind, and not the Protestant settlers alone, had helped fashion America.

What the "German Jews" found harder to face was the question of the foreignness of the newly arriving Jewish masses. Here the Jewish situation was unique. All of the other ethnic groups which had come to the United States in large numbers after the middle of the nineteenth century did not find well-established predecessors who were expected to take responsibility for the newcomers. The descendants in Pennsylvania of the Hessian mercenaries of German stock who had remained in America after the Revolutionary War had been too poor and isolated to become the responsible elite of the millions of German immigrants who came to the United States in the next century. Others, like the handful of English Roman Catholics in Maryland, were too few, and too different from the Irish, to become the leaders of the millions who fled to America during the Potato Famine and thereafter.

The Jewish situation differed because the earlier and largely successful immigrants lived "uptown" in the very same cities where the newly arrived East Europeans were working "downtown," in sweatshops. Many of the newest Jewish arrivals worked, first, for German Jewish employers. Even if the older arrivals would have wanted to disclaim connection, as some did, it would have made no difference.

Gentiles, both friends and foes—and most Jews—persisted in regarding Jews of all provenances as belonging to one community. The "German Jews" were thus trapped: they were inevitably involved with the "Russian Jews," but they wanted to keep their distance. They told themselves that they were "better people," and they told it to anti-Semites. Let the critics of the Jews be aware that their distemper was caused by the uncouth newcomers and that it should not extend to the proper, older arrivals.

As early as 1881, the year of the great wave of pogroms in Russia, spokesmen for the "German Jews" were saying such things in public. The *North American Review* was then the leading organ of opinion. A German Jewish writer argued that "no people . . . is willing to be judged by its immigration." He exhorted the American majority to stop social discrimination against Jews of his class, who were respectable Americans, because the "unfavorable impression of the Jew" they harbor was formed by their observing the immigrants. Another writer suggested that year that the best way to protect existing American Jewry against the problems that would come with the arrival of many immigrants from Russia would be "to send American Jewish missionaries to Russia to civilize them there rather than give them an opportunity to russianize us in the event of . . . a colossal emigration." This suggestion was, on the face of it, empty rhetoric. There were hardly enough "missionaries" available among a Jewish community of perhaps a quarter of a million in 1880 to go to Russia to teach six million Jews middle-class table manners, American-style, and Tevye, and his children, were hardly waiting for such instruction. To learn to copy "German Jews" was not their most pressing concern. This suggestion about a mission to Russia was an outburst of pique—and of a sense of trap. The resident American Jews knew that they were landed with a problem they could not escape.

In those painful, earliest years, the committees in Germany and France that were helping the Russian Jews had essentially one solution, to send the runaways from Russia forward to America. The Americans soon ran out of resources with which to help the new arrivals. Even the most charitable were afraid of the bad impressions the newcomers were making on the Gentiles. As early as October 1881, M. A. Kursheedt, the secretary of the Russian Emigrant Relief

Fund, wrote from New York to the Alliance Israelite Universelle, in Paris, that many of the Jewish refugees had become peddlers, thus representing a "great source of annoyance to us as they have settled in this city and crowd the filthy tenements in a certain section of the East Side." Kursheedt had evidently forgotten that the "German Jews," for whom he spoke, had begun as peddlers less than forty years before, and that some of them had lived, in the 1840s and 1850s, in the very streets that now housed the poor Russians.

Though Kursheedt and his colleagues were ever more upset by the tide of immigrants, they would not, and could not, abandon them. The next month, in November 1881, a group of prominent Jews established the Hebrew Emigrant Aid Society to help the new-comers. A few weeks later, these very circles, acting under another organizational label, wrote a formal letter to the alliance announcing that American Jews would accept no more refugees. By the spring of the next year, as more Jews came in flight from renewed pogroms in Russia, frantic appeals for money appeared in the Jewish press; if the newcomers were left to their own devices, "an element of Jewish tramps and paupers . . . will disgrace the name Israelite through the land."

The Hebrew Emigrant Aid Society disbanded early in 1883, prob-ably out of the fear that if it continued to do such good work, it would attract more immigrants. Augustus A. Levey, the secretary of the aid society, resigned, saying that "only disgrace and a lowering of opinion in which American Israelites are held . . . can result from the continued residence among us of such wretches." A few years later, in 1890, Oscar Straus, a leading figure among the Jews of America, asked the Belgian-Jewish philanthropist Baron Maurice de Hirsch not to "foster, encourage or stimulate emigration to Amer-ica." Straus feared that further increase in the numbers of Russian Jews in America "would be a calamity and a misfortune, not only for the immigrants, but for all American Jews." And yet in the very midst of their ambivalences about the refugees, the established Amer-ican Jewish community actually did extraordinary service in the dif-ficult crisis years of 1881–82. Some nineteen thousand Jews arrived during those two years, and fourteen thousand of them were helped with money, until they could find jobs, by the Hebrew Emigrant Aid Society alone.

II

Though the "German Jews" were almost unanimous in regarding themselves to be a different breed, they were also very nearly of one mind in accepting responsibility for the "Russian Jews." This concern was only in part a form of self-defense against the anti-Semites, as a way of keeping these "Russian Jews" from being too embarrassing. There was an element of wanting to behave, and to be seen to behave, in the way expected of "better people" in the America of the last decades of the nineteenth century.

On the surface, the proper "German Jews" were behaving like their Gentile peers. The turn of the century was the era of the "Social Gospel." The "best people" among the Protestants were translating their Christianity into a set of obligations to help the poor. A wide variety of institutions, from charity hospitals to soup kitchens, were established all over America. The "German Jews" soon did exactly that for their poor "coreligionists." But there was one essential difference between the Christian and the Jewish endeavors. The Jewish philanthropists were very much more involved in the Jewish masses than the Christian "best people" were in the Christian poor. It was not only that the behavior of the Jewish masses would reflect on the older settlers. It was more than that: if the leadership of the Jewish elite was not accepted by the newer masses, then the "German Jews" had no real role in American society. The "German Jews" were expected by everyone, especially by Gentiles, to lead their own kind. If they did not, they could be attacked as an overprivileged, small group of still semiforeign rich people.

In the 1880s and 1890s, the "German Jews" created a network of charity organizations to take care of the "Russian Jews." In every major city, they founded free medical clinics, relief agencies, and an increasing variety of social services, including classes in Americanization, to teach immigrants English, and American ways of behavior, and to prepare them to pass the test for citizenship. In New York, the United Hebrew Charities had been created in 1874, when the first trickle of immigration from Eastern Europe had begun. By the 1890s, this organization was raising and spending a million dollars each year, a very large sum for those days. In Boston, a federation of all the various philanthropic bodies was created in 1895, and by the next decade, such federations existed in Chicago, Philadelphia, St. Louis, Milwaukee, and Cleveland. The newest Jewish arrivals were glad to use these facilities, but for the most part the "Russian Jews" resisted the idea that they should obey the wishes of the philanthropists. These two communities had different agendas. The older settlers wanted Jews to be quiet; the newer arrivals had not yet made their way in America, and so they could hardly avoid the noise of social and economic conflict. The older settlers were, at least in theory, Jews by religion ("Americans of the Jewish faith," in Isaac Mayer Wise's formulation), while the newer arrivals thought of themselves as a people, a national minority, not all of whose members were religious believers, not even in theory.

Social class was equally important. The poor have never liked the rich, and the immigrants on the Lower East Side were a prime example of this rule. The East Europeans had brought substantial class angers with them to the new land. The overwhelming majority of these immigrants had scores to settle with the communal leadership of their former homes. Many were to transfer these angers to America, especially to the "Germans," the rich Jews they found in America. Here effective revolt against those who claimed authority in the community could be mounted more easily than in Europe.

Yet, despite these early skirmishes, the "German Jews" needed the immigrants—the poverty of the newcomers guaranteed the class status of their benefactors. Still, it is too shallow to think that the "German Jews" helped the poor simply to ward off anti-Semitism or to guarantee their class status in America. Their passion for such good works had deep roots in a very old Jewish tradition which had been transplanted unimpaired from Europe. The commandment of the Jewish religion to be charitable to the poor had been reinforced through the centuries by the insistence of a hostile world that it wanted, least of all, to be troubled by Jews with problems. For many centuries, the *parnassim,* the leaders of the ghetto, had accepted responsibility for the poor, even when the rich did not feel charitable, as an act of conscience. In the open society of the New World, observing all of the other commandments of the Jewish tradition had become matters of personal choice, but concern for poor Jews was the one *mitzvah* (religious injunction) which anti-Semites enjoined. When the first group of Jews came to New York in 1654, they were allowed to remain because the leaders of the Jews in Amsterdam promised the hostile governor of New Amsterdam, Peter Stuyvesant, that they would provide for those who might become indigent in America. In the 1780s, Haym Salomon reminded hostile critics that Jews continued to take care of their own; so did Mordecai Manuel Noah and Uriah Phillips Levy in the 1830s, and Jewish leaders after them in all succeeding generations. Throughout the ages, the well-to-do Jews have often complained about these obligations to the poor. Some even tried to avoid them, but religion and custom—and anti-Semitism—were firm in teaching that the poor were, unavoidably, the responsibility of the rich.

Jacob Schiff, the leader of the "German Jews," was very self-consciously a *parnas* in the European mold. Schiff was different from most other German immigrants. In 1865, at the age of eighteen, he had come to the United States from Frankfurt, Germany. Schiff did not come from the poor, but descended from a very distinguished family. Eminent rabbis were among his ancestors, and his father had been associated with the Rothschilds in the banking business. Upon arrival in New York, Schiff did not peddle or open a store; instead, he went to work in a brokerage firm. In 1875, after marrying Solomon Loeb's daughter, he moved to the Wall Street firm Kuhn, Loeb and Co. Ten years later, Schiff was made head of the firm. Under his leadership, Kuhn, Loeb and Co. was particularly important in financing several of the major American railroads and in floating loans for both the American and for foreign governments.

Schiff used his wealth like a *parnas,* in the grand manner. He gave princely gifts to such causes as the American Red Cross, Barnard College, and Harvard University, and to almost every charitable and religious institution, of whatever shade of opinion and belief, among American Jews. The dominant passion of his life was to exercise the responsibility that he felt for the Jews of Russia. Schiff took the lead in underwriting a Japanese bond issue of two hundred million dollars in the winter of 1904–5, when Japan was fighting its war against Russia. He fought hard against any American financial support for the czarist government. More quickly than any other leading "German Jew," Schiff understood that the tide of immigration could not be stopped. He felt the moral responsibility to help more Jews escape from oppression and to help the masses who were arriving. His towering personality helped sweep away the initial desire among a few "German Jews" to pretend that the Russian immigrants were a different tribe.

When the 1903–5 wave of pogroms occurred in Russia, the "German Jews" reacted almost as one. They were outraged, and they hastened to help both the victims who were still in Russia and the many immigrants who were fleeing to the United States. Schiff and his colleagues fought hard against any restriction of immigration, and especially against the attempt to impose quotas based on national origins.

All of these attitudes were expressed in a very high moment, the celebration that was held on Thanksgiving Day, 1905, in Carnegie Hall to celebrate "the two hundred and fiftieth anniversary of the settlement of the Jews in the United States." This was a date of convenience, for the first boatload of Jews had arrived in New Amsterdam in September 1654. The organizers of the celebration chose to commemorate the formal decision by the Dutch West India Company, on April 26, 1655, that gave the Jews the right to remain. Carnegie Hall was crowded on this festive occasion. There was an address by Grover Cleveland, a former president of the United States, as well as speeches by the governor of New York and the mayor of the city. President Theodore Roosevelt sent a letter, and Vice President Charles W. Fairbanks sent a telegram. Dr. David H. Greer, the Episcopal bishop coadjutor of New York, spoke in the accents of a liberal Christian, and the rabbi of Temple Emanu-El, Samuel Silverman, prayed for the well-being of American democracy. These dignitaries, together, were declaring Jews to be part of the very essence of America, past and present. Theodore Roosevelt wrote what this assemblage wanted to hear, that "even in our colonial period, the Jews participated in the upbuilding of this country" and that "they have become indissolubly incorporated in the great army of American citizenship." He went on to confront the critics of the new immigrants squarely: "This is true not only of the descendants of the early settlers and those of American birth, but of a great and constantly increasing proportion of those who have come to our shores within the last twenty-five years as refugees reduced to the direst straits of penury and misery."

Roosevelt's letter echoed the themes that were stated in the opening speech of that celebration by Jacob Schiff who chaired the gathering. Jews have been part of "the developement of the New World" and, therefore, they "believe that we are justified in the claim that this is our country." Schiff made no claim that "the Jewish citizen has done more than his civic duty," but he felt the need to emphasize the significant role of the Jews in the making of America, to counter "the attempts so frequently made to consider us a foreign element." Jews everywhere are ardent admirers of America, and everywhere they set their faces "longingly and hopefully toward these shores."

Perhaps the most interesting speech of this celebration was made by Oscar Straus, not in New York, but in a parallel celebration the day before in Boston's historic Faneuil Hall. Straus had long repented for his letter in 1890 to Baron de Hirsch which expressed deep fear of further Jewish immigration. On the contrary, he talked with pain and passion about the "massacre of thousands of helpless men, women and children in Odessa, Kief, Kishineff, and a hundred cities, towns and hamlets throughout Russia." Speaking in Boston, Straus appealed to the tradition of the Pilgrims who, so he asserted, had come to "our continent, that it shall ever be a shelter for the poor and persecuted." Therefore, he concluded, America must remain open to those who need its freedom and hospitality:

> To bar out these refugees from political oppression or religious intolerance, who bring a love of liberty hallowed by sacrifices made upon the altar of an enlightened conscience, though their pockets be empty, is a grievous wrong, and in violation of the spirit of our origin and development as a free people, for they, too, have God's right to tread upon American soil, which the Pilgrims have sanctified as the home of the refugee.

The leaders of the "German Jews" had a vision of America: immigrants came, bringing with them foreign ways, but they soon unlearned them and became Americans. The one distinction among its citizens that America permitted was religion, so Jews were Americans of the Jewish faith. They, the "German Jews," were proud of their achievement in becoming such Americans, and they fully expected the "Russian Jews" to remake themselves in this long-existing pattern. Had not the Jews of colonial and revolutionary times regarded themselves as Americans of the Jewish religious persuasion? This assertion about the past was not true. Colonial and revolutionary America had been untidy societies where identities were not clear-cut. The separation of church and state in the Constitution did not mean that religion was the only difference among its citizens that the United States would tolerate. As James Madison noted in *The Federalist Papers,* that clause in the Constitution meant simply that the government was barred from legislating for or against religion, as it was forbidden to curtail freedom of speech. The law did not enjoin the supremacy of Anglo-Saxon culture.

In 1905, the "German Jews" could advance no such interpretation of the earliest definition of America. This was the heyday of nativism, and of other forms of distaste for foreigners. It was simplest to agree with the superpatriots that America was a social club, while insisting that the whole history of the New World was one of receiving immigrants and quickly transforming them into members.

This doctrine about America was expressed most clearly by the speech that Louis Marshall, a brilliant lawyer closely associated in Jewish affairs with Jacob Schiff, made at another celebration in Albany. Marshall said frankly that these meetings had been organized across the country for a reason:

> It is . . . to prove that the Jew is not a parasite, an exploiter of the country, or a newcomer within its gates, that we are celebrating on this occasion. It is not to call attention to the Jew as a religious factor, but as a civic element in the grand composite of American citizenship. He is an American of the Americans—a Jew by faith and religion, an American in all that that term can betoken.

The immigrants from Russia, so Marshall insisted, "when transplanted to American soil in a few years, become dignified, industrious, patriotic, self-respecting and productive citizens." In the climactic paragraphs of Marshall's oration, he referred back to the promise the Jews had made in 1655 to the Dutch West India Company, "that the poor among us should not become a burden to the community but should be supported by us." Marshall stood tall as he proclaimed that this promise had been kept for two and a half centuries. The burden has been heavy and it will probably remain so, but "to me it is a source of pride and exaltation that, although we are citizens of a common country, the religious duty of caring for our own . . . had been especially imposed upon us." Fulfilling this obligation was his generation's continuity with the first Jewish settlers, who had made such a covenant with America, expressing "the gratitude that we owe to the God of our Fathers Who has led us out of Egypt to this land of freedom."

The response of the "German Jews" to the anti-Semites and to those who would stop immigration had thus been made. Schiff, Strauss, and Marshall defined America in 1905 as a country of immigrants, all of whom, regardless of when they came, both contributed to America and were remade by it. In these celebrations, the "German Jews" were promising to do their utmost to hasten such transformation of the "Russian Jews" into "America." As one could have expected, the organizers of these grand celebrations convinced themselves, and their existing friends in the majority society, that Jews were cofounders of America and that America would be enriched by the energies of the newest Jewish immigrants. However, the enemies of the Jews remained unconvinced.

III

Henry Adams, grandson of John Quincy Adams and great-grandson of John Adams, thought himself a "rather superior person," but he thought that his sister, Louise Catherine, was far brighter. She married a Jew, Charles Kuhn of Philadelphia, and some of the earliest references to Jews in Adams's writing seem to have been influenced by the presence of a Jew in the family. In 1864, he had written that "fashion was not fashionable in London until the Americans and the Jews were let loose." Adams depicted Jewish figures in his novel, *Democracy,* without rancor and even as allies in the fight for political reform. Nonetheless, in 1879, the year before he published the novel, Adams wrote from Spain: "I have now seen enough of Jews and Moors to entertain more liberal views in regard to the Inquisition." Adams remained ambivalent about the kind of Jew who tried to enter society. He was wary but interested in such people as the young art critic Bernard Berenson, or Sir Francis Palgrave, the historian of early England who had been born "Cohen." He disliked Vienna because its cultural life was dominated by Jews. Adams was hostile to Westernized Jews, though he was not totally on the warpath against them, but he hated the East Europeans. He, and other aristocrats like his brother, Brooks Adams, and his friend, Henry Cabot

Lodge, became vehement, often to the point of hysteria, at the sight of beards and caftans.

In 1901, Henry Adams visited Russia. The first sight that he saw after crossing the border, was "a Polish Jew . . . in all his weird horror." The sight of such figures, so he wrote in a letter from Warsaw, "makes me creep." In his most famous book, *The Education of Henry Adams,* published in 1918, Adams contemplated the flood of such immigrants to the United States, who numbered by then more than two million. Adams lamented the death of his America; the future belonged to the unwashed: "Not a Polish Jew fresh from Warsaw or Cracow—not a furtive Jacoob or Ysaac still reeking of the Ghetto, snarling a weird Yiddish to the officers of the customs— but had a keener instinct, an intenser energy, and a freer hand than he—American of Americans."

But Henry Adams was, indeed, a descendant of Puritan ancestors. It had been bred into him that Jews were heirs to those who had written the Hebrew Bible, and in that role they were dangerous, because they were counterclaimants to being the true scriptural elite. Adams's description of himself on the very first page of his auto-biography, as an alienated aristocrat, reached back to the Puritan encounter with the Jews of the Bible: "Had he been born in Jerusalem under the shadow of the Temple and circumcised in the Synagogue by his uncle and high priest, under the name of Israel Cohen, he would scarcely have been more distinctly branded, and not much more handicapped in the races of the coming century, in running for such stakes as the century was to offer." Two ancient stereotypes about Jews were thus alive in Henry Adams: Jews are an all-too-talented, wrongheaded competing elite, and they are, at the same time, dirty and disease-bearing, the heirs to the "synagogue of Satan." On both counts, Jews had to be kept at bay. In 1894, several of Adams's friends joined other young Boston aristocrats in organizing the Immigration Restriction League. They wanted to limit the admission of "unhealthy elements," which meant Jews, Slavs, and Italians.

In those days it was not even necessary to be an overt hater to claim that the health of the United States was based on the "men of the sturdy stocks of the north of Europe" and that "the more sordid and hopeless elements" which came from southern Europe had to be kept out, because they had "neither skill nor energy nor quick intelligence." These anti-Italian remarks were made as self-evident and beyond need of any proof by Woodrow Wilson in his professorial *History of the American People.* But there were countervoices among American intellectual and social aristocrats. Thomas Wentworth Higginson, a Brahmin peer of Adams and Lodge, wrote in 1897 that there was no such thing as pure-blooded English, for the ancestors of the majority of the American colonists represent "a race so mingled and combined . . . that it can claim no purity of strain, but only the strength of composite structure." Higginson was bold enough to say that America had not been made great, at least in its economy, by the original settlers, but rather by the immigrants. Everybody, including the patricians of that day, were descended from immigrants who came poor, just like the millions who were arriving these days. To be sure, there were more criminals among the immigrants than among the older settlers, but crime is always more present among the poor and "the eminent scoundrels, who are rich and shrewd enough to keep out of prison, are rarely foreigners."

Those who wanted to restrict immigration found allies among the nativists, the Populists, and in the labor organizations. Tom Watson, the Populist leader from Georgia, incited his followers against the immigrants. He wrote in the 1890s: "The scum of creation has been dumped on us. Some of our principal cities are more foreign than American. The most dangerous and corrupting hordes of the Old World have invaded us. The vice and crime which they have planted in our midst is terrifying." Watson blamed "the manufacturers and bankers" who then "wanted cheap labor and did not care how much harm to our future might be a consequence of their heartless policy."

These attacks were directed against all foreigners, not primarily against Jews, but Populism did have its anti-Semitic element. Ignatius Donnelly, a former congressman from Minnesota, published a novel in 1891 called *Caesar's Column,* in which he warned against "Jewish bankers" who were helping "to turn the farmers into serfs." Other Populists were even more violent. Those who demanded freedom from Wall Street bankers very often identified these bankers as Jews. Even the very Gentile firm of investment bankers, J. P. Morgan and Company, which had no Jew on its staff even as an office boy, was slurred as a Jewish house. The poor immigrants arriving from Eastern Europe could be imagined, in anti-Jewish fantasy, as recruits for ever more powerful and more dangerous Jewish forces. Yet, despite the

anti-Semitic fringe among the Populists, and the specific attacks on Jews by some of the nativists, Jewish immigrants were not the sole target, or even the principal one, in the era of mass migration.

The Italians, who were by far the largest group of newcomers, were under the fiercest attack. In 1891 in New Orleans, eleven Italian immigrants were lynched, in a riot led by patricians, after they had been acquitted of a charge of murder. This lynching was the only such outbreak in those years. It was an American pogrom, but it was directed against Italians, not Jews. Even though they were Catholic, the Irish took little interest in the Italians and essentially wished that they would stop coming. Cyrus Adler, the president of Dropsie College in Philadelphia, complained in 1912 that there was no interest among the Irish in that city in joining a coalition with other minorities to oppose restrictions on immigrations.

The essence of the battle against immigration was the repeated attempt to enact legislation requiring that newcomers prove their literacy. The proponents of such a law presumed that their favorite stock, the Aryans from Northern and Western Europe, could read; "inferior people" from other regions were much less literate, and so nearly half of those who arrived at American ports would be sent back. American business and industry generally opposed such a law. In good times, more labor was needed; in bad times, as the Knights of Labor charged repeatedly, cheap immigrant labor was useful in lowering wage rates and in breaking strikes. Enlightened opinion, for which Higginson had spoken, continued to believe that immigrants of any provenance were a useful addition to America. No matter what the immigrants might seem to be, their children would become, as many had already proved, upstanding Americans. Moreover, the immigrants mattered increasingly as voters, and so those who would push restrictions had to contend with their displeasure. President Theodore Roosevelt was himself ambivalent about the new immigrants, but, in a bid for the Jewish vote, he chose Oscar Straus, the first Jew to serve in a United States cabinet, to be secretary of commerce and labor, and thus the chief immigration officer of the United States in 1906. Roosevelt wanted the votes of the Jews for Charles Evans Hughes, the Republican candidate who was running for governor of New York against William Randolph Hearst.

In the course of the battle over immigration, there was a growing majority in Congress for restriction, while presidents stood firm for

twenty years, from 1897 to 1917. Legislation requiring the immigrants to prove literacy passed four times in Congress, and it was
vetoed by four presidents, two Democrats, Grover Cleveland and
Woodrow Wilson, and two Republicans, William Howard Taft and
Theodore Roosevelt. The difference between the presidents and Congress was in the nature of their constituencies. The White House was
sensitive, even under Democrats, to the needs of big business, which
wanted large immigration to provide workers for industry, but also
to the growing numbers of recent immigrants who were becoming
citizens and voters. Jews had already become, by 1910, a political
factor in such major states as New York, Illinois, Pennsylvania, and
Ohio, because they were roughly ten percent of the population of
Chicago, Cleveland, and Philadelphia, and more than a quarter of
the inhabitants of New York City. Most congressmen, on the other
hand, came from districts with few Jews, or other recent immigrants,
or they represented sections of the big cities which felt threatened
by the expanding immigrant ghettos. The presidential vetoes of restrictions on immigration were a first instance of the growing importance of the "Jewish vote." All of the four presidents were men
of goodwill, though only Grover Cleveland was entirely free of
personal ambivalence about immigrants in general and Jews in particular. The vetoes were proof that power counted—the power of
the National Association of Manufacturers in unusual alliance with
Jewish immigrants who were beginning to matter in American politics.

Despite the restrictive majority, a strong minority in Congress,
enough to sustain these vetoes, held to the ideal of generosity and
openness. Joseph G. "Uncle Joe" Cannon, the legendary Speaker of
the House, began on the side of the restrictionists, but by 1906 he
had changed his mind. Cannon snorted that if illiterate immigrants
had been excluded from the United States in the past, his ancestors
would have been rejected. The implication was clear: the partisans
of literacy tests had fraudulent memories of their own forebears.

Senator Henry Cabot Lodge did try, during the first attempt to
enact literacy restrictions, to sneak in a clause aimed directly at Jews.
In 1896, during a Senate-House conference on the first such bill,
Lodge framed the clause to permit entry to the United States only
to those who were literate "in the English language or the langua
of their native or resident country"; he had the phrase "or in s

other language" deleted. The chief sufferers would have been the Jews, for most of those who were fleeing Russia were literate in Yiddish but not in Russian. The Jewish lobbyist in Washington, Simon Wolf, challenged Lodge; he denied that he had any anti-Jewish intentions, but Wolf did not believe him, then or later. The outcry against the proposed law sent the bill back to the conference committee, and the second session restored the pro-Jewish formula: "or in some other language." President Cleveland nonetheless vetoed the law, because, so he said, he did not believe that the "new immigrants" were an inferior breed.

Lodge's assault on the "Russian Jews" united the "German Jews" in total resistance. Isaac Mayer Wise, who despised Yiddish, nonetheless wrote with contempt of the action Congress was contemplating. The literacy test had almost been accepted by Jewish opinion when it was first proposed, but Lodge's anti-Jewish version convinced the "German Jews," in the language of an editorial in the *Jewish Messenger,* that the "test of illiteracy is an unworthy standard for the American public." Other groups joined the fight. In 1906 the National Liberal Immigration League was formed, including Poles, Italians, and Germans, along with some Protestants from the older America, such as Charles Eliot, the president of Harvard, and Woodrow Wilson, the president of Princeton (who had moved away from his earlier near nativism). Jews were the effective leaders and most active members of this association. The continuing fight for an "open door" was widely understood to be a matchup at the very top between Jews and Boston patrician anti-Semites.

The end of the battle over literacy tests came in February 1917, when Congress overrode President Wilson's veto. The bill that was sustained had exempted from the literacy test those aliens who could prove that they were "seeking admission to the United States to avoid religious persecution—whether such persecution be evidenced by overt acts, or by laws, or governmental regulations." Illiterate Jews from Czarist Russia thus had precedence over illiterate Italians from Sicily. But this "victory" was temporary. The tide had been running toward the limitation of immigration as the older American stock was feeling increasingly threatened. Frightening statistics were being published to prove that a few more years of unrestricted immigration would make the older stock a minority in the land.

In 1911, after years of study, Congress had issued the Dillingham

Report, in forty-two volumes, on the whole question of immigration. The underlying premise of this study was to set up the older America as the preferred America and to cast doubt on the abilities of the new immigration. One of the more seemingly objective attacks was the proposition that the new arrivals were bad for the economy. The American Jewish Committee, which had been organized in 1905 to protect the rights of Jews, commissioned an answer. In 1914, Isaac Hourwich argued, in a book entitled *Immigration and Labor,* that the newer immigrants were adjusting to America and rising in the economy as quickly and as constructively as the older waves of immigration. He denounced the Dillingham Commission for writing "upon the supposition that immigrant races represent separate zoological species." In those very years, Franz Boas, a professor of anthropology at Columbia University who was a "German Jew," was busy measuring hundreds of immigrant crania to prove that there was as much physical room for brains in the skulls of these unwanted newcomers as in the supposedly "better heads" of the Aryans—but, unfortunately, nobody except those who agreed with him before he began his labors paid much attention to these "scientific" results.

So long as Jews were under attack together with Slavs and Italians, they were not the worst off of the three. The decent mainstream of American opinion, which might be prepared to believe bad things about all the new immigrants, was persuaded (as the vote in 1917 proved) that Jews were owed special consideration, because they were the object of persecution. The rise in a very few years of the first group of Jewish immigrants to come to affluence—by the early 1900s, some sixty thousand had moved out of the Lower East Side to the middle-class environs of Brooklyn and Queens—made it hard to doubt that the "Russian Jews" had brains and talent. The continuing, intense concern of the "German Jews" provided the "Russians" with charitable and political protectors of the kind that no other group in America enjoyed.

This era ended in the immediate aftermath of the First World War, after the Russian Revolution. Jews like Leon Trotsky were prominent in the making of that revolution. The "Red Scare" identified the "Russian Jews" in America with the threat of Communism. The continuing fight to restrict immigration was, then, directed at Jews more than at any other group. The "German Jews" still fought beside the recent immigrants and their children, but there was a note of tiredness and even of embarrassment among some. The battle had become primarily that of the "Russians."

The "Russian Jews" would soon stand alone for internal reasons as well. There had been continuing tensions even when the "German Jews" were the undisputed leaders of the community. Only in 1902, after a furious fight, did the United Hebrew Charities in New York admit a very few newly well-to-do immigrants to its board. The leadership of the American Jewish Committee remained entirely in the hands of the "German Jews" until well after the First World War. Socially, in the Reform temples, and especially in the clubs that had been established by the older Jewish settlers, the barriers had remained nearly impenetrable. Some "German Jews" did identify with the "Russians" very personally. In Baltimore, Henrietta Szold taught English to immigrants in the 1890s, and she soon very nearly became one of them. In New York, Judah Leon Magnes, the rabbi of Temple Emanu-El, led in the founding of the Kehillah, the overarching Jewish community organization, and he kept moving ever closer to the East Europeans.

Despite these exceptions, "German Jews" and "Russian Jews" remained separate communities. The "Germans" continued to hope that the "Russians" would follow after them and become, or at least talk as if they had become, "Americans of the Jewish religious persuasion." But this rhetoric was irrelevant to the mass of the "Russian" immigrants and to their children. They were trapped by prejudice, in an essentially narrow enclave in America, and they had to fight their way out. They could not wait to be accepted, first, by the "German Jews" and then by Gentile America. For the children of the ghetto, there was no profit, or balm, in respectability.

12.

The Invention of the Jewish Mother

I

The children of the immigrants had no role models. They resented the traps into which they had been born, and they were angry with the powerless fathers who could not liberate them. They had no choice but to invent themselves, as Jews and as Americans.

The most serious and symbolically most important breaks between the generations occurred at the doors of the synagogue. The young refused to follow their parents to regular prayers in the hundreds of conventicles that the immigrants had established. The religion of the father was destroyed in America, but it was replaced by the religion of the mother. This was the fateful shift in the New Land.

The evidence of the destruction of the role of the father is overwhelming. As is well known, the Lower East Side of New York attracted the attention in the 1890s and early 1900s of some of the most incisive observers of American society, men such as Hutchins Hapgood, Jacob Riis, and Lincoln Steffens. What struck all three with particular force was the break in religion between fathers and sons. Steffens described it in his autobiography as a "tragic struggle." "We would pass a synagogue where a score or more boys were sitting hatless in their old clothes, smoking cigarettes on the steps outside, and their fathers, all dressed in black, with their high hats, uncut beards and temple curls, were going into the synagogue, tearing their hair and rending their garments. . . . Their sons were rebels against the law of Moses; they were lost souls, lost to God, the family, and to Israel of old."

Sholem Asch, one of the most famous of the Yiddish writers, confirmed these observations. He did not settle in America until after the First World War, but in 1910 he paid a visit of five months. Asch found that Jewish parents from the Old World and their Americanized children were more alien to each other than Jews anywhere else in the world. Asch made these points, both directly and with very transparent symbolism, in a short novel called *America 1918*. "In the children there awoke a yearning for unshackled liberty" and "their fathers' piety became a matter of jest." Children made a point of not going to synagogue with their parents on the Sabbath but of running off to football matches: "Father, mother, and son were mourning a home that had been and was no more." The one son who did remain true to the old religious and family traditions died after a few months in America.

The revolt of the young against the inherited religion represented the destruction of the authority of the father within the immigrant family, and not only in the realm of religion. Upon arrival in the United States, fathers accepted upon themselves the burden of making a living for their family, but many failed. In the early 1900s among working-class families, less than one-in-five could support themselves on the father's earnings. The immigrant Jewish family was, if anything, a bit worse off than the average of the working class, both native and immigrant, as a whole. In innumerable families wives and children had to do piecework at home. More often, to make ends meet, children had to take to the streets very early to shine shoes, sell papers, or do anything that might come along. To survive economically, many fathers abandoned the Sabbath and disregarded other traditions. Fathers who could neither protect the family nor hold themselves up as a model of values often felt that they had no choice but to withdraw into themselves in silent despair. That helpless father recurs again and again in the many memoirs that were written by the children of the immigrants.

With the destruction of the father, the "Jewish mother" was invented in America. Contrary to popular mythology, the Jewish-American immigrant mother was not a transplant from Europe; she never existed in the traditional Jewish culture. This figure made her appearance in this time of dislocation, the era of mass migration. The immigrant mother became the source of family loyalty for her children because she was their protector. Her labor helped eke out the family budget and made survival and schooling possible. Her own anger with the schlemiel, the father, helped to feed the rebellion of the children. She raised her sons to achieve for her what her husband had failed to do. But this Jewish mother was not simply a goad to success. She had Jewish purposes of her own. They included, at very least, that the children not intermarry, and that some decent formal respect be paid to the Jewish proprieties, and that they succeed. This was the folk religion of the mothers.

These immigrant mothers brought much less knowledge of the religious traditions to America than even their unlearned husbands. In the nineteenth century the majority of East European Jewish women, certainly among the poor, were illiterate. Nearly half of the women who came to America could not read or write in any language. To be sure, some of the immigrant mothers betrayed their families. One of the staple plots of the Yiddish popular stage was the love affair between the married immigrant woman and one of her "boarders." Men, by the tens of thousands, had come ahead of their families, to accumulate some money so that they could bring their wives and children to join them in America. These "boarders" took rooms with established immigrant families who needed the extra income. Young women were thus in close contact with men away from their wives. Some complications and tragedies ensued, but such love triangles in the home affected only a few, and the children did not always know what was happening. The image of the Jewish mother was barely dented by such incidents.

The shift of children's loyalties from father to mother was not the only strain on the family. The most pervasive problem was desertion. As men arrived, leaving families behind, some simply broke connections with their wives and children in Europe. Many others brought their families over, or got married in America, but ran away when they failed in the task of fending for their wives and children. The Jewish charities in the major cities spent so much money to help deserted wives and children that they united in 1911 to found a National Desertion Bureau. This agency existed into the 1930s, until roughly twenty years after the end of the mass migration. Cumulatively it dealt with a hundred thousand cases. In the majority of the situations, it located the runaways and got them at least to contribute to the support of their families.

In human terms, the National Desertion Bureau made an enormous contribution, but this agency has been the least noticed among all the bodies that served the mass migration. The problem that it addressed is discomforting even in memory. One hundred thousand cases of desertion during the era of the mass migration means that at some point at least one-quarter of the Jewish fathers in America deserted their families, either the ones they had left behind in Europe or the ones they had established in the New World. Because the subject is so painful, there is little oral tradition in American Jewish families about desertion. The proof that it was a serious problem is incontrovertible. The evidence of these traumas is not to be limited solely to the files of the National Desertion Bureau. Rabbinic literature of the first decades of this century, both in Eastern Europe and in the United States, contains a flood of references to the problems of abandoned wives, who were appealing to the rabbis to find ways of freeing them from the bonds of marriage by securing a religious divorce (which could not be issued, in Orthodox Jewish law, without the active consent of the husband).

Contrary to the established cliché, the Jewish family was not largely intact in the time of mass migration. Many Jewish mothers, in fact, raised their children alone. One suspects that the insistent emphasis on the intact Jewish family as part of the explanation of Jewish success is self-serving: it underlines a difference between the Jewish ghettos of the Lower East Side two generations ago and the impoverished African-American ghettos of today, where the majority of families are headed by women. The situation was never that grim among the East European immigrants. Most families were headed by men, but, between desertions and early deaths, a large number, perhaps on the order of one in five or, at the very least, one in six of the immigrant young were raised by their mothers.

Poverty and desertion were not the only assaults on the immigrant family; there was also disease. "Consumption," or tuberculosis, was the great scourge of the workers in sweatshops. The cure in those days was to leave the city for the cleaner and purer air of the mountains. The beginnings of Jewish settlement in the Catskill Mountains near New York were often boardinghouses that were created for sufferers from consumption. The need for such facilities soon spread to the Rocky Mountains, where the National Hospital for Consumptives was established in Denver in the 1890s.

Not all of the immigrants from Eastern Europe remained poor, or ill. Some succeeded with astonishing speed. By the mid-1880s, rich "Russian Jews" were moving to New York's Upper East Side, the very citadel of the "German Jews." As early as 1886, they founded an Orthodox synagogue, Kehilath Jeshurun, in that neighborhood. Recent immigrants were the initial guarantors of the salary of the chief rabbi of the Orthodox community in New York, Rabbi Jacob Joseph, who was brought to the city from Vilno in 1888. Abraham Cahan's *The Rise of David Levinsky* is, in part, about the economic success of such an immigrant. The children of these parents did not have to attend the public colleges. Some simply entered the family business; others were among the first Russian Jews to enter the elite American colleges.

All of the families, rich or poor, were deeply and inevitably divided by the Americanization of their children. The most obvious attacks on the integrity of the family were the dance halls and the street culture, including Jewish gangs. But the educated minority were also very much a problem to their parents. Merit examinations had been instituted in New York in 1901, and Jews immediately began to find their way into the school system. By 1905, Jewish students were already a majority in the City College of New York; they were nearly half of the student body at the Normal School, the teachers' college for women that was the predecessor of Hunter College. The men and women followed different paths. The men were struggling through college in order to make careers in honorific professions; by 1910 Jews were already roughly one-quarter of all the students in American medical schools. Very few of the women were raised with such ambitions. Those who went to college were preparing themselves for secure "feminine" jobs as teachers. In the early years, these were mostly women graduates of the Normal School. Here, too,

Marie Antin's autobiographical writing is most instructive. She tells that parents "in their bewilderment and uncertainty, had to address their children to learn from such models as the tenements afforded. Parents had to take the law from their children's mouths because they had no other means of finding out what was good American form." The result was "an inversion of normal relations" which strained and often broke up the family.

The role models that young Jews could not find at home, they inevitably looked for elsewhere. In the immigrant ghetto itself, the revolutionary movements, socialism and anarchism, offered alternatives to the helpless fathers. There was a role to be had in society for those who were heroic enough to dare to remake the world. Revolutionary ideology was never, not even in its heyday at the turn of the century, as dominant among the immigrants as many observers maintained both then and later. On the contrary, the large majority of the immigrants adhered to the traditional religious forms as best they could, and they worked toward leaving the proletariat as quickly as possible. But socialist and anarchist agitation did play a role in the destruction of the Jewish father, of nullifying whatever authority he might have brought with him from Europe, and of replacing him. The revolution demanded new role models. A new society could best be made by the young; a new dispensation required defiance of fathers rather than deference to whatever authority they might still represent.

In reading the writings of antireligious Jews of the 1890s and of the early 1900s, one is impressed by their sense of themselves as being part of a worldwide battle to release men from the bonds of the past. These atheists and anarchists thought of themselves as doing among Jews what leading American agnostics such as Robert Ingersoll and, soon, Clarence Darrow, were doing among Christians. Left-wing Jews regarded all eight of the Haymarket martyrs in Chicago, the four who were hanged, the one suicide, and the three who went to jail in 1886 for the throwing of a bomb during a strike rally which killed policemen, as heroes to be revered. These revolutionary immigrants were imparting freedom to their children—not the freedom to open a shoe store, but the hope of making in America the revolution that had not yet happened in Russia—and which seemed hopeless before it did happen in 1917.

Almost all of the earliest Yiddish poets and novelists were socialists or anarchists who wrote from the sweatshops. Such writing was usually lurid, but it did reflect, in a heightened, declamatory way, the lives of its readers. One of the favorite themes was the oppression of the workers by the Jewish bosses. This class struggle within the ghetto was understood, as a matter of course, to reflect the inequities of capitalist society as a whole. Hope was to be found only in the possibility that an end would be made of capitalism. The immigrants knew that they could not make the revolution because they were too foreign. They could not lead in America, but their "American" children were sworn to the task.

Morris Rosenfeld, the first of these proletarian poets to be translated into English, railed at the meaninglessness of a life spent tending and feeding the sewing machine. The message was clear: there had to be a world that was better than this oppression. The novelists took this theme of social protest further. Leon Kobrin was perhaps the most prolific of all the Yiddish writers in America. In one of his stories, entitled "A Common Language," which was written in the 1920s, the hero is a night watchman who catches a thief and begins to beat him. "Suddenly it struck me. Maybe he had no home for himself and his child? Who knows what kind of place this Ameritchke is? Maybe that's why he went out to steal on a night like this? Maybe he had done it for the sake of his child." The thief was an Italian. "We talked, he in his language, and I in mine." In the end, the hero gets fired for helping the thief.

Moshe Nadir was much more self-consciously political. It was inevitably so, for he wrote for the Yiddish Communist daily, the *Morgen Freiheit*. In one of his stories from the 1920s, Nadir told about a workers' strike. The story, entitled "Thoughts About Forty Cents," was written, ironically, from the perspective of a capitalist. "With the fish course my wife also served me a bit of news about a town called Roosevelt where they had shot into a crowd of strikers without any rhyme or reason. I felt my blood begin to boil." As Nadir's capitalist "hero" eats on, through the various courses of a sumptuous meal, his sympathies gradually shift against the workers and toward the employers. He lights up a Havana cigar and makes himself comfortable in an easy chair. "And at this point I saw how trivial those workers are, to risk their necks for a measly forty cents a day." Even in the writings of the socialist novelists, the workers failed more than they succeeded.

But the socialist novelists and essayists wanted the immigrants to fight back. Revolutionary consciousness meant that Jews should not be passive as they had been throughout the centuries in Europe. They should stand up against the bosses for the rights of labor, as the workers had done in Nadir's story, but above all, Jews were enjoined not to cower before anti-Semites, as they had in Europe, but to confront their tormentors. In one of the numerous stories that revolve around this theme, Joseph Opatashu described the ambivalent response of Jews to anti-Semitism in America: they tried to ignore it, to pretend that it was not there, until on occasion the provocation became too great to be avoided. In "How the Fight Began," a gang of children is teasing an old Jewish peddler, and only one young Jew among the onlookers has the courage to get up to defend him. "The few Jews in the car buried their heads deeper in their newspapers, looking up nervously at the scene, trembling in fear and angry agitation. But fear was strong enough to keep them frozen in their places." Then this gang of young hooligans began to tease a young Jewish woman. At that point, "the Jews behind their newspapers threw them away and clenched their fists, and that is how the fight began." America, the "golden land," was thus an arena of struggle, of pain, and even of defeat. In the sweatshops the bosses were "bloodsuckers," and on the streets the Jew-haters were always mocking and harassing "kikes" and "sheenies." The passivity of the immigrant fathers was irrelevant, or worse, in the New Land. Their children had to find their own courage to fight back, and, in fighting back, they taught at least a few of the fathers to be "Americans."

II

Riis, Steffens, and Asch had observed that the children belonged much more to the culture of the streets than to that of their families. David Nasaw, in his book *Children of the City*, has recently confirmed Riis's contemporary accounts: "The early twentieth-century city was a city of strangers. Most of its inhabitants had been born or raised elsewhere. Only the children were native to the city—with no memory, no longing, no historic commitment to another land, another way of life. . . . Work, money, and the fun that money bought were located on the streets of the city."

The streets have never taught immigrants to America primary lessons in virtue. On the contrary, some of those who were raised on the streets, without strong role models at home, have turned, generation after generation in America, to crime. Young Jews, children of immigrants, followed the pattern. Almost always, except perhaps in Puritan New England, crime has been a major avenue for quick material success in America. There has usually been no generational succession in crime, for western gunslingers who consistently outdrew their enemies sometimes ended their careers as sheriffs, and some of their children became governors. Jews were not exempt from this rule. In the era of the mass migration, the Irish had at first dominated the criminal scene in the big cities. So it was with the Jews. Large-scale prostitution had not existed in pre-emancipation Jewry, though there were, of course, many individual examples of sexual misconduct. In the late nineteenth century, with Jews moving into the big cities of Eastern Europe, and away from the constraints of their native smaller towns and villages, prostitution began to appear in Europe. There was Jewish prostitution in Warsaw and in Odessa. In Moscow and St. Petersburg there was both real prostitution as a trade and the pretense of it: some respectable Jewish women accepted internal passports as prostitutes, because that "trade" was one of those which conferred special permission on Jews to reside in areas from which they were excluded.

But Jewish prostitution, and several other kinds of crime, were prevalent in the New World. At least one-third, perhaps half, of the known prostitutes of New York, then, in the early 1900s, were Jews. The French, Irish, Germans, and Italians were next in order, but the Jewish proportion seems very nearly to have equaled the total number of all the rest put together. The explanation for this anomaly is probably to be found in a demographic fact; unlike all the rest, Jewish immigrants were coming to the half-dozen largest cities, led by New York, where perhaps seventy percent of these immigrants were settling. Big cities are the locus of crime, as small villages, towns, and farms, where many of the other ethnics were settling, are not. The most striking aspect of these statistics is that more of the Jewish prostitutes seem to have been native than foreign-born. The native-born seem to have had the initial skills of language, at-homeness, and streetwiseness, which their parents, as immigrant newcomers, did not have.

How much crime was there really on the Lower East Side of New York? This was a painful issue in the years of mass migration, and it has been debated since by historians. In September 1908, the police commissioner of New York, Theodore A. Bingham, published an article in *Harper's,* under the title "Foreign Criminals in New York." Bingham argued that in New York, the Jews and the Italians, two of the largest communities, were the source of numerous gangs and that these "criminal organizations" needed to be watched by specially trained police details. He went on to say that with a million Jews now in New York, perhaps a quarter of the population, "it is not astonishing that half the criminals should be of that race." He attributed this supposed propensity to crime to the foreignness of those Jews, and he went on to assert that "Jewish criminals tend not to attack people but rather to commit crimes against property." He was particularly sulfuric about Jewish juveniles under sixteen: he asserted that they were especially prominent among the offenders.

This article aroused a storm. The Jews of the Lower East Side reacted to it as a portent of American anti-Semitism, parallel to the kind that they had been experiencing in Europe. They protested with fury. The leadership of the older Jewish settlers, including Jacob Schiff, who was by then the universally acknowledged "king of the Jews," joined the outcry against the assertion that Jews were the main source of criminality in New York. In a few days, Bingham withdrew the remarks "without reservation," but the question remained alive. At the time Bingham spoke, he was probably telling the truth. There was quite a large amount of petty juvenile crime, such as stealing from pushcarts and picking pockets, but the overwhelming bulk of the young people who engaged in such endeavors did not graduate into careers in crime. The young Eddie Cantor, who was later to become a famous entertainer, was a leading member in a gang called, of all things, "Pork-faced Sams." One of the principal tricks of this group was to steal from stores and then sell the owners their own stock.

Gambling was a pervasive Lower East Side recreation. The numerous regular games in homes or other gathering places were largely innocent, but the ghetto did breed professional gamblers. The flashiest of New York's big-time gamblers, Arnold Rothstein, had been born in Philadelphia in 1892 to a respectable, pious family of Jewish immigrants from Eastern Europe. Rothstein could have followed after his father, and become a moderately successful businessman, but he chose instead to be a high roller and casino gambler. Rothstein bribed police officers and judges, he helped support the Tammany machine, and he hobnobbed with the titans of American industry, if only to gamble with them in his own establishment. One famous night, Percival H. Hill, the head of the American Tobacco Company, lost a quarter of a million dollars to Rothstein. This was not the only occasion when the upstart gambler took the leaders of American industry to the cleaners. For that matter, Rothstein was also a famous pool player, and he became even more of a "name" when he defeated a professional from Philadelphia in a game which lasted thirty-four hours. The most famous sports scandal in American history, fixing the World Series of baseball in 1919, was a gamblers' coup engineered by Arnold Rothstein. He arranged to bribe a number of key players on the Chicago White Sox to throw the series. This "feat" earned Rothstein a fortune in bets. In his personal habits, Rothstein had learned from his big-business clients to act the swell. No less an authority than Lucky Luciano, one of the leading criminals of the 1920s and 1930s, paid Rothstein a tribute in his memoirs. Luciano reported that Rothstein had taught him "how to dress, how not to wear loud things, and how to have good taste."

Is is even true, contrary to Jewish apologists then and later, that the immigrants were indulgent to certain kinds of crime. Violence was universally deplored, but clever fraud was for some a way of survival. A little arson to collect insurance was acknowledged as something which occurred with some frequency; the perpetrators were not universally condemned by the community. A contemporary joke told of a petty businessman who had committed arson several times. When he could no longer get fire insurance, he turned inquiringly to one of his friends and asked, "How do you make a flood?" Arson got to be so much of a nuisance and danger that in the early 1890s eighteen of New York's worst arsonists were sent to jail, some for life. The attitude among the immigrants toward such crimes was rooted in centuries of Jewish experience in the Diaspora. The law had always been the enemy of the Jews; to circumvent it was often the only way to survive, and, therefore, to outfox authority was a praiseworthy act. Such an attitude was, of course, to be found among other immigrant groups. Poor peasants everywhere had survived through the centuries by poaching on the estates of the rich.

Criminality was not limited to New York's Lower East Side. There were comparable, though smaller, groups of offenders in Chicago and in Philadelphia, as well as in Cleveland, Boston, Detroit, and Newark. Surprisingly, Minneapolis, which had a comparatively small Jewish community, produced an outsize number of youth gangs and criminals. There may have been as much crime in New York as Bingham had charged, but something was happening that he could not predict: crime was a half-generation occupation for almost all of the young who engaged in it. It created no model for the next generation.

The more socially respectable avenue to quick fame and fortune was sports. The Jewish immigrants had no tradition in sports activities. In Europe, sports had belonged to the Gentiles, and even among them, not to the poor. The children of the immigrants, however, became almost immediately avid participants in sports, especially in those that required little space and equipment, both of which were in short supply in the Lower East Side. The sports in which Jews excelled early were those in which the individual engaged in a kind of "free enterprise," and which might lead quickly to large rewards. Thus, there were no Jewish tennis players or golfers, for these sports were, then, entirely amateur. Those sports were doubly alien to the children of the immigrants because they required courts, or many acres of ground, and this much room could not be found among the tenements. Tennis and golf would later be picked up avidly by many of these second-generation immigrants as one of the marks of their arrival in America.

Despite the strong and ingrained religious tradition against doing physical harm to others, many of the young in the ghetto took to boxing. Training space was minimal: all that was needed was a ring and a place for a punching bag. Such room could be made in any decrepit building. For at least two decades, the Lower East Side was the breeding ground of great Jewish fighters, such as Abe Attell, Benny Leonard, Ruby Goldstein, and Barney Ross, all of whom were children of immigrants. At one point in the 1920s, seven of the nine boxing championships were held by Jews. The striking exception was the heavyweight championship, simply because the Jews did not produce many physical specimens in that weight range. Even so, one of the leading champions of the 1930s, Max Baer, pretended to be a Jew, because Jews were so prominent among the fight fans.

It was an advantage for a fighter like Baer to say that he belonged to "this well-known line of Jewish champions and hopes."

Sports are very often on the border of criminality, because they have always been the object of betting and of fixing. Entertainment was on a higher level of legitimacy, but, like crime and sports, it, too, offered the possibility of success in one's own lifetime. To be sure, there had been a tradition of entertainment in Eastern Europe. Klezmer musicians had performed, especially at weddings, and there was usually a *Badchen,* a composer of impromptu verses, who both praised and mocked the assemblage. These are, perhaps, the cultural ancestors of America's Jewish music-makers and stand-up comedians. The immediate models for the young Jews who tried to sing and dance their ways to fortune were the Irish entertainers, who dominated the vaudeville stages at the turn of the century. The great wave of Jewish immigration came when the main forms of entertainment were theater and vaudeville. Live entertainment was a mass industry, which the older Protestant America had left to the Irish. Jews moved very rapidly into vaudeville. The new Jewish entertainers even brought with them a new audience, their contemporaries from the Jewish ghetto. "Pat and Mike," who made jokes about the rubes and the camaraderie between Jews and Irish, became a favorite team on the circuit. At the turn of the century, "Jewish" figures were widely expected to be part of every program on the vaudeville stage.

Some of the song and dance men and women and the comedians became stars. There is no way of estimating the proportion of Jews among the performers on the vaudeville circuit after the turn of the century. We do know, however, that by around 1910 something on the order of sixty percent of vaudeville houses in the ten largest cities were owned by Jews. Most of these owners were not new immigrants. They descended from the older "German Jews," who had come to the United States before or immediately after the Civil War. But these older Jewish settlers held no monopoly. Soon, by 1900, such people as the Balabans, more recent immigrants who had begun as children of the ghetto, had made their way into this expanding business.

Jews were much more important in the newest entertainment enterprise, the movies. At the beginnings of the movie industry, Jews did not figure as actors or directors. Hollywood was then producing pictures that supposedly mirrored the mainstream of American life. Authentic American was, then, white and Protestant. It took very nearly a generation for Jewish actors and directors to play a role of significance in Hollywood, and, even then, the vast majority of these figures anglicized their names and their total demeanor. Even Paul Muni, who was the superstar among the serious actors in the early days of talking pictures, worked hard not to mention that he had come to Hollywood from the Yiddish stage on Second Avenue in New York.

During the earliest years of Hollywood, Jews rapidly became the large majority of the entrepreneurs. The business of moviemaking was dominated by such men as Louis B. Mayer, Samuel Goldwyn, Adolph Zukor, David O. Selznick, Harry Cohn, the Fox Brothers and the Warner Brothers—to mention only the most prominent. They built the major studios, and they presided over Hollywood at its most flamboyant. What these men put on the screen was very smoothly American, but what they spoke among themselves was an English accented by the Yiddish that had been the first language for most of them, including those who had been born in America.

At the inception of the movie industry, it was Jewish entrepreneurs more than anybody else who seized the opportunities of the new invention and took the risks. Some became glitteringly wealthy, if only for a while. These men were themselves the incarnation of the very Horatio Alger myth which Hollywood often celebrated. Yet, even as they told the story of poor farm children rising from the log cabin to the presidency, or to a Fifth Avenue mansion, they were not yet ready to tell their own story, of rising from the streets of the ghetto to sit beside the swimming pools of Beverly Hills. Some of these men failed, or they destroyed each other. Ultimately, all of the major studios would be controlled, directly or indirectly, by the bankers who provided them with capital. The story of the rise and fall of the Hollywood moguls would eventually be told by some of their children in memoirs or in novels, often with bitterness, as the recurrent tale of unslakable hunger for success.

Recently, the early days of Hollywood have been examined again, with new respect for the astonishing creativity of those who invented the first and still dominant form of worldwide mass entertainment. There is even increasing reference to the yearning of some of the Hollywood moguls for artistic respectability. From Jewish perspectives the movies have been seen as another example of how the Jews, when society was intent on excluding them from established businesses, found their way into the American economy. Jews had to take the risks of beginning new pursuits. The movies were exempt from the endemic anti-Semitism which kept Jews out of white-collar jobs in the banks, the insurance companies, the railroads, steel making and coal mining.

What did the entry of many of these children into largely unprecedented pursuits mean for the shaping of American Jewish experience? The point has already been made that religiously traditional lives were inconceivable in any of these endeavors, even though there is an account of at least one Jewish gangster from Cleveland who wore a skullcap at all times, and who was totally observant of Jewish rituals, as he plied his violent trade as "enforcer." This interesting gangster may have had a parallel or two among Jewish entertainers or Hollywood moguls, but, altogether, such "orthodox" Jews were the merest handful. Those who ventured out farthest from the immigrant ghetto, to Hollywood or into the boxing ring, had to invent a new persona for themselves. There were no models in the Jewish past for the behavior of fighters, gangsters, or movie moguls. All of these new Jews (so they have told in their many autobiographies) had ineffectual fathers; they were their own ancestors.

They also imagined America, for they did not know it. The movie czars, the entertainers, the boxers, and the criminals were usually school dropouts. These were the people who had taken to the streets rather than finish high school and go on to college. They had thus not been reached by American middle-class norms, which the schools imparted. Some of them rose to finance movies about the American gentility they had never encountered. They imagined an America that never was, and hoped that this mythic America would accept them.

III

F. Scott Fitzgerald's famous novel of the 1920s, *The Great Gatsby*, considers this problem. The hero of the novel is supposed to have been fashioned after Arnold Rothstein. In Fitzgerald's story, the Rothstein figure is called Jay Gatsby. He came to Long Island, a precinct of established American society, to win acceptance through his wealth and his manners. Gatsby failed, for, in a moment of crisis, he was brutally reminded that he remained an outsider. The story of Gatsby is thus the tale of an assimilationist who has abandoned his past and who has nothing left to live for when he is rejected. This may have been true of Arnold Rothstein, that he wanted to be accepted by the swells whom he aped, and from whom he won money gambling, but it is not likely. No matter what his surface manners might have been, Rothstein, the gambler, was twice an outsider, and his gambling coups had about them an air of defiance and a suggestion that the America which was fascinated by him, and held him in contempt, was not as righteous as it pretended: the titans of industry came to his casino, and baseball idols were for sale. One cannot know whether Rothstein harbored within himself some Jewish "island within" of defiance and pride, but it is possible. Such feelings were present in most of his generation, even among those who tried to assimilate.

Jewish pride—and guilt—were imparted by almost all of the Jewish mothers, and not only by them. In theory, socialism was a universalist ideology which taught the abandonment of all ethnic distinctions, but most of the spokesmen of socialism among the Jewish immigrants insisted on the importance of maintaining Jewish group feeling, and even of holding onto some respect for the religious heritage. There are many exchanges on the subject of Jewish continuity in the famous letter-column, the "bintel brief," of the *Jewish Daily Forward*. A son of unbelieving parents discovered that his parents, who had always treated even the Day of Atonement as just another day, were upset that he wanted to marry a non-Jewish young woman. He wrote to the *Forward* on the presumption that he would find sympathy and support, only to discover that the socialist and freethinking editors of the paper insisted, with the same seeming illogic that the letter-writer attributed to his parents, that it was imperative that he marry a Jew and that he continue to identify with the Jewish community. This was no isolated exchange, for the *Forward* took a comparable attitude even in its earliest years, when it was most ideologically socialist and secularist. In response to numerous questions about proper behavior for secular nonbelievers, in order not to offend the sensitivities of the vast mass of Jews on Yom Kippur, the *Forward* insisted that nonbelievers should be enormously discreet in their refusal to fast and to attend synagogue on that day.

The editors of the *Forward* did not doubt that the children of the immigrants would move from Yiddish to English as their primary language; they actively encouraged such Americanization. This newspaper preached to the largely Jewish labor unions and to the Jewish socialists (most of whom were organized into a party of their own, apart from the main body of American socialists) that they were not a separate enclave; they were part of all the forces that were fighting for a just society. And yet, those who read the *Forward* knew that the commitment of Jews to remain Jewish was beyond question and discussion.

Even the pleasures that Jews enjoyed in the immigrant ghetto helped maintain some feeling of continuity between the generations. In the 1880s, near the very beginnings of the mass migration, Jacob Riis reported that "the young people in Jewtown are inordinately fond of dancing." By 1900, when the Jewish population of the Lower East Side was some four hundred thousand, there were so many dance halls in the neighborhood that one or two of them could be found on every block. These were frequented by the young. The parents objected, at very least because spending time and money on such endeavors was regarded as wasteful. But all the objections were of little avail. A rage was exploding in America, among the immigrants themselves and especially among their children, for whatever pleasures could be enjoyed in the present. This passion emerged from a desire that had been pent up among the European Jewish poor for many generations; they had been double barred for centuries from "this world," both as poor people and as Jews. Now, in America, the passion for enjoyment had at last found the opportunity to express itself, because here no one was limited to making do with devotion to the spirit. In the dance halls, the young sought to learn how to enjoy pleasure in an "American" way, but they were moved by a hunger for this world that they shared with their parents.

The men and women of the older generation expressed this desire, in part, through their passion for the Yiddish stage, and especially for those sentimental productions, such as plays about the sweatshops or about the clashes between parents and their "Yankee" children, that mirrored their own lives. The big occasions, not only in New York but also in Chicago, Philadelphia, and Boston, were Friday nights and Saturday matinees, when such performances were being held in contravention of the religious injunctions which prescribed the observance of the Sabbath. In the synagogues, the immigrant years before 1914 were the high point of the era of the virtuoso cantors; tickets were sold for the services that they conducted. Those who mobbed such services by superstar cantors, such as Yossele Rosenblatt and Zanvel Kwartin, came to pray, and to be entertained and moved by the talents of these men, who were called "sweet singers of Zion." Giant ads appeared in the Yiddish press inviting people to buy tickets for the services that these cantors conducted. There were often policemen at the doors of the synagogue to make sure that those without tickets were not admitted.

The parents who went to the Yiddish theaters or to the synagogues, and the children who went to dance halls and Broadway shows, did meet in the catering establishments. Weddings, bar mitzvahs, and other family occasions were celebrated with ever greater elaboration. In his memoirs, Dore Schary, of movie fame, tells of his parents' catering business, which opened in the Jewish ghetto in Newark just before the outbreak of the First World War. Schary Manor was a roaring, stormy success from the very beginning. Jewish families flocked to it for their sons' bar mitzvahs, their daughters' weddings, their own anniversaries, or for charity banquets. Business grew so that within a few months, the Manor had to be moved to a large mansion.

Schary's grandfather was a Jew of the old school, and the move away from the older life began when the grandfather died. Schary's father lived an "American" life: "Papa believed in full and generous living. His wardrobe was huge and chosen with great taste. Though he didn't drink and smoked few cigars, he was an avid and reckless pinochle player and a ravenous eater. He was courteous and particularly gallant to women, who were as attracted to him as he to them. On those holidays or for family celebrations when he took us to New York, he arranged for orchestra seats in the theater and the best table at Delmonico's or Lorber's, ordered the finest food and champagne, and tipped the waiters lavishly."

Jews who had had little to eat in Europe had thus created the caterers' culture with its outstanding characteristic of eating too much at every family occasion. The stuffed derma, the knishes, and the "sweet tables" became the assurance that the world was now different. In the language of Yiddish theater ditties of that era, "stuffed geese is no longer a delicacy for the rich; in the golden land everyone can enjoy this dish." Overeating was the revenge, and the apotheosis, of the poor. Among heaping platters of Jewish foods (some of which had never existed in Europe), two or even three generations of post-immigrant Jews could meet on a mutual ground of feeding their bodies, and thus giving assurance to their souls. Here a view of America was asserted that both generations held in common: in the old country poor Jews could only dream of joy in the world to come; the New Land was the place in which the Jew could attain pleasure in this world.

These pleasures of the catering halls could not be divorced entirely from the synagogue. To be sure, political radicals and secularists of several varieties avoided religion and devised forms of their own for celebrating marriages and conducting funerals, but this was not the practice of the overwhelming majority of the immigrants and their children. On the great occasions in the personal lives of individuals, and of families, even the children whom Jacob Riis had seen sitting on the steps defiantly smoking cigarettes on Sabbath morning were in the congregation. The young came with their parents to worship services on the High Holy Days, they attended the Passover Seder at the family table, they were married by Jewish clergy, and they observed the rituals of mourning as prescribed by the tradition. These rituals were practiced out of family feeling. The Jewish God was not entirely absent, for those who observed this regimen felt that they were giving Him the minimum that He was due. Even those who had no faith were in synagogue to appease the father, to be less guilty toward the mother for having inflicted the pain of abandoning her for the wider world, and to demonstrate how far the child of the ghetto had gone in conquering America.

All of these themes came together in the famous first talking picture, *The Jazz Singer*. It was produced in 1927 and premiered in New York in February 1928. Al Jolson, the best-known Jewish entertainer of the day, played the son of a cantor who abandoned his father's calling to sing on the American stage. The theme of *The Jazz Singer*, the pain of loss, and of longing for the Jewish certainties of childhood, had been a major subject of American Jewish writers in the three languages—Yiddish, English, and Hebrew—in which they wrote. And yet, the appearance of *The Jazz Singer* marked a turning point in American Jewish life. For the first time, the Jews who dominated

Hollywood came out of the closet as Jews. This self-revelation of the children of the immigrants was possible because 1928 was the high point of the economic "boom." Jews were well-off: they were, at that moment, less afraid of anti-Semites than ever before, or than they were to be again in two years, after the Crash.

Al Jolson was, himself, the son of a cantor in Washington, D.C. Like the hero of the movie, Jolson had begun as a performer by singing in a synagogue choir, but he had reached the height of his stage career as a minstrel, singing "Mammy" in blackface. Suddenly, in 1928, Al Jolson told the essence of his Jewish autobiography on the screen for all America to see. Being Jewish, especially as it expressed itself in the inner torment of what was lost when the Jewish past was forgotten, had become a subject that could be discussed in front of Gentile America. In the movie the son of the cantor returns home from his "American" life, at least for the Day of Atonement, to replace his dying father in the synagogue, while the mother looks on with tearful blessing from the ladies' gallery. The mother approved of the son, as the father could not, both because he had succeeded in America, and because he returned home for the Day of Atonement. The silent, weeping mother in the ladies' gallery is thus archetypal: it is her Jewishness that *The Jazz Singer* represented.

In 1928, the very year in which *The Jazz Singer* was being screened all over America, Ludwig Lewisohn, who was then one of the best-known figures in American letters, published a call to return to Jewish identity under the title *The Island Within*. Lewisohn was not an East European, for he came of German Jewish stock. As a young man in the early years of the twentieth century, Lewisohn had made a career as the most important interpreter in America of modern German literature. He was involved in political and social causes, and he even served for a short while after the First World War as literary editor of *The Nation,* which was then the most important liberal journal in the United States. In midlife, Lewisohn suddenly returned to Jewishness. *The Island Within* was a plea for the return of the Jew from the inhospitable Gentile world to the inner life of the Jewish community (the hero was, like Lewisohn himself, unhappily intermarried). In a few years the result of Lewisohn's own turning was that he became a Zionist and that he grew ever closer to East European culture in Yiddish. Lewisohn soon became an editor of Zionist journals, and he kept attacking the Jews among the Marxist and Freudian intelligentsia for their alienation from Jewishness. But Lewisohn's career was of concern only to small coteries, even among Jews. The assimilating Jewish intelligentsia, whom he attacked, essentially ignored him, and the organized Jewish community which became his home was, to use his own term, an "island within." It was then a private preserve in which some Jews asked and debated questions about themselves, in substantial isolation from all of America.

By their very nature, intellectuals and ideologues leave a paper trail, for a large part of their trade is to write. The documentary record of the immigrant generation is full of the writings of socialists, anarchists, and of an infinite variety of other movements and cliques. The mass and the passion of this writing have seduced some historians of the immigrant past into believing that new ideologies dominated the ghetto, and that the bulk of the children of the immigrants were raised in left-wing, secularist, Yiddish-speaking families. Some were, but most were not. *The Jazz Singer* offers a much truer picture of the mainstream. The Jewish masses were to be found in the congregation of the old cantor, the father of the "jazz singer." The young Jews who attended sometimes wished that they had other options. Some were proud of what they had made of themselves in America. Whatever their inner feelings about their Jewishness, most knew that they could be neither "German Jews" nor Gentiles. The children of the immigrants had only one option, to be exactly that, children of the Jewish ghetto in the New World. They could make their way into America only by force, by acquiring power.

13.

The Russians Defeat the Germans

I

Between 1914 and 1918 the "German Jews" lost control of American Jewry. The "Russian Jews" rebelled, and won, in the name of Zionism. This fight involved the most serious of all issues: how should Jews behave before the eyes of the American majority? Did they have to play the game by some supposedly "American" rules? Did they always have to appeal to the majority in the name of "freedom and justice for all" like the "German Jews"? Did they have to agitate for the freeing of Jews from the sweatshops in the name of the universal rights of labor? Or could they press, forthrightly and avowedly, for the Jewish interest?

Before 1914, the Zionists were a negligible force in America. When war broke out, the Zionists persuaded Louis Dembitz Brandeis to place himself at their head, and thus a new chapter began in the history of American Jewry. Brandeis, a famous lawyer and a friend of President Wilson, gave Zionists instant respectability. Under his leadership, Zionism was transformed from a movement of small, overwhelmingly "Russian" immigrant groups, who were not even on the margin of American politics, into a viable public force.

On the surface Brandeis was a strange kind of leader for the Zionists. Born in Louisville, Kentucky, in 1856 to recent immigrants from Bohemia, who were not much involved in Jewish life, Brandeis had a brilliant career at Harvard Law School, and by the late 1880s had become a successful Boston lawyer. True, many of his initial clients were "German Jews" to whose social set he inevitably belonged, but he was even more peripheral to the Jewish community than the most assimilated among them. There was some memory in his family of its origins in Prague in a circle that still harbored loyalty to the memory of Jacob Frank, the false messiah who had appeared in Poland in the latter half of the eighteenth century. Brandeis's mother was very opposed to Jewish particularism. In his earliest Boston years, he was to be found, at least once, on the list of contributors to the First Unitarian Church. On the other hand, he had been deeply influenced in his earliest years by an uncle, Louis Dembitz (whose family name he adopted as his own middle name), a learned, Orthodox Jew.

After 1900 Brandeis began to get involved somewhat tentatively in Jewish affairs. The turning point came in 1910, when a bitter garment workers strike, involving both Jewish workers and Jewish employers, was being fought out in New York. Brandeis was known as a leading Progressive, and as an eminent lawyer who had represented capitalists. He was approached to help resolve the conflict. Brandeis succeeded in negotiating an agreement that was a first in labor/management relations in America. The workers and the bosses signed a contract to standardize working conditions throughout the industry, and they agreed to refer all disputes to binding arbitration.

Brandeis was transformed by this encounter. He had come to know the recent immigrants, and he "was impressed, deeply impressed, that these Jews with whom I dealt showed in a striking degree·the qualities which, to my mind, make for the best American citizenship, that within them there was a true democratic feeling and a deep appreciation of the elements of social justice." Brandeis was particularly moved by the fact that even the employers were not totally obdurate, "that each side had a great capacity for placing themselves in the other fellow's shoes . . . That set these people apart in my experience in labor disputes."

At the same time, Brandeis started to become alienated politically from the bulk of the "German" Jews; they were overwhelmingly conservative in their politics, and he was an ever more passionately convinced Progressive. As he was settling the garment workers' strike, Brandeis began to believe that the East Europeans were better Americans than the impeccably "American" Jewish bourgeoisie into which he had been born. These new and, on the surface, very foreign immigrants represented "the age-old ideals of the Jews," which were identical with "the twentieth century ideals of America."

In 1913 Brandeis surprised everyone, including his own family, by joining the Zionist movement. There was some evidence that he found in Zionism a way of expressing his own alienation, and even anger, with the German Jewish leaders. That year he had all the more reason to be angry. Brandeis had worked very hard in the election campaign of Woodrow Wilson. The president-elect was known to be contemplating appointing Brandeis to the cabinet as secretary of the interior. Jacob Schiff, the acknowledged leader of the "German Jews," was rumored to have informed Wilson that the leadership of American Jewry did not regard Brandeis as a representative Jew. Schiff supposedly even hinted that such an appointment would cause trouble, because of Brandeis's supposedly pronounced "leftist" views, and that the possible fallout in anti-Semitism would be an unwarranted and unnecessary problem for American Jews.

There is no proof beyond rumor that such representations were made, but the leading figures among the "German Jews" were known to hold such views. The overt opposition to Brandeis's being offered a cabinet post at the beginning of the Wilson administration came from the Democratic party establishment, which vetoed him as a Progressive and a radical. Brandeis did not react to this defeat by becoming angry with Woodrow Wilson, who had made the decision to exclude him. Brandeis was in and out of the White House within days of the beginning of the new administration. It is, however, not entirely fanciful to suppose that he displaced his anger at the defeat in 1912 on those to whom Wilson had listened, and especially the Jews among them. To lead the East European immigrant masses against the German Jewish classes was a conceivable counterattack.

The private representations against Brandeis in 1913 had not been the first time that the Jewish establishment had sided against him. In 1906, when the "German Jews" had organized the American Jewish Committee, Cyrus Adler had suggested Brandeis's name as a founding member, but the nomination was rejected. This internal rift became public in 1916 when President Wilson nominated Brandeis to the Supreme Court. Brandeis was the first Jew to be named to the high tribunal. His enemies saw in Brandeis a radical, a role model of disrespect for authority, and subversion of established order. Brandeis knew very well why his opponents hated him. Writing in the third person during the battle, he said, "The dominant reasons for the opposition to the confirmation of Mr. Brandeis are that he is considered a radical and is a Jew."

Jacob Schiff and Louis Marshall did not dislike Brandeis because he was a Jew, though they kept complaining to both Jews and Gentiles that Brandeis had been a marginal, uninvolved Jew until he turned Zionist. The clear implication was that such a Jew should not be usurping leadership from them, the legitimate leaders of "Americans of the Jewish faith." Schiff and Marshall privately asked President Wilson to withdraw the nomination. As the controversy heated up, they remained silent in public. They did not testify against Brandeis in the confirmation hearings or send negative letters to the Senate committee. Nonetheless, the opinions of this circle were expressed for all to read in a May 26, 1916, editorial in *The New York Times*. The editorial reflected the views of its German Jewish publisher, Adolph Ochs: "Mr. Brandeis is essentially a contender, a striver after changes and reforms. The Supreme Court by its very nature is the conservator of our institutions." There were "German Jews," such as Henry Morgenthau, Sr., who were Democrats and supporters of Brandeis, but the establishment had made its view clear. It wanted to be perceived as completely "American," and it was distancing itself from Jews who were shaking up past custom and privilege. In the mind of America, and not only of anti-Semites, Brandeis was cementing the identification of Jews with "radicalism." The line of cleavage had been reached in American politics, between the "German Jews" and the leader of the "Russians."

The bitter, public, Gentile opposition to his nomination came from Boston. Brandeis was not some decorous, conservative lawyer who had supported the privileged classes in return for their approval. Though he had been no consistent white knight—he had taken cases in which he defended corporations against their workers—Brandeis had risen to national fame in fighting for restrictions on child labor, in battling for civil service reform, and by befriending the unions. He had fought against the New Haven Railroad, in which many Boston patricians had stakes. The president of Harvard, A. Lawrence Lowell, circulated a petition against Brandeis, and a large number of Brahmins signed with him. On the other hand, the president emeritus of Harvard, Charles Eliot, wrote the Senate committee in favor of Brandeis, and so did nine of the eleven professors at the Harvard Law School. A. A. Berle, who was then serving as a Congregationalist minister in Boston, offered the best and oft-quoted summary of the attitude of the enemies of Brandeis:

> Long and unchallenged control of everything in the Commonwealth has given many of these gentlemen the perfectly natural feeling that whoever is not approved by them is ipso facto a person who is either "dangerous" or lacking in "judicial temperament" . . . They simply cannot realize, and do not, that a long New England ancestry is not prima facie a trusteeship for everything in New England. That is in my judgement the real spring of most of the opposition.

Hillel Rogoff said the same that spring in the *Zukunft,* the monthly of the Jewish socialists: Brandeis was opposed by those who refused to accept that a Jew who wanted to change society belonged in that ultimate temple of America, the Supreme Court. Seats on that bench were reserved, so they insisted, for people like themselves. Walter Lippmann, defending and supporting Brandeis, expressed this opinion in *The New Republic:* Brandeis was feared and distrusted only by "the powerful but limited community that dominated the business and social life of Boston. He was untrustworthy because he was troublesome." The Brahmins of Boston had thus split in public over Brandeis's nomination. President Lowell of Harvard wanted only respectable Jews, and not too many of them, on America's public premises. Ex-President Eliot saw America, past and present, as constantly refreshing itself from new, even sometimes untamed, energies.

On June 1, 1916, after a bitter and bruising fight, Brandeis was confirmed. The battle that preceded the vote in the Senate was even more of a watershed than it appeared to be at the time. For years, the Jews of "downtown" had been railing against the paternalism of the "uptown" Jews, but there had been little criticism of their political attitudes. The "German Jews" had led the "Russians" in their fight against the czar, and against home-grown anti-Semitism. Now the Yiddish press was full of attacks on "Sha-sha Jews," that is, on those who wanted the Jews to be inconspicuous and to make no waves. This attitude continued to harden following Brandeis's confirmation. After he had been elevated to the Court, Brandeis had resigned all his other public positions, but he remained the undoubted, active leader and role model of the "Russian Jews."

II

In providing political legitimacy for the East European immigrants and for their children, Brandeis was far more important in the critical second decade of the twentieth century than much more "Jewish" figures, such as Stephen Wise and Judah Leon Magnes. Both of these men were Reform rabbis who had begun their careers in leading congregations of "German Jews," but they had moved away, very quickly, to identify with the East Europeans. Wise was one of the earliest American Zionists; he had joined the movement for the creation of a Jewish national home in Palestine before the turn of the century, and he was present in Basel as a delegate from America at the Second Zionist Congress in 1898. Wise came back to New York in 1907, after more than six years in Portland, Oregon. A few months earlier, he had been the leading candidate for the pulpit of Temple Emanu-El in New York, but he refused to agree that the lay board could censor his sermons. Wise made a public scandal of this altercation and he proceeded to create a platform of his own, the "Free Synagogue." Wise was a major figure in the fight for the American Jewish Congress, but the leader was Brandeis. Magnes had begun his public career as one of the rabbis of Temple Emanu-El in New York, the "cathedral" of Reform Judaism. In 1910, he had left that pulpit because he was ever more uncomfortable with the anti-Zionism and anti-Orthodoxy that pervaded the congregation. Magnes identified ever more with the new immigrants. For the next years, until he became embattled and marginal as a pacifist opponent of America's entry into the First World War, Magnes, the well-connected and well-established "American" Jew, was one of the preeminent leaders of the Yiddish-speaking ghetto.

Nonetheless, neither of these figures could stare down such powerful representatives of the "German Jews" as Jacob Schiff or Magnes's brother-in-law, Louis Marshall. Brandeis was the only American Jew who could challenge them from the left and in the name of the masses. He was the type of alienated aristocrat about whom Karl Marx had once talked when he explained the role of the Marquis de Lafayette in helping the dispossessed make the French Revolution. Jacob Schiff was Brandeis's major target. Schiff was a man of enormous presence and of princely charity. Though he was personally the leading member of Temple Emanu-El, Schiff helped in 1900 to reorganize the traditionalist Jewish Theological Seminary. Schiff had been born in Germany in an Orthodox family, and he retained much of the religious outlook of his youth. Schiff never did business on the Sabbath, even as he made it a practice to take a ride, grandly, in his carriage through Central Park on Sabbath afternoons. He went frequently to the Lower East Side, where he supported many social services and cultural institutions, to visit with his poorer brethren, and even to debate with them.

On one fabled occasion Schiff announced at the Educational Alliance, in the very heart of the Lower East Side, that he could not possibly be a Zionist because his sensibility was divided into thirds: one part American, one part Jewish, and one part German (that of the *Kultur* of his origins). A distinguished Zionist figure who was then living in America, Shmarya Levine, is reputed to have heckled him by asking: which third is which? Levine is supposed to have added, with vulgarity as well as irreverence: are the thirds divided horizontally or vertically? Reminiscing at Columbia University in 1968, near the end of his life, David Dubinsky, leader of the International Ladies Garment Workers Union, told of clashes with the police, when he led demonstrations against the capitalist bosses in his radical youth. Often, he and his comrades were jailed—but they were soon bailed out by Jacob Schiff, the archcapitalist Wall Street banker. These stories are worth telling because they help to bring to life the figure of an imperious hidalgo who did not avoid the immigrants by barricading himself in his Fifth Avenue mansion. Even his critics and enemies knew that Jacob Schiff was the towering figure in American Jewry and by near total consent the greatest lay figure in all its history.

Schiff had unbounded and very personal concern for all kinds of

Jews, even for those with whom he vehemently disagreed, but he drew the line at the nationalist theories of Zionism. Schiff supported the Jewish Theological Seminary generously until 1906, when he fell out with its president, Solomon Schechter, over Zionism. He then cut off support, and he ceased coming on Sunday mornings to board and committee meetings. Instead he used that time to go to the Montefiore Hospital in the Bronx, making a point of letting it be known that he was helping to count the linen in the laundry. He soon relented and came back to active involvement in the seminary, but his opinions did not change. An American Jew could not be a Zionist, so Schiff argued, because that would call into question his loyalty to the United States; one could not be, as the Zionists would have it, part of the Jewish nation and an American patriot at the same time. In 1916, at the height of the fight with the Zionists over "the war aims" of the Jewish people, Schiff pronounced:

> It is quite evident that there is a serious break coming between those who wish to force the formation of a distinct Hebraic element in the United States, as distinct from those of us who desire to be American in attachment, thought and action and Jews because of our religion as well as cultural attainments of our people. I am quite convinced of it that the American people will not willingly permit the formation of a large separate Hebraic group with national aspirations, and that if not we, our posterity are to become sufferers in consequence.

Schiff and his peers were, of course, responding to the outcry at the turn of the century against "hyphenated" Americans. They feared that Zionism would help "prove" the nativist case, that Jews had a different agenda than that of the American majority, as defined by the nativists. Schiff did push, sometimes even imperiously, to get the American government to help Jews in distress, but he and his colleagues spoke always in the name of such general American values as freedom and equality for all. He never demanded of America that it change its own self-definition in any respect.

Schiff was the "king of the Jews" until his authority was challenged by Louis Dembitz Brandeis. That Schiff would lose was inevitable, for by 1914 the "Russians" outnumbered the "Germans" by ten to one. Some of the East Europeans had quickly prospered in America. The more affluent had already established "second settlements" in

Brooklyn and Harlem. Nevertheless, August 1914 was a turning point, and not merely because the events of the next three years hastened the process of this "ethnic succession." What happened during the war years was no mere change of leaders; it was a revolution in the very content of American Jewish politics. The "Germans" had labored to achieve acceptance in America; the "Russians" pushed their angularities on the American majority.

III

The heightened vulnerability of the Jews in Eastern Europe after the outbreak of the First World War brought on the shift to Zionism in America. The front of hostilities between the Central Powers (Germany and Austria-Hungary) and the czarist empire ran through Poland and the Ukraine. This was the major center of Jewish population in the world, for it included the Russian "Pale of Settlement," the part of the czar's domain in which Jews were permitted to live; it also included Galicia, the southern part of Poland, which had been acquired by the Austrian Empire in the Partition of Poland at the end of the eighteenth century. Most of the hundreds of thousands of recent Jewish immigrants to the United States had come from this region. Every family had immediate relatives in the path of war. The situation of Jews in the war zone was particularly bad because the czarist regime had not relented in its anti-Semitic policies. It was all the worse for Jews because the advancing German armies were received as liberators; as the tide of battle changed and the Germans and Austrians retreated, Jews were attacked by the returning czarist authorities as spies and traitors. Even where there was no direct persecution, the Jews lacked food, shelter, and medical attention. Hundreds of thousands of underemployed Jewish poor had had all too little of the necessities of life in peacetime. In war, when there was no work, the situation was simply disastrous—and it was all the more so because the disruption of communications largely stopped the normal remittances from relatives in America.

The immediate reaction of American Jews to the war was to organize several relief organizations. The German Jewish leaders, Jacob Schiff, Louis Marshall, and Felix Warburg, Schiff's son-in-law and banking partner, convoked a meeting in October 1914 to establish the American Jewish Relief Committee. At the same time, the Orthodox community founded its own body, the Central Relief Committee. Within a month these two groups agreed to create the Joint Distribution Committee of American Funds for the Relief of Jewish War Sufferers. The Jewish unions remained aloof for a year; they supported their own People's Relief Committee. By 1915, they, too, agreed to work through the Joint Distribution Committee. All three of these groups which constituted the "Joint" (as it was popularly called) raised money separately, but their representatives sat together on the board of the operating agency. The lion's share of the money (more than two-thirds of the thirty-eight million dollars that was raised and spent between 1914 and 1920) came, of course, from the rich, who were the "German Jews." The other groups deferred to them—but the creation of the "Joint" was a turning point. It was the first major step forward for the East Europeans. The "monopoly" of the "German Jews" in the field of Jewish foreign policy had ended. The "Germans" and the "Russians" had sat together in the New York Kehillah, but the "Joint" marked the first time that the "Russian Jews" were admitted as equals in an endeavor on behalf of the Jews of the world.

Most of the "German Jews" remained opposed to Zionism, but one cause involving the Yishuv, the settlement in Palestine, did unite all elements of American Jewry. In 1915, after the Turks entered the war, they became highly suspicious of the Jews of Palestine, on the correct assumption that the new Zionist settlers favored the Allies. The Turkish military governor ordered all the Jews out of Palestine, and eighteen thousand were actually forced to leave. The majority went to Egypt. This expulsion was ended by the intervention of Turkey's principal ally, the German government; it did not want the Jews of America to be alienated. The ambassador of the United States in Constantinople (now Istanbul), Henry Morgenthau, Sr., spoke forcefully to the Turkish government but, even more important, he helped to organize relief for the Yishuv. A neutral, American ship, the *Vulcan,* came through the Mediterranean in 1915 with food and medical supplies. The bill was paid by the Joint Distribution Committee, the organization in which German and Russian Jews collaborated. Indeed, the "Joint" spent almost fifteen million dollars in support of the Yishuv during the war years. The rationale for this action was that those who were not Zionists—that is, those who did not share the state-building purposes of the Zionist settlers—would not, on that ground, discriminate against these pioneers when they were in need of humanitarian assistance. Some of the "German Jews" saw beyond the rhetoric of "humanitarian aid" to recognize that the "Russian Jews" had won yet another battle. The Zionist efforts in Palestine were now on everyone's budget.

A pattern was set for the future: financial aid would be extended to the Yishuv by a united American Jewish community so long as humanitarian concerns would be used as the explanation. On this basis, the Zionists could tap the resources of those who opposed nationalist ideology, and the non-Zionists could express their belonging to the extended family of all Jews while talking about the universal value of kindness to the downtrodden. This pragmatic alliance, to cooperate in relief efforts, worked well, then and later, but the Zionists and their opponents could not help but engage in raucous public battle with each other.

The big question was political, the future of East European Jewry: Could their lives be restored and even improved after the war in the places in which they lived? Was it more likely that many Jews would not be able to find a place for themselves when the hostilities ended? Should the Zionist solution, of establishing a Jewish homeland in Palestine, be embraced even by those who were not in ideological sympathy with Jewish nationalism, because such a homeland would offer a place for many Jews who would have to leave the countries of their birth? Should one, indeed, agree with the Zionists that the only permanent solution to anti-Semitism, and to the homelessness of the Jews, was in a Jewish state?

The preliminary skirmishes on these issues occurred almost immediately, in the fall of 1914. The "German Jews" had fought hard in America against restrictive immigration bills, and they were to continue the fight during and after the war. This battle was a matter of honor; they really did not want more immigrants. The existing East Sides were problem enough. The consensus in German Jewish circles was that Jews in danger in the war zones should not be encouraged to emigrate; they needed to be supported until a better time would come in their own countries. The old-line American Jews were not merely afraid of another wave of mass immigration to the United States. They refused to abandon the battle for a worldwide democratic order, for that would imply a lack of faith in the future of democracy even in America. One simply could not surrender on the insistence that Jews had as much right as anyone else to a future in their native lands.

This was not simply or even primarily an ideological debate about what direction American Jews would give their "unfortunate brethren" in Europe. In practice, both sides soon agreed to help both those in need in Europe and the emigrants regardless of destination; few doubted that there ought to be special concern for the settlers in Palestine. But, unlike the "German Jews," the immigrant masses were using their allegiance to Zionism to say something about themselves. They felt themselves to be an ethnic group, an extended family, a "peculiar people" in America. They would not pretend, as the "German Jews" more than half believed, that they were a religious denomination or a bunch of believers in universal abstractions about justice and democracy. Their chosen leader, Brandeis, might talk in such rhetoric, as he defined Zionism as a variation on the ideals of Progressivism in American politics. But the mass of East Europeans knew better. Zionism was for them a way of asserting folk feeling. American Zionism was an emotion and not an ideology. Zionism, in theory, insisted that the Jews were everywhere in exile, even in America. The recent immigrants, and their children, who were beginning to edge their way into American life, believed that proposition no more than they believed the rhetoric of the "German Jews." Despite their problems with sweatshop owners and with anti-Semites, the immigrants believed that America was different from all the previous habitations of the Jews.

Before 1914, Zionism in America had thus already defined itself as fundamentally different from Zionism in Europe. For the Europeans, Zionism meant that its adherents had banged the door shut on the surrounding culture, and that they looked to the possibility of emigrating to a new life in Palestine. In America, the bulk of the Zionists were immigrants who had made the decision not long before in Europe to leave for the United States and not for Palestine. They could hardly be asserting that their coming to the New World had been a mistake, and that Zionism required of them that they repack their bags and leave for Palestine. American Zionism existed to help the pioneers and to take pride in them.

Those who were constructing this sentimental, unideological program knew that theirs was a different brand of Zionism, and they were capable of self-mockery. The remark was going around in American Zionist circles as early as the 1890s that an American Zionist was someone who gives someone else a five-dollar contribution to send a European Jew to Palestine. But after 1914, those five dollars meant much more than the gibe implied. The donors were now bonding together to throw off the yoke of the "German Jews" and to enter the American political process.

The late summer of 1914 brought with it a further and decisive turning point in the self-understanding of American Zionism. The issue was power—and powerlessness. For twenty centuries, Jews in the Diaspora had been dependent on the goodwill of others. They were a people without a country of their own and without an army; they could only implore aggressors to be kind. Even after the Jews were made, by law, into equal citizens, their powerlessness remained a problem. The laws might proclaim the right of Jews to absolute equality, but these laws were not obeyed, or ignored and flouted. The modern Zionist movement arose out of a tragic assessment; wherever the majority society was heavily influenced by anti-Semitism, laws that proclaimed equality would not be heeded. Jews had to acquire some power which was securely in their own hands.

The identification of the "Russian Jews" with Zionism was deeply rooted in anger at their powerlessness. They were being told repeatedly that they were inferior both by the "German Jews" and by Gentiles. By acting as Zionists, these immigrants ceased being silent protégés of the "German Jews." By demanding power in the American Jewish community, and by refusing to let the "German Jews" speak for them to the Gentiles, the immigrants had taken the first major step toward refusing to remain "on approval" in America.

IV

On August 30, 1914, there was a Zionist meeting in New York to face the new problems that had been brought on by the outbreak of the war. The headquarters of the World Zionist Organization were in Berlin, and the members of its executive were scattered on both sides of the war fronts. The American Zionist movement, because it was situated in the greatest of the neutral countries, was asked to take over many of the responsibilities of the World Zionist Organization, especially the concern for the nascent Zionist settlements in Palestine. At this meeting Brandeis was elected chairman of the Provisional Executive Committee for General Zionist Affairs. In effect this meant that he had become the leader of American Zionism. In his acceptance speech, Brandeis spoke with total frankness. He admitted that he had been "to a great extent separated from Jews" and that he was "very ignorant in things Jewish." He had become identified with Jews because of their "deep moral feeling" and he cared about "the young Jewish Renaissance in the Holy Land." Brandeis warned that this "child of pain and sacrifice faces death from starvation." He accepted the office because he had come to "feel that the Jewish people have something which should be saved for the world; that the Jewish people should be preserved; and that it is our duty to pursue that method of saving which most promises success." Until that day in August 1914, Brandeis's East European followers were the poor relatives of the World Zionist movement. They had provided little money and no political or intellectual distinction. Suddenly they were the custodians of the whole of the Zionist future. Brandeis, a great name in America, one of the "German Jews," a kind of Moses who had grown up in the court of pharaoh, and then returned to them, had come to lead them.

That August day held another critical turning point. By his own confession, Brandeis was ignorant of things Jewish, but he felt no need to study Talmud or learn Hebrew as a prerequisite to Zionist leadership. It was more than enough, in his mind, that he identified Jews and Judaism with a passion for morality and intelligence, and that he set before himself, and American Jews as a whole, the labor for Zion as their common task. In effect, Brandeis had presented Zionism in America not as an outgrowth of Jewish history and tradition, which he did not know, but as their total replacement. Brandeis defined Zionism as a set of high-minded political and economic labors for Zion.

Thus, while Brandeis provided prestige to the masses, he was even more important to them because he helped them define themselves. It was Brandeis who made legitimate in American Jewry the severing of Jewishness from Judaism, including even the new Judaism of the Zionist settlers in Palestine—in the name of Zionism. The founder of the modern Zionist movement, Theodor Herzl, who was almost totally removed from the religious and cultural aspects of Jewish life, had done this before, but the bulk of his followers had opposed him on these issues. The European Zionist movement had identified itself ever more closely with the building of national Hebraic culture. Zionism without culture, a movement that had fund-raising and the mounting of political pressure as its content, existed only in America.

The American environment as a whole played a shaping role in defining this local brand of Zionism. European Zionists lived in countries where ideologies were taken seriously; the New World has very seldom been the home of deep ideological ferment, for Americans have usually been doers rather than thinkers. Even recent immigrants, such as the first generation of American Zionists, responded to the majority culture by fashioning their Zionism into a set of tangible acts instead of a national ideology. Deeds were, of course, more accessible to the mass of Jews than ideas. These predispositions were accentuated, and very nearly cast in concrete, by the events of the war years. This was not the time for publication of a grammar of modern Hebrew, or for engaging in deep reflections on the meaning of Jewish history. The Yishuv, the Jewish settlement in Palestine, was under the hostile rule of the Turks, and it had to be safeguarded. The time demanded that American Jews come to the rescue by exerting political pressure and sending money and supplies.

In the early months of 1915 agitation began first in England and then in the United States for the Zionist movement to identify with the cause of the Allies. The British government was pressured to accept an all Jewish detachment into its armed forces. If Jews fought in the war as a national unit, so the argument went, then the Jewish people would be recognized as a cobelligerent with a right to make claims at the peace table. The men available for such a unit were Russian immigrants to England (until late in the war, the British army was all volunteer) and their cousins in the United States, before it entered the war in 1917. Young Jews who had been born in Czarist Russia were not eager to go fight for the Allies. A Jewish formation was therefore proposed; the Jews as a people could point to their share in the victory and they would have the right to ask at war's end for a homeland in Palestine. The Zion Mule Corps was organized in 1915 among the Russian Jewish immigrants to Great Britain. This supply unit took part in the Gallipoli campaign, the abortive attempt by Britain to force the Dardanelles Straits. Because the Zion Mule

Corps was in action against Turkey, which possessed Palestine, Jews had at least shared in a battle for the liberation of their homeland. Jews had fought under a battalion flag of their own on a war front that included the ancestral home of the Jews.

After the failure of the action at Gallipoli, Great Britain disbanded the Zion Mule Corps. Its volunteers went back to England, but the notion of helping the military liberation of Palestine was not dead. Quite on the contrary, two young men who were then already leading figures in the Yishuv, Yitzhak Ben-Zvi and David Ben-Gurion, arrived in New York from Palestine in 1915. They came to organize a Jewish unit to fight as part of the British army on the battle line between the British and Turks on the very borders of Palestine. It took more than two years of effort to persuade the British to accept such a unit, but the result was two battalions which were attached to the Royal Fusiliers. Ben-Zvi and Ben-Gurion, and a number of men whom they had enlisted while America was still neutral, found their way through Canada to the recruiting offices for these two battalions; one of the two units consisted mainly of volunteers from America. In the spring of 1918, these two battalions were sent to Egypt. These Jewish units actually fought on the front in the campaign to conquer Palestine, and they were in the country by the end of the war. The Balfour Declaration had already been issued on November 2, 1917. Great Britain had declared, through its foreign secretary, that it favored the establishment of a Jewish national home in Palestine. Thus the presence of a Jewish military formation under its own flag was of great symbolic and emotional significance to the Jews. Here was the kernel of a Jewish army in the Jewish Palestine.

The number of Jews who actually went to fight in Palestine was not large. There were some eight hundred, of whom about two hundred came from the United States, but hearts were lifted in America by high-flown words about "the first Jewish army since Bar-Kochba" (he had been the commander of the last revolt against Rome in the years 132–35). There were meetings all over the country in praise of the soldiers of the Jewish people. The American Jews had helped out with money. They had saved the Jewish settlement from hunger and expulsion by the Turks, and they had supported the cause of the Jewish fighting battalions. In return, American Jews received a glorious sense of their own power and of their participation in the renaissance of Jewish power in the land of the ancestors.

V

The skirmishes, the guerrilla warfare, and the pitched battles between the "German Jews" and the "Russians" culminated in one titanic fight: whether to organize a countrywide, representative body, the American Jewish Congress. Of their own free will, American Jews had created many organizations, both large and small, but there was no structure that encompassed all American Jews. Therefore, no orderly way existed to create a consensus about the "war aims" of the American Jewish community. This situation was essentially comfortable for the "German Jews," who had created the American Jewish Committee in 1906 to represent their political views. The members of this body were a small, self-chosen elite of the rich and "American" Jews, and they preferred to continue to make policy without interference from the Jewish masses. The only way in which Brandeis and his associates could challenge this plutocracy was by insisting on the pernicious doctrine of "one man, one vote" in Jewish affairs. This meant that those who had money would be expected to continue to pay the bills for Jewish needs while being denied control of Jewish political policy.

The Zionists had the upper hand almost from the beginning. Emotions were running high at the sight of European Jews in trouble, but, more important, it was difficult to argue in a democratic America against democracy in Jewish life. There was much infighting and intrigue, but within two years, the "German Jews" had lost the battle. In the end, the "Germans" had to agree to the calling of elections throughout the United States for an American Jewish Congress, in which the delegates would vote on the "war aims" of American Jewry.

A preparatory session of the American Jewish Congress took place in Philadelphia in 1916, where Stephen Wise spoke for the Zionists; they wanted, "not relief but redress, not palliation but prevention, not charity but justice." Thus the Zionists, who were at the head of the vast majority of the East Europeans, announced their independence from the German Jewish philanthropists. Internal Jewish politics made it difficult to proceed to immediate elections for the American Jewish Congress. President Wilson intervened in this internal affair of the Jews (this was the first such act in American history). Wilson suggested to Brandeis that such a Jewish demonstration would be inopportune at that stage of the war. The elections were postponed until the spring of 1918. One element in immigrant Jewry, the left-wing socialists, boycotted the election because it was, then, still opposed to the Zionists, who were in control of the movement for the American Jewish Congress. The masses refused to follow this socialist splinter among the immigrants. Hundreds of thousands of votes were cast, and it was a nearly complete victory for the Zionists. In an imperfect world, it could not be doubted that the results were largely representative.

When the meeting finally took place in December 1918, the American Jewish Congress agreed by overwhelming majority to push for a Jewish national homeland in Palestine. The representatives of the American Jewish Committee, who were present under the leadership of Louis Marshall, succeeded in softening the resolution so that it was not an outright insistence on a Jewish state. On this basis, they were able to agree to a united American Jewish delegation to lobby at the future peace conference. There were, however, some people in this group, most notably Cyrus Adler (speaking, so everyone presumed, for Jacob Schiff), who remained in opposition. In Adler's view, if Zionist aspirations were a cause of any prominence at the peace conference, the anti-Semites in the new successor states to the Austro-Hungarian and Russian empires would simply be able to say to Jews: "Get out to your own homeland."

On March 2, 1919, a delegation from the American Jewish Congress presented a memorial to President Wilson asking him to support the Balfour Declaration. The anti-Zionists in the American Jewish Committee, including Adolph Ochs, the publisher of *The New York Times*, refused to go along with their own more moderate leaders, who had participated in the American Jewish Congress. On March 5, 1919, they published their own memorial of "warning and protest." They were opposed to the "demands of the Zionists for the reorganization of the Jews into a self-governing, ethnic entity in America and to the creation of Jewish territorial sovereignty in Palestine."

The American Jewish Congress had been envisioned as a continuing body, a voluntary parliament of American Jewry. This did not happen, because after the war almost all the groups, except the Zionists, preferred to go their own ways. Nevertheless, the victory of the Zionists in forcing even this one meeting in Philadelphia was a

great turning point in American Jewish life. The East European immigrants had used the only weapon that they really possessed, their
numbers and their passion, in the only forum in which these assets
mattered, in the first election that American Jews had ever held on
a nationwide basis. The moderate majority among the "German
Jews" did not simply walk away, not then, during the fight for the
American Jewish Congress, or later. They led in supporting relief
efforts which helped Jews in need everywhere and especially the
Zionist settlements in Palestine.

Numbers mattered. The Zionists had acquired mass support. In
1914 the enrolled strength of the American Zionist movement had
been less than 12,000; within four years there were 176,000 members
in the American Zionist Federation, and more belonged to a variety
of smaller Zionist bodies. In the next several years, Zionist strength
grew some. Membership then dropped dramatically. But, despite
ups and downs in the Zionist rolls, the feelings of the East European
majority of American Jews remained consistent: the Jews were a
worldwide people, and Jews in trouble were safest and best off in
their own land.

At times of upset and danger like the First World War (or, later,
in the Hitler years), this emotion translated itself into rising Zionist
membership. Whether organized or unorganized, the masses of the
East Europeans had made an irrevocable choice: they thought of
themselves not as "Americans of the Jewish faith," but as members
of a people. The mainstream of the German Jewish establishment
moved toward the "Russian Jews," for they would not abandon or
alienate themselves from their larger family. The self-definition of
"Americans of the Jewish faith" remained in force in theory, but in
real life it was displaced by the label, non-Zionist—not an opponent
of Zionism, but a fellow traveler, who cared about the Jews in Palestine, but who did not adhere to a nationalist definition of the Jewish
people.

Some years earlier, before the rift over the calling of the American
Jewish Congress, Louis Marshall had even learned Yiddish in order
to be able to communicate with the immigrants; his influence in the
American Jewish Committee was toward moderate, nonconfronta-
tionist policies. Felix Warburg, Jacob Schiff's son-in-law, continued
to cooperate with the Zionists in nonpolitical concerns, including the
physical and cultural renaissance in Jewish Palestine. Men like Louis

Marshall and Felix Warburg were religious believers; they knew that helping people (and especially Jews) had been commanded by God. But they also wanted to belong to the Jewish people—and the masses of that people, the immigrants, had moved in a few short years from being a protectorate of the "German Jews" to the very center of Jewish and American life. The total opponents of Zionism among the "German Jews," the old believers of Reform Judaism, had been pushed to the margin.

Virtually all the "Russian Jews" would remain poor, and all would be semi-alien, for another generation, but by the early 1920s, they had become the dominant force in American Jewry.

14.

Closing the Gates

I

The children of the immigrants had to fight for power in America, not least because Congress kept telling them that they were really not wanted. The Constitution of the United States guaranteed equality for all citizens, but even in law that promise was not kept until 1965. For more than forty years the immigration law had been biased, overtly and without apology, against Jews, Slavs, and Italians. They were admitted to the United States in small numbers to ensure that the population of the country would continue to be dominated by the descendants of immigrants from Northern and Western Europe. Congress had implicitly declared that some people were better than others; America wanted more tall, blond, blue-eyed immigrants, and fewer short, dark-skinned brunettes.

During the war over American immigration policy which had begun in the 1890s, two propositions had been advanced by those who wanted to close the doors of America. The first was a basic premise, thought to be so self-evident that it needed no proof: the American population must continue to consist, in its majority, of descendants of the earliest, prerevolutionary white Anglo-Saxon Protestants. Statistics were produced, with supposedly impressive scholarly authority behind them, to "prove" that American society was barely in its majority of such composition, and that further immigration of Slavs, Italians, and Jews would tip the balance in an "un-American" direction. It was argued, further, that the original American stock would be flawed by the introduction of more such immigrants, because Slavs, Italians, and Jews were of a lower intellectual and moral stature—and statistics were invoked to "prove" that Slavs, Italians, and Jews were unintelligent, indeed that they were the least bright of all the groups in America except for the Native Americans.

In the war years, immigration became a more important issue. Most of the Jews of Europe lived in the borderlands where the Russians fought the Austro-Hungarians and the Germans. By 1917, at least one million on both sides were refugees. Jewish relief efforts, which emphasized the great suffering of these refugees, could only suggest, both to friends and enemies, that there would be large-scale emigration as soon as the war was over. This became even more certain after the armistice in November 1918. The Bolshevik Revolution was at that time a year old. Several counterrevolutionary armies were trying to overthrow the Reds, and the newly created Polish army was attempting to advance into Russia. Between 1919 and 1921, at least sixty thousand Jews were slaughtered in this region, some by the Poles and most by the Ukrainians, often under the pretense that Jews were supporters of the Bolsheviks.

Both Zionists and "German Jews" were eager to help the sufferers, but in radically different ways. The Zionists maintained that Jews in trouble in Europe should go to the nascent national home in Palestine. Zionists and non-Zionists joined in fighting hard and successfully for guarantees of equality before the law in all the states, including Poland, which had been created by the peace treaty of 1919. These men sincerely believed that Eastern Europe would settle down after the war into a culture of parliamentary democracy. Many even added the hope that the Bolshevik regime, which they did not like because it was Communist, would in its own way treat Jews with fairness and equality. For a very short while, a wish bordering on fantasy existed among those who opposed the pessimism of the Zionists about the future of the Jews in Europe that many who had already come to the United States would want to return to their original homes.

The reverse was true. Jews in Eastern Europe were undergoing no renaissance; they were being murdered by the thousands. The Joint Distribution Committee acted courageously, sending relief wherever possible during the fighting between the Bolsheviks and White Russians, and during the Polish-Russian War. The Jewish effort was "legitimate," because the American government itself, much as it detested Bolshevism, had allowed a commission under Herbert Hoover to raise and spend millions between 1919 and 1921 in revolutionary Russia to alleviate suffering. Jewish relief continued even after the Hoover Commission ceased to function. These humanitarian endeavors were not attacked in the United States, even at the height of the Red Scare of 1919–21. The leaders of the Joint Distribution Committee were "German Jews" who were beyond suspicion of Communism.

The sight of the horrors in Eastern Europe moved the chairman of the House Immigration Committee, Albert Johnson, to propose a two-year suspension of immigration, as an emergency measure until a permanent policy could be worked out. Early in 1921, Johnson reported to the House that East European Jews had come through Ellis Island in great numbers in the previous few months. He quoted an unnamed officer of the Hebrew Immigrant Aid Society as saying, "If there was in existence a ship that would hold three million human beings, the three million Jews of Poland would board it to escape to America." More damaging still to the cause of the Jews, Johnson quoted Wilbur S. Carr, the head of the United States Consular Service. Carr had surveyed the conditions at a number of ports in Europe, and found that the Polish Jews were the worst of all the potential immigrants. They were "filthy, un-American and often dangerous in their habits . . . lacking any conception of patriotism or national spirit." As we have seen, something like this had been said almost a century earlier, in the 1830s, by a British traveler—and repeated by American observers—about the "German Jews," who were then trading on Chatham Street in New York.

Though the forces pushing for immigration restrictions had not forgotten their distaste for Slavs and Italians, Jews were still their main target. When hearings were held in the Senate on the proposed legislation, Jewish representatives testified, chiefly to deny that there was any probability of large-scale immigration from Poland. Some of the Jewish leaders, even among the "Russian Jews," were admitting in private that such immigration would be difficult to digest, but they opposed quotas on Polish Jews as an affront to the Jews already in America. The Senate committee heard comparable opinions from representatives of American business, and it therefore agreed that there was no immediate emergency. The Senate substituted its own proposal for an immigration law—it decided to limit the numbers of new arrivals to three percent of the foreign-born of each national group who were present in the United States according to the census of 1910. The House concurred in the Senate version. This bill was signed by Warren Harding in May 1921. For the first time in all of American history, immigration restrictions based on national origins had become law. The editorial writers of the Yiddish press knew exactly what had happened. In the words of the *Morgen Journal:* "Our kin is fleeing from persecution both individual and governmental, and the question of emigration is to most of our brethren one of life or death, not merely of economic betterment. We are more hopeful than others that in the end the portals of our country will remain open for victims of political and religious persecution."

This hope would not be realized. On the contrary, the pressure kept mounting for an even more restrictive immigration policy. There were two new notes in the antiforeign outcry: the fear of the Bolsheviks, that more radicals would come from Russia to join the deplorable number who were already present in the United States, and the supposed certainties of eugenics as a way of controlling the quality of human population.

In 1919, A. Mitchell Palmer, the red-baiting attorney general of the United States, went looking for the Bolsheviks in America. He used the Justice Department's Bureau of Investigation (forerunner of the Federal Bureau of Investigation) to help in the tracking down of Communists. Palmer had no particular bias against the Jews, but his campaign against Communism lent itself to such uses. Jews were prominent among Communists, both in Russia and in the United States. A forgery of a generation earlier, the *Protocols of the Elders of Zion,* was published in the United States in 1919. The document asserted that Jews were all part of a conspiracy to dominate the world, and that this conspiracy was directed by a central body of influential Jews. The *Protocols of the Elders of Zion* had most probably been concocted twenty years earlier by the secret police of the Russian czar to justify his anti-Semitic policies. Henry Ford, the most famous industrialist in America, financed a daily newspaper in his hometown of Dearborn, Michigan, *The Dearborn Independent,* which had this fantasy reprinted in hundreds of thousands of copies. The *Protocols* made it possible to believe that Jewish capitalists like the Rothschilds and Communists like Leon Trotsky were all part of the same power directorate, and that these known leaders were controlled by even more mysterious and remote figures. This theory of Jewish world conspiracy would thus "explain" the success of the Bolshevik Revolution—and it could act as a warning against allowing the Jews to extend their wealth and power in any society, including the United States. On the basis of this forgery, Ford's paper became the chief trumpet of anti-Semitism in America in the 1920s.

The trouble with the accusation of Jewish Communism was that it had just sufficient truth in it to make the tale plausible to Jew-haters. Though Communism was never a strong force in America, not even in its salad days before and during the Russian Revolution, Jews were very prominent in the movement. In the 1920s, there were approximately fifteen thousand enrolled members of the Communist party of the United States; the Yiddish-speaking section represented about one-tenth of the membership, but Jews were also very important in the English-speaking section which numbered, by 1925, 2,282 of the total membership of 16,325. This rising membership was motivated by domestic exclusions in America, but it reflected, as well, the large initial sympathy within the Jewish community for the Bolshevik Revolution. In the earliest years of the new regime, both Jewish religion and Jewish nationalism were persecuted, and their institutions were essentially outlawed, but the Soviet Union did allow and encourage secular Jewish culture in Yiddish. In the 1920s there was substantial sympathy for the Soviet Union among many Jews who abhorred Communism and were outraged by the persecution of religion. The Bolshevik regime was perceived, then, as the one government in the world which actively fought anti-Semitism and fostered Yiddish culture. Jews were thus a striking, obvious, easy-to-find element in American Communism, and the "defense" of the country against subversion could, and was, easily translated into lessening the numbers and the power of Jews in America.

The old outcry against Jews, Slavs, and Italians was given additional respectability by the supposed science of eugenics. In 1911, the American Breeders Association had commissioned a study to find "the practical means for cutting off the defective germ-plasm in the American population." The conclusions of the study were published three years later. The authors were supremely confident that they could point out scientifically the bearers of defective genes, such as "the feeble-minded class" and the "pauper class," as well as the bearers of epilepsy and insanity. Sterilization was the defensive measure of choice to protect the population. Such thoughts were sufficiently respectable so that Louis Marshall, a longtime leader in the fight for open immigration, was a member of the expert advisory committee. He clearly did not foresee that theories about eugenics would be used in a very few years to help curtail the immigration of "undesirables" from Europe.

The secretary of the committee, Harry H. Laughlin, was the scholar who would reassure the House Immigration Committee in 1924 that it did well by the Republic when it passed the new immigration law in the spring of that year. Under this bill, quotas were now based on figures from 1890, when the foreign-born from Southern and Eastern Europe were much fewer. The result was that less than 6,000 Jews could be admitted in any year from Poland, about 2,000 from Russia, and 600 from Romania. These were the countries from which almost all Jews had come in the past. Italians were no better off; less than 4,000 would be allowed to come to America in any one year. In contrast, the quota for Germany was 51,000, for Great Britain and Northern Ireland, 34,000, and more than 28,000 for the Irish Free State. Switzerland was allocated almost as many places as Russia; Norway had more than 6,000 and Sweden had more than 9,000.

The bias of the law was clear. Hearings were held in November 1924, when the committee already had in front of it the figures on arriving immigrants in the fiscal year which had ended June 30. More than 60,000 Italian immigrants and 50,000 Jews had arrived. Henry Laughlin told the committee the truth when he defined the basis of the new law as the assertion that "immigration into the United

States . . . is primarily a biological problem, and secondarily a problem in economics and charity." The committee had adopted an immigration policy on "the biological basis."

Lest the committee have any second thoughts about the "biological basis" of the quota law, Laughlin used very recent "scientific" evidence from army experts which "proved" that people from Southern and Eastern Europe were intellectually and morally inferior. He paraded the results of standardized intelligence tests which had been given to a random group of about a hundred thousand draftees into the American army after the United States entered the war. The categories of analysis ranged from the "very superior," persons who were "capable of high-class creative work," to "very inferior," that is, the kind of person in whose case it was "doubtful if the value of labor equals cost of supervision." In five elaborate tables Laughlin reiterated the same message: of all the recent immigrants, the English were the most intelligent, and Russians, Greeks, Italians, Belgians, and Poles were almost totally stupid. American Negroes, though much less intelligent than native-born whites, were three times as bright as the Belgians, seven times as intelligent as the Poles, and fifty percent brighter than the Russians. It did not seem to have occurred either to the army psychologists or to Dr. Laughlin that the intelligence tests were based on schooling in, and comprehension of, standard English, and that Negroes and recent immigrants, even the Einsteins among them, were at a marked disadvantage. One suspects that the authors of this study, and those who used it against the people whom they regarded as "undesirable," were not motivated by pure, self-critical zeal for scientific truth. There was more than a breath of the doctrine of Aryan supremacy in the air.

Congress overwhelmingly supported this law, while the opposition to it was divided. Though the National Catholic Welfare Conference had called the Johnson Act of 1921 racist, and the Federal Council of Churches, of the Protestants, asked for restrictions on immigration not based on race, neither group testified at the congressional hearings in 1924. Even Jewish congressmen, such as Emanuel Celler of New York, were willing to accept immigration quotas if the base year were kept at 1910, and not the much more restrictive 1890. On the surface, all Jews, "German" and "Russian" alike, were united in opposing the law, but the "German Jews" were visibly upset by the Red Scare. In January 1919, the *American Hebrew* had published an editorial in which it warned that "the immigrants from Russia and Austria will be coming from countries infected with Bolshevism and it will require more than a superficial effort to make good citizens out of them." Two years later, in September 1921, this same journal was busy trumpeting the one hundred percent Americanism of the Jews. Louis Marshall, who remained firm in opposing any attempt to restrict immigration, wrote in 1921 to Israel Zangwill, the Anglo-Jewish man of letters and politics, that a large number of Jews who disliked the new immigrants were actually on the side of restriction.

In the mid-1920s, the second generation, the children of the immigrants, was still young and largely inarticulate. Its spokesmen did not participate in the debate about immigration, but the passage of the law taught these children of immigrants a bitter lesson. They were second-class citizens in America. They were, at best, on approval. To be sure, Henry Ford was forced in 1927 to recant his anti-Semitism. It was bad for business. Ford cars were being boycotted by Jews and by some liberal Christians. Ford wrote a letter to Louis Marshall withdrawing his anti-Semitic allegations, and he closed down *The Dearborn Independent*. This was a victory of sorts, but fundamental damage had been done. Red-baiting and nativism set the seal on a conviction that was widely held in the 1920s by people who did not consider themselves Jew-haters. Jews were not seen as individuals; they were attacked as a group for being different and clannish, with a tendency toward political radicalism. But the Jews learned something. Jews read the victory as a result not of a change of heart by Ford but as his bowing to the power that they had marshaled against him. This incident was an important lesson in a truth about America: it is better to depend on power than on goodwill.

In the face of attacks by the anti-Semites, the Jewish leadership of the 1920s was back where their predecessors had been in the 1890s. They were again forced to "prove" their patriotism and their contribution to the making of America. The American Jewish publications of those years were full of lists of Jews who had achieved honorific positions in politics and in law and medicine. These lists were sad reading, and not only because such apologetics could never convince anti-Semites that they were wrong. The numbers that could be found were small, far less than the proportion of the Jews in the

American population as a whole (it was then three and a half percent).

Three centuries earlier the Puritans had created their commonwealth to include only the elect. Jews were particularly alien, because only the Puritans understood the truth of the Bible; unconverted Jews were subversive. In the 1920s, these notions, in up-to-date versions, now dominated immigration policy and much of American social thought. There were inferior races who had to be kept out, and kept at a distance even after they arrived. Jews were particularly problematic, because they had a marked propensity to radical or revolutionary ideology. Before the onset of the Second World War, almost no Jew could make a free, personal decision about his education and career. At every turn, the fact of his Jewishness meant that many, if not most, options were simply not available to him. There was a fence around Jews.

II

In the 1920s and 1930s, American-born Jews in New York and Chicago were almost as much in the ghetto as Polish-speaking Jews in Warsaw or Romanian-speaking Jews in Bucharest. To be sure, there were no pogroms in America and little physical violence, but many occupations excluded Jews entirely. Despite the protests of their enemies that the Jews controlled banking and finance, the opposite was true. Jews had remained a minority on Wall Street, even as America was experiencing its stock-market fever in the years before the Crash of October 1929. There was an effective ban on allowing the Jews into the banking business. Banks could be created only through state or national charter. Only one such charter had ever been issued to Jewish owners, to a New York concern called the Bank of the United States. After the crash of 1929, this bank was actually among the most solvent. It was forced into bankruptcy because none of the larger banks would give the Jewish-owned bank any help in weathering the crisis. The few Jews who held jobs in banking, even at the lowest rungs of management, were usually those who hid their origins. In the insurance industry, almost no Jews could be found in the central management of the various firms. Thousands of Jews were independent agents. Such endeavors were white-collar versions of pushcart peddling; the insurance companies were willing to make a profit on whatever policies these petty Jewish businessmen would sell. The situation was the same in heavy industry; the management of the steel and the coal companies, and the auto manufacturers, were simply closed to Jews.

The barriers in education were equally formidable. Before the early 1920s, Jews who applied were admitted quite freely to Ivy League schools. The Jewish proportion at Yale rose from two percent in 1901 to thirteen percent in 1925. At Harvard the proportion was seven percent in 1900 and twenty-one and a half percent in 1922. In 1922, it leaked from Harvard that a Jewish quota was being imposed. Jews had become so prominent that they were changing the character of the colleges and challenging Gentile supremacy. President A. Lawrence Lowell of Harvard, who had led the attack against Brandeis, defended the idea of a quota by suggesting that if "every college in the country would take a limited proportion of Jews, we should go a long way toward eliminating race feeling among the students." Lowell was forced to retract his view because of public outrage, but in actual fact the proportion of Jews in the Harvard student body went down after this incident. At Yale, a decision was made that students should henceforth be admitted on the basis of "character" rather than strictly on scholarship. Dean Frederick Jones had found that "every single scholarship of any value is won by a Jew" and "that we could not allow that to go on, we must put a ban on the Jews." He agreed that "in terms of scholarship and intelligence, Jewish students lead the class, but their personal characteristics make them markedly inferior." At Columbia a Jewish proportion of forty percent in 1920 was cut in half within two years.

The quotas in the medical schools forced many hundreds of young Jews to go abroad, to schools in various countries in Europe, especially to Italy, for their medical education. Even after they graduated, Jewish doctors were still in trouble; the Gentile-controlled hospitals allowed very few Jews to join their staffs. In the 1920s and 1930s, Jewish hospitals existed not so much to take care of Jewish patients as to provide places in which Jewish doctors could practice. There were so few Jewish professors in the American medical schools that medical education and research were essentially closed to Jews. Jewish doctors had little choice but to enter private practice. This was equally true of the Jewish lawyers, for there were very few Jewish firms—and the non-Jewish firms simply did not hire Jews.

A Jewish lawyer could only hang up a shingle and hope to build a personal practice.

These increasingly severe quotas in the colleges and universities were a lesser part of the problem. At least in theory, the administrators who had enacted these exclusions had tried to "explain" that Jews could be assimilated only in small, dispersed numbers. There was no such pretense at the top of American intellectual life. The most modern American writers, Ernest Hemingway and F. Scott Fitzgerald, mentioned Jews only to insist that they were irretrievably outsiders. The English departments of the universities refused to have any Jewish teachers on the premises. By anti-Semitic definition, no matter what he knew or thought, a Jew was simply incapable of entering into the spirit of Anglo-Saxon literature, or, for that matter, of American history. Lionel Trilling worked at his alma mater, Columbia University, as an instructor in English between 1932 and 1936, but was not reappointed. The spokesman of the department explained to him that he would not be happy there "as a Freudian, a Marxist, and [a] Jew." It took the personal intervention three years later of Columbia's formidable president, Nicholas Murray Butler, to force Trilling's appointment as assistant professor in Columbia's English Department. Even so, Trilling's painful victory was rare. The existing American intellectual establishment of the 1920s and 1930s never made room for Jews. Some American intellectuals had found Jews interesting, in early immigrant days, as exotics who wrote in Yiddish and lived in a pulsating ghetto. Their children were no longer exotic. They were American-born and educated, brilliantly so, but their very achievement in becoming "Americans" stood against them. They had become potential competitors of their Gentile fellow students—and even of their teachers. Almost without exception these young Jews were kept out of America.

But academically trained Jews who were trying to enter the professions were a minority. The majority of the children of the immigrants, and of their parents, were going into business in the 1920s. In the years before the Crash of October 1929, many were getting rich. This contradicts one of the accepted "truths" about the history of the Jews in America, that the "German Jews," who arrived in the middle of the nineteenth century, became rich in their own lifetimes, but that the East Europeans did not achieve wealth until the next generation. Supposedly, they had to wait because there were so many of them. This construction offers a partial explanation of the differences between the "Germans" and the "Russians," but it leaves out a significant and little remembered part of the story. It skips from the sweatshops of the 1910s to the mass unemployment of the 1930s, without paying attention to the 1920s. In that decade, the Roaring Twenties, as the stock market rose steadily from 1924 until the famous Crash in October 1929, a considerable number of the East European immigrants were becoming wealthy all over America. These new rich were the immigrants themselves and not their children, who were then still too young to be making fortunes. It was not until 1940 that a bare majority of all American Jews were native-born.

Those who devised the questionnaires for self-studies of Jewish communities almost never asked questions about income and wealth: don't let anti-Semites know that the Jews are doing "too well." The several studies that were done by outsiders were no more informative, for Jews were even less likely to tell Gentiles the truth about their earnings. Consequently there is no direct evidence to support the assertion that a considerable minority of the East European immigrants were becoming rich in the 1920s. But rising gifts to Jewish charities make this assertion highly probable. Between 1918 and 1926, the donations to domestic Jewish charities nearly doubled. In 1918 the Jewish federations (community chests) of the four largest Jewish communities—New York, Chicago, Philadelphia, and Boston—disbursed a bit over $4.8 million to the local agencies they supported; in 1926 the disbursements had reached $8.5 million. These figures, which came from a set of tables published each year in the American Jewish Yearbook, appeared for the last time in 1926: they were growing at a rate which the yearbook's editors, always concerned about anti-Semitism, did not want used by enemies of Jews and "Wall-Street bankers."

It can be argued that these contributions to domestic charity came in those years primarily from the rich "German Jews" (there is no breakdown by origin of the contributors). However, the formation of new congregations and especially the erection of new synagogue buildings in that decade point to an increased wealth among the "Russian Jews." In 1908 there were only seventeen hundred permanently organized Jewish congregations in the United States; ten years later, at the end of the war, there were two hundred more. In the years 1917–19 a building boom began; seventy-three new synagogues were dedicated in those years, and no more than ten were Reform. By 1928, the number of organized congregations had jumped to three thousand. These new synagogues were not being organized by "German Jews," who had more than enough space in their existing temples. Over a thousand new congregations, with the budgets that they required, were funded in the 1920s by recent immigrants who suddenly had the necessary money.

The boom in synagogue building was even more striking. A number of Reform congregations built new buildings in that decade, moving with their congregants to more elegant surroundings, but the new synagogue buildings, in their vast majority, were paid for by recent immigrants. A large number of imposing synagogues were built in the 1920s in the neighborhoods of "second settlement" into which East European Jews were moving. Whether on the Grand Concourse in the Bronx or on Park Heights Avenue and Forest Park Avenue in Baltimore, the newly affluent "Russian Jews," by placing their synagogue buildings on the most public thoroughfares, were announcing their presence on the American scene, just as the "German Jews" had done in the 1860s and 1870s.

The pitched battles of the early 1920s over the exclusion of Jews from the "best" colleges is another oblique proof of the rise of the East Europeans to affluence. Two decades earlier their children had been going to the city colleges; by the early 1920s many were still poor, and their children made their way to the Ivy League schools by winning the competition for scholarships. However, there was not enough such aid to poor, bright Jews to explain the Harvard class of 1922, in which very nearly one out of every four students was a Jew. Most were paying tuition, there and elsewhere among the Ivies, because their parents could now afford the bills. The economic profile of immigrant Jews as a whole had been transformed in twenty years. In 1900, the immigrants were two-thirds workers and one-third in white-collar pursuits. By 1920 two-thirds were in business or white-collar jobs and only one-third were still workers. When the best private colleges more than half-closed their doors to Jews in the early 1920s, this was a blow not only to poor Jews but also to newly affluent immigrants and their children.

Many immigrant Jews participated in the bull market of the mid-1920s. In the era of speculation, poor Jews of yesteryear had a particularly passionate need to believe that the future was unbounded. But, of course, the immigrants who became rich in the 1920s did not all engage in speculating on the stock market. In a buoyant economy hundreds upon hundreds entered the risky business of manufacturing clothing, and they did very well until the Crash came and consumers had no money with which to buy new clothes. Numerous other kinds of small businesses and retail stores prospered before 1929. The massive move of Jews to new neighborhoods provided large opportunities in real estate. New buildings were going up in the Bronx and on the Upper West Side of New York, and in equivalent places in all the other cities in which there was large Jewish population. The builders of these high-rise apartment houses, or of row houses in Brooklyn, were almost all Jews. So long as the economic situation was on the upswing, apartments were in demand, rent was paid on time, and the assets of the entrepreneurs kept growing. After the Crash, many of those who had built these buildings were very soon bankrupt. Their tenants could not pay rent, and soon the landlords could not meet obligations to the banks which held the mortgages. The Jewish labor unions, which had felt powerful and rich in the 1920s, could not keep up with the payment of benefits to members out of work. Jewish charities had much less money to pay for social services for the poor, and their money now came mostly from the "German Jews," who, being better established, were weathering the Depression.

The Crash of 1929 aborted the dash of a significant minority of East European immigrants to affluence in their own lifetime. They, the parents, were bankrupt, and they would not be able to pass on functioning businesses and fortunes to their children. Many of the American-born young who had been enjoying the pleasures of the Jazz Age had to find jobs in the America of the Depression years, in which anti-Semitism was rising. They were suddenly poor and defenseless Jews, even in America.

III

In discussing anti-Semitism in America before the Second World War, too quick a jump has often been made to 1933, the year in which Hitler came to power in Germany. The story of anti-Semitism in the United States between the two wars has thus tended to become an account of the effect in America of reechoes first of Bolshevism and then of the Nazis. It is, of course, undeniable that anti-Semitic propaganda played a large role in whipping up sentiment, for the propagandists provided a rationale for excluding Jews. The anti-Semites were in agreement on one central point: the Jew is alien, subversive, and dangerous; he cannot be allowed the freedom of unfettered competition to achieve a place in society. The American economic pie had shrunk, and Jews were cast for the role of aliens who were eating an undeserved share of the scarce food.

After 1929, American anti-Semitism arose not in the areas where Nazi propaganda was the most virulent, in big cities such as New York and Baltimore, but in the Farm Belt and the Far West. The editors of *Fortune* magazine, who in 1935 conducted a survey of American anti-Semitism, devised an indirect question: Do you think that Germany is being helped or hurt by the Nazi exclusion of Jews? Across the country, the results were much less encouraging than the editors of *Fortune* tried to make them out to be. Over half the respondents answered that Germany had been hurt by its policies. About a third were indifferent to the question, and some fifteen percent nationwide answered that Germany had been helped. In the Farm Belt and Far West the indifferent and the antagonistic added together to more than half of those who answered the questions.

The 1930s were the time of massive disaster in the Farm Belt, both because prices had fallen drastically and because of the drought which had reduced the farmland to dust. Hundreds of thousands of dispossessed farmers, the Okies, took to their Model Ts and drove west to California. It was easy to suggest to these pained and bankrupt farmers that the Jews were somehow behind their downfall. George Winrod and Gerald L. K. Smith, the most extreme voices of anti-Semitism in the Midwest, used the rhetoric of Populism. Winrod and Smith were not, however, the most prominent preachers of anti-Semitism in America in the 1930s. That role was seized by a Catholic priest, Charles Coughlin. His prime audience was not the farmers, but rather the industrial workers. Coughlin was the pastor of the Shrine of the Little Flower in Royal Oak, Michigan. He had taken to the radio as an advocate of the New Deal, but he soon turned to preaching anti-Semitism. His message was popular in Detroit, where the auto industry was in ever-greater trouble, and among the industrial unemployed throughout the country, for until the Second World War most had little hope of returning to their jobs.

To be sure, other factors were important in the growth of anti-Semitism in the 1930s. Much of the population of the Midwest was of German extraction and preferred to think well of the mother country, even under the Nazis. The blue-collar workers to whom Coughlin appealed were predisposed to think in terms of race, because many, both white and black, had their roots in the South. Those who were striking in Detroit against the auto manufacturers risked being injured or sometimes even being killed on the picket lines of the 1930s. Jews were prominent among union officials and strike organizers, but that did not endear them to the workers. Here were "New York Jews" with white-collar jobs in the union bureaucracies, trying to tell blue-collar workers who had been fired how to fight the bosses. Many were predisposed to make Jews the scapegoat for their woes, because it was safer and more emotionally satisfying. As always, anti-Semitism was rising in America among the masses during times of economic dislocation.

As the recovery from the Great Depression began, Jews were visibly better off than most other groups. Toward the end of Franklin Delano Roosevelt's first term, the depression in production had not yet ended, but white-collar jobs were beginning to increase, if only in the staffing of the New Deal bureaucracies. The steelworker in Pittsburgh who had not had a job in six or seven years was usually interviewed for home relief by a newly employed caseworker, who very often was a Jew. Indeed, social work began to flourish as an "industry" under the New Deal. Before the advent of Roosevelt, caseworkers had been employed in very small numbers by private charity agencies. The new governmental bureaucracies for administering relief required thousands of such functionaries. Inevitably, a large number of Jews sought these new jobs. All of the New Deal agencies were staffed by a notable number of Jews, for Roosevelt had opened these newer bureaucracies to the "merit system." Roosevelt was thus the major employer in America who did not discriminate against Jews, and he was, inevitably, their hero. An age-old drama repeated itself; Jews were being hired in a new "industry," the government agencies which had just been created, because the older pursuits were keeping them out. These new jobs were insecure, but the Jews who held them were resented by those who had no jobs at all.

The net result of the Jewish experience in the decade during the Great Depression was the conviction among Jews that they remained outsiders in the American economy. Their security could come only if the government itself consciously tried to include them in the promises it had made to all Americans. Jews could not afford a laissez-faire government. They required a share in political power; they had to be indispensable to the coalition which elected the government, and that government had to act to widen the field of possibility for Jews. Otherwise, no matter what the children of the immigrants might do, their successes could be taken away from them. The way to fight the systematic exclusion of Jews was politics.

In the mid-1930s the respectable representatives of American Jewry were still trying to finesse the difference between Jews and all other Americans by insisting that there was no difference. The "German Jews" kept repeating the doctrine that being a Jew was like being a Methodist, that is, it meant belonging to one of the many religious denominations in America. But the mass of the East Europeans and their children knew that none of this was true—and so did the most perceptive Gentiles. In America the Jews were a sui generis minority; for them, and for all those who related to them, whether friend or foe, this was not a multireligious or multiethnic country; it was a Jew/Gentile country. But in their need to "arrive" in America, Jews kept hoping that this was not so, or, at the very least, that Jews could persuade the Gentile majority of some definition of American society that would obscure this line of cleavage.

15.

Children of the Ghetto

I

Jews never had an alternative to America. They could not go "home," because they had none in Russia, Poland, and Romania, which remained hostile to Jews. Therefore, Jews needed acceptance in America more than any other minority.

Many Gentiles, of all the ethnic groups, could, and did, go home when times were bad and they could find no work. Others returned after they had succeeded in making enough money to buy a farm or a business. But not the Jews, neither the poor nor the successful. The most telling proof of this difference is to be found in the statistics for the last year of mass migration to the United States, the fiscal year which ended on June 30, 1924. The restrictions of the new quota law hit the Italians as hard as the Jews. Those who returned to Europe from both groups knew that they would have great difficulty being readmitted. Nonetheless, while 23,000 Italians went back home that year, only 260 Jews returned to their place of origin. Even the Irish, few of whom had ever gone back, had a higher rate of reemigration; more than 1,500 returned to the home country in 1924.

Jews not only needed acceptance in America more than any other ethnic group, they also needed it more quickly. The Irish, Slavs, and Italians came from the farms, and most were willing to remain farmers or laborers for at least a generation after they arrived in America. Jews had lived for centuries in the cities and small towns of Europe, on the margin of the economy and society. The New World meant, for them, the chance to achieve in New York what they could not reach in the Moscow of the czars: to become professors, merchants, and white-collar bureaucrats. In the early 1920s, Harvard, Yale, and Columbia did not feel constrained to impose quotas on Slavs, Irish, and Italians, because few of their children were then applying to universities. Jews were the first ethnic group to try to breach the American Establishment. They were the first to be told that they were not true Americans. Inevitably, they were the first of all the ethnic groups to counter this attack by trying to remake themselves, and to redefine America, so that they would be "just like everybody else."

Their German Jewish predecessors had solved the problem of self-definition by insisting that Jewishness had no cultural or ethnic content; they were Jews by religion. This formula was borrowed from Europe, where Jews had tried to present themselves in the nineteenth century as Frenchmen or Germans of the Jewish religious persuasion, just like other Frenchmen or Germans, who were Christians. The Gentile majorities in Europe were not convinced. They continued to feel that being French or German meant that the individual had age-old roots in the culture and religion of the majority. In America, opinion was not quite as firm, but even the friends of the Jews did not contest the proposition that America was, culturally and historically, largely Christian.

Theodore Roosevelt was not an enemy of the Jews; he had even vetoed a bill restricting immigration, and as we have seen, he had written a warm greeting to the celebration in Carnegie Hall of 250 years of Jewish settlement in the United States. But Roosevelt thundered, again and again, against "hyphenated Americans," by which he meant anyone who did not quickly sever ties with his past and assimilate into American society. Roosevelt did not specify that this American society was determined by Protestant Christian norms, though he probably felt that it was at the essence of true Americanism. Roosevelt would have felt at home with Ezra Stiles. That ex-

Puritan divine had proposed in the earliest years of the Republic that America was a redemptive society to which all newcomers would have to conform.

The repeated demand, by the Puritans, by Ezra Stiles, and by Theodore Roosevelt, that newcomers assimilate, was demeaning. It suggested that nothing that an immigrant might bring with him was of value to the existing society, except, perhaps, as an exotic curiosity. The older, "German Jews" had made no such total concession to the majority, for they had insisted that their Judaism, even as they reformed it into American respectability, was the equal of Christianity. The "Russian Jews" had to preserve a comparable dignity. Some rejoiced in getting rid of their Jewish past, but most could not accept the thought that they should be ashamed of everything they were before landing on Ellis Island. Even assimilation could not be allowed to mean total self-abasement.

But how does one retain some pride in being Jewish and become an American? The first formal attempt by some "Russian Jews" to answer this question was the theory of the "melting pot." This notion was invented in the early 1900s at the height of mass emigration. The United States was imagined as a big pot seething with various nationalities, both old and new. As new elements were tossed into this pot, the stew kept changing in flavor and composition. The "American" was, therefore, not a fixed, existing type; he was always still in the process of becoming. This formula was a bold attempt to make Pilgrim Fathers and sweatshop workers into equally important actors in the making of the "American." The theory of the melting pot accepted the premise of the nativists about society: to be an "American" meant not merely to obey the law; one had to belong to American society. But there was a basic difference between the nativists and the proponents of the melting pot. The nativists said that American society had been defined permanently by the older America; the supporters of the melting pot argued that American society was constantly evolving.

Very little has been said about the other implications, at least for Jews, of the notion of the melting pot. All the other immigrants bore no responsibility for the future of the culture from which they came. Germany, Russia, Italy, and all the other European countries would continue to safeguard their various languages and traditions even if everyone who went to America transmuted his origins into knock-wurst, vodka, or marinara sauces. Jews had a "homeland" in Eastern Europe, but they were everywhere an embattled minority. Indeed, all of the Jewish ideologies of that day, from revolutionary socialism to Zionism, began with the premise that the existing Jewish life in Eastern Europe was not viable and that in its present form it was not worth preserving. The suggestion that the Jews in America should assimilate was therefore based only in part on any certainty that Jewishness was safe in its older centers in Russia and Poland.

The idea of the melting pot was not conceived in America. This new definition of America was constructed in England by Israel Zangwill, from the same intellectual material which Theodor Herzl had used when he designed his version of Zionism. When he published *The Jewish State*, in 1896, Herzl had posed these alternatives: Jews should choose either national existence in Palestine or assimilation; they should finally reorganize themselves, "normalize," and become "like everyone else." In 1914, Zangwill said exactly this in an afterword that he wrote to his drama, *The Melting Pot*, which had been produced six years earlier. The point of the play had been its advocacy of intermarriage between Jew and Christian as a way of dissolving even the greatest of differences among Americans. In the last lines of the play, the Jewish hero addresses his Christian wife. He regards the New World as far more glorious than even Rome or Jerusalem because America is the place where "all races and nations come to labor and look forward." Zangwill remained convinced of this idea; he defended it again in 1914, in the afterword to the new edition, by insisting "that the conditions offered to the Jew in America are without parallel in the world." In the New World, the Jew is a "citizen of a republic without a state religion." All of those who were speaking for maintaining some form of Jewish apartness were missing the meaning of this messianic moment: "In America . . . the Jew, by a roundabout journey from Zion has come into his own again." The rabbis who had denounced Zangwill for proposing the "solution of the Jewish problem by dissolution" were wrong, because Zangwill did not believe that assimilation is "universally applicable." In the play itself, its hero had asked his uncle, "Why, if he objects to the dissolving process, did he not work for a separate Jewish land?" Throughout this essay, there is a presumption about the mass of Jews in Eastern Europe: they are kept separate by anti-Semitism; they should be saved by being given the choice between national life in Jerusalem or "the melting pot" in New York.

The concept of the "melting pot" established a premise which would be the basis for all the other Jewish theories about the nature of America: the New World was not merely a place to make a living or to be free from persecution; becoming part of America was to participate in the drama of redeeming the Jews in this world. Jews could no longer be hectored by the older America as latecomers who were bringing their supposedly uncouth and pushy ways to an existing and defined America which they had not helped to run. This was heady stuff for some Jews; they could assimilate into America in good conscience, and even in glory. But his formula of the melting pot did not persuade many leaders of the old American Establishment, not even liberals such as Theodore Roosevelt.

The concept of the melting pot was rejected by Jews as well. The existing Jewish life in America was in trouble; it was threatened by its foreignness and its shallowness, but most Jews were not going to abandon their Jewishness for assimilation. Some were at war with themselves and with the world about their Jewishness, but most accepted it as a fact of nature.

Horace Kallen and Mordecai Kaplan, the first intellectuals among the children of the immigrants to think about America, began with the presumption that Jews were in America to stay—as affirming Jews. Kaplan had been brought to New York in 1887, at the age of eight, by his father, who was a distinguished rabbinic scholar of the old school. Kaplan himself was raised on the Lower East Side of New York on the Talmud, and he was ordained as a rabbi in 1902 at the Jewish Theological Seminary, but he also studied at Columbia under John Dewey, whose philosophy of pragmatism Kaplan embraced. Kaplan was unshakably a Jew, but he wanted to enter the mainstream of American life. Along with Horace Kallen (who had studied at Harvard under William James, another important American philosopher of pragmatism), Kaplan proposed a theory of "cultural pluralism." Kaplan and Kallen defined America as a creation of all the various ethnic groups which came to the New World. They denied the melting pot because they insisted that each of these groups had the right to cultivate its links to its origins. The force of this assertion was to dethrone the Protestant Anglo-Saxons, who were the earliest arrivals, from their self-assumed position of being the only true Americans. The Talmudic learning of Kaplan's father was thus pronounced to be as much a part of the American heritage as the Puritans' Calvinist theology. Kaplan imagined an America in which both traditions lasted, side by side, as equals.

Writing in *The Nation* in February of 1915, Horace Kallen defied the older America, and those who were decrying "hyphenated Americans." He conceded (in my view, wrongly) that "the writers of the American Declaration of Independence and of the Constitution of the United States were not confronted by the practical fact of ethnic dissimilarity among the whites of the country." The situation was different now: "Their descendants are confronted by it." Kallen refused to back down and accede to the doctrine of assimilation in any form, including the melting pot. He insisted, passionately and vehemently, that inherited identities are inalienable:

> Men may change their clothes, their politics, their wives, their religions, their philosophies, to a greater or lesser extent: they cannot change their grandfathers. Jews or Poles or Anglo-Saxons, in order to cease being Jews or Poles or Anglo-Saxons, would have to cease to be, while they could cease to be citizens or church members or carpenters or lawyers without ceasing to be. The selfhood which is inalienable in them, and for the realization of which they require "inalienable" liberty is ancestrally determined, and the happiness which they pursue has its form implied in ancestral endowment. This is what, actually, democracy in operation assumes. There are human capacities which it is the function of the state to liberate and to protect in growth; and the failure of the state as a government to accomplish this automatically makes for its abolition. Government, the state, under the democratic conception is, it cannot be too often repeated, merely an instrument, not an end.

As the model for the new America, Kallen proposed Switzerland, with its three languages and cultures. There was, however, one critical difference: "The common language of the commonwealth, the language of its great tradition, would be English, but each nationality would have for its emotional and involuntary life its own peculiar dialect or speech, its own individual and inevitable esthetic and intellectual forms." Kallen knew, clearly and unmistakably, that he was proposing an unprecedented structure of society, a new "symphony of civilization" that would be composed of differing nationalities. He did not pretend for a moment that he was affirming a process that had been in motion since the beginnings of America. Kallen was clear and forthright in presenting cultural pluralism as a new idea. It was the contemporary way to assure everyone his full human rights in a democracy, for each American would be encouraged to have a direct and respected relationship to his ethnic group. Kallen knew that the older America would resist: "The question is, do the dominant classes in America want such a society?"

Kallen addressed this question to the Gentile Establishment, but that was not the only question that he and Kaplan had to answer. They had to explain what it meant to be a Jew in this culturally plural American democracy. How could one demand equality, and the role of a cocreator of America, and yet continue to insist on the classic Jewish faith in the "chosen people"? How could one accept this doctrine, even in the attenuated version of the immigrant family, that Jews were, somehow, unique? Kallen had no problem. As a completely secular person, Kallen distinguished between "Judaism," which he used as a name for inherited religion, and "Hebraism," which meant for Kallen the cultural expressions of Jews as a community. Kallen was persuaded that all American identities were rapidly becoming secular. In the New Land, Jews would behave like the Irish, the Italians, and all the other ethnic groups by using only those elements of their past which spoke to their present needs in America.

Kaplan, the rabbi, insisted that Jewishness had religion as its central element, but his definition of religion was unprecedented. Having become a philosophical pragmatist, Kaplan had ceased believing in a transcendent God, the Person who had spoken at Sinai to His creatures and who had revealed His will to them. Kaplan's God was "natural," which meant that He was conceived as a word which summed up the highest values of a community. All of the ethnic minorities in America, Kaplan argued, shared the basic values of American democracy, but each subgroup expressed these values through a different set of symbols derived from its history. Kaplan had thus ruled out the most striking of all Jewish doctrines, the faith of Jews that they were the "chosen people." In practice, he conceded even more. Kaplan wanted no segregation from the cultural life of the majority. He asserted that "Jews have no intention of following the example of the Catholics in contesting the prior right of the State to the education of the child." He thus refused to use private education to preserve Jewish culture. He was too busy entering America, by differentiating himself from Catholic separatism, to ask an obvious question: What about boarding schools such as Groton and Andover, which continued to be the training schools of the Protestant elite?

Both Kallen and Kaplan were thus eager to present the Jews as the model for all other ethnic minority identities in America. Kaplan and Kallen had produced a set of definitions of America, and of the Jews, which seemed to solve the question of how one can be both a Jew and an American.

Kallen helped Brandeis win the fight for the American Jewish Congress (in which, in effect, Jews had declared themselves to be an ethnic minority with its own political agenda), but, overall, his impact on the organized activities of the community was not large. Kaplan did have at least one important success in shaping American Jewish institutional life. Right after the First World War, he founded the movement for the creation of "Jewish centers," and he continued to be the inspiration for the many dozens that were being created in the next several decades. These "centers" were different from the Americanization agencies that the "German Jews" had put up at the turn of the century. The purpose of the new Jewish centers was to provide a place of Jewish assembly, where ethnic and family loyalties could be cultivated through recreation and cultural endeavor. In Kaplan's earliest formulations, these centers were to exist as extensions, and even transformations, of the synagogue; religion played the most prominent role, but even so, it was only one of many elements in the "reconstructed" synagogue. Many centers were not, however, affiliated with synagogues. They were created as secular expressions of Jewish ethnicity. In both sets of institutions, there was large emphasis on providing programs which would attract people to the building, with the implicit assumption that the old Jewish learning and piety were too forbidding, and too identified with guilt, to be, now in America, the cement which held Jews together. The pervasive contemporary jibe at Kaplan's synagogue-center was to call it "The Shul [synagogue] with a Pool."

Kaplan knew that he was creating the Reform Judaism of his own day for the East Europeans, and that he was, thus, reenacting what Isaac Mayer Wise had done two generations earlier for the German Jews. Like Wise, Kaplan insisted that his version of Judaism affirmed American democracy, and that he had redefined Judaism in America as an active, forward-looking, and optimistic faith. Kaplan was less clear, even to himself (and in this, too, he repeated Isaac Mayer Wise), that he was essentially acceding to the nullification of rabbinic authority. Kaplan was constructing a new model of American Jewish life which, because it was not bound by the past, had no need for those who had been its guardians. In his own, "reconstructionist" synagogue, Kaplan even abandoned the title "Rabbi." For a number of years, in the 1930s, he followed the example of the Ethical Culture Societies in which the clergy were called "Leaders." In theory, Kaplan kept insisting that decision making in his "synagogue-centers" was a democratic enterprise and that rabbis could, at most, offer some informed opinion, but that theirs was never the deciding vote.

Kaplan never really believed these theories, for his own heritage and temperament stood against them. He was the descendant of many generations of rabbis, and he was personally a commanding, often intolerant presence. More importantly, even as he asserted democracy in religion, Kaplan was a deep traditionalist. He fervently believed that his very modern formulations would lead his American Jewish contemporaries to accept the major forms of their inherited tradition, not as divine commandments but as "folkways." Jews would no longer look at Judaism and feel guilty because they were disobedient. Kaplan's reconstructed Judaism would supposedly be so attractive that Jews would affirm it with joy. Here, too, he was repeating Isaac Mayer Wise, who had announced eighty years earlier that the American Jewish "temple," with which he was replacing the synagogue of old, would represent a new Judaism, without tears, rejoicing in democracy. Jews would no longer be compelled to come to synagogue out of guilt, or fear, or even the compulsion of Orthodox fundamentalism; they would come to Wise's temple rejoicing in its beauty and in the uplifting quality of the music and decorum of the service. Kaplan, eighty years later, was offering the joys of togetherness and the warmth of selective memory of the Jewish past.

Kaplan's most difficult problem of self-definition in America was that he was a Zionist. Indeed, by the 1920s he had been adopted by the mainstream Zionist organizations, the men's Zionist Organization of America, and the women's group, Hadassah, as their official thinker. These organizations invited him repeatedly to their platforms, to provide the intellectual rationale for Zionism in America. He talked away the stark assertion of the European and Palestinian Zionist ideologies that Jews were irretrievably different from Gentiles. Kaplan refused to accept the fundamental Zionist assertion that it was better for a Jew to live in his own homeland, in a majority culture which was his, than to live in a minority, even if it was a democracy. This might be true of European lands, but America was different. Indeed the nascent Jewish majority in the ancestral land had much to learn from those Jews who were, like himself, being refashioned by their unique experience of American democracy. But, above all, Kaplan used Zionism as a "task" to preserve Judaism in America. It did not matter, for Kaplan, whether a Jewish majority and state were ever achieved in Palestine—and before the 1940s, that hope did seem distant. Judaism was to be a pragmatic, "American," problem-solving faith; its major continuing Jewish preoccupation, one that would last and keep Jews busy for generations, was the Zionist endeavor.

The theories of cultural pluralism, defined by Kallen and Kaplan, served to "legitimize" Jews in America, and to make them comfortable with themselves: they sanctified what the mainstream of the Jewish community wanted to feel. Jews were just as good Americans as everyone else; Jews had the right to think of themselves as a group, with a past. Still, the theoretical formulations by Kallen and Kaplan were never really believed. Most Jews never accepted the all-too-logical assertions by Kallen and Kaplan that the price of equality in democracy was, at the very least, the abandonment of any thought of "chosenness." The mainstream of American Jews never doubted that they were special, and different, from all the other minorities. Why suffer from anti-Semitism, which one could avoid by assimilation or, if need be, religious conversion, just for the sake of asserting an ethnic identity that was as important, and as unimportant, as that of the Sicilians, the Slovaks, or the Albanians?

The rhetoric of cultural pluralism did have its uses. It was convenient when demanding equality from an unfriendly majority, and it helped in forgiving oneself for straying away from the older religious norms. Nevertheless, it was never dominant among American Jews, because the evidence of their own lives was against it. American society was not becoming more plural and more open. On the contrary, it was keeping Jews at arm's length, even as they were increasingly the most educated, culturally creative element in America.

II

Most of the young Jewish intellectuals could not understand America as a melting pot, for it kept refusing to melt them in. Cultural pluralism was irrelevant, not least because most of the younger intellectuals were refusing to adhere to any discrete ethnic culture. This intelligentsia had no other option but to make its alienation into a form of heroism.

Before the Second World War, ideologues, from anarchists and Communists to psychoanalysts, were proposing to fashion a reborn world in America, a new Garden of Eden, each according to his own doctrine. Almost all of the Jews among them knew that they were "other," and that this otherness was linked to their Jewish origins. In theory, these dreamers dealt with their Jewishness by preaching its abandonment; the Messianic Era could come, as Paul of Tarsus had once said nineteen centuries earlier, only to a world in which there was "neither Jew nor Greek." But Paul in his day had continued to insist that this new age for all mankind could happen only if the Jews exercised special leadership in bringing about the new dispensation. A comparable notion about the special role of Jews existed, though it was sometimes disguised even from themselves, among Jewish Marxists, Freudians, or modernists in art and literature. They thought of themselves as the prophets of the new in politics and culture. They needed this grandiose self-image, for this was a generation which was without fathers, either Jewish or Gentile; these intellectuals stood alone. As Isaac Rosenfeld wrote in those days: "A Jewish writer feels that he may at any time be called to account not for his art, nor even for his life, but for his Jewishness." But this Jewishness was no continuing commitment to a separate Jewish identity and tradition. It meant standing over against society for a while to exhort it to create a new age in which there would be neither Jew nor Gentile.

As both friends and enemies knew, Communism was especially attractive to this dispossessed Jewish intelligentsia. Karl Marx was a formidable "ancestor," and Joseph Stalin was already, in the Communist clichés of the 1930s, the "father of all the peoples." Though the mid-1930s were a high-water mark for adherence to Communism among the children of the immigrants, they also signaled the beginning of retreat and falling away. The Great Depression had caused growth in the influence, and numbers of domestic radicalism. The call from the Soviet Union for a "popular front" against Nazism reechoed even in non-Communist circles. But there were also the purge trials in Russia in the late 1930s. Stalin was consolidating his personal power by accusing those whom he did not trust of spying for the Nazis. Fabled figures in the making of the Bolshevik Revolution were tried and shot; tens of thousands were sent to jail. In Arthur Koestler's phrase, there was "darkness at noon." (This was the title of a novel that he published in 1937 in Europe, but the book was read, widely and immediately, in America.) Koestler himself had been a Communist; he left the movement in outraged disbelief at the purge trials.

In the United States, many of the Jews who followed Communism were motivated by immediate "Jewish" concerns; the Soviet Union was supposedly free of anti-Semitism. This faith was shaken by the purge trials, because some of the major makers of the Bolshevik Revolution who were Jews, such as Lev Kamenev and General Jan Gomarnik, were shot as traitors who had supposedly conspired with Hitler. Even the Communist Yiddish daily in New York, the *Morgen Freiheit,* which had been siding with Arabs against Jews in Palestine, was shaken by controversy. The paper followed the Stalinist line, but some of its contributors resigned, and more left after the signing of the Stalin-Hitler pact in August 1939. Nonetheless, the majority of Jewish Communists remained in the party into the next decade. Aging immigrants could not give up a lifetime of psychological investment: many lived together in housing which had been built in the Bronx by Communist-dominated unions. Adults and children spent time together in Yiddish-speaking summer camps, which were creations of the party. Those who abandoned this immigrant, Communist subculture were shunned by the friends whom they had known best and longest.

The second generation, the American-born, were less concerned about the status of Jews in Russia. They were concerned about themselves. Many Jewish teachers, doctors, and lawyers joined the party in anger at their great difficulty in finding a place in America. Jewish teachers, who were entering the profession in the Depression years, were the first to be fired when budgets were cut. Doctors and lawyers had difficulty gaining appointments to hospitals or law firms. These young professionals thought they needed the revolution in America, or they would spend their lives out on the street, looking through the window at America. Many such young Jews, who were given their first jobs by the New Deal, moved to support Franklin Delano Roosevelt, but a significant number continued to believe that they would have an equal chance only in an American equivalent of Russian Communism. A significant minority of bright Jews thought that they would rise by merit, and unencumbered by anti-Semitism, to high places in society only after a revolution in America.

A small but intellectually significant group of these left-wingers were not Stalinists but Trotskyites. Some had recoiled early from Stalin, recognizing him to be a Communist Russian czar, and not the leader of a universal ideology. A handful of Jewish intellectuals identified passionately with Trotsky, who was like them, or like what they wanted to be: an intellectual of Jewish origin, a revolutionary thinker who could be mentioned in the same breath with Karl Marx, and a fighting Jew, unprecedented for many centuries, who had been the commander of all the Bolshevik armies. This Trotskyite handful condemned both the Soviet Union, under Stalin, and the democracies, which were dominated by appeasers in Europe and isolationists in America. One could only hope for a new age when both rotten structures, Stalin's Soviet Union and the capitalist West, would be replaced by a decent, worldwide revolutionary order.

In all their clashing varieties, these intellectuals and professionals were all alienated from America. There was no home-grown revolutionary tradition into which they could fit, not even American Populism. In the Depression years the Populist impulses were tainted with antiforeignism and anti-Semitism. These Populists were mostly midwestern radicals, and they were not imagining an America in which they would be led by the Jewish intelligentsia. Even within the Communist party, which was based in the cities, mostly on the East and West coasts, some Gentiles, blacks among them, refused to accept the dominance in the party of white-collar Jews. Radical Jews in America, therefore, did not derive their radicalism from older American left-wing traditions or constituencies. The Jewish radicals were "cosmopolitans"; they could not really feel that they were the unquestioned leaders of the American radicalisms. The Communist party made a great point of having a Gentile, Earl Browder, as its head, and the leader of the socialists was a former Christian minister, Norman Thomas. Jews were very nearly forced to look toward Europe for inspiration and legitimacy. Moscow was the capital for the Communists. American Jewish Trotskyites were emotionally "in exile," together with their leader, who was chased from country to country by pressure from Stalin after he expelled Trotsky from Russia in 1926. The Jewish socialists in the Bund looked to Poland, where the party was strong and creative even in the bad times for Jews in the 1930s. The believers in modernism in art and literature looked to Paris, Berlin, and Vienna for inspiration, for the center of these movements was there and not in America.

The advent of Hitler was, therefore, not so paradoxically, a spiritual milestone for all these "post-Jewish Jews." More than two hundred thousand Jewish refugees were admitted to the United States between Hitler's ascent to power in 1933 and America's entry into World War II at the end of 1941. Those who came were largely middle-class people from Central Europe. An extraordinarily significant minority among these refugees were scholars and artists who were the very glory of European culture. These newcomers were different from all the earlier immigrants. There were ranking scientists, artists, and social thinkers among them, such as Albert Einstein, Marc Chagall, Theodor Adorno, Max Horckheimer, and Hannah Arendt. These people were not only incredibly learned. They were perceived by young American-born Jewish intellectuals as light bearers of modernity. In the 1930s and the 1940s, they provided legitimacy for the American Jewish intelligentsia.

They were teachers who could be adopted as fathers. Growing up in Europe, these Jewish intellectuals had already faced the question of where to situate themselves in a hostile culture; they had solved the problem by extolling their "marginality," and by inventing the "international style." It was painful to be on the margin, but it was also ennobling. Franz Kafka, who had become the most read and quoted writer of the displaced European Jewish intelligentsia in the 1930s, had lived on the margin of both the German and the Czech communities. These Europeans brought Kafka with them to America. They did not read him as a Jew who moved from the margin in search of community but rather as the archetype of an alienated man who was condemned to sit forever outside the majority culture. In his novel *The Trial,* he wrote of the individual who waits endlessly outside the door of a judgment chamber, hoping to be admitted to face the judges and, at least, to be told the name of the crime for which he is accused. Even though the word "Jew" is not once mentioned, this was a very "Jewish" tale. It could, and was, read as a parable about a Jew waiting for the Gentiles to tell him on what terms they might accept him—but the answer never came. The story cried out for some resolution. One could not live forever in limbo with Kafka's antihero. Perhaps he could discover his "crime," if some skilled physician would sit with him and help him look into his soul. Perhaps this unfortunate sufferer would then be welcomed by the nameless judges as one of their own, when he would have become, like them, untormented and cheerful.

"Marginality" helped the native-born Jewish intellectuals to explain their own situation in America: Jews were excluded by the capitalists, who dominated the society (and Jews even had some trouble with the poor), but Jews were the people who were most attuned to the newest, most cosmopolitan currents in culture and thought. In America in the 1930s, Jewish intellectuals who did not believe in the Jewish God were thus asserting that they were the true prophets of Western culture, the breakers of the existing idols, and that they were being persecuted by anti-Semites for their prophetic role. Here, under fairly transparent cover, the un-Jewish Jews among the children of the immigrants were replaying the classic themes of Jewish history: exclusion and chosenness.

This self-definition as "alienated prophets" was especially strong in the 1930s among the Jewish disciples of Leon Trotsky, who were editing and writing for the *Partisan Review.* Sidney Hook, Irving Howe, and a number of others who were a part of that circle as young men have attested to a pervasive alienation from America. Hook has written that the editors of the journal were "almost exclusively European in their cultural orientation," and that "they were largely ignorant of and indifferent to American traditions. . . ." Howe has told that the editor of the *Partisan Review,* Philip Rahv, was among those in the circle who "took an acute private pleasure, through jokes and asides, in those aspects of intellectualism that mark Jewishness: quickness, skepticism, questioning." However, on the pages of the journal in its heyday, Jewish issues were never discussed directly. Rahv himself made one glancing reference, in all of his writings, to the "cleverness" of Jews, and that remark was not meant entirely as a compliment. These young intellectuals, in Howe's words, "refused to acknowledge ourselves as part of a Jewish community encompassing all classes and opinions." They had chosen to belong to the "straggling phalanx" of the international Stalinist Left. And their heroes were such "non-Jewish Jews" as Rosa Luxemburg and Leon Trotsky.

This Trotskyite splinter group of the intelligentsia was surer that it was bringing the light of the revolution to the world in the 1930s and into the 1940s than the much more numerous Stalinists. The rightness of their politics was confirmed in their minds by the treason trials of the late 1930s, when Stalin shot almost all of the surviving leaders of the Bolshevik Revolution, and even by the murder of Trotsky by Stalinist agents in Mexico in 1940. But America was not moving toward the revolution. The New Deal and the onset of the Second World War gave American capitalism another chance, even as Jews were still semioutsiders in America. The question had to be posed: Is marginality, in and of itself, a light-bearing mission?

Ultimately it is not. As Jewish intellectuals found out from some of their European teachers, a passion for the revolution can be sustaining, but the sheer loneliness of being outside of society is unbearable. Abraham, the ultimate ancestor of all Jews, including these brilliant young writers, had known some thirty-five centuries earlier that to represent a minority opinion against the reigning idolaters is a dangerous role, but Abraham had been sustained by faith in the one God. As world revolution tarried, what sustained "marginal" intellectuals, both the European "fathers" and their new American "children," for whom the Jewish God was an outworn myth and for whom Communism was becoming a failed faith? The door was now open for psychoanalysis.

In 1938 Sigmund Freud had fled from Vienna to London. In 1939 he published *Moses and Monotheism,* a book in which he tried to "cure" the Jews of their "illness," as Freud diagnosed it. Moses, so Freud asserted, had been an Egyptian, and not a Jew, and the doctrine of monotheism was not Jewish. It had been proclaimed first by a young revolutionary pharaoh, Akhenaton, and had been brought to the Jews by Moses. Jewish tribalists had murdered the bearer of this universalism. The hidden trauma of the Jewish people was the "suppressed memory" of this murder. The only way for Jews to return to health was to admit the crime, and to abandon their ethnic separatism. Freud's fanciful, and totally unsupported, "historical" reconstruction of the biblical drama of Moses and the Jews was a plea for assimilation, with the clear implication that "cured," that is, de-Judaized, Jews would stem the tide of Nazi anti-Semitism. This assumption was obviously wildly wrong, for the Nazis hated assimilated Jews even more than affirming ones. Assimilated Jews were more likely to occupy central positions in contemporary culture and politics.

Nonetheless, despite the illogic of Freud's argument in *Moses and Monotheism,* psychoanalysis became the "religion" of elements of America's Jewish intelligentsia. The psychoanalysts were not only an alternative to the agents of Stalin; they seemed to have an answer to the most pervasive, personal problem among many younger Jews, the question of their relationships with their parents. This pain lent itself to analysis in terms of one of Freud's basic insights, the supposed desire of the child to destroy his father and to possess his mother. As the revolution tarried, it seemed ever less likely that a classless America, according to Karl Marx, would free these children of immigrants from the woe of their Jewishness. Some hoped that Freud might purge them of their pain by freeing their inner selves of their ancestors. "Analyzed" young Jews would finally be able to realize Mary Antin's dream of walking into the warm sunlight of a joyous America. But the analysts, and their Jewish analysands, could never shake off Freud's own bitter knowledge, that psychoanalysis was an overwhelmingly Jewish cult.

Psychoanalysis as theory promised a universalist salvation; it suggested that it might achieve the Enlightenment's world of reason, now renamed superego. Psychoanalysis as cult reinforced a feeling, deeply embedded in the psyche of its believers, most of whom were Jewish, that they were at war with society, and that they had only their Promethean "chosenness," as the bearers of the truth, to sustain themselves. The Freudians, too, were sectarians, very much on the margin of society, and certainly "foreign" in the eyes of even the most literate Americans. Jewish intellectuals of the 1930s did, as Trilling's enemies at Columbia had told him, belong to Marx and Freud, and not to established America. They were in the same situation as their brothers and cousins in business; they were enraged by their exclusion from the promises of America, and they were sustained by feeling (no matter what its rationalization) that they were special.

But what were their Jewish roots? Looking back on those years, Irving Howe has written that he thought of himself, then, as descending from such archetypes as Solomon Maimon, the Lithuanian Jew who had come to Germany in the last years of the eighteenth century and transformed himself into a serious philosopher. Maimon had lived a picaresque and miserable life, outside both the Jewish and the German communities. Howe asserted that Maimon prefigured those in America who, though they wrote about politics and culture, had left the Jews, and were disregarded by the Gentiles. This assertion of intellectual affiliation was basically false. Solomon Maimon, and the far greater figure of Baruch Spinoza a century earlier, had both been educated, first, in a classic yeshivah, where they had learned the sacred texts in Hebrew. Both Spinoza and Maimon are intelligible only if one takes into account the tension between the religious and intellectual culture of Judaism, which they actually knew, and the new thinking and forms of living to which they found their way. In class terms, for that matter, Spinoza and Maimon— and such contemporary European figures as Ahad Ha-Am (pseudonym for Asher Ginzberg), the founder of cultural Zionism, and David Ben-Gurion, the first prime minister of Israel—came from the middle class, while the parents of the new American Jewish intelligentsia were almost without exception from the less-educated poor.

In the 1920s and 1930s, there were already some such classical scholars, and even a few writers in modern Hebrew, in America, but they were an ignored handful. Few among the immigrants, and even fewer of their children, knew Hebrew, except to say prayers by rote. The overwhelming preoccupation in the New Land was to survive and to succeed, and Jewish learning was not a useful tool in these endeavors. Secular learning, the kind that one acquired in college, was clearly useful; there was hope that it would lead to a career; it was a way to "America." But Jewish learning was held to be irrelevant. The secular intelligentsia simply ignored the bearers of Hebrew as museum pieces. No one adopted them as "fathers" to be emulated. They could have taught the intelligentsia the classic culture of Judaism, but no one came to listen, except some candidates for the rabbinate and a small handful of intellectual oddballs. Thus, the children of the immigrants learned to be intellectuals, either from books or from Gentile professors. Their own Jewishness was constructed out of ideological slogans and pronouncements about Jews by often unfriendly outsiders, in tension with childhood ghetto memories of fear, shame, pride, and defiance.

Most Jewish intellectuals of the 1920s and 1930s knew no Jewish world before the arrival of their parents on Ellis Island, or their own entry into City College. They did not rebel against the world of the Talmud, for they never knew it. The young Jewish writers were, almost without exception, children of parents who had brought very little formal Jewish education with them to the New World. A few of the fathers did know the Hebrew texts, but generally they did not transmit the learning that they had once acquired; most knew very little. Irving Howe's father ran a grocery store in the Bronx, and the Jewish culture that he imbibed was Yiddish; it was the world for which the *Jewish Daily Forward* spoke. Nathan Glazer has given a comparable account of his own parents. Even Alfred Kazin, who had a somewhat different personal history, is a case in point. He told, in his autobiographical memoir, *A Walker in the City,* that his father was a house painter who was almost totally silent. The son did not discover until near the end of the father's life that the older man had had some rabbinic education in his youth in Russia, and that he had buried that secret during his son's formative years because he wanted his son to be an "American." Those of the immigrant parents who were different from the majority, like Kazin's father, most often accepted the notion that their heritage was useless in the New World. They wanted their sons to find new "fathers" in Gentile America.

Kazin went to school in a very tough neighborhood in Brooklyn. His parents kept reminding him that if he did not do well in class, there "yawned the great abyss of a criminal career"; school was for him, therefore, "the stage for a trial." Immigrant parents—silent fathers and dreaming mothers—drove their children to succeed because, as Kazin observed, these children were their "America."

I worked on a hairline between triumph and catastrophe. Why the odds should always have felt so narrow I understood only when I realized how little my parents thought of their own lives. It was

not for myself alone that I was expected to shine, but for them—
to redeem the constant anxiety of their existence. I was the first
American child, their offering to the strange new God; I was to
be the monument of their liberation from the shame of being what
they were. And that there was shame in this was a fact that everyone
seemed to believe as a matter of course. It was in the gleeful dis-
counting of themselves—what do we know?—with which our
parents greeted every fresh victory in our savage competition for
high averages, for prizes, for a few condescending words of official
praise from the principal at assembly.

Such parents did want their children to remain Jews, but the Jewish
education that almost all the immigrants gave their children, including the intellectuals-to-be, was only sufficient to teach them to mouth
the rituals at bar mitzvah or, at most, to say some of the liturgies in
Hebrew without understanding the words. The rest of their exposure
consisted of folk religion and family memory. Thus, in their flight
from the "Lower East Side," such American-born intellectuals carried with them the pain of their immigrant Jewish beginnings, but
very little of the dignity that the yeshivah conferred even on those
who rebelled against and abandoned it.

The new, young, Jewish intelligentsia believed neither in the melting pot nor in cultural pluralism. Whether left-wingers or not, the
dominant mood among them in the 1930s was assimilation. Jews in
arts and letters almost always wrote and composed as "general Americans"; they were at great pains to avoid any reference to Jews in the
characters that they depicted. George Gershwin, for example, talked
occasionally about composing an opera on biblical themes, but that
work was never begun. The opera that he did compose was *Porgy
and Bess,* which was set in Charleston, South Carolina; it was about
the agony, the blasted hopes, the dreams of plenty, and the ultimately
triumphant courage of at least one heroic figure among the Negroes
in Catfish Row. The libretto for the opera was written by a white
Gentile, DuBose Heyward, and his subject had been Negroes. It is
no surprise that Gershwin found this tale suitable for his first opera,
for Jewish artists and performers had a particular affinity in those
days for expressing their Jewish angst through Negro characters.
Gershwin composed *Porgy and Bess* in the very years in which Al
Jolson and Eddie Cantor were appearing on vaudeville stages all over
America in blackface. In Cantor's most famous movie, *Whoopee,* he

alternated between blackface and Indian red, while throwing in an aside or two in Yiddish.

George Gershwin was a Jew from the Bronx, the child of Yiddish-speaking immigrants—and the Negroes in *Porgy and Bess* seemed to be Jews in blackface. Gershwin had rarely seen any of the tormented Negro characters whom he described so eloquently; it was in the Bronx ghetto of his childhood that the composer had seen picturesque criminals like the villain, Sportin' Life, and tragic men of principle, many of whom had been stunted by poverty and exclusion, like his crippled hero, Porgy. In the Bronx there were many women like Bess, the heroine of the opera, who was torn between the fast-talking Sportin' Life and the good and faithful Porgy. It was on their journey from the Bronx that invisible "cripples," the children of immigrant Jews, had traveled the hard road, on their knees, to New York and to America.

This process of avoidance, of masking the Jewish origins of his characters, is nearer the surface in the work of a younger contemporary, Clifford Odets: "I have a serious artistic problem. I don't feel I write completely American characters; they always come out a little Jewish." Odets knew enough about himself to admit that he "was really trying to disavow being a Jew. If the truth must be told, I yearn for acceptance like a youth of eighteen." What he ultimately hoped for, as he often said, was the Anglo-Saxon Protestant respectability of a Sidney Howard, a Maxwell Anderson, a Robert Sherwood. This passionate desire to annihilate the Jewish self was expressed in the names that he gave some of his characters. The protagonist of his play *Golden Boy* (1937) is named Joe Bonaparte, but in his notes for the play, Odets wrote, "Papa Bonaparte is sort of a Jacob character." The family in *Paradise Lost* (1935) is called Gordon, as an antidote to having identified the family in his first play, *Awake and Sing!* as Jews named Berger.

The Odets of the 1930s did write some plays which were overtly about Jews of his generation trapped in the Bronx, but his solution to their problem was assimilationist. In *Waiting for Lefty* (1935), the workers, who are Jews, were asked to rally against the bosses. When the Gentile Dr. Barnes fires the Jewish Dr. Benjamin from the staff of the hospital, Benjamin knows that he is meeting "an old disease, malignant, tumescent," and that he had met this disease before. He is losing his job, despite his seniority, because Jews are let go first—but Odets cannot let it go at that. Dr. Benjamin is surprised that there is "such discrimination, with all those wealthy brother Jews on the Board." Barnes replies that there "doesn't seem to be much difference between wealthy Jews and rich Gentiles. Cut from the same cloth." In two lines Odets, who was then a Communist, thus summarized the doctrine that Karl Marx had propounded a century before in his essay, "On the Jewish Question"—there really are no Jews or Gentiles, there are only capitalists and workers. Jews will solve their problem, anti-Semitism, only through social revolution. They can bring that revolution closer by giving up on any notions of Jewish group solidarity.

By the end of the 1930s, American Jews of the second generation were intellectually in an ever more untenable position. Their fathers had failed them. The path to America, through education, remained blocked. The revolution had, at very least, not yet succeeded; its tarrying was the cause of desperation in the very midst of rhetorical bravado about the dialectic certainty that capitalism would soon collapse. To be sure, the intellectuals were really better off than they were saying. They had not arrived at the center of American thought and literature, but many had jobs. They were working for New Deal agencies and so they were not starving. The most striking problem of this intelligentsia was its alienation from the Jewish community, but that was a problem that most refused to recognize. The active involvement in any separate Jewish existence was left to the "backward."

III

Almost all the neighborhoods, even the newer ones, in which Jews lived in the 1930s were still overwhelmingly Jewish. This living together was the major form of personal association. People met each other on the stoops in front of their houses, and in the candy stores. There were organizations of many kinds, from "friendly societies" to political groups. The synagogues did not seem, then, to be the dominant expression of Jewish identity. The formal memberships—as opposed to those who "bought tickets" or congregated outside on the street during the High Holy Days—were small. Nonetheless, the changing nature of religious life was the most accurate indicator of the future shape of life of the mainstream American Jews.

In the 1920s and 1930s, the Reform temples still seemed powerful, but they were increasingly becoming relics. The Reform movement had denounced Zionism when it first appeared, and the majority of the rabbis had remained hostile, even as the major lay leaders were becoming moderates. The Central Conference of American Rabbis, the organization of Reform rabbis, had made anti-Zionism into an article of faith. At their annual conventions the rabbis resolved again and again that Judaism was a "religion of universal significance" and that ethnic loyalties were both regressive and un-American. Many of the Reform temples were reluctant to admit the East Europeans, but they could not keep the doors tightly closed. Their memberships were dropping. The grandchildren of the original "German Jews" were intermarrying with non-Jews at the rate of one in three. The "German Jews" had fewer children, and they generally cared less about their Jewish identity than their parents or grandparents. The Reform temples were attractive to some of the nouveaux riches among the children of the immigrants. These "Russian Jews" did not accept the anti-Zionism that still pervaded many of the temples, and they were not comfortable with being snubbed. Yet, they fought to be admitted as members, or at least to send their daughters to the Reform Sunday schools, so their children might arrive among the "better Jews." In the 1920s and 1930s the social clubs which the "German Jews" had created a generation or so earlier, because they were excluded by the Gentiles, still stood firm in refusing to admit East European Jews. One might pray beside the "Russians" on the High Holidays, but it was still not conceivable that one would play golf with them on weekends. The story was told in those days of the "German Jew" who blackballed an affluent recent immigrant from membership in his country club, saying that "a man who speaks with an accent cannot possibly play golf."

But the 1920s and the 1930s were the last hurrah of old-line Reform Judaism. The Zionist minority among the Reform rabbis was increasing. In 1922, Stephen Wise established a new rabbinical school called the Jewish Institute of Religion which proposed to train rabbis for all the shades of Jewish belief, on the basis of an overarching commitment to the "unity of the Jewish People." Obviously, no one in the Orthodox community regarded rabbinic ordination from a liberal seminary as valid; in practice, this school was oriented toward a Zionist Reform Judaism. Its library never rivaled the great collections at the Hebrew Union College or of the Jewish Theological Seminary of America, but it was the preeminent place in America for books of modern Hebrew literature. The students at the Jewish Institute of Religion were themselves children of East Europeans; so were most of the congregants in the newer Reform congregations which they led.

Change was remaking even the older establishments of Reform Judaism. Very early, even before 1900, the Hebrew Union College had been forced to recruit its students not from the Reform laity but from the various immigrant East Sides. Though many of these men would play it safe for years, and preach "universalism" from their pulpits, their ingrained particularist feelings about the Jewish community could not be silenced forever, and especially after Hitler appeared in 1933. The formal reversal took place at a meeting of the Central Conference of American Rabbis in 1937 in Columbus, Ohio. There was a hard and bitter fight; hundreds of rabbis divided evenly, and the tiebreaking vote was cast by the president, Felix Levy. The resolution avoided the issue of a Jewish State, but the creation of a Jewish national and cultural center in Palestine was declared to be one of the aims of Reform Judaism. Even more bitter and divisive battles would yet come, but the antinationalist upholders of "classic Reform Judaism" had become a shrinking minority in their own house. Henceforth, Reform Judaism took greater pride in Jewish ethnic feeling, and pretended less that it stood for prophetic "ethical monotheism."

In the 1920s and the 1930s American Conservative Judaism also defined itself. The Jewish Theological Seminary had been founded in 1886 by a handful of rabbis and laymen of the older America settlement, the few who refused to go along with the then triumphant Reform Judaism. Their purpose was to create a Westernized, English-speaking Orthodox rabbinate to serve congregations in America. Very few such synagogues had resisted the tide to Reform, but it was hoped that their numbers would increase. By 1900, the seminary had very nearly evaporated. It was then revived by the leaders of the Reform "cathedral" synagogue, Temple Emanu-El, and moved from Philadelphia to New York. Solomon Schechter, a distinguished rabbinic scholar and historian (in religious practice he was a liberal traditionalist), was called from Cambridge University in England to New York to head the revived seminary. At its new beginnings, in 1902, it was not imagined that a new denomination was arising, for avowed Orthodox Jews, some of whom were even among the founders of the Union of Orthodox Jewish Congregations, taught on its faculty.

The new seminary began, at least in the minds of the laymen who refounded it, on an ill-defined premise. Jacob Schiff, Louis Marshall, and their friends wanted to produce Westernized rabbis who would help in the grand task of Americanizing the East European Jewish masses. Such English-speaking traditionalist rabbis already existed then in England, Germany, and France. They had defined decorous, mildly Orthodox congregations which were not socially embarrassing. Schiff and Marshall did not imagine that the American version of such synagogues would be centers of Jewish nationalist feeling, but the Conservative synagogues were soon out of control. The faculty and the students of the Jewish Theological Seminary were almost all from Eastern Europe; most were themselves recent immigrants. They had brought to America a Jewish identity which had been fashioned in the Austro-Hungarian and Russian empires, where Jews were still treated not as a religious denomination but as a national minority. On the immediate level of religious practice and observance, the Conservative synagogue was particularly comfortable for the children of the immigrants. The traditions and the rituals of Orthodox Judaism were upheld there, with one striking change— the separation of sexes at worship was abolished almost everywhere. The individual laymen were also subject to very little pressure about their personal religious conduct. But there was more to the Conservative synagogues than religious adjustment. The essence of the faith of Conservative Judaism was passion about the intense, and unique, history of the Jews. The effort for Zionism came naturally to such believers. Many of the members and sympathizers of the Zionist Organization of America, and Hadassah, belonged to Conservative synagogues. The home for a Zionist meeting, especially when a visiting emissary from Palestine was on tour, was most often the local Conservative synagogue.

Throughout the 1920s and the 1930s membership in the Conservative congregations kept rising, both in absolute numbers and in relation to the Orthodox and the Reform. In 1935 a reasonably reliable estimate showed a million Jews who identified themselves as Orthodox. The Conservative synagogues, the newest denomination, claimed three hundred thousand members, and Reform had only two hundred thousand.

Group emotion was, of course, powerful among the small minority of the American-born who had remained Orthodox in religion. A yeshivah had been established in New York as early as 1886; another was founded in 1897. These two institutions merged in 1915. This school encouraged its students to acquire a secular education. Its president, Bernard Revel, was not content to send his students to City College for their academic degrees; he wanted a college as part of his Talmudic school. By 1928 Revel had succeeded. The Yeshiva College, the first such school in all of Jewish history, accepted its first students. The motto on the seal of this new institution indicated that knowledge of the sacred literature and meticulous observance of every ritual of the Jewish tradition would be combined with secular learning. But there was suspicion regarding this new institution among the immigrant rabbis who ministered to Yiddish-speaking congregations. The new, "modern Orthodox" rabbis were competitors, and they were less learned in the Talmud. Most of the older men refused to accept these college-educated rabbis as true representatives of the Orthodox faith.

All of the religious communities, of all the clashing persuasions, had been transformed in America. In none of them, not even the Orthodox, was there any serious expectation that the laity would be trained in Jewish learning. The differing religious groups represented degrees of intensity of immigrant memory. The Orthodox congregations housed the immigrants, while the Conservative synagogues were becoming the religious home of their American-born children.

IV

The morale of Jews was lower in the 1930s than at any time ever. The Depression seemed endless for everybody, but Jews had a unique problem: anti-Semitism was more threatening than ever before in American history. Jews had withstood poverty and exclusion many times before, but the threats in America were especially upsetting.

If not here, where could Jews ever hope to attain equality among the Gentiles?

Looking inward, Jews felt more fear than hope about the future of Jewish culture. The 1930s were the tipping point for the population of American Jewry. The census of 1940 was the first to show a preponderance of native-born Jews. The institutions that the immigrants founded were still flourishing but they were clearly past their peak. The circulations of the Yiddish dailies kept dropping, as the immigrant subscribers died. The theaters on Second Avenue were closing one by one. By 1940, no more than four or five were open at any time, as compared to the roughly twenty that had existed in the heyday of the Yiddish stage. The immigrant culture was dying, and there was little sign in the 1930s of the rise of an American Jewish culture in English of comparable viability.

The news from abroad was even bleaker. To be sure, tens of thousands of Jews from Germany were arriving in the United States, but these were not the immediate relatives of the East Europeans. Their own brothers and cousins were mostly in Poland or Romania. These immigration quotas were oversubscribed, or blocked by instructions from Washington. Applicants from Poland, where homegrown anti-Semitism was as hurtful in those years as that of the Nazis, were told to wait for twelve to fifteen years before the American consulate in Warsaw could consent even to interview them. Jews could do little about their immediate relatives in Europe except send them a few dollars.

There was also growing fear about the new Zionist settlement in Palestine. Murderous riots had taken place in 1929. Arabs had killed Jews, most notably in Hebron. The tensions kept getting worse. The essential response of the British, who held the mandate for Palestine, was to appease the Arabs by trying to limit the growth of Jewish numbers in the land. Right before the war began in 1939, this process reached its climax when the government issued a White Paper in which Jews were given seventy-five thousand more places in Palestine during the next five years, after which the door to Palestine would be closed to Jews. The Yishuv, the Zionist settlement, was endangered and friendless. The declarations in favor of Zionism that were made by American politicians, especially at election time, were ritual rather than serious politics. The Middle East was remote from the United States; it was in Great Britain's sphere of influence. In the decade between 1929 and 1939, even the most Zionist American Jews had few illusions about their power to help the Jews in Palestine with anything more than money. Such funds were very short during those years of the lingering Great Depression.

The most searing heartache of the 1930s was the gulf between parents and children. The parents had come to America "for the children," but most of the children were not succeeding. The immigrants had wanted some kind of continuity with their own Jewishness, but the most intellectual of their children were alienated, on radical principle of one kind or another. Parents wanted *naches* (joy and continuity) from their children, but there was very little *naches* to be had. Never mind all the theories about the melting pot, cultural pluralism, or world revolution, which promised to confer equality on Jews. The Gentiles were not listening, American Jews felt powerless, and they were afraid.

At this worst of times Franklin Delano Roosevelt was the source of hope.

16.

FDR:

The Benevolent King of the Jews

I

The Jews loved Franklin Delano Roosevelt with singular and unparalleled passion. Most Americans admired Roosevelt for leading the country out of the Great Depression, and they gave him an unprecedented landslide victory in 1936, but the Jews felt that he was their special protector. No president of the United States had ever surrounded himself with so many Jews. Benjamin V. Cohen and Samuel Rosenman were among his most trusted lieutenants. His friend and neighbor in Dutchess County, New York, Henry Morgenthau, Jr., was secretary of the treasury. Felix Frankfurter, the famous professor of law at Harvard, commuted regularly to the White House. Jews were thus very visible, almost defiantly so, in the upper reaches of the Roosevelt administration. These men were not always heeded by Roosevelt, for he was a master of playing off his advisers against each other, or of eliciting from them the kind of advice that he wanted to hear. The Jews fared no differently from all the rest in his inner councils, but their presence in the President's entourage was a signal of hope to the masses of Jews, when they felt endangered by anti-Semitism at home and by the Nazis abroad.

It was at least equally important to Jews that Roosevelt broadened the Civil Service. Members of minorities who could pass examinations had a chance at many jobs in government and in education from which they had previously been excluded. Jews were especially delighted, because they were, in the 1930s, the single largest pool of underemployed college graduates. A host of young lawyers was hired by government agencies, especially by the new ones that were created by the New Deal. To be sure, Roosevelt pushed very few Jews into the older, existing bureaucracies. The Departments of State and War remained bastions of older establishments, but that was barely noticed by anyone. Roosevelt's coming to power represented the first entry of Jews in numbers into the government. The overwhelming majority of these "new men" were the children of recent immigrants; they were ever more grateful to Roosevelt.

So were their parents. Their culture, in Yiddish, had been regarded as exotic, and as their own private business. Valid American culture was not in the language of the immigrants; it was in American English. Roosevelt, the patrician from Groton and Harvard, of impeccable old American pedigree, acted in disregard of this prejudice. One of his most decisive acts in combating the Depression was to create the Works Progress Administration (WPA) soon after he came to power. This agency paid for numerous endeavors which put people to work at government expense. The WPA even financed theaters and writers, and not only in English. Unemployed Yiddish writers worked together in a study of the many hundreds of *Landsmanshaften,* the associations of immigrants from the same town or area, which existed in New York in the 1930s. The result of the study was published, under the imprimatur of the WPA, in a volume in Yiddish. The experience and the language of the Jewish immigrant ghetto had thus been pronounced by the United States government itself, for the very first time, to be part of the expression of American life. The Yiddish writers project of the WPA was moral recompense for the discrimination against Jews in the immigration laws.

Thus, during his first term, Roosevelt was perceived by Jews to be surrounded by Jewish courtiers, to be the protector of the Jews against their enemies, and even to have respect for their culture.

Roosevelt was the special shield of the Jews—or so they thought.

Even as he was doing little for the Jews of Europe, the Jews of America continued to believe in his "special" love for them. The root of the attitude toward Roosevelt was deep in many centuries of Jewish experience. As an endangered and often reviled minority, Jews had depended on "benevolent kings" to protect them. In many societies, both in Christian Europe and the Muslim Middle East, Jews had been the king's financiers, businessmen, physicians, and advisers, men who depended on the king's favor. They were on his side against noblemen, merchant guilds, and peasants, who generally did not want to pay taxes or to support the king's wars. To be sure, the king was often not as well disposed to the Jews as they wanted to believe. On occasion, he simply milked them for money and then expelled them from his domain. But the Jews wanted to believe— indeed, had to believe—that the king really respected them, and that he had been misled by wicked advisers. So, for example, when King Ferdinand and Queen Isabella expelled the Jews from Spain in 1492, Jews blamed the royal court and the Church for having given the royal family bad advice. This half-truth, half-fantasy about "benevolent kings" was enshrined in the prayer for kings, emperors, and even czars in the synagogues of Europe. The formula was a prayer that the ministers and the advisers of the kings might be enlightened by God to give the ruler, who is, by definition, benevolent, the kind of advice which would make him look kindly on Jews.

During Roosevelt's first term, as he became their "protector" in America, the Jews reenacted this ancient psychodrama. They believed, on the evidence of all the good things that Roosevelt did do for them, in the "good king Roosevelt." They hoped that he would eventually save their brethren in Europe. Jews attributed Roosevelt's inaction to the cabals of bureaucrats in the State Department, the present-day "successors" of the king's unfeeling, or anti-Jewish advisers. They preferred not to see him as a politician who balanced his political need of the Jews against the interests and the prejudices of all his other constituencies. They preferred, instead, to rejoice in the New Deal as their own, almost messianic deliverance in America.

The special passion of the Jews for Roosevelt was strikingly clear in the election of 1936. In 1932, when Roosevelt had run against Herbert Hoover, he had supposedly won over seventy percent of the Jewish vote, but they were not then his greatest supporters. The Italians were even more enthusiastically on his side; nearly eighty percent voted for Roosevelt. In 1936, the Jews were in the lead among his supporters. They gave him ninety percent of their votes, a bit more than he got from the nearly as enthusiastic Irish and Italians. Roosevelt received an unprecedented number of endorsements that year, across the entire Jewish political spectrum.

The mainstream of the Jewish community was almost entirely for him, but even many of the Communists, most of the Socialists—and almost all the rabbis—joined the chorus of those who praised him. Although the *Morgen Freiheit,* the Communist daily, railed against Roosevelt as an instrument of American capitalism, many of its subscribers voted for Roosevelt and not Earl Browder, the party candidate. Among the Socialists, the split of opinion was open and pronounced. In 1932 at least one-fourth of the 900,000 who voted for Norman Thomas, the Socialist candidate for president, had been Jews. Four years later, almost all had abandoned Thomas. In April 1936, the *Zukunft,* the Socialist monthly journal in Yiddish, endorsed Roosevelt, writing that he "has no fixed philosophy or fixed convictions concerning all of the difficult problems which confront the country. But, he has a good heart. Until now, sympathy and compassion have been his compass; he has listened to his more liberal advisors." Even *Der Freind,* the official organ of the Workman's Circle, endorsed Roosevelt; only a strong leader can rally America against the Fascists; the workers ought to vote for Roosevelt because he has put them to work.

Even more surprising endorsements came from the editors of small Hebrew journals, which had never before spoken out on politics. *Hadoar,* a secular weekly devoted to literary and cultural matters, endorsed Roosevelt, calling him "a leader and prophet, who had arisen to take the people from the desert to the promised land." They praised the President for his efforts in combating the economic Depression, and for his leadership for the "light and good" of democracy against the "darkness and evil" of Fascism. The most unexpected support appeared in *Hapardes,* a Hebrew monthly for rabbis. Its editor, Rabbi S. A. Pardes, endorsed Roosevelt not only as a champion of democracy and the savior of the country from the Depression, but as a protector of threatened Jews in Europe.

Roosevelt received a copy of this editorial in English translation. He responded with a letter thanking the author for "his pledge of loyalty and confidence and for his generous appraisal of his administration." But there was no response at all to Rabbi Pardes's concern about the Jews in Europe, not even a ritual expression of sympathy for their plight. The editor printed Roosevelt's letter, and added the hope that "we trust that President Roosevelt will stand by us [the Jews] not only in America but also beyond its borders." Rabbi Pardes had a hard time finding proof of this assertion from the very general letter that Roosevelt had written—but it was wonderful, so Pardes implied, that a president had responded to an Orthodox rabbi.

The near worship of Roosevelt was possible in the first five or six years of his presidency even among those, like Rabbi Pardes, who were most concerned about the Jews in Europe. In the mid-1930s, the temperature of anti-Semitism in Europe had not yet become uniquely searing. It was still possible for American Jews to think that the situation of their brothers and sisters in Europe was grave but not catastrophic, that there was still some time to find means of relief, and that Roosevelt, the "benevolent monarch," would take pity on his Jewish children. This was, in fact, a role he loved to play, and not only for Jews. He liked to hear his visitors call him "Papa," or Chief, and come to him as suppliants, asking for protection. It was unimaginable to Jews that such a leader would fail to protect the victims of the Nazis if their dangers increased. Therefore, Jews felt that they could in good conscience worry most about their own problems in America.

As the Depression hung on, anti-Semitism was on the rise in the United States. Public opinion polls showed that roughly one-third of the respondents thought that "Jews had too much power." There was substantial sentiment, on the order of one in five, to restrict the role of Jews in politics and even in business. Father Charles Coughlin, the radio priest from Royal Oak, Michigan, had an average of a quarter million subscribers to his largely anti-Jewish weekly, *Social Justice*. The Ku Klux Klan claimed more than one hundred thousand members. Though the Klan had begun in the South, which was still its major base, it was acquiring many members in the big cities where Jews lived. The German-American Bund, the Nazi party in America, though much smaller, was visible and virulent. There were many fistfights in those years between American Nazis in uniform and young Jews who were outraged by the presence of Hitler's followers on American soil.

In October 1935, the editors of *Fortune* magazine published a large study of anti-Semitism in America. This account argued that anti-Semitism was widespread, especially among the poor, and that the poor might turn violent if they remained hungry. A few months later, *Fortune's* editors followed up their survey of anti-Semitism with an analysis of Jewish power. *Fortune's* researchers had found that though Jews were concentrated in white-collar pursuits, they dominated nothing of any consequence in American life. This article was an attempt to answer the anti-Semites, and to calm the fears of Jews, who were described by the editors of *Fortune* as overreacting and thus inviting more trouble for themselves. But the Jews were not overreacting. *Fortune* itself soon proved that the Jews had real worries. In February 1936, the editors defined the Jew in America as still a "universal stranger." *Fortune's* pundits added that the "Russian Jews" had not yet been absorbed in America, and that many insisted on retaining their Jewish identity. They were in need of "toleration and respect."

It was dangerous, then, for an embattled minority to push for the unpopular and losing cause, to try to open the door wider to refugees. Roosevelt's own political calculations produced essentially the same results. He could not annoy the labor movement, which was opposed to more immigration, and he did not want to lose votes to the anti-Semites, who had taken to calling him Rosenfeld. He had sinned in their eyes by appointing a number of Jews to visible roles in his administration.

The Zionists offered an alternative policy, to ask for the quick establishment of a Jewish state in part of Palestine which would accept those who were in danger in Europe. In 1936, there was reason for such optimism. The British commission under Lord Peel to consider the future of the land recommended in the spring of 1937 that Palestine be partitioned, and that a Jewish and an Arab state be established. It was not ignoble in the mid-1930s for some American Jews to take their energies away from a losing battle for large-scale immigration into America and to turn toward the fight for Zionist immigration into Palestine. There was a special dignity to pleading not for refugees but for a people who were reestablishing their ancient home. Roosevelt helped the Zionists by issuing declarations of support, especially at election time. In 1936, in their election platform, the Democrats did not advocate easing immigration restrictions, but neither did the Republicans. The Democrats demanded that Britain, the power that held the mandate to Palestine, refrain from restricting the immigration of Jews. Here, too, the Republicans agreed, but that could not gain them any votes away from Roosevelt. He spoke for this plank in public, and even in private representations to the British government. Roosevelt easily played the "benevolent monarch" for the Zionists, too.

II

American Jews have been accused in numerous recent studies of having done too little for the Jews of Europe. This charge is essentially not true. The one or two attempts that were made in the 1930s to loosen the restrictions on immigration backfired. The Congress of the United States was simply not susceptible to Jewish pressure. The only path that was open to Jews was to attempt to persuade Roosevelt.

The Jewish figure who was personally closest to Roosevelt was Felix Frankfurter. He was born in Vienna and came to the United States in his early teens. Hitler's attacks on the Jews of Germany were for him a very personal and painful issue. Frankfurter raised the matter with the President as early as April 7, 1933, barely a month after Roosevelt had assumed office and less than a week after the boycott of Jewish businesses that Hitler's government had organized for April 1. After hearing nothing for two weeks, Frankfurter sent the President a telegram, asking for "some word of progress." He finally received an answer, not from the President but from the secretary of state, Cordell Hull, who assured Frankfurter that there were plenty of unused quota numbers for people who were born in Germany who wanted to come to the United States. When Frankfurter wanted to save a relative of his from Vienna, he went to an English contact, Lady Astor, for help, and not to Roosevelt. After this effort succeeded, he sent a copy of the document to FDR. Frankfurter felt let down throughout the Roosevelt years by the lack of large action, but he believed, or wanted to believe, that Roosevelt was blameless and that the good intentions of the President were being blocked by State Department bureaucrats. Frankfurter, too, was behaving as a Jew who had been fashioned by the myth of the "benevolent king."

The leaders of the American Jewish Committee kept intervening in private. In the 1930s, that organization still spoke for the "German Jews," who believed that Jews should talk in universalist accents about the rights of individuals, and that anti-Semitism, as such, was best not mentioned. The leaders of the American Jewish Committee were afraid that given a choice between the cause of the European Jews and Nazism, the Jews would not necessarily win in American public opinion. In contrast, the major spokesman of the "Russian Jews," Rabbi Stephen S. Wise, insisted on public action. A coalition of organizations under his leadership organized a massive protest meeting at Madison Square Garden in New York on March 28, 1933. The tens of thousands who gathered there knew that they had little influence on Hitler; their main purpose was to move the newly inaugurated President to denounce the Nazi regime. They failed, because the United States was still trying to have "correct relations" with Germany. But the American Jews were not indifferent. They raised impressive amounts of money in the years of the Depression to help the Jews of Germany emigrate. Between 1933 and 1939, the American Jewish Joint Distribution Committee spent nearly twenty million dollars, an impressive sum, particularly during the economic Depression.

After the election of 1936, despite the massive support he had received from Jews, Roosevelt did not move to do more for the "non-Aryans" who were being persecuted by the Nazis. He was limited by anti-Semitism, which was actually getting worse in the United States. In 1937, the American Institute for Public Opinion found that nearly two out of five Americans thought that anti-Jewish sentiment was increasing. In a poll in March 1938, forty-one percent thought that Jews had "too much power in the United States"; almost half thought the Jews were at least in part to blame for their persecution in Europe. In those days, everybody read the novelist Sinclair Lewis. It was Lewis's judgment that the triumph of anti-Semitism in America was a real possibility. That was the message of his topical novel, *It Can't Happen Here,* which appeared in 1935. American Jews read the book and they were both fearful and angry.

Soon after the election, Roosevelt himself was in a weakened political condition. In the first year of his second term, in 1937, he proposed adding to the number of justices in the Supreme Court, in order to overcome the existing conservative majority, and he lost the fight. The years 1937–38 were a time of economic depression— the "Roosevelt depression"—and parts of his own party, especially the Southerners, were in rebellion against the New Deal. The limit of Roosevelt's power was evident on the one occasion when he actually proposed a major act to help the Jews. In March 1938, Germany invaded Austria and its Jews were immediately in danger: some were mistreated or beaten up; others were sent to concentration camps. Within a few days Roosevelt floated the idea at a cabinet meeting of special aid for refugees from Austria. The cabinet advised him that he could not get a bill passed in Congress to increase the immigration quota. The public opinion polls proved most Americans were then opposed to such action. In April 1938, Roosevelt called for a conference of all concerned governments to find ways of helping the refugees. This meeting was convened in Evian-les-Bains, France, in July.

It came to very little. Few of the assembled nations, some thirty-two of them, wanted any new immigrants. Australia promised to admit 15,000 in the next three years, and it actually did admit some 5,000 before war broke out in the Pacific on December 7, 1941. The Dominican Republic made a dramatic offer to accept 100,000 refugees, but the structure to receive them did not exist in the primitive economy of the island. Some 500 families did arrive. The Netherlands, which had already accepted 25,000 refugees from Germany, offered temporary housing to those on their way to other countries. Denmark, with its already dense population, announced that it would continue to be as hospitable as it could to refugees. No other country responded with anything more than words. The United States, the principal convener of the meeting, did not offer even to consider changing its restrictive immigration policies.

Even Rabbi Stephen Wise was upset when a Jewish congressman from Brooklyn, Emanuel Celler, introduced a bill to waive all limitations on refugees who wanted to come to the United States. Wise was certain that such a bill would arouse the many enemies of immigration, and the ensuing outcry would block all possibility for quiet acts of favor by presidential instruction for all the refugees, including not only Jews but also other opponents of Nazism. The only real hope, against an increasing majority of the people, and the insensitivity and hostility of many of Roosevelt's advisers, was the personal benevolence of the President.

On the night of November 9–10, 1938, when the Nazis made a massive, nationwide pogrom in Germany, called Crystal Night, the problem became more acute. Almost all of the synagogues in Germany were burned or vandalized, and many Jews were beaten. After this outrage, it was clear to all the world that the Jews had to be gotten out, and quickly. Roosevelt recalled Ambassador Hugh Wilson, and issued a strong statement condemning Nazi barbarism, but he did not move to change the immigration laws. Under pressure from the secretary of labor, Frances Perkins, who, along with Henry Morgenthau, Jr., was most concerned about the victims of the Nazis, Roosevelt did extend visitors' visas for German refugees, for many had come to the United States on such visas. This action amounted to letting nearly fifteen thousand people stay on in the United States, almost all permanently.

By late 1938 Roosevelt was already mentally prepared for war in Europe. He did not want to add to the venom of the isolationists by being too involved in the question of Jews; he did not want to annoy the large majority of Americans who professed some sympathy with the victims of the Nazis but did not want them in the United States. In a radio speech in late November 1938, Myron Taylor, Roosevelt's principal representative to the Conference on Refugees in Evian, assured the American people that nothing would be done for the Jews who wanted to get out. The language was very thinly veiled:

> Our plans do not involve "flooding" of this or any other country with aliens of any race or creed. On the contrary, our entire program is based on the existing immigration laws of all the countries concerned, and I am confident that within that framework our problem can be solved.

Nonetheless, more was done for Jewish refugees that year than ever before. Roosevelt was behaving with far more concern in private than in public. The bureaucratic delays in issuing visas were made much less severe. For the first time, the whole of the quota that had been assigned to Germany and Austria by the immigration law of 1924, nearly twenty-eight thousand, was used in 1939. A bill to add twenty thousand additional places in the next two years for children under fourteen failed to get anywhere in Congress. In this very bitter time for Jews, Roosevelt nominated Felix Frankfurter to a seat on the Supreme Court, in actual, though not direct, succession to Louis D. Brandeis. Though Frankfurter was then perceived to be a radical, as Brandeis before him, Roosevelt insisted on appointing him. This action was widely interpreted both in America and abroad as an assertion by Roosevelt that he would not countenance the down-grading of Jews in America. The "Chief" had refused to be intim-idated by anti-Semites. The difference between nominating Frank-furter and avoiding the issue of the immigration law was political calculation: the arguments about Frankfurter would soon go away, for they involved very few people directly; a more liberal immigra-tion policy could have cost Roosevelt votes.

The most pointed and most poignant proof of Roosevelt's un-willingness to fight with the enemies of immigration on behalf of Jewish refugees was the *St. Louis* affair, in May 1939. At that time the Nazi government was pushing out every Jew who held a doc-ument which might entitle him to land somewhere. The *St. Louis,* which was owned by the Hamburg-America Line, sailed for Havana, Cuba, carrying more than nine hundred people, most of them Jews. Well over seven hundred were eligible for admission to the United States; they had already filed affidavits of support with American immigration officers, and were awaiting a "quota number." These refugees proposed to land in Havana, with the prior agreement of the Cuban government, until there would be a place for them in the United States. While the ship was at sea, however, the Cubans changed their minds. The "tourist letters" of admission to Cuba that the passengers had bought from the steamship line were no longer acceptable. When the *St. Louis* arrived in Havana harbor, almost no one on board was permitted to land. Privately, the American embassy in Havana tried to persuade the Cubans to let the passengers disem-bark. The American Jewish Joint Distribution Committee offered to pay bond so that the passengers would not be a public charge in Cuba, but the amount that the Cubans demanded kept rising, and the request for large bribes became increasingly more outrageous. All the negotiations failed, and the *St. Louis* was ordered out of Havana. The captain of the ship then headed for the coast of Florida, but the United States Coast Guard made sure that he would not make port in America and that no passenger would swim ashore.

This drama became headline news in America. The White House and the State Department were barraged with telegrams. At one stage of the negotiations with the Cubans, while the *St. Louis* was still in Havana harbor, American Jews tried to guarantee the bond. Leaders of the Joint Distribution Committee asked the embassy in Havana to arrange for them to see Cuba's president, Federico Laredo Bru. The head of the visa division of the State Department, Asa Warner, telephoned the counsel general in Vienna, Coert du Bois, to instruct him that "under no circumstances" should he "intervene in the landing of the *St. Louis.*" Warner made it clear that this instruction came directly from the secretary of state and the White House. Roosevelt and Cordell Hull had thus been willing to say a private word to the Cubans, but not to act in public. The desperate passengers on the *St. Louis* telegraphed the President, but he ignored them. The ship had no choice but to go back to Hamburg; most of its passengers ultimately perished in Nazi-held Europe.

It was not noticed at the time that the voyage of the *St. Louis* was an eerie, but tragic, reenactment of the very first journey of a boatload of Jews to America. In 1654, the *Ste. Catherine,* carrying twenty-three refugees from Recife, Brazil, had stopped in Cuba and been turned away, like the *St. Louis* almost three centuries later. But, when the *Ste. Catherine* arrived in New York, Peter Stuyvesant did not send out the "Coast Guard" to force the ship away. He eventually agreed to let them stay, on the assurances by the Jews of Amsterdam that they would not become a public charge. In 1939, a more "enlightened" government in America was infinitely less decent.

III

By 1939, when the Second World War began, and the situation of the Jews in Europe became catastrophic, Roosevelt had already defined and redefined this attitude to Jewish refugees. He was personally sympathetic, provided he could express that sympathy through quiet administrative action. In fact, Roosevelt had become more sympathetic personally, as the situation of the Jews in Europe was becoming radically worse. The proof is in the immigration statistics. In the years 1933 through 1937, fewer than 40,000 Jews had been allowed into the United States. These numbers represented less than twenty percent of the room for immigrants that existed even under the Immigration Law of 1924. From 1938 through 1941, when America entered the war, 110,000 Jews entered the United States as immigrants. The numbers increased because the visa section of the State Department knew that the President wanted to stop putting obstacles in the way of refugees. Roosevelt could change administrative procedure, as an act of conscience and to satisfy his Jewish constituents, without courting political trouble.

The onset of the Second World War essentially relieved Roosevelt of this problem along with many others. He was soon claiming the United States was "the arsenal of democracy," and he insisted that the defeat of the Nazis was now the democratic world's only concern. The Jews, who were the targets of Hitler's fiercest invective, certainly could take no exception to Roosevelt's seemingly single-minded passion for victory, especially because he promised that after the war all the wrongs that the Nazis had inflicted would be righted. At the beginning of the war, almost all the Jewish leaders in America agreed that the Jews of Europe should not be a "special case." The first bitter fight within American Jewry began in October 1939, over this very issue: Should Jews obey the blockade of Nazi Europe that Great Britain had announced, or should they, as neutrals, send food packages and other help to the Jews in Poland? The Jewish Labor Committee, which had direct links with occupied Poland, insisted that it was the duty of American Jews to send all possible help into Poland. But Dr. Joseph Tenenbaum, who was both the president of the Federation of Polish Jews in America and the chairman of the Joint Boycott Council, insisted in agreeing with the British that "the responsibility for feeding occupied Europe rightfully rests with Germany." Tenenbaum, therefore, urged Jews to cease contributing to the relief of their brethren in Poland. Rabbi Stephen Wise was even more vehement. He thundered that Jews could not afford "to run the risk of alienating the already dubious good will of the British government to our people," and therefore, as "president" of the American Jewish Congress, he issued "the order of immediate discontinuance."

The Socialists of the Jewish Labor Committee defied Tenenbaum and Wise, but they eventually directed their help to Jews who were taking refuge in neutral countries or in Vichy France. Uncompromising defiance came from ultra-Orthodox of the Agudath Israel. By the summer of 1941, only the Agudath Israel was still sending food packages directly to Poland. The Joint Boycott Council, which represented most of the organizations in America, picketed the offices of Agudath Israel in New York for three weeks—but this Orthodox body refused to knuckle under. At the beginning of the war, while America was still neutral, choices were made: almost all of the leaders of the Jewish establishment were loath to proclaim the Jews to be a special case. The Socialists and the Orthodox (in both groups most still spoke Yiddish) were emotionally closest to the Jews of Eastern Europe; they cared least about offending London or Washington.

This quarrel during the two years of American neutrality was conducted in the awareness of some random murders of Jews in Eastern Europe, but before the decision by the Nazis in January 1942 to establish the death factories. It was therefore still possible to believe that the Jews of Europe would come out of the war battered but not destroyed. The news of systematic murder began to leak to the West by July 1942. The Jewish Labor Committee received a report from Poland that seven hundred thousand Jews had already been killed. (We know, now, that this number was an underestimate.) But this report was not believed. By the fall of 1942, such accounts could no longer be disregarded. The government of the United States knew, as did the leaders of the American Jews, that the Nazis had embarked on systematic mass murder and that the killings had begun in January 1942 in makeshift gas chambers near Auschwitz. By midsummer the operation was at full speed. The news was brought to Switzerland by a German industrialist, Eduard Schulte. Through intermediaries the story soon reached Gerhart Riegner, who represented the World Jewish Congress in Geneva. Riegner brought this seemingly unbelievable information to the American consulate in Geneva and asked that it be sent on to Rabbi Stephen Wise in New York.

Riegner's story was not believed by anyone in the State Department's chain of command; it was characterized in an internal document in Washington as a "wild rumor" inspired by Jewish fears. Several levels of bureaucrats, reaching up to the under secretary of state, Sumner Welles (who was personally very sympathetic to the plight of Jews in Nazi Europe), decided that Riegner's story was inflammatory, and that such questionable information should not be passed on to Rabbi Wise. But Wise soon heard the story. Riegner had also informed another official of the World Jewish Congress, Samuel Sydney Silverman, who was a member of the British Parliament, and Silverman sent the telegram on to Wise. Almost immediately Wise called a meeting of leaders of the major American Jewish organizations to tell them of the Riegner cable, and to relay news from other sources, that there was mass carnage in Warsaw. In early December, a delegation of American Jewish leaders was received by President Roosevelt at the White House. He assured the delegation that he would do all in his power "to be of service to your people in this tragic moment." Two weeks later, on December 17, he and Churchill issued the one statement that the Allies ever made in the course of the war in which they expressed their concern for Jews by name. Rabbi Wise and the others had left the meeting with Roosevelt encouraged, but all that the President had really promised was punishment for the Nazi criminals after the war. In actual practice, Roosevelt reassured Congress, at the very moment of these expressions of sympathy and concern, that he had no plans for proposing the lifting of immigration restrictions.

Roosevelt may not yet have been aware of the full extent of the tragedy in December 1942, though there is abundant evidence in wartime intelligence documents that the American government was well-informed, both directly and through the Vatican. But there cannot be the slightest doubt that by midsummer 1943, Roosevelt knew everything. He heard directly in July 1943 from an eyewitness to the horrors. Jan Karski, a lieutenant in the Polish underground, gave the President a personal account of what he had witnessed some months before in Belzec. Karski actually had seen railroad cars full of corpses; he attested, as beyond doubt, to the existence of gas chambers. Karski told the President that the horror tales reaching the West were not exaggerated: more than half of Polish Jewry was already dead; the Nazis intended to exterminate every Jew in Europe. Roosevelt didn't comment on what he'd heard; he simply assured Karski that the Allies would win the war.

It is equally beyond doubt that the Jewish leadership in America knew the extent of the tragedy, as it was happening. Riegner and Karski were not the only sources. The Polish government-in-exile in London included two Jewish members, Szmul Zygielbojm and Ignacy Schwarzbart. They tried desperately to make the West pay attention to the news of the slaughter of the Jews, but they were ignored. On May 12, 1943, Zygielbojm committed suicide, leaving behind letters condemning the Allies for their failure to do anything to stop the murders. Zygielbojm already knew that his family in Poland had been completely wiped out, and that the Allies were refusing to do anything directly to save the Jews who were still alive. The day before he committed suicide, Zygielbojm was told by a young officer of American intelligence, Arthur Goldberg (who would later become a member of Kennedy's cabinet and a justice of the Supreme Court), that the American Air Force would not be instructed to bomb the railroad line to Auschwitz. Goldberg did not know who had made this decision, and so he could not have named names, but he suspected privately that the question had been decided by Roosevelt himself. Zygielbojm went home from his meeting with Goldberg—it was dinner at Claridge's—knowing that the Allies would not use force to symbolize any specific concern for Jews. The Western press took note of Zygielbojm's suicide, but it largely ignored the cause.

Among the Jews in America, all the leaders knew. The Orthodox Jewish community was particularly well-informed. Jacob Rosenheim, the international president of the Agudath Israel, the most Orthodox Jewish organization, was in close touch with developments in Europe through his representatives in Switzerland. The Labor Zionists in America knew, because they were told over and over again by the intellectual leader of the movement, Hayim Greenberg, through their publications, *Jewish Frontier* and *Yiddisher Kemfer*. Greenberg wrote in *Jewish Frontier* in 1943 that he was in shock that "Jews have not produced a substantial number of mentally deranged persons." The "full even temper" that prevailed was much more abnormal than "hysteria."

Knowing as much as they did, why did Roosevelt—and the Jews—do so little? When the United States entered the war at the end of 1941, it was far from certain that the Allies would win. During the first eighteen months of American participation, the Japanese dominated eastern Asia; the Germans were deep into Russia, and their Afrika Korps had driven across North Africa very nearly to Cairo. The Allies were the losing side until November 1942, when Montgomery stopped Rommel at El Alamein, and February 1943, when the Germans surrendered at Stalingrad. Roosevelt and Churchill began to feel like winners in Europe in the course of that year, as the Russians kept rolling back the Germans, and the Allies made their first landings in Italy. Millions were dying on all the battle fronts; it was difficult to cast the Jews as a special case. Indeed, until the death camps were opened after the German surrender, American public opinion did not believe the accounts of the atrocities. The one poll that was taken before the end of the war showed that most Americans guessed that perhaps one hundred thousand Jews in all had been killed by the Nazis. Jews in Europe were imagined to have been victims of the massive pogrom, but that was not unprecedented; some sixty thousand Jews had been killed between 1919 and 1921 in the wars on the Russian-Polish border. Such suffering, if that was all, was minor, by the standards of the mass slaughter of the war.

Roosevelt's convenient and comforting answer to others—and undoubtedly to himself—was that he was concentrating on winning the war, and he was hoping that victory would come quickly enough to save many of the Jews of Europe. In fact, if the war had been one year shorter, this hope would have been realized, for in mid-1944, two million of Europe's Jews were still alive. Roosevelt refused to permit the use of money or supplies to bribe Nazis to let some Jews live. He did repeatedly alert the Nazis that they would be held accountable for their murder of the Jews, but only once did he mention the Jews as such. Though Roosevelt has been severely criticized in retrospect by many historians, it is hard to see what a specific statement could have accomplished. The Nazi "war against the Jews" was so central to Hitler and to his followers that they pursued it to the very last days of their power. This was the "war" that they could win, and, as Martin Bormann is reputed to have said, they would "jump into their graves laughing." The Nazis knew that Roosevelt would treat them as war criminals for all of their crimes, and not only those against the Jews. Some lower-ranking officers occasionally behaved better than they might have, because they feared Allied retribution, but those who ran the Nazi government took no notice of these threats until the very last months of the war, when total defeat was imminent.

The pained and elaborate discussions in recent years about whether the Jews of the United States did enough to save their brethren in Europe are therefore essentially unhistorical. Jews had no power to do more. Jews protested in public many times during the war years. Individuals and delegations went to see the President and many high officials of the government. Coordinating committees were organized several times by the major national Jewish organizations to work to rescue the Jews in Europe. These bodies fell apart over differences in policy and tactics. The Orthodox went their own way, insisting on contravening the law against sending bribe money into Nazi-held territory. The Zionists agitated for making a Jewish state in Palestine the "war aim" of the Jewish people. Though they succeeded in winning overwhelming endorsement for their platform in the meeting in January 1943 at the American Jewish Conference, a body in which all the organizations participated, the endorsement was not unanimous. The representatives of the American Jewish Committee walked out rather than agree to this nationalist aim. The dissenters preferred to hope, then, for the restoration of democracy all over the world and the repatriation of the people whom Hitler had displaced.

But even if the groups had been united and single-minded, it is hard to imagine a different outcome. Had the American Jews dared to stage a sit-in at the White House or to engage in civil disobedience in the major cities of the country, the catastrophe in Europe would have received much more attention. Indeed, one such effort was made by the Orthodox, in alliance with the Palestinian representatives in America of the right-wing Revisionist party. Four hundred rabbis marched from the Capitol to the White House on October 6, 1943, the day before Yom Kippur, "to protest the silence of the world when an entire people is being murdered," and to assert that this "is a crime and that all who tolerate it are equally guilty." Roosevelt did not receive the rabbis, in large part because his closest Jewish advisers did not like the organizers of the protest march. This action did move some members of Congress to consider a special, separate effort for the rescue of Jews, but nothing happened until Roosevelt was persuaded to act—and he did not change his mind until victory seemed secure.

In January 1944, Roosevelt was persuaded by Henry Morgenthau, Jr., to create the War Refugee Board. This body was allowed to "trade with the enemy." Its major success was to save the lives, by bribery, of tens of thousands of Jews out of Hungary and Romania. In Hungary, in the spring of 1945, Raoul Wallenberg, a young Swedish diplomat, protected thousands of Jews in Budapest from deportation, only to disappear at the end of the war behind Russian lines;

Wallenberg operated with American Jewish money. The work of the War Refugee Board was the one major achievement of the Roosevelt administration in rescuing Jews from the Nazis. It was possible because the fears of domestic disunity had lessened, as worry about the outcome of the war was essentially gone.

Roosevelt ran again, for his fourth term, in the fall of 1944. He again lost votes among most of the minorities; five percent of the Irish and ten percent of the Italians moved to the Republicans. But the Jews gave him the largest proportion of their vote ever: ninety-three percent. They wanted to believe that he was extending himself to save the Jews in Europe. Most Jewish leaders knew even in 1944 that Roosevelt had done much too little, but the Jewish masses were more adoring than ever of the "benevolent king."

The experience of American Jews with Roosevelt was paradoxical. After his death, when the Jews began to reflect on the Roosevelt years, they discovered that he had taught them a deep truth about America: it is power that really counts, and they had not had enough. Roosevelt had paid his political and emotional debts to Jews by opening doors in government and in the economy—and they were deeply grateful. But, during the Holocaust, Jews had not been powerful enough among all the factions and fractions of America to make the President and Congress feel their Jewish pain. In the 1940s, this knowledge was not yet spelled out in public. Jews continued to speak the language of goodwill, and of "Americans all," but Jews would spend the next two decades making sure that power in America was not the monopoly of the uncaring.

17.

After the War

I

During the Second World War, the Irish had no love for Great Britain, many of the Italians admired Mussolini, most of the Slavs hated Stalin, and the blacks were still victims of almost total segregation. The Jews were different—they hated Hitler—but they shared with the other minorities the feeling of being outsiders in America. Yet everyone rallied to the flag with enthusiasm. The rhetoric of the war effort promised everyone equality in America after the war, if only the children of minorities would behave like "Americans." Most accepted this bargain and, at the war's end, they demanded payment. But they soon felt betrayed when the deal was not honored.

The bargain between the majority and the minorities was made by the new wartime American nationalism. Roosevelt took the lead in proclaiming America's mission as the "Bearer of Democracy" for all the world. This nearly messianic self-image reached back to one of the deepest themes in American history—the certainty of the Puritans that they had come to the New World to create a society which would redeem the Old. In a time of total war, this vision could no longer be defended by American aristocrats alone. The United States could save Europe from the Nazis—and itself from the Japanese—only if everyone, without exception, fought in the common cause. The "Bearer of Democracy" could succeed only with the participation of "Americans All." During the war, blacks continued to protest against the indignity of segregation in the military; Americans of Japanese origin were put in concentration camps as security risks. But even blacks and Japanese, who had the greatest immediate scores to settle with the American majority, eagerly enlisted. They were sure that in victory they would not be excluded again from all the benefits of America. Very consciously, they were earning due bills on the American future.

The war movies made during this era expressed this new American nationalism. The three major outsiders in American society were Catholics, Negroes, and Jews. Every embattled platoon contained at least one of each: a second-generation Irish Catholic who still spoke with a light brogue, or a Polish Catholic from the coal mines of Pennsylvania; a street-smart Italian-American, an inner-city or southern black, and a white-collar Jew who turned out to be as heroic as the rest. These heroes, regarded as aliens by their white, southern sergeant, usually started out distrusting each other. But under fire, in the movies' final scene, the protagonists coalesced. After one of them died heroically saving the sergeant's life, they were transformed into equally worthy examples of "Americans All."

There was thus room in America for people of diverse backgrounds and origins—but this ideal could be interpreted in contradictory ways. Did it mean that there was now a new, triumphant "religion of democracy" to which all Americans were supposed to belong? Or would each group now be free to be itself, at its most angular? The wartime vision of American nationalism was basically assimilationist. The standard movie plot contained more than a hint of the suggestion that the fast-talking kid from Brooklyn was learning to behave like the archetypal American from Kansas, or perhaps even a Yankee aristocrat from New England. All past separate accounts with the American majority would end, if only society agreed to accept suitably assimilated individuals of whatever origin.

But the separate accounts of the minorities of Jews with America could not be ended so easily. For Jews in 1945 it required a conscious act of looking away, of instant group amnesia. Perforce, American Jews looked at the death camps which had been discovered by the Allies in 1945, but they preferred to bury the issues raised by the newsreels of bodies stacked like cordwood in Bergen-Belsen, or of the ashes in the ovens of Auschwitz. American Jews did not want to stand aside from the rest of America. In their deepest souls, the sight of the death camps had suddenly made them very lonely in the world. As "cobelligerents," the Jewish people had lost their war. But American Jews needed to feel that they were part of America, that they were among the victors. Possible American complicity, by inaction, in the murder of the Jews of Europe could not be discussed. If such an accusation were true, America's Jews would have had to continue to think of themselves as deeply alien. In the midst of the euphoria of the spring of 1945, American Jews would have been left to imagine themselves as stepchildren, more of a nuisance than a source of pride, to America as a whole, and even to the "gracious king" Franklin Delano Roosevelt.

Nor did Jews want, then, to examine their own conduct. They could have offered the excuse immediately that as outsiders, beset by anti-Semitism and concerned about their own status, they had been powerless to act boldly, but they preferred to suppress the subject. The Jewish agenda was dominated by one desire, to expand the place of Jews in America. They wanted to be accepted by the Gentiles, not to confront them—at least not then.

This was the message in those years of the most talked about novel about anti-Semitism, Laura Z. Hobson's *Gentleman's Agreement.* (It was published in 1947.) The hero of the story is a Gentile who disguises himself as a Jew. This thoroughly likable and decent Gentile is mistrusted only because he is thought to be Jewish. The point of Hobson's story is that the hero, who was played in the movie version by Gregory Peck, one of Hollywood's cleanest-cut "American" actors, was really no different from everyone else, that his Jewishness was label-deep. This treatment of anti-Semitism in America encouraged Jews to behave like Gentiles, and it avoided the question of whether Jews really were different from Gentiles, or whether America should be hospitable to those who did not play the game of assimilation. According to *Gentleman's Agreement,* for Jews to succeed in America, the remains of their immigrant and ghetto past had to be driven deep underground.

No one had any illusions that *Gentleman's Agreement* was an important work of literature, but it did express the dominant mood, even among serious writers. During and immediately after the war many younger Jewish intellectuals, who had been born and raised in the immigrants' ghettos, were eager to accept what the new American nationalism seemed to offer: minorities would be allowed into society if they adopted the manners and culture of Protestant Christians, or if they became "universal men." This "bargain" was accepted, with variations, by two brilliant young Jewish writers of the war years, Arthur Miller and Saul Bellow.

Bellow's first book, *Dangling Man,* appeared in 1944. Joseph, the protagonist and narrator of the novel, is caught in a state of ambivalence and self-questioning, torn between the desire to find a "group whose covenants forbade spite, bloodiness, and cruelty" and his own anger at what he perceives to be violations of the rules of humanity. The author reveals nothing about Joseph's origins. What we know about Joseph is that he is an ex-Communist, that he wants a life which is not hemmed in by choices which are made for him, and that he wants to find his way to the moral leadership of a regenerated humanity. This description is unmistakably that of a Jewish intellectual in 1944, who had become disillusioned with Communism.

Arthur Miller, who began his career in the war years, was equally uncomfortable with his Jewishness. Miller's first play, *Focus,* which appeared in 1945, is the story of Lawrence Newman, a bigoted organizational man of the 1940s. Newman is especially repulsed by Jews, until he needs to wear glasses and begins "seeing a Jew" every time he looks in the mirror. His self-loathing creates paranoia; he hears and sees everything as anti-Semitic reaction to him. Newman tries to return to mainstream society by joining a group to drive away a Jewish neighbor, but ultimately, he cannot bring himself to persecute someone who has done him no wrong. The anti-Jewish group assaults him. At one point, Newman addresses the Jews and wishes that they would "for God's sake go away, let everybody be the same! The same, let us all be the same!" Nor does Finkelstein, the sole Jewish character in the novel, defend his right to be a Jew. He pleads only that people not be lumped together under one stereotype. He wants to be seen as an individual without any reference to his Jewishness: "You can look at me and you don't see me. You see something else." In an early issue of *Commentary* magazine, *Focus* was praised for attempting to enlighten the non-Jewish community about the evils of anti-Semitism. There was no ringing defense in the review of the right of Jews to be themselves, but rather an acceptance that Jewishness is best forgotten. Jews would arrive in America in the name of "brotherhood," that is, by finding acceptance in the existing bourgeois society.

Miller has confirmed the assimilationist thrust of his early work. In his autobiography he recounts that as a college student he struggled to identify himself "with mankind rather than one small tribal fraction of it." He asserted that for him Judaism had become "dead history." For Miller, Orthodox Jews "had always seemed like atavisms, fossils of a long-dead past . . . they were either collecting alms or were too sharp as businessmen." Such a memory had gone beyond assimilation; it had internalized more than a bit of the anti-Semitism of the WASPs. Bellow and Miller thus announced a new direction for their generation: some of the intellectual children of the immigrants no longer railed against America or wanted to make the Communist revolution. They had abandoned the community of the political Left, but they had not moved to the Jewish community. They wanted simply to be liked by the existing bourgeois America.

This assimilationist agenda lasted into the 1950s and it is at the core of Arthur Miller's most famous work, *Death of a Salesman* (1949). Though Willy Loman and his son, Biff, are presented as Americans, we are given no clues as to their provenance. Here again, Miller suggests a smoothed-out society in which people have jettisoned their pasts and belong to no subgroup. And while Willy Loman was portrayed as a "general American" type, he is most intelligible as a Jewish immigrant. Of the many productions of this play, perhaps the most memorable was in Yiddish in the mid-1960s. Willy Loman was played by Joseph Buloff, one of the last great classical actors of the Yiddish stage. Watching Buloff's performance, one knew that the family's deepest, most repressed pain came from the Jewishness Willy had surrendered. Biff knew, perhaps better even than the author who created him, that the sacrifice had been wasted, that the approval of the Gentiles did not offer the content of a life and, above all, such approval would not be offered.

In their rush to arrive in America, the Jews of all varieties were embarrassed by the Communists. They needed to say to America as a whole that Jews abhorred Communism even more than other Americans. The more sophisticated knew that most of the Jews who had survived Hitler owed their lives to the Soviet armies, and that the vote of the Soviet Union at the United Nations in November 1947 was crucial to the creation of the State of Israel. These were historic debts, and they would be acknowledged some decades later, in different times, but in the immediate years after the war, the domestic needs of American Jews took precedence. The Jews wanted to get rid of their image as outsiders in America.

The lure of revolutionary ideologies that had seemed attractive to much of the Jewish intelligentsia in the 1930s was fading in the 1940s. Most of the Communists of the 1930s and 1940s simply drifted out of any strong ideological commitment as they found a place in America's booming, postwar capitalist system. Others were frightened out of left-wing ideology by the Cold War. When Senator Joseph R. McCarthy was roaming the country, conducting hearings to hunt Communists, many youthful believers in Communism tried to bury their past; others made public recantation. The most interesting group of all was a handful of Jewish intellectuals who had been Trotskyites before the war. As believers in Trotsky's vision of world revolution, they had been bitterly opposed to Stalin's imperialism. When the war was over, world revolution of the proletariat was clearly not going to happen, for capitalist America was the world's dominant power. Though Communism was spreading through Eastern Europe, it was Stalin's Communism. To oppose Stalin's imperialism, this group thought that they had only one option—to join the American side in the Cold War. Under the leadership of Elliot Cohen, the editor of the newly established monthly *Commentary*, they organized the Committee for Cultural Freedom. In 1951 the flagship publication of this body, *Encounter*, was launched in London. The budget of the Committee for Cultural Freedom came from American intelligence sources. From the perspective of the American cold warrior, this money was well spent. The committee was the most sophisticated intellectual front against the Russians. Through this association with the American Establishment in the battle against Stalin, some ex-Trotskyites, such as Irving Kristol, began the journey that would take them to neoconservatism.

The transformation of the Jews into respectable American bourgeois society was symbolized in 1951 by the conviction of the Rosenbergs. Julius and Ethel Rosenberg, a Jewish couple in their early thirties, were tried and convicted as spies who had given the Soviet Union sensitive atomic secrets. They were sentenced to death, and, after repeated appeals, were executed in 1953. The nature and the extent of their guilt have remained in controversy. It is clear, in hindsight, that the making of atom bombs could not have remained an American monopoly for very long. Any help the Soviets got from spying on the Americans had little effect on their entry into the atomic age. In the atmosphere of those years, however, the Rosenbergs were judged guilty of fundamentally altering the balance of power. They became the only Americans ever put to death for spying in peacetime.

Whatever the actual extent of their contributions to Soviet knowledge, the Rosenbergs' trial gave the Jewish community the opportunity to prove its patriotism. Near the surface of the trial there was a Jewish motif. The case was heard in New York, before Irving R. Kaufman, a district judge, who in his personal life was very much part of the Jewish establishment. The prosecuting lawyers (and, for that matter, the attorneys for the defense) were all Jews. An unmistakable message was being conveyed: the Jewish community was not to be identified with the Rosenbergs. Judge Kaufman announced that he prayed for divine guidance before passing the death sentence. He certainly was aware of the fears in the Jewish establishment that Jews as a whole might be held responsible for this act of treason. The Rosenberg case was the purgation in which Jews "proved" to the country that the political radicals who had once dwelt among them had either converted or that they had been cast out.

It is unfair and untrue to suggest that the young writers and intellectuals of those days, children of immigrants, were motivated simply by the desire to surrender their Jewishness to America on any terms. On the contrary, during the years immediately after the war, the passion to enter the mainstream swept along even some writers whose language was Yiddish. America itself had become an ideal rooted in the same premises that Jews had once heard from the God of their ancestors. H. Leyvik, the leading Yiddish poet, had been seared by the Holocaust, and inspired by the creation of the State of Israel. In September 1954, near the end of his creative life, Leyvik wrote a poem, *To America,* in which he made his final peace with his adopted country:

For forty-one years I have lived under your skies,
For over thirty years I have been your citizen,
And until now I have not found in me the word, the mode
For painting my arrival and my rise on your earth
With strokes as broad and revealing as you are yourself,
America
As soon as speech would shift toward you, I would curb
My words, rein them in with austere restraint,
Bind them in knots of understatement.
My whole world and my whole life
I held under secret locks, far from your wide open breath

Leyvik continued to imagine that "the moment of farewell" could happen within America's boundaries, that he might again be an alien in America; or he might choose to leave and be part of the new Jewish life being born in Israel, but these options now seemed more imaginary than real. The new reality was America. At the end of the poem a faint trace of ambivalence remained, but his last lines were an affirmation of this land in which neither he nor his ancestors had been born:

In days of old age, when I stand in the bright vision
Of one or another shining farewell, I recall again
The moment, forty-one years ago, when I reached
Your shore, America, and I wanted to and should have
Fallen prostrate to your earth and touched it with my lips,
And in confused embarrassment I did not do it,—
Let me do it now—as I stand here truthfully,
Embracing the glare of intimacy and farewell, America.

II

After the war, however, the promises of equality were not kept. Racial segregation continued, and there remained prejudice against Catholics. Jews were no better off, at least not in the public regard. In February 1946 nearly sixty percent of all Americans surveyed agreed that anti-Semitism was increasing in America. During the war, anti-Semites had claimed that Jews were either avoiding service or were finding their way into rear-echelon jobs. In 1946 the Jewish Welfare Board, the body which had served the Jewish soldier in all the theaters of operation, felt the need to publish two volumes of lists of Jews who had distinguished themselves in combat. Nearly 11,000 had been killed, 24,000 had been wounded, 36,000 had been decorated. All told, more than 500,000 Jews served in uniform during the war. Such lists (like those which Haym Salomon had made in 1784 and Simon Wolf in 1891) were necessary not simply as a memorial to the dead and as a celebration of living heroes; they were evidence that the Jews had earned an equal share in America's future.

When the vast wartime bureaucracies were disbanded, Jews feared and even half-expected that they would be beaten back into the ghetto. This did not happen. On the contrary, Jewish academics, professionals, artists, and technocrats maintained their newly earned intellectual status. After the war, there was a sudden expansion in higher education, publishing, and other semiacademic endeavors. Through the GI Bill of Rights of 1946, the government offered returning veterans the cost of their higher education in America's colleges and universities. Hundreds of thousands of young men were coming home to finish college. Hundreds of thousands more, who had previously not thought of higher education, entered the colleges on government scholarships. Jewish veterans comprised a strikingly large proportion of these students, and especially those among them who were studying for advanced degrees. The existing faculties were far too small to cope with this influx, and thus Jews who had waited in vain to be hired by academe in the 1930s were now in demand. The new availability of academic jobs attracted thousands of Jews to the graduate schools; by the mid-1950s, many had acquired doctorates. In 1940, Jews had comprised less than two percent of the faculties in all the institutions of higher education in America; by the 1960s the number had risen to at least 20 percent of all the faculty appointments in the schools which were not church-related. Young Jews were an even higher proportion of those newly hired by the most prestigious faculties.

Jews in retail business had made a significant jump during the war. Consumer goods were scarce and rationed, even in America. It was a seller's market. Stores which had made no money in the 1930s turned their owners into rich men by the mid-1940s. The newly well-off could expand their businesses and move into new endeavors. They had the money to begin the flight from apartment buildings in the cities into houses in the suburbs.

One bastion of established America where circumstances of the war did not forge opportunity for Jews was the corporate and industrial world—the banks, the insurance companies, the steel mills, the motorcar manufacturers. American big business was doubling and redoubling in those years. Between 1945 and 1959 the gross national product of the United States quadrupled, but the bureaucracies of the major companies continued to exclude Jews from upper-level jobs. Unlike colleges and universities, the giants of "free enterprise" could not easily be brought to book. But there was hope that big business would accept "White Jews," that is, those who behaved like "general Americans."

But what did it mean in the 1940s and 1950s to become a "general American"? Who were the other Americans? Some parts of the organized Jewish community, especially the elements that were led by the American Jewish Committee, continued to believe that doors would be opened wider for Jews through persuasion and appeal to democratic conscience. It published together, in 1950, five volumes on anti-Semitism which had been prepared under its auspices by several Jewish scholars who were refugees from Nazi Germany. The essential thrust of these volumes, at least in the public mind, was a definition of anti-Semitism as a disease, an expression of an "authoritarian personality." This analysis suggested that healthy people—like, presumably, the Americans—could not possibly be guilty of such prejudice. If there were any pockets of hatred, these were a residue from less enlightened, past ages. Anti-Semitism would be dissolved by education, goodwill, and appeal to democratic principles. These learned volumes were, of course, a restatement of an old assimilationist theme: the Jews would be accepted by society if they and the majority together gave up most of their past memories and behaved like "enlightened" bourgeois.

The counterview was held by the old enemies of the American Jewish Committee, the "Russian Jews," for whom Stephen S. Wise still spoke. These forces believed that the Gentile majority would yield only if it had no other choice. The reigning Establishment might give away positions which it had not preempted, but it would yield a share in what it already had only if it was forced. The American

Jewish Congress, under Wise's leadership, accepted a suggestion of several brilliant young lawyers who were on its staff in the mid-1940s: use the courts; demand the equality that was promised in the Constitution of the United States. The first public expression of this new tactic was the threat by Wise to sue to deny Columbia University its tax-exempt status. Wise's legal staff argued that undeniable evidence existed of quotas both in admissions and in hiring policies; the university was, therefore, not a public body but a private club. Wise's argument did not reach the courts, for Columbia preferred to drop the quotas. The shock waves went out to the rest of academe: discrimination against Jews, either as students or as faculty, became a risky proposition. For a number of years thereafter, many of the colleges and universities continued to discriminate against Jews, but the practice was fading. The universities became the first established American institutional arena in which Jews entered and even joined the elite.

Wise had shown the way to force doors open, but the activist and confrontationist appeals to law had as their purpose the very same agenda as the assimilationist preaching of goodwill and democracy: to ease the entry of Jewish individuals into careers equal to their talents. Their Jewishness was their own private business, which America as a whole was not supposed to notice, at least not in the job market. Jews thus cast themselves as the greatest partisans in America not only of equality but also of the total separation of church and state. Jews thus assumed the role again (as Isaac Mayer Wise had in the 1850s, when he went to court in Ohio against prayers in the public schools) of constitutional purists.

But America was not simply a Jew-Gentile country. There were Catholics and blacks, major "outsiders" like the Jews, who represented one-third of the American population. They had their own postwar agendas, and their desires clashed not only with the wishes of the Protestant majority but also with the aims of the Jews. The Catholics were the clearest, and the boldest. They interpreted their American situation as offering them the right to be themselves. No matter that they were annoying other groups who comprised, together, a large majority of all Americans. In 1947, the Supreme Court decided *Everson* v. *the Board of Education,* the first major case involving public education. Though it set forth a strict definition of the "wall of separation" between church and state, it sanctioned the use of public funds to bus parochial schoolchildren. The immediate response from Protestants and secular liberals was outrage; it was feared that Catholics would ultimately find a way of gaining tax support for the parochial schools, at least for their teaching of reading, writing, and arithmetic. Even James B. Conant, then president of Harvard, attacked the Catholics; he called the parochial schools a threat to national unity, and he praised the role of the public schools in assimilating immigrants (even as he looked away from his own college, where the dominant minority of its students came from boarding schools). The attacks upon the Catholics were all the more pointed, because the liberal community had long been angry with the Church: Catholics had been perceived as major supporters of General Franco against the Spanish Republicans. They had not silenced Father Coughlin, who had opposed the New Deal after 1935 and had become a public anti-Semite by 1938. The Catholics had crusaded in the 1930s against birth control and they were even more intransigent in the 1940s and 1950s about very strict standards of public propriety.

These Catholic positions had evoked vehement opposition, but the Church had chosen to fight rather than to draw in its horns. In the words of its most eloquent and most liberal spokesman, Father John Courtney Murray:

> The American Proposition makes a particular claim upon the reflective attention of the Catholic insofar as it contains a doctrine and a project in the matter of the "pluralistic society," as we seem to have agreed to call it. The term might have many meanings. By pluralism here I mean the coexistence within one political community of groups who hold divergent and incompatible views with regard to religious questions—those ultimate questions that concern the nature and destiny of man within a universe that stands under the reign of God. Pluralism therefore implies disagreement and dissension within the community.

Murray was very much aware that there had to be a set of principles on which religious groups participated in one community, but he felt that these common grounds did not have to conflict with any group's individual expression. To be sure, there were younger Catholics who disagreed with the Church. As early as 1953, the liberal Catholic journalist, William P. Clancy, accused both Catholic au-

thoritarianism and doctrinaire secularism as "the fruit of that total-
itarian spirit which, hating diversity, demands that all existence be
made over to conform to its own vision." The Catholic position was
itself, thus, judged to be too intransigent. Catholics were asked to
pull in horns and to put less pressure on the rest of America, but
Clancy spoke for a minority then. The thrust of the Catholic mainstream, or, at very least, of the clergy, was toward using the new
freedom and equality as the chance to buttress and secure Catholic
separateness.

In those very years, blacks inevitably made the contrary choice.
They had started so far outside American society, as the National
Association for the Advancement of Colored People asserted in its
program statement in the early 1940s, that the troubling immediate
questions—discrimination in "jobs, housing, the vote, education"—
had to be their primary concerns. This agenda remained constant
until the mid-1960s, when serious advocates of black separatism appeared. Before then, most of the efforts of the black community
were variations on a theme that had been stated in 1944 in the anonymous preface to a collection of essays entitled *What the Negro Wants*:
"Race relations in the United States are more strained than they have
been in many years. Blacks are disturbed by the continued denial of
what they consider to be their legitimate aspirations and by slow,
grudging grant of a few concessions."

The earliest "official" strategy of blacks had been that of Booker
T. Washington. At the turn of the century, Washington had coun-
seled his brethren to make themselves "worthy" of acceptance by
the white majority. By the 1930s, the black organizations, and especially the intelligentsia, knew very well, and with great bitterness,
that white racists were not waiting for the appearance of black men
and women with polished manners, so that they could cease practicing racism. In the 1930s, a few blacks, like some of the Jewish
intellectuals, had flirted with the revolutionary Left. Even a Swedish
Social Democrat, Gunnar Myrdal, insisted that the mass of the blacks
everywhere could be helped, as he proved in his study of *An American
Dilemma* (it was published in 1944), only by radical change of the
whole social structure.

Myrdal's book was one of the turning points in moving the black
community away from Washington's philosophy. Even during the
war there were race riots in several black neighborhoods. The expres-

sion of black impatience had, thus, become overt and even shocking. The declared purpose of the Negro community had become at once grandiose and simple: to make race irrelevant to the life and career of every individual in America. One of the leading black intellectuals, the historian John Hope Franklin, defined this purpose in an immediately famous essay that he published in 1964, entitled "The Transformation of the Negro Intellect":

> Surely, one of the great tragedies of American life has been the manner in which one's intellectual resources, whether they be of the order of a moron or a genius, have been used up in the effort to survive as a decent, self-respecting human being. Negro intellectuals in increasing numbers have come to appreciate this as one of the stark, grimly tragic facts of life. In increasing numbers they have come to regard this fact as a challenge which they would not escape, even if they could. Until they can live as other human beings—pushing back the frontiers of knowledge, writing a great novel, composing a beautiful symphony—Negro intellectuals have come to realize that they must carry on the fight, in concert with others, to make America true to her own ideals of equality and democracy. The realization of this fact and the continued preoccupation with a program to achieve success constitute the transformation of the Negro intellectual.

In the postwar years, black leadership thus moved away from any hope of acceptance by the America that had existed in 1939. The battle was to make society live up to its rhetoric about equality. The battle was not for black culture; it was for jobs, education, and an end to segregation.

The major Jewish organizations vied with one another to be helpful, even filing supportive amicus curiae briefs in the cases the Urban League and NAACP brought to strike down poll taxes in the South and to end segregation in education. The rationale was that ending any form of discrimination was also a victory for Jews in their own fight for total equality. And yet, Jews were different from blacks. In the 1940s most blacks were little concerned about "black culture." Most Jews, even when they were rapidly on the rise after the war, never abandoned some pride, even if it was ill-defined, in their Jewishness.

Inevitably, also, Jews chose up sides against the Catholics in the battle over state aid to parochial education. This was not a new battle. Jews had made the decision in the nineteenth century to enter the public schools; Catholics had chosen to put their efforts into keeping their children out of these Protestant-dominated institutions. These choices were rooted in each group's reasons for coming to America. The Irish, who were the dominant element among the Catholics, had fled the Protestant British. On arrival, they labored hard to stay away from the pressure of Protestant institutions which dominated America—and never mind that the price included an extra generation or two of remaining in the blue-collar classes. During their mass migration, Jews had come to America to escape the czar of Russia and the king of Romania, both of whom belonged to the Orthodox Christian faith. The ancestors of the American Protestant majority had not recently oppressed Jews. One had no reason for erecting barriers against this culture, and especially not if the main purpose of coming to America was to succeed in the "Golden Land." Therefore, after 1945, when the choices had to be made, the Catholics reenacted their earlier decision, and so did the Jews—but with a difference.

Catholics could not easily make the distinction between public devotion to the religion of "freedom and democracy" and private allegiance to the teachings of the Church—but that is what they were soon constrained to do. The hierarchy and much of the laity wanted to secure a separate Catholic culture, but Roman Catholics in America were haunted by the memory of Alfred E. Smith. Smith had run for president in 1928 as the nominee of the Democratic party. He had lost in a very ugly campaign in which the Protestant majority had made it clear that it did not regard a Catholic as a true American. By the 1940s and the 1950s the Protestants had not relented; their passionate battle against state aid for parochial education proved that their anti-Catholic emotions had not weakened.

In the years immediately after the Second World War, the blacks campaigned to enter the majority. Their ideal, then, was the day when the black organizations and the black community as a whole would dissolve into America. The Catholics wanted to make America accept, and make room for, their separate identity as a community. Most Jews tried to have it both ways: to become part of the majority society while keeping some kind of Jewish communal life alive.

18.

The Conquest of the Suburbs

I

The children of the East European immigrants were now, in the 1940s and 1950s, in midcareer. They were numerous and increasingly wealthy, and ever more "Jewish." Every sociological study made in the 1950s (and they were made by the dozens) attested to the fact that they were most comfortable with other Jews, and that they regarded the Jewish community as their primary home. Yet, they were deeply ambivalent, often without admitting it even to themselves, about their most Jewish emotions. They eagerly seized the pragmatic, "American" responsibilities of philanthropic and political leadership of world Jewry, but they regarded it as unthinkable, and even anti-American, to use any part of their new wealth to create boarding or parochial day schools in which separatist Jewish culture and values might be cultivated. What they did as Jews—and, more revealing, what they chose not to do—had to fit their dominant purpose: to "arrive."

The transforming moment for this generation can be dated precisely: the three years between 1945 and 1948, the time of the creation of the State of Israel. The children of the immigrants took the lead in this fight, and in the process, they settled their scores with other Jews. In the 1940s the "German Jews," well into their third generation, were still the richest members of the Jewish community. Though the "Russians" had comprised the vast majority of the Jewish population in the 1930s, dominating the community's public agenda since Brandeis's days, they had remained poor relatives. They were patronized too by Europe's Jews. Before the war, the European Zionists, without exception, regarded the Americans as intellectually and even politically irrelevant. They were the source of a few dollars, but the real action was in Europe and Palestine. The United States was largely on the margins in the fierce battle waged in the 1930s by the moderate Chaim Weizmann and the militarist Vladimir Jabotinsky over the future of the Zionist movement. The Halutzim, the pioneers who settled Israel, came from Europe and not the United States.

The first battle within American Jewry erupted over the future of the refugees in Europe. Little more than a million Jews remained of a European community that before the war had numbered over seven and a half million. The attempt was begun everywhere to reconstitute the broken pieces of Europe's Jewish communities. The "German Jews," represented primarily by the American Jewish Committee, felt that the refugees should return to their former homes. Those who could not return, they thought, could go to Australia, or the United States, or perhaps, as individuals, to Palestine, but not to a Jewish state there. A more extreme ideological group, the American Council for Judaism, split off from the American Jewish Committee. This group, led by Rabbi Morris Lazaron of Baltimore and Lessing Rosenwald of Philadelphia (an heir to the Sears, Roebuck fortune), was loyal to the pronouncements of "classic Reform Judaism" as enunciated in the Pittsburgh Platform of 1885: Judaism was a religion, and not a nationality; to constitute a Jewish national community in Palestine would make every Jew in the Diaspora suspect of dual loyalty. The "Russian Jews" were furious. They took to reprinting Brandeis's pronouncements that Zionism is the best form of Americanism. They knew that establishing a Jewish state was a popular cause. Americans admired fighters. More negatively, it was an open secret that the United States, which was engaged in demobilizing and finding place in the economy for some fifteen million soldiers, was in no mood to open its own door to hundreds of thousands of immigrants. The Zionists had little trouble persuading America that the Jewish state was a moral necessity—and that those who were supporting this endeavor were good Americans.

The "Russian Jews" in America especially identified with the Jews in Palestine. Most of the heroes who fought the battles of Israel's first war were from Eastern Europe. To be sure, young Jews from Germany, and from the rest of Central Europe, were doing their share, and perhaps even more, in the dramatic battles for the creation of the Jewish state. In the mid-1940s, Teddy Kollek, of Viennese origin, was the emissary of the Haganah, the mainstream Zionist army, to the gunrunners in America. The fabled Brecha, the underground which guided thousands of Jews across European frontiers and past the British blockade into Palestine, had many young Jews of Central European birth among its emissaries. But the dominant majority of the Jews in Palestine in those days, and almost all of their leaders, from David Ben-Gurion to Golda Meir, were from Eastern Europe. So were most American Jews. There was, of course, no equality of sacrifice between Americans and Israelis. The Jews in the United States were providing money and political support, but the Jews in Palestine were fighting the war. The Americans played a supporting role, and they knew it—but this role was sufficiently dramatic to make their leaders the most important Jews in America.

The successful battle for a Jewish state was not only a victory over the "German Jews"; it was, on many levels, a very American endeavor. These were the years of the Marshall Plan and the rebuilding of Japan by American occupation forces under General Douglas MacArthur. The creation of Israel was the equivalent task for American Jews. Those who engaged in it felt themselves cutting no less a figure in the Jewish realm than the American leaders were cutting on the wider stage. What a metamorphosis this was for the children of the immigrants who had been poor in the Bronx in the 1930s.

The effort for reconstituting a Jewish nation was even more "American" because of the Holocaust. The murder of six million Jews in Europe had been the ultimate demonstration of Jewish powerlessness. American Jews were doubly uncomfortable: they were suppressing their own immediate memories of not being able to help, and they suspected that American anti-Semites were more contemptuous than sympathetic to Jews who had not fought back in Europe.

It would take a generation before American Jews would even want to understand the impossibility of armed valor by the victims of the Nazis. In the years immediately after the war, only the few examples of armed resistance, such as the revolt in the Warsaw Ghetto, in April 1943, were remembered and celebrated. In American terms, the Warsaw Ghetto was the Jewish Alamo.

The fighting Jews of Palestine, at war with both the British and the Arabs, were even stronger proof that Jews were a heroic people. They were having their own Valley Forge and crossing of the Delaware—and the Jews of America were sharing in the glory. Settlers fighting Indians and establishing civilization in unfriendly territories were another American myth, and the battle for the State of Israel could be told in those terms. The Jews of Palestine could be cast as pioneers on an unfriendly frontier. The story of the creation of Israel soon was made into the Wild West in the Middle East by a Hollywood writer, Leon Uris, in his novel *Exodus*. As soon as the book was published in 1956, it became very nearly the "Bible" of American Jews. In the film version, the hero, Ari Ben-Canaan, was played by Paul Newman, a young American Jew. During those heroic, early years of Israel, American Jews were hoping to imitate the Israelis. They wanted to be believable to themselves as "cowboys" in America, as active wielders of power on American soil.

The Zionist effort in the mid-1940s was helped by a deep anti-British strain in American history. Had not the United States been created in rebellion against Britain? Never mind that America had just fought a war as Great Britain's ally. At war's end, the British still held a worldwide empire, and the United States was no defender of British power. It wanted that empire to dissolve—in large part so that America might inherit the role of primacy in the world. Various American ethnic groups, and especially the Irish, had more immediate reasons to dislike the British. Indeed, American sympathizers with the Irish Republican Army announced their admiration in the 1940s for the Zionists. For American Jews to help push the British out of Palestine was, therefore, on several levels a very "American" act.

The creation of Israel solved another basic problem for American Jews, the question of a homeland. In the immediate postwar years, it was no longer "anti-American" to remember one's origin. Individuals now looked with fondness to their ethnic pasts. All of these

Americanized ethnics, precisely as they were becoming more American and more remote from immigrant life and culture, needed the legitimacy of a homeland. They could not be less than the descendants of the earliest settlers who looked back to England. The Irish marched on Saint Patrick's Day; the Italians gloried in their kinship with the country which had been the home of culture and art since Roman times. Even the Germans claimed descent from the tradition of Goethe and Beethoven, as they insisted that Hitler had been a temporary aberration.

America's Jews, however, had no homeland in which they could take some pride. The vast majority of recent immigrants had never had positive feelings about their countries of origin. They could not look back to anti-Semitic Czarist Russia, or to interwar Poland. And many of the places from which they had come had either been destroyed by the Nazis or taken over by the Soviet Union. As Marc Chagall hinted at in his paintings of Jews floating in the air, Jewish life in prewar Europe no longer existed in the towns and villages to which Jews had clung for a thousand years.

The creation of Israel thus offered the Jews of America a place, a homeland, in which they could take pride, and thus nurture both their Jewish inner selves and their need for "normal" status in America. It was inevitable that American Jews would conceive of their old-new homeland as uniquely heroic. This nation had arisen again after a hiatus of two thousand years. This "miracle" had more than a hint of "chosenness" about it. Those who identified with the new State of Israel could feel very special as Jews, even as they were becoming Americans with roots in a homeland of their own, just like all other Americans.

All of these themes were symbolized in the fall of 1947. Abba Hillel Silver, the elected leader of the American Zionists, took a seat at a table in the United Nations. He was one of the speakers, along with Moshe Shertok, the political secretary of the World Zionist Organization, to present the case for creating an independent Jewish state. Silver was a distinguished and striking figure, of matchless eloquence. Though a Reform rabbi, he was an East European who had been brought to the United States as a child. Silver was an American, but he spoke not on behalf of the United States but rather as a principal representative of the Jewish people. As Silver spoke for Zionism in an American accent before the United Nations, he carried with him the ultimate dream of his generation: he had shifted the leadership of American Jewry away from the "German Jews." This son of immigrants to America was speaking for all the Jews of the world, as an equal to princes and prime ministers.

II

In less dramatic ways the children of the immigrants remade themselves on the domestic scene to suggest that, in their very Jewishness, they were behaving like all other Americans. Even as they were constructing institutions to serve their inner needs, the newly rich of the 1940s and the 1950s used these institutions as their "calling card" into America.

They began by repeating a maneuver used by the "German Jews" nearly a century earlier. The "Germans" had become rich during the Civil War, and they soon fought their way into the "best neighborhoods." They announced their success by building ornate synagogues on prominent thoroughfares in all the major cities of America. In the era after the Second World War, the East Europeans followed suit. Between 1945 and 1965, about a third of all American Jews left the big cities and established themselves in suburbs. The small-town synagogues which already existed in these areas were transformed into large, bustling congregations, and hundreds of new communities were created. The new synagogues were located in very visible places. The formula was an old one: American society might be prejudiced against Jews, but it respected religion. In the 1950s and 1960s, at least a billion dollars were raised and spent building a thousand new synagogue buildings. It was the largest building boom in the history of American Jews.

In the transplantation of Jews to suburbia in those decades, the Orthodox synagogues were essentially left behind. The bearers of Orthodoxy were the immigrant parents who continued to live in the Jewish enclaves that they had established in the big cities. As the Lower East Side in New York City was being taken over by Spanish and Chinese speakers, the electric sign in Yiddish atop the building of the *Jewish Daily Forward* on East Broadway became increasingly forlorn. Few among the aging immigrants moved to the suburbs. The older generation was attached to the established institutions of

Jewish life, to the older synagogues, the kosher butchers, and the meeting places in the corner candy stores. Even in areas of second settlement, such as the Bronx in New York or Park Heights in Baltimore, the sermons were still, at least some of the time, in Yiddish. Of all of the institutions of the Jewish ghetto, the Orthodox synagogue was the most vehement that Jews stay out of the American mainstream. Such separatist rituals as the Sabbath and kosher law expressed and enforced an attitude: to be a true Jew meant to live apart in a Gentile world, even in America.

Such sensibilities rarely came along to suburbia in the 1950s. The move from the old neighborhood into upper-bourgeois areas, where Jews had never been before, was a move into America. The Conservative and the Reform synagogues were suited to the task of helping this move. Their rabbis, trained in America, were more versed in the arts of congregational leadership than in the difficulties of Talmudic law. The inner convictions of these rabbis were, more often than not, as separatist as those of the older, Yiddish-speaking Orthodox rabbinate. This younger generation (and of course those of their peers who had remained Orthodox) still thought that America, like all of the rest of the world, was divided into only two camps: "we," the Jews, and "they," the Gentiles. This emotion was shared by the bulk of the laity, but it was a feeling held in reserve. The public policy of the new communities in suburbia was to "arrive." The synagogue of the 1950s (like the temples of the 1870s and 1880s) acted out a lead role in a very heady drama: Judaism was now being legitimized as a major American faith, on a par with the Protestant and Catholic versions of Christianity.

Though the Jews who were moving into suburbia were often invading restricted enclaves, the cult of "Americans All" dictated to the churches that they had to exercise neighborliness. Whatever the theological differences, they were now expected to behave, in practice, as if they accepted each other as equals. President Dwight David Eisenhower drove home this point. Just before coming into office, Eisenhower had joined a church. He never defined the specifics of his own religious view, and he did not seem to want to be troubled by any angular doctrines of other people's faiths. The President, acting as leader of opinion, and even as "High Priest" of Americanism, had pronounced all religion to be good, provided that the sects did not squabble with each other, and that they joined in teaching their believers to take pride in the United States. Eisenhower himself provided the best definition of this ideology: "Our government makes no sense, unless it is founded in a deeply felt religious faith—and I don't care what it is."

This "civil religion" that had been fashioned during the Second World War was now the "official" religion of American society. It was best expressed and symbolized by the story of the four chaplains. In 1942 an American troop carrier, the *Dorchester*, was sunk in the North Atlantic by a German submarine. There were not enough life jackets to go around. The four chaplains on board gave up theirs to four enlisted men. The chaplains—two Protestant ministers, a rabbi, and a Catholic priest—were last seen standing together in prayer on the deck of the ship. This heroic tale was told and retold in the 1940s and 1950s. In the postwar years the ministers and the priests were not called upon to die together with rabbis, but, at very least, they had to welcome the newly arrived Jewish clergy as colleagues.

The time was right in the 1950s for a social theorist, Will Herberg, to sanctify these events by pronouncing America a tri-faith society. Herberg had come to Judaism as religion in those very years, after spending all of his adult life as a secularist in the service of the labor movement. In 1955, Herberg published a book entitled *Catholic, Protestant, Jew*. The recent declaration of the State of Israel, and its heroic early years, made little impact on Herberg, for his prime concern was the state of American society. Herberg argued that religious differences were not only tolerated in America, but even expected. The synagogue could be cast as the most "American" of all Jewish institutions. Jews were less than three percent of America, but as a religious group, they could be defined as one of the three major faiths which the society had recognized and respected. Joining the synagogue was the way to be a respectable "American" in those Eisenhower years.

In the 1950s and 1960s, the rate of synagogue affiliation climbed from twenty percent in the 1930s to nearly sixty percent of all American Jews. Membership was highest in smaller and middle-sized cities and lowest in New York and Los Angeles. For example, in 1963, in Providence, Rhode Island, including the suburbs, eighty percent of the men and seventy-five percent of the women reported themselves as members of synagogues. In New York itself the enrollment never reached fifty percent, but in the suburbs, everywhere, it averaged two out of three Jewish households. These figures were even larger than they seemed, because of the "revolving door" nature of synagogue enrollment. Many joined synagogues when it came time to prepare their oldest child for bar mitzvah or bat mitzvah, and they left soon after the celebration of that ritual for their youngest child. All of the communal studies of the 1950s showed that more than eighty percent of American Jewish children were receiving some kind of exposure to Jewish religious education and that, therefore, at one point or another, their parents had belonged to a synagogue. The supplementary schools which taught Yiddish, under the auspices of what remained of the Jewish labor movement, were waning in numbers, and the few Jewish day schools were just beginning to increase in the 1950s by those founded by the newest arrivals to America, the survivors of the death camps who had arrived after 1945. The dominant form of education was the synagogue school which offered supplementary classes on weekday afternoons, after public school, or on Saturday and Sunday mornings.

But was this boom in affiliation a religious revival? There was no return to such traditional values as observance of the rituals and the study of sacred texts. Even as synagogue enrollments were increasing, fewer of their members obeyed the restrictions on forbidden foods or observed the Sabbath. The adult groups in the suburban synagogues were much more likely to discuss current events, or busy themselves with bowling, than to study the Bible. What was reviving, or, to be more exact, what was being expressed in a new way, was Jewish group feeling. The children of the immigrants were reexpressing, in wealth, the Jewish emotions of their parents.

In their youth, they had dreamed of both entering American society and retaining a closeness with other Jews. The suburban synagogue was their "city on the hill," the symbol of the achievement of this dream. In the new suburbs, as Nathan Glazer observed at the time, the synagogue was necessary even to Jews who had never attended its door when they were young in the ghetto. In Flatbush in Brooklyn, or in Rogers Park in Chicago, the candy stores and the delicatessens had been places of assembly for Jews. In suburbia people lived in one-family houses, surrounded by grassy lawns. There was little street life. This new environment was not like the Bronx; one could not walk out the front door of one's apartment house and encounter only Jews. Therefore, Jews built synagogues to swim together, to play mah-jongg, or to attend an almost endless variety of meetings.

Even those Jews who affirmed neither religious nor ethnic identity admitted that they were most comfortable with other Jews. Even the most "anti-Jewish" Jews reported that at least four out of five of their friends were Jews. This was true even of people of Jewish origin who had converted to one of the branches of Christianity. Jewish businessmen and professionals did establish themselves by the tens of thousands in the middle class, and they did business much of the time with Americans of all origins and persuasions. They lunched often with their customers or clients, but they went home to have dinner and play cards, or to play golf on weekends, or to go to the theater and the symphony, with other Jews.

In the spring of 1953 the United Synagogue of America, the central lay organization of Conservative Judaism, did a self-study of the leaders of the synagogues. Though 9,100 questionnaires were mailed out, only 1,800 questionnaires were returned. The professionals at Columbia University's Bureau of Applied Social Research were persuaded that the sample, though skewed because the leaders of the smaller congregations were not adequately represented, presented a picture that was essentially correct. About one in three of these synagogue leaders attended "the main Sabbath services" of their congregations with any frequency. About one in five came often, and nearly half showed up infrequently or not at all. Essentially, this profile of the synagogue leadership is not different from the results of a questionnaire about synagogue attendance among the laity as a whole.

The private religious habits of the leaders of the congregations were equally revealing. The Sabbath candles were lit in three-quarters of their homes, but three out of five did not make a sufficiently festive affair of the family dinner to chant the kiddush, the prayer over wine which is ordained by ritual custom. Only one-third of these board members kept a kosher home; there was a middle of one-fourth that was "partially kosher" and another third which made no effort whatsoever toward the ritual restrictions on diet. This profile of typical children of the immigrants is to be compared with the 1880s and the 1890s, when at least four out of five immigrant homes kept kosher. The figures from 1953 mean that the next generation (for Conservative Judaism was, then, the majority option) had largely moved away from obedience of this ritual—and that the stage had been set for further erosion in the next generation. There is a hint of this in the 1953 survey in the answer to the question about the attendance of children at the synagogue service. Only twenty-eight percent of the board members usually took their children on the occasions when they went to Sabbath services; as many as fifty-eight percent went by themselves, leaving their children the option to go shopping, to play in Little League baseball, or to attend ballet classes.

The force of the religious commandments of the Jewish tradition was weakening even among the leaders of the Conservative synagogues. In the survey they were asked whether they would support a requirement that board members regularly attend synagogue. Less than a third, probably those who themselves did come regularly, were for such a proposal; almost all of the rest were opposed. Indeed, there were wars in the boards of synagogues of all the denominations over the issue of what the requirements were for admitting a child to the rituals of bar mitzvah or bat mitzvah. Rabbis and religious school principals, and some of the lay leaders, wanted to make it mandatory that the child, and preferably the entire family, attend Sabbath services for a year or two prior to the ceremony. Wherever this rule was proposed, there was controversy. The parents were overwhelmingly in opposition. Most wanted to "buy" a service from the synagogue. Had not many of these parents themselves been "bar mitzvahed" (to use the phrase that was coined in those days) in a synagogue to which their parents did not belong, after instruction by a tutor who was hired for the occasion? Now, as adults in the 1950s, they wanted essentially to rent such facilities for their children, to let an institution "prepare" their children for bar mitzvah or bat mitzvah without any pretense of accepting any religious authority. Most synagogues did not dare impose such a rule.

The impression that most of the board members of the Conservative synagogues had become board members in order to be board members is illustrated by the behavior of these men and women outside the synagogue. Only a quarter of them claimed to read books or magazines of Jewish content, except for the information bulletin of the congregation which they helped lead, but most were active in some other Jewish organization, and often in more than one. The author of the survey summarized the figures with a certain sadness:

True, the bulk of community involvement shows a heavy con-centration on fund-raising efforts, such as the U.J.A. or the local community chest! Yet, the active "side interests" in Zionist en-deavors, fraternal associations, service organizations and other na-tional agencies are formidable. The figures of participation add up to "astronomical" percentages (totaling 290) and indicate a pa-thetically harassed leadership group, relentlessly driven by the forces of social pressure and relentlessly driving itself to the point of exhaustion. They further demonstrate a fragmentization of at-tention which accounts for the present character of our communal organizations.

The writer of the report could not refrain from adding that no one complained that organizational meetings interfered with the time that these men and women wanted to set aside "to acquire information about Jewish affairs and to study them."

These synagogue leaders were asked what motivated them to work for the synagogue. Three-quarters asserted that they regarded the synagogue as the most important of all Jewish institutions. Many asserted that the synagogue is the primary agency for "perpetuating a Jewish way of life," but just as many said that the synagogue "raises the level of Jews in the American community" and that its existence "makes for a better America in which the Jews shall be well inte-grated." The suburban synagogue was thus defined as both a temple of Jewish togetherness and a bid for acceptance by the Gentiles.

This study was published in mimeograph form in 1953 by the sponsoring organization, but it was almost immediately buried. The results were too plain; they pointed to many problems which the author of the report, Emil Lehman (he was then assistant director of the United Synagogue), did not cover over with the rhetoric of self-congratulation. The people whom Lehman surveyed were of the second generation, the children of the immigrants. The members of this generation were then at the zenith of their lives. Nine out of ten of these board members of synagogues were between thirty and fifty-nine years of age; their children were still young. Educationally, almost half of the respondents had been to college and three out of ten had graduated (be it remembered that these men and women had struggled their way to an education before World War II, in the Depression years). Family income was reported as being over ten thousand dollars a year for a quarter of the respondents, and over fifteen thousand dollars a year for three out of ten. These were high figures in those years, when middle-class incomes were still under ten thousand dollars. No doubt, the synagogue board members were chosen for being, on average, wealthier than the bulk of the members of the congregation, but these respondents were most likely to have been even wealthier than they admitted. There certainly was enough money around those days to build hundreds of new synagogues. By the spring of 1953, among the Conservatives alone, the membership of the United Synagogue, their association of congregations, had risen from less than 200 in 1945 to 443 congregations.

This passion for belonging was a reflection of the problem of rootlessness, of anomie, which pervaded much of American society in the postwar years. In 1956, at the bicentenary of Columbia University, J. Robert Oppenheimer, the physicist who had been chief scientist among the makers of the atom bomb, described the present as a time when "diversity, complexity, richness overwhelm the man of today." His prescription was: "Each . . . will have to cling to what is close to him, to what he knows, to what he can do, to his friends and his tradition and his love, lest he be dissolved in a universal confusion and know nothing and love nothing." Oppenheimer spoke from very high philosophical ground about the need for educated men and women, intellectuals like himself, to define their values and to live by their ideals in the company of fellow believers.

Lesser souls had more tangible problems. America as a whole was moving to new neighborhoods, and thus new associations had to be formed by tens of millions of people. Membership in Christian denominations was rising in those years as dramatically as among the Jews. The Protestants claimed that for the first time in American history over half of those who had been born into Protestant families were formally associated with organized congregations. This would seem to indicate a religious revival, especially in the light of the results of a *Time* magazine poll in 1952 that almost all Americans of Christian birth believed in God.

The difficulty with this explanation is that the 1950s were not a period which was marked by religious fervor. On the contrary, middle-class America, which furnished the laity for the "main-line" Protestant churches, was increasingly self-satisfied and materialist.

In the South, in the Bible Belt, the young Billy Graham, the first of the modern revivalists to achieve a national audience, had barely made his mark before the mid-1950s. Whatever tremors were being felt within American Protestantism involved the issue of race. The central establishments of the main-line churches, especially as represented by the National Council of the Churches of Christ in the U.S.A., were strongly on the side of equal rights for all, but the bulk of the individual congregations, even in the North, did not make fighting for the rights of blacks into a central concern. Those who were joining the congregations, then, in unprecedented numbers were not repentant sinners who had suddenly become twice-born. By joining churches they were asserting not their Christianity but their Gentileness, just as the new, large synagogues of the Jews were an assertion not of their faith in Judaism but of their Jewishness.

Only seventy percent of the Jews answered the *Time* pollsters that they believed in God—and so, clearly, some, perhaps even many, unbelievers were joining synagogues. The difference between Jews and Christians in their answers to the *Time* poll was essentially rhetorical. When Jews were asked about their identity, it was possible for many of them to assert that their loyalty was to the Jewish people, and never mind faith in God. The sense of being one people, one family, as the seed of Abraham, had always been central in Jewish consciousness. This self-definition had become more pervasive in the 1950s, as American Jews increasingly identified with the new State of Israel. In Israel, all Jews belonged to the nation, even though many were indifferent to the Jewish religion.

Christians had no such readily available self-definition; they had always thought of themselves as belonging to a church, to a community of believers, and not to a people. When American Christians wanted to say, in a changing America, that they were Gentiles and not Jews, the rhetoric of Christianity dictated that this be expressed through asserting a belief in God. In the 1950s the Protestant Church in America, which had traditionally represented the dominant American Establishment, housed a laity which was being severely threatened in its role as the unquestioned American elite. Catholics, blacks, and Jews were all on the attack. The churches, even though they joined in an occasional interfaith service, became, like the country clubs, defensive bastions against the attackers. Looking back in 1968, in an essay entitled "Social and Intellectual Sources of Contemporary Protestant Theology in America" (published in a work by many hands entitled *Religion in America*), the Christian scholar and theologian Langdon Gilkey wondered why an increasingly secular America had been experiencing a revival of the churches:

> In recent decades this has created in this least of all ecclesiastical cultures a new species of ecclesiasticism, one stripped of all the dogmatic, priestly, and sacramental elements that have characterized other kinds of ecclesiastical systems. As of now, the variety of American church life has little theological, liturgical, pietistic, or even Biblical content, but it is nonetheless burgeoning with air-conditioned sanctuaries, ladies' and men's societies, large Sunday-school plants, "holy name" baseball teams, and innumerable suppers and dances. It is a "religious" institution of immense power, wealth, and prestige, but one characterized largely by secular values such as recreation, sociability, and sporadic good works in the community. The social value of such an institution is undoubted in our mobile, rootless, suburban culture. Whether it has any real religious character—whether it manifests a presence of the holy in its midst or offers a higher ethical standard for man's daily life— is something else again.

These words could, of course, have been applied without change to the contemporary synagogue. The main-line Protestant Church in decline, and the suburban synagogue on the rise, thus were mirror images of each other—temples of competing ethnics, bastions not of Judaism and Christianity but of Jewishness and Gentileness. Jews would feel more equal and even contentious in the next decade as their power grew and as they became less likely to think of the Protestant Church as everybody's host in America.

III

But there were limits, as much self-imposed as imposed by anti-Semitism, as to how far these Jews could go in becoming "just like everybody else." Jews were marked as Jews, at very least, by their drive to escape their early poverty. Jews were uniquely visible in this stampede toward wealth because they were moving more rapidly upward from the poverty of their youth than any other group in America. This intense passion for success was noted by others, and not always with approval.

The great majority of Jews willingly proclaimed that they were "proud to be Jews." But this American Jewishness was radically different from any Jewish experience of the past: it was situational; it had little to do with a tradition of Jewish learning which had been at the center of the life of all previous communities in the Diaspora. Eli Ginzberg, one of the most astute observers of the American Jewish scene, defined it in those very years. He published a short book in 1949 entitled *Agenda for American Jews*. Ginzberg was more concerned than almost anyone else in those days with strengthening the historical consciousness of the next generation of Jews. He was pointedly critical of the almost total preoccupation with anti-Semitism by the organized Jewish community.

> Today at least among large numbers of American Jews, the "defense activities" have usurped a position of priority. This was more or less inevitable since many of these Jews have lost all interest in positive Jewish values; their entire adjustment is externally oriented. Finally, we are confronted with the amazing belief among American Jews—and it is quite prevalent though it contradicts the inner wisdom of Judaism—that the basic attitudes of the Gentiles toward the Jews can be significantly altered, if only the right "techniques" are discovered and employed.

Nonetheless, Ginzberg concluded his book by insisting that "as Americans, we have not only the right, but the responsibility to be concerned with the future of our democracy." Ginzberg knew that Judaism and democracy were not the same. He used the most immediately available rhetoric of cultural pluralism: "The true strength of a democracy is its highly variegated and diversified culture which permits each sub-group to develop its maximum potentialities and thereby contribute to the whole." Ginzberg had thus paid some lip service to the clichés of cultural pluralism, but what really concerned him was the shallowness of a Jewish community which was largely organized on the domestic front as a society of anti-anti-Semites.

If the Jews to whom Ginzberg was speaking had paid any heed to his agenda, they should have thought about the question of schools. Ginzberg was writing at the beginning of an era when Jewish education was in the ascendant; the 1950s and the 1960s were the heyday of the supplementary Jewish school in America. Ginzberg expressed the hope that these schools would have intensive curricula and that they would succeed in imparting some classic Jewish learning. It was a vain hope. The after-hours schools in the synagogues were being used by the Jewish parents for their own ends. What the mass of parents wanted, apart from a decent performance at bar mitzvah, was that the school impart to their children enough of the sense of Jewish loyalty so that they would be inoculated against intermarriage, that is, that they should remain part of Jewish togetherness. Once that inoculation had supposedly taken hold, the Jewish child could then be launched on his next task, to succeed in being admitted into a prestigious college.

It is revealing that Eli Ginzberg, in his *Agenda for American Jews,* had not recommended, or even mentioned, the educational institution to which his analysis pointed, the Jewish parochial school. If the deepest problem of Jews was, in Ginzberg's words, "to strengthen the historical consciousness of the next generation," the institution within which such sensibility is best formed is a Jewish parochial school. There were a few such schools in existence in 1949, under Orthodox auspices, but Ginzberg's imagination did not have to be tied to this model. The American elite, the seemingly unattainable WASP Brahmins, had been educating their young for almost three centuries in elegant boarding schools which were avowedly Christian, or in their counterparts in private schools in the cities, such as the one conducted by Trinity Church in New York City, for students who lived at home. The creation of Jewish equivalents of these educational institutions was not a question of money, for the generation to which Ginzberg was speaking was finding hundreds of millions with which to build new synagogues and Jewish community centers. The fundamental decision about education, not to engage in private Jewish education, was not even discussed. It was self-evident to the newly affluent East Europeans that their children had to go to the public schools, or to the private schools which would admit them, for there they would encounter their Gentile peers.

In 1949 Ginzberg was pleading for Jewish intellectual seriousness. The tone of his writing suggested that he expected not to be heeded, but that he was sure that he was at least keeping some bad conscience alive. He was wrong. The truth was being foreshadowed by the board members of the synagogues: American Jews were going to make their "spiritual life" out of solving their problems or other people's problems. They would become the audience for numerous novels, sociological surveys about themselves, and for a growing literature about Israel. The American Jewish community had decided, with little deliberation and very much as a matter of course, that its inmost Jewish content was activism.

19.

With JFK, to Power

I

By the late 1950s American Jews imagined that all would soon be for the best in the best of all possible worlds. Anti-Semitism in America had not yet vanished, but it was consistently decreasing, and Jews could imagine that the problems were vestigial. American Jews had adopted Israel as their homeland and blacks as their principal allies. These were the Eisenhower years, when America was at the height of its power and its horizons seemed unbounded. Jews shared in the optimism. But, even as Jewish power and influence were cresting, snakes were growing in their Garden of Eden. The problems came from blacks and Israelis, the very people who were the closest allies of this generation of American Jews.

The established leaders of the black and Jewish communities still agreed, in the 1950s, that they shared the same agenda, but the official words barely masked the differences in real life. The agency which spoke for the Jewish community was the National Jewish Community Relations Advisory Council. This coordinating group included all of the Jewish organizations, both national and local, which dealt with American domestic affairs. Each year, these bodies met to redefine their objectives and priorities for action. In 1953, the NJCRAC asserted: "A fundamental objective of Jewish community relations is equality of opportunity for all, regardless of race, religion, color or national origin. In a still imperfect democratic society, Jews, together with many other groups, suffer from inequalities of opportunity and other forms of discrimination. They are among the victims of the intergroup tensions and antagonisms that exist in our society." In the text, the NJCRAC went on to argue that it was to the advantage of Jews to fight side by side with blacks against discrimination in housing and in jobs. This was true in law, for anti-discrimination legislation applied equally to every social and economic level, but it was not true in fact. Jews were then doing battle in suburbia, or in posh neighborhoods for apartments in the cities, against "restrictive covenants," which obligated the owners not to sell to Jews or other "undesirables," but the Jewish upper middle class was not out on the street, without possibility of buying adequate housing. Blacks were trapped in crowded slums. The drive to move out was motivated mostly by the sheer need for space. Jobs, too, were a different kind of issue for Jews and blacks. Jews were troubled by still existing discrimination at the very top of the American economy, in "executive suites." Blacks were fighting to leave the most menial jobs in America.

In those years, at the very height of the alliance, there was one marked note of dissonance among Jews. The southern Jewish communities were under fire from southern racists, who were angry with the Jews for leading in the battle against segregation. This ire was directed at the national Jewish organizations, which were all without exception based in the North and run by leaderships and bureaucracies which were overwhelmingly northern. A few southern Jews were prominent in the battle for racial integration. In Nashville, Tennessee, Dan May, a leading industrialist, was chairman of the school board in 1954, and he took the lead in fostering a plan for integrating the public schools, one grade at a time. This modest suggestion did not endear him to the local racists, and he had to be guarded by police for a while. In Atlanta, Jacob M. Rothschild, the rabbi of the Reform congregation, was an ardent supporter of the cause of blacks. He was himself in some danger, and the temple building was dynamited in 1958. Nonetheless, despite such exceptions, the overwhelming majority of southern Jews tried to avoid the racial controversy. Almost none shared in the most rampant prejudice. Many had close personal relations with blacks, because the typical southern Jew in the 1950s was a storekeeper whose clientele was often in part or even entirely black. The mainstream position among southern Jews was "gradualism," that is, that the progress toward racial equality should proceed in such fashion as not to evoke rage in the white majority—the very "gradualism" that Martin Luther King would mock and denounce at the end of the period, in 1963, in his letter from a Birmingham jail, which was addressed, in the first instance, to a coalition of clerics of all three faiths.

Southern Jews often suggested to the national Jewish organizations to which they belonged that they dampen their rhetoric in support of blacks, but, even as these pleas were not heeded, there were few defections. In their conscience, the Jews in the South knew that the misery of the blacks cried for better treatment, and so, even as they did very little, the southern Jewish communities did not dissociate themselves from the official Jewish position of alliance with the blacks. In 1955, the NJCRAC reaffirmed the alliance with some pride. The framers of the NJCRAC plan for the year took note of the discomfort of Jews in the South, but proposed an additional reason for remaining firm. The price was worth paying because "As the Asian and African colonial peoples pursue their inevitable course toward emancipation and political independence, they will grow increasingly aware of the role of distinctions based on race and color in most parts of the world; and their attitudes toward various nations and peoples—including their attitudes toward Jews—will be deeply influenced by their observations." Thus, strengthening international support for Israel became, probably for the first time, a reason for Jews to support America's blacks.

Still, the "black-Jewish alliance" was not, in the 1950s, and it had never been from its very beginnings as self-evident as the NJCRAC would have liked to think. On the contrary, the formal alliance had arisen only after the Second World War and, even as this cooperative relationship was being defined and celebrated, the memory of past difficulties was very much alive. Blacks, the weaker partner, remembered even better than Jews all of their hurts and disappointments. In the 1930s, as Walter White, the executive head of the National Association for the Advancement of Colored People, had attested, "Negroes were concerned only when Negroes were attacked; Jews became alarmed only when Jewish toes were trod upon." In those years, Jewish leaders, so he told, refused to join the NAACP against antiblack housing restrictions, even though White pointed out that such restriction "would in time be used against Jews and other minorities." Later, in 1943, White still did not think that the time was right to suggest joint action: "I do not advocate here a Jewish-Negro coalition." But he pleaded that Jews should at least learn from their own experiences not to "indulge in any form of prejudice or superiority to others who are victims of the same evil forces of oppression."

The race riots in Detroit in late June 1943 and the even more devastating outbreak in New York's Harlem in August of that year had marked components of black anti-Semitism, but this knowledge was largely unreported. Most of the businesses on the main shopping streets of black Detroit and of New York were then owned by Jews. In its lengthy account of the Harlem riot, the closest that *The New York Times* came even to hinting at these facts was to mention the destruction of a pawnshop on 125th Street owned by someone called Sobel. During the riot in Harlem a number of stores had put out signs NEGRO–OWNED AND OPERATED. Such establishments were not looted. Though the Jewish-owned stores soon called in the glaziers to install new windows and reopened for business, most of the owners had decided to get out. Jewish businesses in Harlem were now up for sale; they ceased being enterprises that fathers might hand on to their children. This was all the more true because by the 1940s there was almost no remnant of the earlier Jewish population in Harlem. Those who had founded the stores when they lived in the neighborhood had already moved out in the 1920s and 1930s, as the population of Harlem was becoming entirely black. They had left behind many ornate synagogue buildings, which were now black churches. Jews still owned much housing, which they were renting out to black tenants, who were often too poor to pay the rent and who, even more often, complained that they were not being provided with adequate services.

All of these tensions persisted in the years after the Second World War, even as the black-Jewish alliance was being made formal. In 1946, Kenneth B. Clark, a young sociologist, published a blunt description of the difficulties between blacks and Jews. He asserted that "in practically every area of contact between the Negroes and Jewish people, some real or imagined ground for mutual antagonism exists." Blacks, of course, were aware that the black entertainer who was antagonistic to his agent also knows that "if the Jews didn't give us bookings or parts we wouldn't work—but they make a gold mine out of us." Clark documented the proposition that blacks were more bitter toward Jews because they were more in contact with them— as merchants and as landlords—than with any other element in the white community. When Jews called conferences about "the Negro in the United States," blacks felt patronized.

Black leaders knew that they needed the Jews, for this was the only white community in which there was almost total support for their cause. But the "patronizing" Kenneth Clark spoke of was becoming ever more irritating. Jews seem to have been largely unaware, then, of these angers. They were persuaded in their own minds that their passion for the cause of blacks was entirely idealistic: Jews were remembering their own past suffering, and thus they were predisposed to be more identified with the blacks than any other group in America. But there was more than a little truth in Kenneth Clark's complaint. Jews were far better educated than blacks, and they presumed without question that they could provide a significant proportion of the highest caliber of leadership for the black cause.

Jews had cast themselves in the 1950s in the role of doing for blacks what blacks supposedly could not do for themselves. This notion seems to have appeared simultaneously both among the intelligentsia, especially among scholars in the social sciences who were Jewish, and among the bureaucrats of several of the national Jewish organizations. The scholars were troubled by the assertion that blacks are, in the aggregate, of lesser intelligence than whites. Writing in 1952, the sociologist Charles I. Glicksberg surveyed the literature on blacks in America. He found that "The Jewish scholar, be he a psychologist, an anthropologist, historian, or a student of public opinion, is drawn to the problem of racism because it furnishes another flagrant example of the violation of the American Dream." Glicksberg quoted Franz Boas, the leading American anthropologist of the previous generation, who had described the Negro past in America as fruitful and creative. Glicksberg listed a number of Jewish scholars of his own time, from the anthropologist Melville Herskovits to the Marxist historian, Herbert Aptheker, as disproving "the myth concerning the Negro past" and establishing "that the charge of inherent racial inferiority is utterly without warrant." Otto Klineberg, who tested blacks who had come to the North from the South, proved that intelligence rose when blacks lived in a freer environment. Glicksberg gloried in the fact that not a single Jewish scholar was to be found among the apologists for prejudice against the Negro. On the contrary: "The Jewish intellectual, steeped in the prophetic tradition of his people, is necessarily a defender of democracy, a champion of justice for all people."

In the mid-1950s, the rhetoric of the Jewish organizations began to shift. They were facing serious trouble within the Jewish community itself. The NJCRAC was forced to fight on behalf of blacks with some of its own Jewish constituents. It had to acknowledge that "when Negroes moved into formerly all-White communities" even some Jews were opposed. These attitudes were condemned because they ran counter "to the Jewish stake in the integration of housing and schools." The opposition among Jews to blacks came up again two years later, as did the same argument: that Jewish interests required them to oppose all forms of housing discrimination. But the Jewish organizational leaders, who were advancing this argument, were not convincing those of their brethren who were fighting against the penetration of blacks into lower-middle-class neighborhoods in New York and Chicago. The Jews opposed to blacks were aging workingmen, or small businessmen, who still lived in the cities. Unrestricted housing was not in their immediate interest. The Jewish leaders urging them to side with the black community were, overwhelmingly, rich suburbanites. Their own immediate, personal interests were not threatened, for blacks were not then competing for their jobs, or bidding for homes on the streets to which the well-to-do had moved.

To be sure, the involvement of Jews in the cause of blacks did not come cheap. Jews paid an outsize share of the financial bill for the black organizations. Few statistics are available, but it is a fair guess that at least a third of the money that financed the NAACP and the Urban League in the 1950s came from Jewish contributors. Thousands of Jews helped organize and participated in the protest marches in the South and in the North. These men and women were most often passionately convinced idealists—but their efforts for the black revolution served Jews in a very deep way. The era after the Second

339

World War was the time when Jews were on the march, with the intention of arriving at the very top of American society. By the mid-1950s, they had made base camp, through their rapid economic rise, for the final assault on the Mount Everest of elite status in America. Now, through their role in the black revolution, Jews were making their first overt bid for a major place in the American elite. They were announcing themselves as a major force for solving America's worst problem, racial tension. The Jews were the only white community in America that was very nearly united—in support of blacks. The great and passionate participation of Jews in the battle for blacks was the very first time, in all of American history, when Jews were not pleading for themselves. They were leaders at the very cutting edge of social change—and thus they had "arrived" at the center of American life.

But blacks would not allow Jews to enjoy this "triumph." The young among them, in particular, could not abide the thought that any whites, and especially the Jews, were an elite to whom they should defer. In 1960, young blacks organized the Student Non-Violent Coordinating Committee. They believed in direct social action, and insisted that the black struggle be led by blacks alone. SNCC led in lunch counter sit-ins and boycotts of businesses which discriminated against blacks. Whites were soon excluded from the organization—but nonetheless, for the next several years, Jews continued to furnish a quarter to a third of its financial support. Some admired the activism of SNCC. Jews were even officially indulgent of more radical black elements, such as the Black Muslims, with more than a hint that adults should understand the growing pains of less-advanced people.

The Jewish establishment and the liberal Jewish intelligentsia were reluctant to stop thinking of themselves as the patrons of the blacks. This attitude colored the NJCRAC program for 1960. But the framers of the "program plan" knew that radical changes were taking place, not only in the relation between whites and blacks in general, but especially between blacks and Jews. They predicted that there would be violence even in the North, and that this was all the more likely because of the new black nationalism: "Taking various forms, these movements are essentially alike in their Negro chauvinism, in their 'anti-Whiteism.' The Negro Muslim movement is also anti-Christian and anti-Jewish. All share the conviction that Negro rights can be achieved only through Negro efforts, that White cooperation or help is a poor reed on which to lean or even a fraudulent and deliberately deceitful mask for White domination and exploitation." The Jewish leaders knew that "the rank and file of the Negro community" had become alienated from Jews, and felt little gratitude for the contribution of Jews to the black struggle. Blacks were boycotting Harlem liquor stores and emphasizing that most of the proprietors were Jewish; there were charges in Harlem that black numbers racketeers were being arrested while Jews and Italians were not being bothered. The Jewish community had to take a new attitude toward blacks and not only by establishing relationships with the newest, most activist, and least "respectable forces" among the blacks.

The Jewish establishment thus admitted as early as 1960 that the relationship with blacks could no longer be defined as comradeship of excluded peoples, as in the first years of the alliance in the 1940s and early 1950s, or as the paternalistic concern of Jews for the less fortunate blacks, as in the late 1950s. The young activist black leaders had revolted, and the black masses were on their side. Blacks were well on the way to becoming a power group in America, if only because of their capacity to make trouble. Other groups in America would have to learn how to deal with blacks who could not be patronized, even by their friends. The Jews, who were closest of all, would have to learn the lesson first. Jews had bid for the role of an elite in America by taking care of the blacks—but the essential meaning of the black revolution had become clear by 1960. Blacks were insisting that America was the place that James Madison had once defined as an untidy collection of conflicting interests. There was no elite to which blacks would defer. Jews could rise in America only to the degree that they, like all other groups, acquired and held onto some power in the continuing jostle of American society.

II

The relationship of American Jews with Israel was just as boobytrapped—with difficulties and conflict—but the American Jewish community had a much larger emotional investment in pretending that this was not so. When conflicts arose, they were swept under the rug as quickly as possible. The essence of the matter was that, even as American Jews were adopting Israel as their "homeland," they were refusing to be Zionists.

In the 1890s, at the beginning of modern Zionism, Theodor Herzl had predicted the absorption of most Jews into a Jewish state and the disappearance of the rest; Ahad Ha-Am, the founder of "spiritual Zionism," had insisted that most Jews would live as Jews in the Diaspora. He suggested that the relationship between the Jewish society in the homeland and the rest of the Jews of the world would be primarily secular and cultural.

It was clear as early as 1949 that the Jews of America were not going to emigrate en masse to the State of Israel, and it was equally clear that this community resented any reminder of Herzl's thesis that those who chose to stay in the Diaspora should help "normalize" the Jewish people by assimilating. Those who made this suggestion, such as the writer Arthur Koestler, were bitterly attacked in the Jewish press as traitors. American Jewry was going to survive, so the critics insisted, by deepening its relationship to Israel. In defense, the name of the founder of "spiritual Zionism" was invoked and reinvoked: the Diaspora would be warmed by the blazing sun of the new Jewish center in the State of Israel. But there was no cultural content to this assertion. The Zionists in America were inventing a peculiar kind of Ahad Ha-Amism. Support for Israel, and not learning Hebrew, was the "spiritual content" of the relationship.

This American version of Zionism—to admire and work for Israel but not to move there or participate in its culture—surfaced in several stormy encounters. On May 14, 1948, when the State of Israel was declared, the World Zionist Organization ceased to be a "government in exile," but it did not cease wanting to exercise political functions. The leader of the American Zionists, Abba Hillel Silver, wanted to continue to have a roll in Israel's political life. Silver argued that the Jews of the world had a very special relationship to the State of Israel; they should have a voice in the decisions that Israel would make about itself. Soon after the War of Liberation was won, David Ben-Gurion, the prime minister of Israel, made an end of this anomaly. He thundered that no one "could sit in Cleveland and give directions to Tel Aviv." Let Silver come to Israel to live, let him join its political process, and then he would be entitled to whatever influence he could gain at the polls. Otherwise, so Ben-Gurion insisted, Silver's claim to a voice in Israel's life was impertinent; it was an assault on the basic character of the independent Jewish state.

Ben-Gurion won this argument because he insisted that the state was now sovereign over all partisan interests in the Jewish world. And yet, the question of the relation between the Diaspora and Israel remained. Ben-Gurion soon "solved" the problem by applying to it the rhetoric and ideology of basic Zionism, in its most uncompromising form. The "founding father" of Israel ruled that Zionism means the demand that all Jews, and not only those in immediate danger, must remove themselves to Israel. Since the Jews of the West were not coming in any appreciable numbers, the hundreds of thousands who continued to call themselves Zionists were simply misusing the term. Jews who remained in the Diaspora would, without exception, be treated as "friends of Israel."

In 1950, a year after Ben-Gurion ended Silver's Zionist career, he began to treat Jacob Blaustein, the president of the then non-Zionist American Jewish Committee, as the effective leader of American Jewry. The two of them soon made clear the meaning of their entente: Ben-Gurion wanted financial and political support from American Jews, but he was intractable in insisting that only the State of Israel could determine the use to which such support should be put. Those who disagreed with what Israel was doing had the right to walk away, but they had no right to object. The Zionists in America chafed under this formula. Even those who had made no claim, as Silver had, on major influence on the life of Israel, resented being downgraded to minor-level fund-raisers, but this unhappiness made little difference. Israel was nearly overwhelmed in the 1950s with the task of absorbing well over a million newcomers. It needed money badly, and most of its major donors were not associated with the Zionist organizations.

Ben-Gurion's solution to the question of Israel-Diaspora relations worked well for thirty years. It was widely accepted, at least in the Diaspora, that the leadership role of Israel's Labor party was permanent. American Jews belonged mostly to the moderate center of the Democratic party. They were sure that Israel, under Labor's management, would pursue policies which they themselves could accept and defend. Even as the Labor party began to splinter in the 1950s, American Jews preferred to know as little as possible about that quarrel. They were essentially happy with Ben-Gurion's formula of support without interference; thus, they could, in good conscience, avoid knowing any uncomfortable facts. The relationship between the official American Jewish community and official Israel was thus defined as an involvement which could be maintained only as long as distance was observed. American Jews were entitled to be proud of Israel, but not to meddle in it. Members of "missions" of the United Jewish Appeal often visited Israel in those years and expressed their identification with its brave new life by donning the tembel, the crushed cloth hat of the kibbutzim, and shouting "we are one" from their tour buses. On occasion, the Israelis asked these Americans whether they were truly one: the Israelis were fighting wars; Americans would fly home to safety in a couple of days.

The first hit movie to be made in Israel in the 1950s, *Salah Shabati,* mocked the American Jews, who arrived one after the other in tourist cars to inspect the name plaques on the trees they had given to the afforestation of Israel. It was the job of the hero to change the plaques in advance of each arrival; of course, he got confused, and thus he upset the self-important donors, who could not find their names on any honorific inscription. But such uncomfortable incidents were soon forgotten to permit each of the parties, American Jews and Israelis, to get on with their separate agendas. Israelis needed help, and American Jews needed to love Israel.

American Jews were sure that the involvement in Israel guaranteed the survival of their Jewishness. The surface rhetoric was the proposition that if things ever got bad in America, Jews could find haven in their own state, but this notion was brushed aside by most American Jews. For many, the labors for Israel provided the major content and the emotional highs of their immediate existence as Jews. It was ever more widely held in the 1950s and 1960s that the effort for Israel would somehow guarantee the Jewishness of the next generation of American Jews. Newly appointed heads of the fund-raising drives for Israel spoke, in the words of one such chairman in northern New Jersey, about "handing on the task of raising money for Israel to my children and grandchildren, so that they will remember that they are Jews."

The labors for Israel had one other important meaning for American Jews. These activities began to be recognized as a vehicle for Jews to rise to prominence in America. It was considered to be an act of anti-Semitism, in the 1950s and the 1960s, for anyone to talk about a "Jewish vote," and any Gentile who did was reprimanded by Jewish organizations, which insisted that Jews voted as individual Americans. This was, of course, not true. American Jewish politicians were very much engaged in cementing the power of the Jewish vote and of Jewish political activity. Increasingly, and ever more overtly, Jews were making the support of Israel into an American political issue, and they were rising to the heights of American politics precisely because of their involvement in Israel.

This did not happen all at once. In the first two decades of Israel's existence, there was almost no direct aid from the United States. Israel's deficits could still be met by privately raised funds, and it was not regarded as politic to push the American government during the Eisenhower years, when the war in Korea remained an ever less popular and more costly foreign entanglement. It was too soon after the poverty of the 1930s and the fears of the Hitler era for Jews, even as they were on the rise in America, to take on a very popular president over a few million dollars of possible aid to Israel.

These fears were evident in the American Jewish response to the events of November 1956. England and France tried to reverse by force the decree of Abdel Nasser, the president of Egypt, nationalizing the Suez Canal, and Israel acted in concert with these two powers by moving southward through the Sinai to the banks of the canal. Eisenhower was angered by this adventure, and he ordered the British and the French out of the region. They quickly complied, for both countries were then very dependent on American aid, but Israel did not. It had entered the war to make an end of terrorist raids from Gaza, and it insisted on holding all the territory that it had occupied until it was sure that it had won an end to hostilities.

The administration in Washington became ever testier with Israel. John Foster Dulles, the secretary of state, called in leading figures in the American Jewish community to put pressure on Israel. At this testing time, Eisenhower and Dulles achieved their immediate objective: the Jewish leaders insisted that Israel had a right to its objectives, but they were willing to tell the government of Israel that it ought to moderate its position. The voices grew louder when the rumor got around in February that the Soviet Union was supposedly preparing armed intervention in favor of the Egyptians. Israel withdrew to its original borders in the spring of 1957, under American pressure and with guarantees from the United Nations that an international peacekeeping force would henceforth safeguard quiet on the border of the Egyptian-controlled Gaza Strip. Israel felt itself too weak to defy the major powers. Its supporters in America were not inclined, then, to oppose the government of the United States, but they were sullen.

John Foster Dulles had played the old-line aristocrat, the representative of long-standing American legitimacy, when he leaned on American Jews. He had suggested, on behalf of an angry President Eisenhower, that the American Jewish community had to choose between defending Israel or following the policy of the government in Washington by joining him in forcing Israel to withdraw. The Jewish leaders waffled, but they resented the trap. It reminded them of their feelings of powerlessness in earlier decades, when they did not dare confront Roosevelt on behalf of the endangered Jews of Europe. It was clear that American Jews had not yet acquired enough power to talk back to Washington. Abba Hillel Silver (a longtime Republican) returned to politics to intervene at the White House, but Sherman Adams, the President's principal assistant, brushed him off with some testiness. He came home to Cleveland repeating an old conviction that Jews could not depend on goodwill.

III

Despite their difficulties with blacks, Israelis, and with the American government in the 1950s, American Jews entered the next decade with confidence and pride. They had ceased being an endangered species, and they had become wealthy and secure enough to have some real power in America. The seal was set on this achievement by the presidential election of 1960. This was the moment when the "outsiders," with Jews very prominent among them, conquered America. John F. Kennedy, the Catholic, won the presidential election by a handful of votes. The breakdown of the vote between him and Richard M. Nixon was striking: Nixon, who had infinitely less charisma than Dwight D. Eisenhower, got as much of the white, Protestant vote as Eisenhower had received in the previous election; Kennedy put together his bare majority by getting just about nine-tenths of the vote of Catholics, blacks, and Jews, and of the blue-collar workers, many of whom belonged to ethnic minorities. Thus, the older America was outvoted for the first time by a majority constructed out of the very elements which had been told, for at least two centuries, that they were on approval in America.

It was particularly significant to Jews that the election was so close that Kennedy could not have been elected without them. Jews, even though they were then already less than three percent of the population, cast at least five percent of the votes, for Jews were almost twice as likely to go to the polls as all other Americans. Jewish votes were the margin of victory in several of the swing states. Jews had been of some electoral importance in Roosevelt's coalition, but they had not been indispensable to any of his four presidential victories. The Kennedy election was different. Jews were proud that they had been so crucial to helping the first Catholic into the presidency and that they had thus helped reshape America. In 1960 Jews had a share in the new national administration, as they never had before.

In office, John F. Kennedy surrounded himself with members of the intelligentsia from the major universities. These included not only such figures as Arthur Schlesinger, Jr., who had Jewish immigrants in his immediate family tree, but also McGeorge Bundy, who was descended from the oldest Puritan families. Kennedy's "Camelot" was, thus, not an unvarnished overturn of the older America by an ethnic "pol" who transferred to Washington the machine politics of his grandfather, the first Irish mayor of Boston, John F. Fitzgerald. The minorities were not now simply being given their turn to stuff themselves at the political trough. Kennedy's "Camelot" thought of itself as a meritocracy, as a national leadership of the ablest mandarins, who were recruited regardless of their origins. This theory of merit was satisfying to Jews, for they had been pushing for two centuries for careers based on talent.

Moreover, the White House as "Camelot," with Kennedy as young "royalty," was a reenactment of Roosevelt's White House in which he had played the "gracious king," especially for Jews. There was a critical difference, though, between the new generation of Jewish advisers in "Camelot" and their predecessors who had followed "good king Roosevelt." The Jews in the Kennedy administration represented independent power. The Kennedy years were the moment when the East European Jews finally reached the top of the mountain and saw the promised land. John F. Kennedy brought with him to his cabinet two Jews, Arthur Goldberg and Abraham Ribicoff, both of whom were American-born children of East European immigrants; they were exact representatives of the generation that was then cresting as the dominant element in American Jewry.

The Kennedy era came to a tragic end when the President was assassinated in Dallas on November 22, 1963. These were the years when Jews became a normal, and even unremarkable, part of the American political scene. But Jews had been moving with equal passion toward the upper reaches of American society. In the early 1960s, the black revolution was denying Jews the special role of patron, but Jews could and did associate themselves with those white leaders, and especially the clergy, who fought for the cause of blacks. The great symbolic pageant had taken place just three months before Kennedy's assassination. On August 28, one of the great moments of American history, the march for civil rights took place in Washington. This was a climactic event not only for blacks but also for Jews. It was strikingly evident that Jews were playing a far larger role in pushing for equality than any other white group. There were many Jews among the leaders and members even of the older black civil rights organizations, and the organized community was represented by many delegations. A rabbi walked at the head of the parade, hand in hand with the leader of the march, Martin Luther King. But Jews and blacks were not even pretending to be in the same situation.

On the platform that day Martin Luther King asked blacks not to "distrust all White people" and he pleaded that "in the process of gaining our rightful place we must not be guilty of wrongful deeds." But the thrust of his historic speech was in a confrontationist early paragraph which was really no different from the angry, Black Power outcries of Malcolm X: "There will be neither rest nor tranquility in America until the Negro is granted his citizenship rights. The whirlwinds of revolt will continue to shake the foundations of our nation until the bright day of justice emerges."

The Jewish speaker that day was Rabbi Joachim Prinz, who had come to America in 1937 as a refugee from the Nazis. As a Jew, he invoked "our own painful historic experience, most recently under the Nazis." What the world should have learned from "those tragic circumstances is that bigotry and hatred are not the most urgent problems; the most urgent, the most disgraceful, the most shameful and the most tragic problem is silence." He pleaded that "America must not become a nation of onlookers." This was required "for the sake of the image, the idea and the aspiration of America itself." Martin Luther King was that day the prophet who chastised America for what it had done to his people. Joachim Prinz, even as he remembered the Holocaust, was not speaking in the accents of a minority. He sounded much like his colleagues from the Catholic and Protestant communions. They too—in the persons of the Roman Catholic archbishop of Washington, Patrick O'Boyle, and of the immediate past president of the Protestant National Council of Churches, Eugene Carson Blake—were speaking from that platform of the duty of white America to bring justice to the blacks.

The March on Washington was a high moment for blacks—but also for Jews. They believed that August day that the future was unbounded—but the worst turmoils of racial tensions were soon to come, and so were the divisions over the war in Vietnam.

20.

Turmoil at Home, Glory in Israel

In the mid-1960s, most of American Jews wanted to stop the clock. The dreams of their immigrant ancestors had been realized: Anti-Semitism no longer troubled their business careers, and their children were going to the best colleges. It was also a quiet time for Israel. The raids from Gaza had been ended by Israel's war with Egypt in 1956. American Jews raised money and visited Israel with quiet satisfaction that all was well with the Jewish homeland. Martin Luther King was beginning to have his troubles with younger militant and sometimes even anti-Semitic blacks, but, in the mind of the Jewish community, he was the leader whom they knew and liked. He was, like them, a liberal and not a revolutionary—and he was a great admirer of the State of Israel. Christianity seemed better disposed to Jews than ever. Interfaith activities had become so routine and institutionalized that the major Jewish organizations were vying with each other to "control" the field. In New York, the Interreligious Affairs Office of the American Jewish Committee and the Synagogue Council of America were at war, inconclusively, over who could properly claim to be the Jewish representative in interfaith activities, but these were squabbles over "turf" and publicity. No one, not even among the English-speaking Orthodox Jews, disagreed with the proposition that Jews ought to find some common ground for meeting and working together with Christians. The atmosphere was all the more positive because the Jews revered Pope John XXIII. The pope was reliably rumored to feel contrite about the role of the Church in the Nazi years and to deplore all the elements in Christian theology which were hurtful to Jews. Vatican Council II that John called together in 1962 issued a near-unanimous declaration against anti-Semitism. The Jewish experts and lobbyists, most of them American, who were present in Rome exulted in the coming of a new age.

Inside the Jewish community, the situation was equally comforting. Intermarriage did not yet seem threatening: it was 1 percent of the grandparents and 5 or 6 percent of the parents. But, some worry was beginning to creep into the organized community. Among the Jewish faculty in the colleges and the universities, the rate was much higher, one in three; these were the people who were often the most admired by the hundreds of thousands of the Jewish young in the colleges. The young, the grandchildren of the immigrants, were already marrying out at the rate of one in three, but few of them were old enough by the early 1960s to be marrying. Thus intermarriage had become a topic for discussion, but it was not yet frightening.

In the congregations, there was increasing bustle, but an essential placidity. The dominant problem was how to take care of ever-expanding budgets and how to pay off the mortgages of the newly built synagogues and Jewish community centers. Rabbis were being called to pulpits, in the rhetoric of those days, not to lead or to teach but to "serve." They were expected to be neither prophets nor teachers of Talmud, instructing their students in how to live. The suburban rabbi was cast as a pastor, but he was not a mentor for troubled souls. That task had been entrusted to psychiatrists who were then in ever greater vogue among the educated urban middle class, in which Jews were so prominent. The English-speaking rabbi of the 1960s often tried to become a "pastoral psychiatrist," but he really existed as synagogue functionary.

In the public life of the Jewish community, confrontations had ceased. In the 1930s and the 1940s, American Jews had been led by colorful rabbis such as Stephen S. Wise and Abba Hillel Silver; feisty labor leaders like David Dubinsky and Adolph Held, and capitalists like Felix Warburg and Jacob Blaustein, who fought with Brandeis or Ben-Gurion about Zionism. By the 1960s, some of these figures were dead, and the rest were inactive and irrelevant. The fights had ended, or seemed to have. "Class struggle" between Jewish workers and Jewish bosses was over, because the children of the immigrants who had worked in the needle trades had become businessmen, or lawyers or doctors. All the polls showed at least nine out of ten American Jews were pro-Israel. The vestiges of anti-Zionism among some of the old-line reform Jews, small circles of Socialists and Communists, and some of the intellectuals had become so marginal that no one even bothered to fight with these elements.

The national Jewish organizations were therefore becoming totally bland. Leaders were being chosen almost everywhere because they were likable and moderate. Almost inevitably, the organizations were soon dominated by professional bureaucracies. The executive directors and executive vice presidents were on the scene every day. They were the natural guardians of public policy, and, to ensure that they had the largest possible outreach, they were geared to mass sentiment. A generation earlier, Jewish organizations had "specialized" in competing causes. By the 1960s, they were all doing the same thing. Everyone of the major bodies was for civil rights, for the cause of Israel, and, of course, against anti-Semites. The competition for money and volunteers was among organizations, each of which claimed that it could do all of these things better than any of its rivals. Both in the local communities and on the national scene, this "end of ideology" (in the contemporary term coined by Daniel Bell, the political thinker and social critic) bred not charismatic leaders but institutional managers.

Amidst this self-satisfaction, some social discomfort continued to exist. Jews expressed their annoyance by founding their own country clubs—and by remaining Democrats in politics. The Republicans whom Jews encountered in the suburbs usually had controlled local politics for generations, but these were often the same people who had tried, just a few years before, to uphold "restrictive convenants," to make it impossible for Jews to buy real estate in the neighborhood. The Republican party continued to hold many of its fund-raisers and social affairs in clubs which did not admit Jews. In some places it was tactically wise to be a Republican on the local scene, but the social distance between Jews and Gentiles, between newcomers and older settlers, was sufficient ground for voting present and past resentments, at least in national elections. Irving Kristol, the leading theoretician of neoconservatism, observed ruefully that "Jews are as rich as Episcopalians but that they vote like Puerto Ricans." In the 1960s, when the Jews became as "rich as the Episcopalians," they were the only group in America which had social prestige that was far lower than its income level. And so the Jews—out of memory of the New Deal, pride in their role in the Kennedy administration, resentment at the remains of social exclusion, and sympathy for the poor (for they had recently been poor themselves), and a continuing re-echo in the Jewish soul of prophetic injunctions to love justice and do mercy—became the richest Democrats in the 1960s.

But even so, Jews had become a special kind of Democrat. They wanted the party to be stable and orderly. They wanted negotiated settlements among all the factions in the party and in the country. The majority of American Jews, as Democrats, had become the party of order: they were the true conservatives. Subject only to some minor changes, they liked their world as it was.

But what was the content of inner Jewish life in these years of quiet? The question of self-definition was being posed in the mid-1960s, but most Jews paid no attention. They were interested in their families, in business, and in their social engagements with each other. They did not hear the radically opposed suggestion that the intellectuals and the ultra-Orthodox were making. Most intellectuals wanted the Jewish community to dissolve. The ultra-Orthodox proposed a return to the ghetto; the Jews should live apart from the rest of America. The mainstream refused to listen to either suggestion. Most American Jews preferred to affirm their togetherness without quite being sure what they meant.

The intellectuals were prime disturbers of the peace. Some were wrestling with their Jewishness, and others were indifferent, but almost all of them disliked or were even contemptuous of the existing American Jewish community. In 1961 Norman Podhoretz, who the year before had become editor of the monthly *Commentary,* organized a symposium on "Jewishness and the Younger Intellectuals." Half a generation earlier, in 1944, the *Contemporary Jewish Record,* the predecessor of *Commentary,* had published a comparable symposium and had found almost total alienation from the Jewish community, and from the Jewish religion, among such figures as literary critic Lionel Trilling, art critic Clement Greenberg, and the essayist/novelist Isaac Rosenfeld. Podhoretz reopened the subject for a younger group, under forty, to find a somewhat less angry version of the same result. These grandchildren and even great-grandchildren of immigrants felt "that they properly belonged to a much larger world than is encompassed by the Jewish community—or, indeed, by America itself." The youngest of the contributors almost totally rejected the idea of the need for attachment to any community of tradition. Summarizing the answers, Podhoretz was encouraged by "the atmosphere of idealism." He found that these young intellectuals were asserting with almost one voice "that the essential tradition of Judaism became to be embodied in modern times not in the committed Jewish community, but in the great post-emancipation figures who rushed out of the ghetto to devour and then to recreate the culture of the West: Marx, Freud, Einstein."

These names kept recurring in the symposium. Raziel Abelson, then an assistant professor of philosophy at New York University, mentioned these names, along with Spinoza, as the figures "to which I feel most directly linked"; the modern Jew, he noted, should be "spokesman for a nationally organized, democratic world society, unfettered by parochial traditions and superstitions." Werner Cohn, then assistant professor of sociology at the University of British Columbia, invoked Marx, Freud, and Einstein, and added Jesus and Trotsky, as role models for the Jews as the "outsider," the one who stands alone. Jason Epstein, then editor in chief of the Modern Library, was detached from the Jewish community: "I have the impression that the traditional human groupings are on the way out . . . Perhaps it would be good to feel oneself engaged in a highly auspicious tradition. But I happen not to and do not feel as one with those who do." Nat Hentoff, a regular columnist in *The Village Voice*, echoed this view: "I feel no more involvement with the Jewish community as a whole than I do with any community." Only two symposiasts were clearly on the other side, Enoch Gordis, a physician whose father was a rabbi, and Malcolm Diamond, who was teaching religion at Princeton and writing on Martin Buber. Neither was Orthodox, but both found their Jewish identity in the Jewish tradition, in its texts and practices.

The fundamental issues about contemporary Jewishness had been raised seriously and precisely in these essays. These questions would appear again two years later in a comparable discussion in the Zionist journal, *Midstream,* which published a symposium on the question of whether American Jews were "in exile." Henry Roth, who had fallen totally silent since the publication of his novel *Call It Sleep* (1934), asserted that he had abandoned the "fairly intensive conditioning of [his] own childhood with regard to Judaism," and now felt himself attached to humanity. He knew that his life and the life of his children were inescapably affected by prejudice, but, because his children had not freely chosen to be Jews, they owed Judaism no allegiance: "I can only say, again, that I feel that to the great boons Jews have already conferred upon humanity, Jews in America might add this last and greatest one: of orienting themselves toward ceasing to be Jews." Though some of the other participants in the discussion in *Midstream* agreed with Marie Syrkin, the Zionist intellectual, that American Jewish life was being strengthened by the growing centrality of Israel in the concerns of the community, the younger Jewish intelligentsia agreed with what the novelist Philip Roth said in the exchange in *Commentary,* that "I cannot find a true and honest place in the history of believers that begins with Abraham, Isaac and Jacob on the basis of the heroism of these believers, of their humiliations and anguish. I can only connect with them, and with their descendants, as I apprehend their God." Since Roth was not a believer, "nostalgia or sentimentality" or even "a blind and valiant effort of the will" cannot connect him to Jews as he is not connected to other men.

Roth was correct: only the religious believers had a clear and unshakable answer to the question of why be a Jew, and such believers had recently appeared in the United States, for the first time in all of American Jewish history, in their most ultra-Orthodox version. They were mounting a serious attack from the religious right on conventional American Jewish life. They asserted the most uncompromising, separatist version of the Jewish religion. This doctrine was brought to America during and after the Second World War by leaders who had previously refused to come to the United States— heads of yeshivoth (the schools for advanced Talmudic studies) and Hasidic rebbes. A few, such as the rebbe of Lubavitch, Rabbi Joseph Schneerson, and Rabbi Aaron Kotler, the head of the yeshiva in Kletzk, Poland, had been saved in 1940–41 from Nazi-occupied Poland and brought to the United States. Most other leaders arrived after the war, when the remnants of European Jewry decided that they could not reconstitute the communities which the Nazis and their collaborators had destroyed.

The Talmudic scholars and the Hasidic rebbes who had survived, and their followers, could choose only between Israel and the United States. Many chose the United States, because they were uncomfortable with or strongly against the new secular Jewish state. In their minds, states were a non-Jewish affair. Rabbi Joel Teitelbaum, the rebbe of Satmar, went first to Jerusalem, but he soon left for New York. A number of other Hasidic figures came directly to America. These rebbes reestablished their "courts" in several neighborhoods in Brooklyn. Satmar and several less renowned groups settled in the Williamsburg section where by the mid-1960s the Hasidic community was estimated at five thousand families. Lubavitch established its headquarters in the Crown Heights section; many other branches of the ultra-Orthodox moved into Brownsville. In less than twenty years, all three neighborhoods were dominated by the ultra-Orthodox. Williamsburg, in particular, had become the urban equivalent of an East European shtetl.

The new arrivals were not necessarily at peace with each other. On the contrary, they brought along to the United States many existing sectarian quarrels. The legalists of the yeshivoth and the more mystical Hasidim continued to feel the distance which had arisen between these two versions of Judaism in the late 1700s in Europe. The adherents of Satmar and Lubavitch quarreled violently over a very contemporary issue; the rebbe of Lubavitch was not totally opposed to the State of Israel; the rebbe of Satmar regarded Zionism as the ultimate sign of rebellion against God, who had commanded the Jews to wait for the Messiah. Nonetheless, despite their quarrels, the ultra-Orthodox held one fundamental value in common: they had come to America not to "arrive" or even to succeed (though some were becoming rich by the 1960s), but to be uncompromisingly religious by their own standards.

In the twenty years after the end of the war, less than one hundred thousand Orthodox came to the United States, but this was the first group of Jews in all of American history to come not primarily in search of bread but to find refuge for its version of Jewishness. The new ultra-Orthodox were reenacting, in mid-twentieth century urban America, and mostly in New York, what the Puritans had done three centuries before in the New England wilderness; they were escaping a hostile Europe and coming to the New World in order to create their own separatist theocracy. Their neighborhoods in Brooklyn were being fashioned as their own "city on the hill."

All the sects of the new Orthodoxy insisted on entirely separatist education. Upon arrival, the ultra-Orthodox had found that the existing, "modern Orthodox" community was educating its children largely in the public schools. Like the Conservative and Reform groups, the "modern Orthodox" depended on supplementary classes in the afternoons and on Sunday to impart the teachings and practices of Judaism. Before the Second World War, there were fewer than 20 Jewish day schools in the country, almost all of which were in New York. By 1944, the number had grown to 55, for the existing Orthodox community had begun to move toward educating the young under Jewish auspices. Nineteen years later, in 1963, according to a survey by the Jewish Education Committee of New York, there were 257 Orthodox day schools in the United States, 132 in greater New York and 125 in other cities. In about half of these schools the language of instruction was Yiddish; these were the institutions that the newly arrived ultra-Orthodox had created. From their poorest beginnings, they had insisted that their children be raised in an all-Jewish and uncompromisingly Orthodox environment. The "modern Orthodox" had little choice but to follow the example of the newest arrivals. Within a decade, by the mid-1970s, almost all children of Orthodox families, including the older, Americanized ones, were attending Jewish parochial schools.

The ultra-Orthodox community was the one group in American Jewry which was opposed on principle to having the young go to college. They were especially opposed to the college under Jewish auspices which had been founded a generation earlier by the oldest yeshiva in the United States, and had become Yeshiva University. Its school for the study of Talmud no longer dominated Orthodox learning in America. By the mid-1960s four out of five of the advanced students of Talmud were attending the ultra-Orthodox yeshivoth. These numbered more than three thousand in all. Television sets were forbidden in the dormitories of these schools, and newspapers were frowned upon. The necessities of making a living forced those who ended their studies into contact with the non-Jewish world, but the alumni of the ultra-Orthodox yeshivoth remained convinced that one meaning of American freedom was the right not to participate in American culture. Other Jews who did not share this view were excluded from their fellowship. This, too, was reminiscent of the Puritan attitude, three centuries earlier, toward all other Protestants.

The ultra-Orthodox picked their leaders just as the Puritans had, by consensus. An individual or several individuals were recognized as possessors of profound Talmudic scholarship and charisma. Such leaders were to be obeyed because they represented the true meaning of "Torah," the cumulative teaching of the whole of the sacred tradition. Among the teachers and students of the American yeshivoth, and the thousands of laymen who belonged to this subcommunity, Rabbi Aaron Kotler was the undoubted religious authority. His decisions were widely accepted in most of the other camps of the Orthodox community in the United States, and they were respected in Israel. After his death in 1962, the mantle passed to Rabbi Moshe Feinstein, the head of a yeshiva on the East Side of New York. The modern Orthodox group increasingly revered Rabbi Joseph Soloveitchik, who was the premier figure among the teachers in the yeshiva of Yeshiva University, but Soloveitchik's authority was not recognized by the ultra-Orthodox. He was exactly the kind of figure they opposed, a rabbi with a doctorate in philosophy. No one doubted Soloveitchik's Talmudic learning, or his Orthodox piety, but he was a man who lived intellectually in both the Jewish and the secular world—and the new ultra-Orthodoxy in America refused to compromise with secular culture or even acknowledge its existence.

Rabbi Menachem Mendel Schneerson, the rebbe of Lubavitch, was an extreme separatist, but he was a unique figure, because he was more involved than any other ultra-Orthodox leader with the non-Orthodox majority of American Jews. He had succeeded as the rebbe of Lubavitch on the death in 1950 of his father-in-law, Rabbi Joseph Schneerson. Though the new rebbe had himself attended university in Berlin and Paris, he had long left that phase of his life behind. As rebbe, he insisted, as vehemently as all other ultra-Orthodox leaders, that his followers should be educated entirely in institutions of his movement, and that secular education should be given only to the degree necessary to satisfy the laws of the state. But the new rebbe turned his movement into a "mission" to the rest of the Jewish world. His disciples were sent out into the "wilderness," to all five continents, to do good works and to propagate the faith. By the 1960s, young emissaries of Lubavitch were to be found on street corners handing out prayer shawls and other ritual objects, and asking Jews to join in saying the prescribed benedictions. Any Jew who was moved to perform even one of the commanded rituals, so the rebbe taught, was opening a gate which would lead him to Lubavitch Orthodoxy. The rebbe had thus announced a new policy: his Orthodoxy was a missionary faith which was now setting out to convert all other Jews.

The prestige of this endeavor was rising in the 1960s. The rebbe was widely revered because he was rumored to control the only effective underground Jewish network in the Soviet Union. But there were deeper, less tangible reasons for the success of Lubavitch, and for the increasing influence of all the ultra-Orthodox. Within the non-Orthodox mass of American Jews, many had always felt that Orthodoxy was the true Jewish religion, and that the more modern forms of Judaism, those that admitted the existence of the secular world, were essentially compromises. Had not the "reformed" Jacob Schiff, a generation earlier, said kaddish for his parents in an Orthodox synagogue? The self-confidence of the rebbe of Lubavitch attracted many. Some joined him, at least in part. The renowned sculptor Jacques Lipchitz made no secret that under the influence of the rebbe of Lubavitch he had returned to saying morning prayers every day in the Orthodox manner. Many others basked in the glow of the rebbe's virtue by giving money to his endeavors.

The new ultra-Orthodoxy in America broke with the modern Orthodox by refusing to cooperate with the more liberal religious groups. The fight began over the Synagogue Council of America, a national organization founded in the 1920s as a joint endeavor of the central bodies of the Orthodox, Conservative, and Reform groups, to be the peer group of the Protestant National Council of Churches, and of the National Conference of Catholic Bishops. Belonging to this body suggested that the three Jewish "denominations" were willing to accept each other as equals, if only for limited representational purposes. In 1962, however, the leading ultra-Orthodox religious authorities ruled that belonging to any body which admitted Conservative and Reform rabbis was forbidden. Though that did not stop the modern Orthodox from continuing to adhere to these institutions, the ruling made clear that the ultra-Orthodox felt secure in the future of their own separate community. One could join the "elect" by conforming to its rules, but this "elect" would never adjust to other Jews—or to secular American culture. The mainstream of the American Jewish community thus had been urged by its intellectuals to dissolve, and by the ultra-Orthodox to live apart from American society. The mass of Jews refused to think such radical thoughts. What came naturally and easily was the customary, well-established option, to affirm "togetherness."

But if Jews were "other" from Gentiles, what made them so? Why did they need to remain together? Was it simply the label Jew, pinned on them by anti-Semites? Was it a residual sense of being unwelcome in Gentile America? It was already clear in the 1960s that the older American elite had lost interest in anti-Semitism. Black angers against Jews had become more overt, and sometimes poisonous and violent, but no one in the Jewish community, not even the poor who were fighting housing battles in changing neighborhoods, could imagine being antiblack as a continuing principle of cohesion.

Jewish "otherness" needed positive justification. American Jews had to find a way of persuading their children to be "proud to be Jews," and not merely to be angry with the enemies of the Jews. A "usable past" had to be constructed.

In the seeming quiet of the early 1960s (when racial confrontations were still confined to the South), this Jewish "past" could not be presented as angry, defiant, and revolutionary, nor could it be based on Prophets and Talmudists who had demanded obedience to the law that God had pronounced at Sinai. This past, edited for American Jews, needed to be sanitized so that it would be uplifting and inoffensive.

This editing of memory had begun almost as soon as Jews began to "arrive," after the end of the Second World War. The Rosenberg affair (a Jewish couple, Julius and Ethel Rosenberg, were convicted of spying for the Soviet Union and passing on atomic secrets) had "corrected" the notion that any substantial number of Jews had ever been Communists. Indeed, Jews insisted that they had always been the most respectable of Americans. The Broadway hit, *Fiddler on the*

Roof, was evidence of this trend. The tens of thousand of American Jews who came to see the play were both remembering and inventing an ancestor. They were remembering correctly that their European grandfathers had been poor and semiliterate like the hero of the play, Tevye, the water carrier in the mythic village of Anatefka. There was psychological truth, also, in the village's fatuous rabbi: the poor of Europe had old scores to settle with the traditional leaders of the community who had failed to save them. But, as Irving Howe, the essayist and socialist intellectual, said at the time, *Fiddler on the Roof,* unlike the Sholem Aleichem stories on which it was based, had very little of the blazing anger of the poor toward the rich. Class struggle was not a "nice" subject. Moreover, it was not a piece of Jewish history that the newly well-to-do wanted to remember as they were joining the middle class. Tevye's piety, in the Broadway version, was equally sanitized. It bore little relation to the original figure in the Yiddish tales, for Sholem Aleichem's hero, even as he misquoted the Bible, knew that it enjoined commandments, and not some vague and sentimental "tradition."

The earthy Tevye was a Jewish version of an American theme. Tevye belonged together with De Lawd, the dignified black man who was God in *The Green Pastures,* Marc Connelly's play of the 1930s about simple black folk; an Irish leprechaun in Lerner and Loewe's *Brigadoon* (1947); and with Zorba the Greek. Like them, Tevye was quaint and undemanding; he was, at once, Jewish and American. Jews in New York and Chicago did not have to ask themselves to behave like Tevye, any more than the Irish in Boston could be expected to take leprechauns seriously. The Jews who flocked to *Fiddler on the Roof,* and brought their children to see the show, were proud of Tevye. He was Jewish in a very American way.

This new American Jewishness of the masses who flocked to Tevye was all too respectable—and boring. By the beginning of the 1960s, the problem was unmistakable. In 1963, sociologist and historian Nathan Glazer summed up his essay on the Jews in *Beyond the Melting Pot,* the book that he wrote together with now Senator Daniel Patrick Moynihan, by asserting:

Neither the synagogues and temples, nor the charitable and philanthropic work, nor the fund-raising for Israel and defense seems sufficiently vital and relevant for the most gifted young people who are emerging from the community. Nor does that other community that was scarcely less Jewish, that of the radical movements and the unions, engage them much.

Speaking of the mainstream of the younger generation, those who were not intellectuals, Glazer added that "a satisfying pattern of Jewish middle-class life has not yet emerged." The Jewish community as a whole had not yet found the balance between its Jewish and American identities. Nat Hentoff echoed this view. He asserted that the vast majority of American Jews possessed an identity with little substance; they have "no permanent psychological barrier to joining the other hollow men."

The middle-class Jews of the mid-1960s might have seemed "hollow," or uncertain of their values, but within themselves they remembered why they were Jews. They had been taught by their immigrant parents that being a Jew meant having *tsuris* (troubles) and complaining about them to other Jews. They had been reminded of this Jewishness by Tevye, whom they had just seen on Broadway. He had been saddened by a daughter who went off with a Gentile revolutionary; he had problems with the Russian peasants who sometimes got drunk and made pogroms. A reenactment of such problems in their own time, here in the United States, was thus an almost comforting reminder to the suburbanites that they, too, were Jews. There were such worries to be complained about in the mid-1960s. Some Jews, and some blacks, were disturbing the peace.

Some "clever" Jews were becoming a problem to the Jewish mainstream. Intellectuals and writers were giving Jews a "bad name." Norman Mailer was a famous novelist, the author of an acclaimed war novel, *The Naked and the Dead* (1948), but the Jewish community deplored him. He was looking for the "apocalyptic orgasm," and he was insisting that affirming the body, and even lust, was a daring proclamation of marginality to American culture. Mailer imagined an individual who left society to set out on an "uncharted journey into the rebellious imperatives of the self," even if that meant "to encourage the psychopath in oneself." He did exactly that in those very years. In a frightening passage in *Advertisements for Myself* (1959), Mailer had found value in the murder of "a candystore keeper," no doubt a Jew, by "two strong eighteen-year-old hoodlums." The murderers have displayed "courage of a sort," because they were murdering "not only a weak fifty-year-old man but an institution as well, one violates private property, one enters into a new relation with the police, and introduces a dangerous element into one's life."

Norman Podhoretz was even more troubling to the Jewish community, because he had *Commentary* as his platform. Early in 1963, Podhoretz published an essay titled "My Negro Problem—and Ours." He argued that the "Negro Problem can be solved in the country" only through "the wholesale merging of the two races." He did not flinch from the conclusion that, despite his own upbringing as a white and a Jew, he would give his daughters parental blessing if they decided to marry blacks. This assertion was denounced from almost every synagogue pulpit in America. How dare a Jewish editor advocate intermarrying and the dissolution of the Jewish people? Those who denounced Podhoretz did not stop to hear the torment in his essay. He had not been at ease with blacks since his childhood, and he refused to make himself comfortable in 1963 as a "white liberal" who wished blacks well from a distance. The mainstream Jewish community heard none of this: it heard only that the most prominent Jewish editor of the day was an anti-Jew.

Even the most serious Jewish novelists made the mainstream community unhappy. To be sure, the literary world, which had long seen Jews as aliens, was now very nearly dominated by them. They were establishing that Jewish immigrant habitations, whether in Saul Bellow's Chicago or Bernard Malamud's New York, were as valid a "region" of American experience as William Faulkner's Yoknapatawpha County in Mississippi, or J. P. Marquand's Yankee Connecticut. But Faulkner could write about drunks and perverts and Marquand could tell stories of disintegrating Yankee aristocrats freely, because they were Gentiles. Was it really necessary to tell the non-Jews about quack psychiatrists, like Dr. Tamkin in Bellow's *Seize the Day* (1956)? For that matter, were Isaac Bashevis Singer's earthy stories "good for Jews"?

Many of the writers and intellectuals were disturbing, but they did not threaten the immediate peace of the Jewish community. Blacks were different. They were no longer willing to accept what the white liberal community, where the Jews were so prominent, was eager to offer them: personal equality, a place at the same starting gate as everyone else in the race for success and honor in American society. In the mid-1960s blacks were articulating a radical new program: not equality at the beginning but equality of result. Blacks insisted that the ladder of "merit" was a set of tests invented by whites to measure not intelligence but assimilation to white culture. The poor results of black children in the schools was the direct fault of an educational system which was, by its very nature, racist: it taught black children to be underclass.

These propositions were articulated in their most challenging form by Malcolm X, the leader of the most uncompromising black nationalists, the Organization of Afro-American Unity:

What do we want? We want Afro-American principals to head these all-black schools. We want Afro-American teachers in these schools. Meaning we want black principals and black teachers with some textbooks about black people. We want textbooks written by Afro-Americans that are acceptable to our people before they can be used in these schools.

The most nationalist element in the black community had thus been told by its leader, at the founding rally of the OAAU on June 28, 1964, that the New York schools, in which Jewish principals and teachers predominated, were an arena in which blacks could wrest control of programs and jobs for themselves. This demand was made by blacks not as individuals but as a community: they were proclaiming themselves to be a national group in America with ethnic roots in Africa.

Six months later, Nathan Glazer told the Jews that there was "a new challenge to pluralism" in their encounter with blacks. The demand by blacks for special consideration, for equal share in all of society, was a direct challenge to the Jews. Glazer was aware that Jews were particularly the gainers of the move "into a diploma society, where individual merit rather than family and connections and group must be the basis for advancement, recognition, achievement. The reasons have nothing directly to do with the Jews, but no matter—the Jews certainly gain from such a grand historical shift. Thus Jewish interests coincide with the new rational approaches to the distribution of rewards." The new demands by blacks, so Glazer asserted, did not simply threaten the "merit system"; they undermined the existence of the Jewish subcommunity and of all other American subcommunities. The demand by blacks for equality of results meant that the neighborhoods, professions, and businesses that the various subcommunities had created for themselves would be breached. "The force of present-day Negro demands is that the sub-community, because it either protects privileges or creates inequality, has no right to exist." Glazer insisted that Jews, despite their concern for the advancement of blacks, were now opposed to blacks: "Thus Jews find their interest and those of formally less liberal neighbors becoming similar: they both have an interest in maintaining an area restricted to their own kind; an interest in managing the friendship and educational experiences of their children; an interest in passing on advantages in money and skills to them."

Glazer was not yet confronting the blacks' nationalism for which Malcolm X spoke, even though it was then transforming most of the black intelligentsia. Glazer focused on the majority view among blacks at that particular moment, the demand for a percentage of place in white schools, neighborhoods, and jobs. But the blacks who had gone to war against "merit"—even the majority, then, who wanted integration with whites—were not at war with the idea of subcommunities in America: they simply wanted the rules to be changed so that their subcommunity could arrive.

Glazer's defense of the Jews was, as he knew himself, unhistorical. Three decades earlier, Jewish intellectuals had been arguing that English literature was not the particular province of Christians, who supposedly best understood its spirit. Blacks were arguing, forty years later, that the system of preferment in America had to change, again, to take account of their particular situation. The supposed culture-free and color-blind exactness of "merit" examination had produced, so Glazer was asserting, a community of Jewish bureaucrats and teachers with an ethos of its own, a subculture which had the right to defend itself—against blacks who wanted to seize the schools for their own subculture! The relationship of American Jews to blacks had now changed; the consistency of the arguments was unimportant. What mattered was that the theories were rationalizations by some Jews, who were fighting to retain posts which blacks were demanding.

To be sure, the Jews on the immediate firing line were middle-class bureaucrats and teachers whose jobs were products of civil service exams in the era of the New Deal. They were threatened, as their richer Jewish relatives in business and the professions were not.

But the genie was out of the bottle: some Jews and some blacks were on their way to open war. Jews could no longer assume that, having fought their way to the top of American society, they would not be attacked from below by blacks on the march into the middle class.

In 1966, the situation became more pointed, when Stokely Carmichael became president of the Student Non-Violent Coordinating Committee (SNCC). Carmichael insisted in the early months there was no anti-Semitism in his "Black Power" outlook. Some Jews, such as the journalist I. F. Stone and the entertainer Theodore Bikel, remained in public support. There were even rabbis, such as Harold Saperstein, who was then in the Reform congregation in Lynbrook, New York, who, while unhappy with the insistence on "Black Power," continued to support SNCC. The real break with black nationalists would not come until the next year, in June 1967, when the Israel-Arab war broke out, and the black radicals and their supporters in the white community sided with the Arabs. Until then, specific groups of Jews—the not very rich who still lived in the cities and the white-collar bureaucrats—were in direct battle with blacks. The richer and better established elements could continue to talk the older language of social conscience. Rabbis had gone by the planeload to join the march on Selma, Alabama, in 1964. Albert Shanker, the head of the American Federation of Teachers in New York, which was beginning to be embroiled with blacks over control of the schools, had joined the march. The National Jewish Community Relations Advisory Council persisted in believing that the riots in the cities, in which Jewish stores in the black ghettos were main victims, were of little importance. In "program plan" after "program plan" the doctrine was reiterated that Jews should remain committed to every form of help for blacks. In late May 1967, the Anti-Defamation League published a study in five volumes of black anti-Semitism, to assert that there was less such prejudice among blacks than among whites. The Anti-Defamation League would soon change its estimate of black anti-Semitism, but in May 1967, this was the dominant "orthodoxy" of the American Jewish establishment. It took until 1969 for Bertram Gold, the executive vice president of the American Jewish Committee, the organization which published *Commentary,* in which Glazer had written in 1964, to say that the Jewish community could no longer remain silent and forgiving of angry blacks. Until 1967, the leaders of the organized Jewish community, those who spoke for the mainstream, wanted to believe the Jews were, somehow, still where they had briefly been in 1963, an elite which no longer had to battle other groups in an often rancorous America.

Important elements of the Christian intelligentsia were siding with the most radical blacks. In the spring of 1968, one of the riots in the cities was in Washington, on Easter weekend. Rosemarie Reuther, a young Catholic theologian who was a partisan of the blacks, wrote a column in the *National Catholic Reporter,* in which she pronounced the burning of the Jewish stores in the black ghetto to be a contemporary celebration by the poor of Christ's Resurrection. This was Reuther's version of a theme from Malcolm X: blacks in the American ghettos were the victims of white colonialism. The exploiters, so he insisted, were none other than Jews, who were "colonizing" the blacks, while the Jews themselves had moved away to better neighborhoods. The implication was clear that burning down stores, some of which Jews might own, was a liberating act.

What was least troubling then, in the mid-1960s, were the young Jews of the New Left. As the political thinker and sociologist Seymour Martin Lipset estimated at the time, these were not very many: less than ten thousand of the nearly four hundred thousand Jews who wer students in the colleges and universities. Thus, very few Jewish families were directly affected by the young radicals. But these Jewish activists did make up a very large proportion of the total leadership of all of the various movements of the New Left. The Jewish community, which was always measuring the temperature of anti-Semitism, feared that the prominence in the New Left of Jews such as Saul Landau and Paul Jacobs in Berkeley and of Abbie Hoffman and Jerry Rubin, who were the founders and the leaders of the Yippies, would arouse anti-Jewish feelings among Gentiles. This did not happen. In the mind of America, the New Left was an American and not a Jewish problem.

A study done in 1968 showed that 82 percent of all Americans regarded Jews as the least troubling and troublesome of American minorities. These opinions were being expressed at a time when Abbie Hoffman was screaming at a Jewish judge in Chicago that judging him for his role in the riots at the Democratic National Convention was a *"shande* [disgrace] before the Gentiles." Hoffman was dragging in his Jewishness; it did not matter even in those most superheated days. Jews had "arrived"; they would not be blamed for outbreaks which some of their children were making together with contemporaries from good or even the best old-line Protestant families.

Until June 1967, when large parts of the New Left became anti-Israel, the mainstream of the American Jewish community had substantial sympathy with its purposes. The first manifesto of the New Left, which was written at Port Huron, Michigan, in early summer of 1962, was, in its language and ideals, a very "Jewish" document: "We are the people of this generation, bred in at least modest comfort, housed now in universities, looking uncomfortably to the world we inherit." What the drafters of the statement affirmed was "human independence . . . a quality of mind not compulsively driven by a sense of powerlessness." They pleaded for community which could be achieved "by improved gadgets but only when the love of man by man overcomes the idolatrous worship of things by man." Their social ideal was proclaimed to be "participatory democracy" in which the individual would "share in those social decisions determining the quality and direction of his life." The group that met at Port Huron was opposed to the "military-industrial complex," to the "cold war," and to "colonialism." It was vehemently opposed to discrimination against blacks. Salvation was to be found in remaking society.

The major drafter of the Port Huron Statement was Tom Hayden, who was a Catholic, but the text echoed the committed language of previous generations of Jewish radicals, in the labor unions and in several varieties of the Socialist movement. A substantial proportion of those who came to Port Huron were, indeed, Jews. The Students for a Democratic Society (SDS) had been founded two years before at a convention in New York, and Robert Alan Haber had been elected its first president. Haber came from the University of Michigan, where his father, William, had been teaching since 1936. The elder Haber was an economist and labor arbitrator, who had helped create the Social Security system in the era of the New Deal. In 1948, the family had spent a year in Frankfurt, Germany, while William Haber was adviser on Jewish affairs to the general who commanded the American forces. These were the very days when the survivors of the concentration camps were finding ways, with some quiet American help, to break the British blockade of Palestine and to help in the battle to create Israel. Haber was thus raised in the home of an American Jew who was a social democrat and a Zionist. When he became "Ann Arbor's resident radical," as James E. Miller called him in *Democracy is in the Streets* (1987), Robert Alan Haber had no opposition at home. On the contrary, the SDS, at its founding, was supported by the League for Industrial Democracy, of which his father was a leader.

Dozens of memoirs, histories, and sociological analyses of the New Left, in all its complicated and often warring parts, have appeared. The explanations vary from psychoanalytic interpretations of Oedipal rebellion by the young, to the "red diaper" theory that many protesters were children of radicals of the 1930s, to the thesis that the young copped out of serious politics by protesting without a serious political program. But the New Left as a whole is not the subject here; it is rather the question of the Jewishness of these young radicals and of their affect on the Jewish community as a whole. The adult Jewish supporters—or indulgers—of the New Left were not only some older radicals. The American Jewish establishment never really distanced itself from these young Jews.

Racial equality was a cause which all Jews shared—or said they did. The war in Vietnam did divide American Jewish opinion down the middle, exactly as it divided all of the rest of America, but by 1968, when the college draft was instituted, American Jewish parents were transformed into opponents of the war, along with the parents of much of the rest of the students of the colleges. The occupation of university buildings and the violence were disturbing, but the mainstream of the Jewish community, as represented by these parents, was more indulgent of the young protesters, who were their children, than were most of the Jewish faculty members. The professors had almost all come to their jobs very recently, in the 1950s when academic appointments were opened wide to Jews; they did not want disruption of the institutions through which they had just entered one of the American elites. Thus, some Jewish professors, such as Edward I. Levy in Chicago, were prominent in opposing the students who took over university buildings: others, like Henry Rosovsky in Harvard, led in the effort to conciliate and to bring peace.

Very "established" Jews figured among the early ideological opponents of the war. The women's division of the American Jewish Congress passed an antiwar resolution in the fall of 1965, associating

itself with the demonstrations against the war which had been organized by students and especially by the SDS. Clergy and Laity
Concerned About Vietnam (CALCAV) was formed in the next year;
rabbis led by Abraham Joshua Heschel, the theologian, were prominent among its leaders. That fall the Reform lay body, the Union
of American Hebrew Congregations, passed a resolution at its bien-
nial convention which asked the President "to declare to the world
that as of a given date, our armed forces would cease firing, our
planes would cease bombing and our representatives would proceed
forthwith . . . to meet with the representatives of the opposing
forces in Vietnam, with the view toward finding a peaceful solution
to this conflict." In January 1966, the Synagogue Council of America,
despite the Orthodox, who tended to be more prowar than all the
rest, issued a statement calling for an immediate cease-fire. There
were countervoices to this opposition to the Vietnam War, especially
among the Orthodox. Michael Wyschogrod, who taught philosophy
in the City University of New York, wrote in the Orthodox quarterly *Tradition* (Winter 1966), that America's presence in Vietnam
was part of the war against the Soviet Union, and that Jews had to
support this war as part of their defense of Israel, which was safe
only if the United States included it under its protective, anti-Soviet
umbrella.

American opinion as a whole, and especially the White House,
was aware that Jews, both established figures and young protesters,
were central to the opposition to the war. This issue came to a head
on September 6, 1966, when Malcolm Tarlov, the national commander of the Jewish War Veterans, reported that President Lyndon
Johnson was "disturbed by the lack of support for the Vietnam War
in the American Jewish community at a time when he was taking
new steps to aid Israel." Inevitably, there was an outcry about this
statement, and the White House soon let it be known that Johnson's
remarks had been "misunderstood" or "poorly interpreted" by the
news media. Tarlov soon took back his words. The essential result
of this incident was to harden the views within the Jewish community
on both sides. The supporters of the war in Vietnam insisted that
the protest movement was "bad for Jews" and "bad for Israel." The
opponents of the war became all the more vehement in their insistence
that Jews should not be singled out by a president who wanted to
quell dissent. So long as the young in the New Left remained con-

cerned with race and Vietnam, the older Jewish community was essentially friendly or at least understanding. The atmosphere changed in May–June 1967. Theodore Bikel and Rabbi Arthur J. Lelyveld, the president of the American Jewish Congress, resigned from SNCC, which was most vociferously anti-Israel. The American Jewish community still cared about social justice in America, and about ending the war in Vietnam, but Jews cared most, and with unique passion, about Israel. This emotion had been largely hidden, even from itself, by the Jewish establishment in the mid-1960s. But suddenly, these newly minted American bourgeois, these "hollow men," as Hentoff described them, were full of Jewish anxiety. The children of the immigrants looked like their parents again. They were no longer solving America's problems; they were worrying about Jews.

Many Jews would never have believed that grave danger to Israel, which was being threatened by Egypt and by all of its other Arab neighbors, could dominate their thoughts and emotions to the exclusion of all else. Many were surprised by the depth of their anger at those of their friends who carried on as usual, untouched by fear for Israel's survival and the instinctive involvement they themselves felt. Almost every observer said, then and later, that American Jews had never behaved this way before. The magnitude of the response was without precedent, because Jews were more numerous, richer, and more powerful than they had ever been—but the response was not new.

Jews had been fighting their government on behalf of Jews in danger since they first quarreled with James Buchanan in 1858 over Edgar Mortara, the child whom the papal authorities refused to return to his parents after a maid had secretly baptized him. In 1903, when a bloody pogrom took place in Kishinev, Russia, the Jews in America protested in mass meetings all over the country, and they raised much money for relief. Since the 1890s, Jews had fought with nativists and some aristocrats, and with most of Congress, to keep the doors to America from closing on other Jews. Thus, the passion for Israel was not born in 1967, and it had not even been born as a passion for Israel. It was the immediate, contemporary version, then, of all the earlier campaigns for overseas relief and for political pressure for Jews in trouble. The Nazi years had been the only exception: Jews had been too weak, too concerned about themselves, and too trusting of Roosevelt to go to war with major elements of American power and public opinion.

In May–June 1967, some atonement was made for those years. The response to the Middle East crisis was a way of saying that, come what might, Jews would not repeat such conduct—but that conduct, in the 1930s, had not been the norm; it had been the sole exception in all of American Jewish history.

The immediate reaction to the Middle East crisis was to give money. Much more money was given by many more people than ever before in history. There were numerous stories from every Jewish community throughout the United States not only of giving on a fantastic scale by people of large means but also of the literal sacrifice of their life's savings by people of modest means. During the little more than two-week period which marked the height of the crisis—between the day when President Gamal Nasser of Egypt closed the Gulf of Aqaba on May 23 and the end of the war on June 10—well over *one hundred million dollars,* the bulk of it in cash, was realized for the Israel Emergency Fund of the United Jewish Appeal. This was a fund-raising effort unprecedented not only in Jewish experience but also in the history of private philanthropy in the United States. Ultimately the UJA drive that year realized the unheard of amount of six hundred million dollars, more than any such appeal in all of American history.

The drive did not begin from the top. On Monday May 29, the national board of the United Jewish Appeal met in special session in New York to launch its nationwide emergency campaign, but by that time—six days after the inauguration of the blockade by Egypt of Israel's southern sea-lane—local campaigns were already under way in dozens of communities which had not waited for anyone to ask them to move. Moreover, it was not only the old-line, late-middle-aged leadership of these communities who were acting in this way. Many people in their thirties and forties who had never participated in organizational Jewish life suddenly emerged to take the lead in giving and in working. The financial contributions of these newer elements were astonishingly large—perhaps because of a desire to make up for past neglect and a wish, or even a need, to be counted in during a moment of manifest danger. If in Israel more reserves showed up in some places than had been ordered to mobilize, American Jewish fund-raising was, in its own way, a comparable phenomenon.

In the last days of May, Israeli consulates and the Hillel directors in the colleges were overwhelmed by hundreds of young people who wanted to go to Israel to take over the civilian jobs of their peers who had been mobilized for the army. By June 5, the day war broke out, some ten thousand such applications had been recorded throughout the country, more than half of them in New York at the offices of the Jewish Agency, the Zionist central body, despite the American ban on travel to the area. A high official of the Jewish Agency told that as he arrived at his office early that morning, a cab drew up and a man jumped out, followed by two younger men. He stopped the agency official and said to him: "I have no money to give but here are my sons. Please send them over immediately." That day this was no isolated incident.

Dr. Arnulf Pins, executive director of the Council on Social Work Education, offered his services to help process the volunteers at the New York office of the Jewish Agency. He had some questions included on the forms they filled out concerning their Jewish educational and organizational background and their involvement in such causes as Zionism, race, and peace. Those who came in May, and who therefore constituted the large majority of the young people who actually did get to Israel before June 5, were Orthodox from yeshivoth, and from the relatively small circle of American Jewish youth whose main interests were Jewish. At least a third of all the ten thousand who ultimately came to volunteer had had a substantial Jewish education and a continuing Jewish concern. In their answers to the political questions, another third showed that they had spent their young adult years worrying about race and Vietnam, and that they now lacked any organizational Jewish ties. Yet even this group had had some Jewish education in childhood or even into the teens. What seemed to be happening to them was that a dormant loyalty had suddenly been stirred, and that it had become at that moment an overriding passion.

The Six-Day War thus united the Jews of America but it also made them somewhat lonelier and even angrier. Most American opinion was enthralled by Israel's victory, but the opponents of the war in Vietnam were divided, and so were the churches and the blacks.

Among Jews, the question of Vietnam was instantly swept aside. But there were immediate jibes at the Vietnam doves now transformed into Middle East hawks. No one had the time or the inclination to produce a theoretical case which would harmonize the two positions. American Jews and some of their friends acted instinctively in the face of a threat to the survival of Israel. Their concern for the life of the beseiged Jewish state was not to be compromised by any embarrassment that might come to them out of any other views on other matters, even one so serious as the war in Vietnam.

Within a very few days, however, a rationale began to be developed. The pro-Israel Vietnam doves argued that American support of the government of South Vietnam represented an involvement in a regime which had no popular roots. The last thing that could be said of the State of Israel, by contrast, was that it lacked popular roots. A similar contrast was drawn between American diplomatic commitments in the two cases: they had always been less than perfectly clear in Vietnam, whereas no one could possibly deny that to support the integrity of Israel had been a solemn American obligation for nineteen years. Why then was it inconsistent to demand that America honor its commitment to a rooted democracy fighting for its life and to withdraw from a dubious venture to prop up an unpopular military clique? This "case" helped persuade even many Jewish radicals, but not all of them. A significant and vocal minority clung to sympathy with the Palestinians as Third World victims of Western colonialism.

The churches were especially troubling to the very Jews who had been most involved in Jewish-Christian dialogue. Despite some vocal opposition among the Orthodox to the broadening of the Jewish-Christian dialogue, the majority view within both religious and secular Jewish organizations had cherished the increasing contact between Jewish and Christian groups. When the crisis broke, Jews found that leading individual figures within the various Christian denominations, such as Reinhold Niebuhr, Alexander Schmemann, and George Higgins, were quick and firm in their public commitment to the cause of Israel, and so were Martin Luther King and John Bennett, the president of Union Theological Seminary. But the formal establishments of both the Protestant and Catholic churches remained largely silent. In the last days of May, as the crisis was building toward war, almost no statements in support of Israel could be elicited from any of these communions. As soon as the war was over, several emergency meetings were arranged between Jewish figures with a large stake in the dialogue and their Christian peers. As individuals (though not as spokesmen for their churches) some of the Christians present had supported Israel's right to exist, but the prevailing Christian sentiments in those tension-filled rooms were directed toward the question of Arab refugees and the status of Jerusalem. Israel was denounced as the aggressor in the conflict, and there was much discomfort in being pressed hard by Jews to think differently.

The Jewish participants in these discussions had not prepared any statements in advance, and yet they were as one in their answers: the existence of Israel was not a negotiable matter for any Jew, and Jews would regard Jewish-Christian relations in America as greatly damaged if the organized Christian community failed to support Israel's right to live. It was made very clear that Christian emphasis on the Arab refugees, no matter how correct the argument might be both morally and politically, would be taken by Jews as an evasion, or worse, if it was not linked to Israel's right of existence. The day had now come when Jews could afford to dispense with goodwill from the churches, if that was the price they might have to pay for their passion for Israel. The Jewish ecumenists did concede that they had been at fault in having failed to make clear to their Christian colleagues in the past that Israel was more important to Jews than the concerns for racial justice and peace that they shared with other Americans. The identification with Israel was their "religion." This connection was the ultimate meaning of contemporary Jewish "togetherness"; this was what set them apart from all other men. And oddly enough, at the same time, the new shining pride in Israel brought American Jews, in one sense, closer to the majority. American Jews were identified with the most successful army in the world. At a time when the United States was bogged down in Vietnam, Israel had again "proved" to the world that Jews were a race of fighting heroes.

The events of 1967 answered some questions that the mainstream of the community had been asking themselves for the several years before: how to define Jewishness in America's open society. In June 1967, the Jews of America were "saved" from having to think about issues of meaning and value that the intellectuals and the ultra-Orthodox had posed. They did not have to face the question that Philip Roth had asked: what is Jewishness to the unbelieving Jew? There was a ready answer: it is glory in Israel.

The spirit of the high drama of June 1967 lasted for months and even years. American Jews thought that they had solved their problems as Americans and Jews. But they had not. They were, in fact, ever more comfortable with their place in the jostle of American society, and ever less secure within themselves.

Conclusion:

The End of Immigrant Memory—
What Can Replace It?

After 1967 the Jews in America were freer, bolder, and more power-ful than any community of Jews had ever been in the Diaspora. And yet, amid the bustle of success, the Jewish community was eroding. Those who had been young in the 1930s still remembered Hitler, and Coughlin, but their children had much less sense of em-battlement as Jews. Some took up causes, such as fighting for the rights of Soviet Jews or rallying to support Israel. Those who took part in the "student struggle for Soviet Jewry," or in the agencies which supported Israel, felt both virtuous and important, but they and their parents knew, if only deep in their hearts, that American Jews would eventually run out of causes. They would have to face the question of meaning. American Jews had solved their problem with the Gentiles, but they did not quite know what to do with themselves.

Jews could be bolder than they ever had before because America was different. There was no longer a stable, self-confident American majority. The oldest American population, which had lost the elec-tion of 1960, could not regain its majority status. Many of the mi-norities were busy emphasizing their angularities: some blacks were taking to wearing dashikis; Orthodox Jews in the colleges were insisting on wearing skullcaps at all times. The young Woody Allen began making film comedy out of the persona of an undersized Jew from Brooklyn who did not know how to behave at dinner in the home of his WASP girlfriend. Though this clash of cultures had been a cliché of the American stage since the beginning of the century, the tone was now different. The wearers of dashikis and of skullcaps were saying that there were no arbiters left in America of what was proper and improper.

America, moreover, was becoming less Western and Judeo-Christian. Large numbers of Asians and Muslims were arriving. The time was coming near when a Buddhist priest and a Muslim imam might be included with ministers, rabbis, and Catholic priests at the most sacral event in America's political life, the inauguration of a president. For the first time in American history, Jews were no longer the only non-Christian minority.

In this untidy America, Jews were a striking and accepted part of the political landscape. In their support of Israel, they were asserting Jewish interests with almost total unconcern as to what the Gentiles, or the government in Washington, might be thinking. In the America of the 1970s, the pro-Israel lobby behaved like the lobbies of big business, or labor, or the farm interest, or the China lobby; each was defending a "special interest."

In 1981, 50 percent of those polled believed that at a moment of confrontation between Israel and the United States, American Jews would side with Israel. Six years later, in answer to the same question, a large majority thought that American Jews would support American policy. These opinions were expressed in the years when all Americans, very nearly nine out of ten (including some of those who thought Jews were more involved in Israel than in America), were willing to vote for a Jew for president of the United States. Obviously, underneath the rhetoric of these seemingly contradictory attitudes, there were two awarenesses: America had become a place in which individuals and communities were affected by conflicting loyalties; Jews were therefore "entitled" to be a one-issue lobby.

In domestic policy, too, Jews behaved like everybody else; they made bargains in their own interest. The most lasting arrangement was with the blacks. Jews were well aware that there was more anti-Semitism among blacks than among whites in America, including greater support for the enemies of Israel, but the organized Jewish community chose to ignore these feelings. In Congress, the Jewish members were consistent and nearly unanimous in voting for social programs; the black caucus was equally consistent and almost equally unanimous in voting for all of the aid packages for Israel. In the election campaigns of 1984, and again in 1988, when Jesse Jackson was a candidate for the Democratic nomination for president, he expressed some public distemper with Jews, and he actively supported the political aspirations of the Palestinians, but he pulled back, very visibly, from questioning the compact that Jews and blacks had made in Congress.

Such enlightened self-interest was basic to the commitment of Jews to the Democratic party. The mainstream remained liberals, at very least, because they feared social disorder. In the 1970s, the circle of writers around *Commentary* preached at American Jews that their interests had changed. They were now one of the richest communities in America; they should be voting their pocketbooks, for lower taxes and for decreased social spending. But the bulk of American Jews did not agree. In every presidential election Jews were securely and sometimes overwhelmingly on the side of the Democrats. In 1968, almost 90 percent of the Jewish vote went to Hubert Humphrey; in the next several elections, Jews voted on the order of two to one against the Republicans. In 1984, when Ronald Reagan defeated Walter Mondale in a landslide, the Jews were the only white community to vote Democratic; in 1988 George Bush received less than 30 percent of the Jewish vote.

But there was also, in this commitment to the welfare state, a reecho of the prophetic commandment to "do justice and love mercy," and to protect the weak, "for you were once slaves in the land of Egypt." Even some Jewish Republicans believed in social welfare. In 1968, in the very midst of the battle between Jewish teachers and blacks over teaching jobs and control of the schools in the Ocean Hill–Brownsville district in Brooklyn, Max Fisher, who was then both president of the United Jewish Appeal and the leading Jewish Republican, insisted that Jews had to continue to support the programs of aid for blacks. "If Jews truly believe that advancing social justice is a Jewish obligation," he said in 1968, "there can be no lingering doubts that helping people in the inner city . . . does represent a genuine Jewish commitment." The pragmatic and materialistic Jewish community of the 1970s could not quite become just another collection of well-to-do Americans with ethnic memories of their own. The social conscience that the Jewish religion taught still lived among them.

But in white America, anti-Semitism was disappearing as an effective force. College students in the 1930s had all known that anti-Semitism barred them from many careers; by the 1970s, this was no longer true. A 1988 survey of the Jewish students at Dartmouth College found not a single respondent who thought that being Jewish made any difference to his or her future. Other studies showed that very few people, less than one in ten, continued to believe that Jews had too much power in America. Other Americans still thought of Jews as Jews, but they were equally likely to think of them as businessmen, physicians, or college roommates.

Even when they admitted to themselves that anti-Semitism was negligible, many Jews kept worrying, deep within themselves, whether the America of the 1970s and 1980s was forever. One could interpret the rise of Jews in America in economic terms: throughout all of their history in America, Jews had leaped forward when the economy was expanding. The "German Jews" had become well-to-do on the frontier. The "Russian Jews" had broken out of poverty after the Second World War, when the United States was booming. In some future economic depression would Jews again be under the kind of attack that they last experienced in the 1930s? No one knew the answer to this question, but few really believed that the 1930s were likely to recur.

The economic boom in America in the 1970s and 1980s was less important for Jews than the fundamental change in the nature of the society. A majority in the Supreme Court had excluded prayer from the public schools and crèches during Christmas from the lawns of public buildings. These decisions reaffirmed that America was not a "Christian country," a point Jews had been arguing since the 1840s when they protested the invocation of the Trinity in a Thanksgiving proclamation by the governor of South Carolina. In the 1970s and 1980s, the "born-again" led a counterattack to permit prayers in the public schools and, in general, to increase the Christian flavor of public life, but Jews remained in the forefront of the forces which resisted this latest attempt to re-Christianize America. They were unwilling to compromise with the fundamentalists even when the prime minister of Israel, Menachem Begin, made them his allies in the cause of Israel.

Jews in America felt they were nearer than ever to helping to make the kind of society that they had last experienced in the third century, in the Roman Empire. Rome had ceased insisting that its culture and state religion must dominate everywhere, and it had not yet itself been dominated by Christianity. Rome's "golden age," however, did not last much more than a century. Will it last longer in America? There is some reason for hope that it will last, for such structures are at this moment the wave of the future. Western Europe is moving toward this third-century Roman model; it is organizing itself as one economic market, and looking toward the possibility of becoming a "United States of Europe." The difference from the past is already apparent among the Jews of Western Europe. Because an increasing number of Muslims from North Africa and Turkey, Buddhists from Indochina, and political refugees from Communism now live permanently in Western Europe, Jews are no longer the only persisting religious and ethnic minority.

America and the West as a whole are still essentially Christian. Some Jews would regret to see the end of the dominant role of Christianity in the West. Christians are supposed to have a special reason for protecting Jews: orthodox Christian theology commands that Jews be present to witness and to be converted at the Second Coming. In the 1970s and 1980s, however, this special relationship was becoming an ever less important concern for Jews. In "foreign policy," Communists and Arabs were more prominent as opponents and as interlocutors than Christians. At home in America, most Jews opposed the entire domestic agenda of activist Christians, including their effort to forbid abortion. American Jews were fighting in the 1970s and 1980s for an objective beyond their old purpose, a neutral public life. Jews wanted a post-Christian American society. It seemed to them to be the logical conclusion to the end of the dominance in American life of those who claimed descent from the overwhelmingly Christian colonial America.

American Jews had thus very nearly achieved their dreams of equality and influence, and they believed, despite some residue of fear, that their future was secure. Moreover, they tried to construct an equally lasting bargain with their own Jewishness. They used the "material" that they knew: they invoked anti-Semitism at a time when it was essentially irrelevant, and they preached and practiced togetherness at a time when Jews were associating more and more with anyone they pleased. By the mid-1980s, it was beginning to be clear that these techniques that were being used to preserve Jewish identity would fail.

In the 1970s, after a generation of avoidance, the Holocaust was reevoked. There were many reasons, but one was the need for the memory of anti-Semitism. The young in the colleges were the most prone to believe that their generation was free of danger, and that they had the opportunity to blend into the American scene. In the many new centers of Jewish studies that were being founded in the 1970s, the Holocaust was the subject that was most taught. In the deepest recesses of their hearts, young Jews were being exhorted to live a contradiction: they should accept, joyously, the liberal America which Jews had helped make, but they should remain afraid. The teaching was that Jews stood, ultimately, alone. This inner, more than half-hidden isolation was their "Jewishness." By 1975, when the interest in the Holocaust was reaching its height, Lucy Dawidowicz published *The War Against the Jews, 1933–1945*. Based on a clear, "Jewish" thesis—"Hitler's idea about the Jews was at the center of his mental world. They shaped his world view and his political ambitions, the matrix of his ideology and the irradicable core of his Nationalist Socialist doctrine"—Dawidowicz depicted a Holocaust that gave grandeur to the rule of the Jew as the persecuted combatant who had to continue the fight.

The Holocaust was a shattering memory. It evoked guilt, compassion, and fear. It said to American Jews, in an essentially optimistic time, that being Jewish is to know that life itself is often about tragedy, suffering, and murderous hatred. Even the new State of Israel, the center of Jewish hope and power, was not merely about glory and triumph; it was endangered by Arab enemies. Jews were called to rally to Israel in the name of the slogan "Never Again." This "army" was united not only in the camaraderie of combat but also in some rituals, such as the Passover seder or the lighting of Hanukkah candles which expressed good feelings about other Jews, past and present. Jewishness in America was thus fashioned, de facto, not as religion but as ethnic community. America's Jews would define themselves by fighting their enemies and clinging to each other.

In the 1980s some Jewish sociologists, led by Calvin Goldscheider, were busy hailing this development. Their basic contention was that American Jewry had "transformed" itself into a form of Jewishness appropriate to America. They insisted this very American Judaism had stabilized: it was being continued, unweakened, by the third and fourth generations. American Jews were not assimilating. On the contrary, some of these sociologists maintained that the rate of intermarriage had leveled off at about thirty percent, and American Jews were observing a few of the festivals—Passover, Hanukkah, and Yom Kippur—as fervently as ever. This generation had even added to its observances a new, unparalleled passion for Israel.

This optimism about continuity was not true. Intermarriage, the single most sensitive indicator of the stability of the Jewish community, was continuing to rise in the 1980s. Even Goldscheider was becoming less positive. In 1987, he conducted (together with a collaborator, Sidney Goldstein), a demographic survey of the Jewish community of Rhode Island. The figures for intermarriage in Rhode Island were 14 percent in the 1960s, rising to 27 percent in the 1970s—and rising again in the 1980s.

> Among the couples married between 1980 and 1987, 38% intermarried. These data do not suggest, as some other studies have, that the rate of intermarriage has plateaued. Indeed, there have been increases in every decade since 1960.

The figures from Rhode Island were part of a pattern. In Boston the overall percentage, for all the marriages including those that were contracted half a century ago, rose steadily from 7 percent in 1965 to 13 percent in 1975 and 18 percent in 1985; in San Francisco in the mid-1980s intermarriage was, overall, 40 percent.

The "transformationists" made much of the fact that younger Jews said that they observed the High Holidays as much as their parents and even their grandparents. But did they, really? As the sociologist Charles Liebman asked: Was there equivalence between the college students who absent themselves entirely on Yom Kippur, and those who drop in on the service on campus between classes? Is a seder on Passover the same when it is observed with all the prescribed rituals as when it is simply an elaborate family dinner? Does the most widely observed of all the holidays, the very minor festival (in the Jewish tradition) of Hanukkah, represent a rebirth of piety, or is it a creation of a Jewish equivalent for Christmas?

In the 1980s, the observance even of the new Jewish *mitzvah*, the commitment to Israel, was becoming more tepid. In 1973, when Israel was attacked on Yom Kippur Day by Egypt, American Jews were less involved than they had been in June 1967. Contributions were just as massive, but there were fewer volunteers among the young. Some American Jews had already begun to question Israel's policies. In 1973, a few hundred American Jews had banded together in an organization that was named Breira ("alternative") to insist that Israel should make peace on the basis of a Palestinian state in the West Bank and Gaza. Breira was effectively "excommunicated"; it was blackballed as an organization by every coordinating Jewish body which it tried to join. Nonetheless, for the first time since the euphoria of June 1967, the government of Israel was under attack on the most sensitive of all issues, its policy toward the Palestinians.

In June 1977, when Menachem Begin took office as prime minister, he insisted that he had been elected to enact the ideology of his Likud party that the land of Israel, west of the Jordan River, was indivisible. But the mainstream of the American Jewish community wanted to believe that Begin was really a hard bargainer, a pragmatic politician in the American mold, who was announcing these ideological propositions in order to negotiate from strength. When Israel went to war in Lebanon in 1982, the American Jewish majority insisted that Israel's move was really an incursion to clean out terrorists from southern Lebanon; any criticism of Israel's actions or motives was misrepresentation by the media. But the war in Lebanon was the first in all of Israel's history that did not evoke massive donations from American Jews. They seemed to have been unhappy, at least subconsciously, in this attempt to end by war any need to negotiate with the Palestinians.

This increasing disaffection was evidence of a deeper process that had been at work for a long time. Near the very beginning of the State of Israel, as early as 1949, several observers had predicted that Israeli and American Jews would inevitably move apart. The cause would not be some definable quarrel, such as Israel's demand upon the Diaspora for manpower to come to settle, or some disaffection in America from specific policies, domestic or foreign, in Israel. Rather, Israelis and American Jews were fashioning two different cultures. The life of a minority in a democracy would be radically different in another generation from the life of the majority in its own, Hebrew-speaking, Jewish state.

Forty years later, Steven M. Cohen, a sociologist who is himself part of this next generation of American Jews, concluded that this had indeed already happened:

> Policymakers in American Jewish life and Israel need to confront the challenge to Israel-Diaspora relations posed by long-standing processes: the fact that Israeli and American Jewry have been parting company politically, culturally and religiously, . . . I would suggest that educators place more emphasis on how Israelis differ from their American Jewish counterparts, and how the possibilities for Jewish living in Israel are really very different from those in the Diaspora. . . .

And yet there are statistics which say that the majority of American Jews, at least nine out of ten, are still as devoted to Israel as they used to be. Indeed, they are—but ever less intensely than in earlier years. The situation is essentially parallel to the commitment of the third and fourth generations to a Passover seder or to fasting on Yom Kippur. Some attention is paid to these observances, but the commitments are impressionistic. The love of Judaism, and of Israel, cannot rest for the future on such unsafe ground. But, the Jewish experience in America could not, so far, have produced a more secure kind of Jewishness. Like almost all the other migrants who came to the United States throughout the centuries, Jews arrived in America as individuals and not as communities. There was no Jewish equivalent of a "Mayflower Compact" until after the Second World War, when organized groups of Orthodox Jews replanted themselves in the United States. American Jewish history is thus the story of Jewish individuals who banded together to form communities, to express their memories, or serve their immediate needs. The ancestors of American Jews did not come to the United States to create a base for a rebirth of their religion or to become the other front for Israel. They came to succeed in America. Their Jewish commitments, including their involvements with other Jews, were ultimately bounded by this vision of themselves. The problem was that Jews kept trying to convince themselves that they had come to America for some good higher than their own success and they kept wanting to believe that they were united by something stronger than fear and memory.

Disillusionment was growing in the 1980s, and anger at the shallowness of the seemingly busy life of the Jewish community. Ethnic tasks and memories, some warm and some angry, could not stop the erosion of Jewishness even at a time when Jews had become powerful and accepted. Ethnic identity is, by its very nature, a free association. It has recurrently become a mix of sentiment and surface decoration. When Armenians move out of their neighborhood in Fresno, California, or Jews leave Borough Park in Brooklyn, or when the young of all the ethnic groups go to college with each other, most associate with people who are not of their own kind. In America, after a few generations, ethnic identities have been either forgotten by individuals or remembered in Saint Patrick's Day parades or Steuben Day observances. Even those who march do not necessarily feel commanded to support the political line of their original homeland. Jewish ethnicity has had a stronger hold than almost any other because Jews had been more alien for centuries, as non-Christians, than any other minority. In fact, the mass of American Jews are only fifty years out of the ghetto, and the form of assimilation has changed. American society no longer forces assimilation into a dominant culture. It is possible in this new age of America to evaporate out of being Jewish without making a decision to be anything else. In fact, the drift of life in contemporary America is toward free association. The older generation of Jews still finds most of its friends among other Jews; the young, so they have told in all the polls of the 1980s, do not. They remain "proud to be Jews" but they are less and less likely to live their lives within the ethnic community.

After nearly four centuries, the momentum of Jewish experience in America is essentially spent. Ethnicity will no doubt last for several more generations, but it is well on the way to becoming memory. But a community cannot survive on what it remembers; it will persist only because of what it affirms and believes.

In the 1970s some American Jews were becoming uncomfortable and even despairing. A few of the young who had participated in the movements of the 1960s were demanding that the organized Jewish community be less pragmatic and more spiritual. Arthur Waskow, who had made his reputation as a leader of the 1960s counterculture, became a kind of rebbe who taught hundreds of followers that such forms as the Passover seder could be made both more immediately political and more mystical. Still, the overwhelming bulk of American Jews were unaffected. Ninety percent of the young continued to receive their Jewish education in some hours of supplementary schooling, essentially as training for bar or bat mitzvah. The Reform movement created almost no day schools. The Conservative group, which did, could not get beyond the number of sixty countrywide; in these schools they were educating less than ten percent of the children of affiliated families. Nonetheless, even in the midst of "business as usual" the question of religion was troubling the mainstream of American Jews. The leaders of the Jewish establishment, those who ran the national organizations and the local fund-raising drives, were busy congratulating themselves that their institutions were the true "synagogue" of American Jews—but they did not quite convince themselves. In 1983 Jonathan Woocher, a sociologist who had praised Jewish activism as the "civil religion" of American Jews, studied the "Jewishness" of these leaders of the establishment. He found one astonishing result: two out of three insisted that the Jews were God's "chosen people." Such an assertion did not belong together with their usual rhetoric about ethnic pluralism. An ethnic group cannot assert "chosenness" without falling into chauvinism or worse. In a democratic society, only a religion dare use this term and only to describe believers who are committed to live spiritual lives. Perhaps a desire to be commanded by God, rather than to keep devising various forms of Jewish togetherness, troubled the people whom Jonathan Woocher interviewed.

Jews who cared about being Jewish knew, if only in their bones, that they had to turn to religion—and most did not know how to begin. They were not heirs to a religious past. Their ancestors who had come to America had brought little learning in Bible and Talmud, and they had imparted less still to their descendants. Mainstream Judaism in America, at its most religious, had emphasized the tangible rituals, the practices, and not the learning that had been accumulated for three millennia. Thus, a community which was uniquely "American"—that is, pragmatic and not intellectual or spiritual, even in religion—knew only that it ought to become "more observant."

The most observant sector, the ultra-Orthodox, who had arrived in recent decades, were an available home for some—but only for a few. Ultra-Orthodoxy was attractive because it posited authority and certainty, but the rationale of that authority could not be accepted by most Jews. The intellectual base of this orthodoxy was unabashed religious fundamentalism. The rebbe of Lubavitch, the most striking leader of the Orthodox revival, had defended the faith by asserting that the world is indeed in its fifty-eighth century since creation, the date given in the Jewish sources. The rebbe insisted that, all of the scientific evidence to the contrary, from dinosaurs to atomic clocks, was planted by God in the universe, in His act of creation, to test men's faith. Most Jews could not accept such fundamentalism. They finally had to ask the inescapable question: can Judaism as religion be renewed? What does Judaism say to modern men and women who come to its texts and to its practices from the outside?

American Jews may be the descendants of not very learned, poor immigrants, but they are Jews, and thus they know that being Jewish is indissolubly connected to moral responsibility and to the inner life of the spirit. Tevye in all his quaintness had not read much Bible, and he misquoted wildly, but it reechoed within him, and the memory of that memory is present among his descendants. They still worry about the poor, and they still think that they are "chosen," perhaps to suffer. The embers of the classic Jewish faith still smolder, but they may be dying among the mainstream of American Jews. The rational evidence is that these Jews will continue, with growing unhappiness, to bet their future as Jews on what they know, their ethnic together-ness. But Jewish experience through the centuries has often been surprising and unpredictable. The need for and the possibility of a spiritual revival are clear. If it does not happen, American Jewish history will soon end, and become a part of American memory as a whole.

When Asser Levy and all the other refugees from Recife arrived in New Amsterdam in 1654, they did not know that the fundamental questions of meaning were then being asked in Amsterdam by Baruch de Spinoza (who contributed that year to the fund for the relief of Levy and all the other stranded Jews). Spinoza insisted that by the light of reason, Jews had only two options, either to assimilate to the majority or to reestablish their national state in the land of their ancestors. But Levy had chosen to come to America, and to remain a Jew. He had fought to join the militia as an equal, but that fight, in all its permutations, is over. Three-and-a-half centuries after the oblique encounter between Levy and Spinoza, the question of faith remains open. It will be answered, if at all, not by politicians and bureaucrats, but by men and women who hear voices—even in America.

Notes on Sources

In both American and American Jewish history, there is no lack of comprehensive bibliographies. The works mentioned here are those that were used directly and that made a specific difference to the arguments that are advanced in the text.

Chapter One: The authoritative work on the early history of Jews in North America, from the beginning of the settlement to the Revolution, was done by Jacob R. Marcus. My account of this period is heavily in his debt, though my interpretations vary some from his. Marcus's most important synthetic work, in three volumes, is *The Colonial American Jew, 1492–1776* (Detroit, 1970). This work supersedes his first attempt at synthesis, *Early American Jewry*, 2 vols. (Philadelphia, 1951, 1953). The early pages of Morris U. Schappes, *A Documentary History of the Jews in the United States, 1654–1875* (New York, 1950), were a useful source. The many volumes of *The Publication of the American Jewish Historical Society* (*PAJHS*), a quarterly which was founded in 1893, are full of detailed information. The following articles were of particular help here: Leon Huehner, "Asser Levy," vol. 8, pp. 9–23; Max J. Kohler, "Jewish Activity in American Colonial Commerce," vol. 10, pp. 47–64; Samuel Oppenheim, "Early History of the Jews in New York," vol. 18, pp. 1–91; Arnold Wiznitzer, "The Exodus from Brazil and Arrival: New Amsterdam of the Jewish Pilgrim Fathers, 1654," vol. 44, pp. 80–97. Another instructive series is the semiannual, *American Jewish Archives*, published by the institution of the same name. J. S. Emmanuel, "New Light on Early American Jewry," vol. 7, pp. 3–64, was particularly useful. The existing overview of the earlier history of the Jews in New Amsterdam, and, later, New York, is in Hyman B. Grinstein, *The Rise of the Jewish Community of New York, 1654–1860* (Philadelphia, 1945). This book was helpful also to Chapters 6–8.

Chapter Two: This study of Puritans and Jews is based on direct reading of many seventeenth-century tracts, some of them to be found only in the British National Library. A technical version of this chapter appeared in *Israel and the Nations: Essays Presented in Honor of Shmuel Ettinger* (Jerusalem, 1987), pp. xxxii–lxvi, under the title, "The New England Puritans and the Jews," with citation of all the sources, both primary and secondary. My views on Puritans and Jews parallel the opinions of Sacvan Bercovitch, *The Puritan Origins of the American Self*, New Haven, Conn., 1975.

Chapter Three: The older Jewish communities which existed in colonial times have all been the subject of numerous books. In addition to Grinstein on New York, see Charles Resnikoff and U. Z. Engelman, *The Jews of Charleston* (Philadelphia, 1950), and Edwin Wolf II and Maxwell Whiteman, *The History of the Jews of Philadelphia: From Colonial Times to the Age of Jackson* (Philadelphia, 1975), and Morris A. Gutstein, *The Story of the Jews of Newport (1658–1908)* (New York, 1936). See also *Letters of the Franks Family 1733–1748*, edited by Leo Hershkowitz and Isidore S. Meyer (Waltham, Mass., 1968). On Ezra Stiles, the early book by George A. Kohut, *Ezra Stiles and the Jews* (New York, 1902), contains all of the relevant diary entries; on Carigal, see Lee M. Friedman, *Rabbi Haim Isaac Carigal* (Boston, 1940). The most recent work on Ezra Stiles was done by Arthur Chiel. See especially "Ezra Stiles and Rabbi Karigal," *Yale Alumni Magazine* (March 1974), pp. 16–19; "Stiles and the Jews: A Study in Ambivalence," in *Jews in New Haven*, vol. 3, edited by Barry E. Herman and Werner S. Hirsch (New Haven, Conn., 1981), pp. 118–34. The standard biography of Stiles is by Edmund S. Morgan, *The Gentle Puritan: A Life of Ezra Stiles, 1727–1795* (Chapel Hill, N.C., 1962). There is no adequate biography of Haym Salomon.

Chapter Four: The single most interesting article, because it contests the myth that all Jews were partisans of the American Revolution, is Cecil Roth, "Some Jewish Loyalists in the War of American Independence," in *PAJHS*, vol. 38, pp. 81–107. Aaron Lopez's biographer is Stanley F. Chyet, *Lopez of Newport: Colonial American Merchant and Prince* (Detroit, 1970). There is much information on Judah Touro in Gutstein's monograph on Newport, mentioned above. There are numerous articles on this period in the *PAJHS*; in other publications, see especially Albert M. Friedenberg: "The Jews of America, 1654–1787, With Special Reference to the Revolution," in *American Jewish Yearbook,* vol. 17, pp. 193–218. David Nassy, before coming to Philadelphia, lived in Surinam and even published a book: see Sigmund Seeligman, "David Nassy of Surinam and His 'Lettre Politico-Theologico-Morale Sur Les Juifs,' " *PAJHS*, vol. 22 pp. 25–38. On the echoes in France of the American Revolution, see Arthur Hertzberg, *The French Enlightenment and the Jews* (New York, 1969). See also the documents in "Miscellaneous Items Relating to Jews in Wars of United States and Correspondence with Washington," in *PAJHS*, vol. 27 pp. 494–96. As always, the work of Jacob R. Marcus is instructive. See *Memoirs of American Jews: 1775–1865,* vol. 1 (Philadelphia, 1955).

Chapter Five: The prime source for American Jewish history in the period immediately after the Revolution is Joseph L. Blau and Salo W. Baron, editors, *The Jews of the United States, 1790–1840: A Documentary History,* 3 vols. (New York, 1963). See also the following articles: Abraham Lewis, "Correspondence between Washington and Jewish Citizens," in *PAJHS*, vol 3, pp. 87–96; Anita Libman Lebeson, "Hannah Adams and the Jews," *Historia Judaica*, vol. 8, pp. 113–34. The discussion by Raphael Mahler of messianic dreams in early America is in Hebrew, *Zion*, vol. 15, pp. 107–31: "The Jews of America and the Idea of the Return to Zion in the Era of the American Revolution." For some thinking of the Founding Fathers about Jews, see Thomas Paine, *The Age of Reason*, edited by M. D. Conway

(New York, 1924). The other quotations in the text are from *The Complete Writings of Thomas Paine,* edited by Philip S. Foner (New York, 1945). Of Irving Brant's multivolume biography of James Madison, the third volume, *James Madison, Father of the Constitution, 1787–1800* (New York, 1950), was relevant here.

Chapter Six: The "hero" of this chapter is Mordecai Manual Noah, on whom an excellent modern biography has been written: Jonathan D. Sarna, *Jacksonian Jews: The Two Worlds of Mordecai Noah* (New York, 1981). See also Sidney M. Fish, "The Problem of Intermarriage in Early America," in Gratz College *Annual of Jewish Studies,* vol. 4 (1975), pp. 85–95. See the early biography by Leon Huehner, *The Life of Judah Touro (1775–1854)* (Philadelphia, 1946), and the material in Bertram W. Korn, *The Early Jews of New Orleans* (Waltham, Mass., 1969). For Isaac Harby, see Resnikoff on Charleston cited above. Two illuminating articles were by Abraham Peck, "That Other 'Peculiar Institution': Jews and Judaism in the 19th Century South," *Modern Judaism,* vol. 7, pp. 91–114, and Edward Pessen, "The Egalitarian Myth and the American Social Reality: Wealth, Mobility, and Equality in the 'Era of the Common Man,' " *American Historical Review* (1972), pp. 989–1034. Despite some inevitable errors, the genealogies by Malcolm H. Stern are important: *Americans of Jewish Descent: A Compendium of Genealogy* (Cincinnati, 1960); and *First American Jewish Families: 600 Genealogies, 1659–1977* (Cincinnati, 1978).

Chapter Seven: The most recent study of the "German Jews" is by Naomi W. Cohen, *Encounter with Emancipation: The German Jews in the United States, 1830–1914* (Philadelphia, 1984). On Belmont, see C. Irving Katz, *August Belmont: A Political Biography* (New York and London, 1968). On politics, see the early pages of Lawrence H. Fuchs, *The Political Behavior of American Jews* (Westport, Conn., 1956). Of the many articles in various places by Rudolph Glanz, the most important for this chapter is "German Jews in New York City in the 19th Century," *YIVO Annual of Jewish Social Science,* vol. 11 (1956–57), pp. 9–39. See also Barry E. Supple, "A Business Elite: German-Jewish Financiers in Nineteenth Century New York," *Business History Review* (Harvard), vol. 21 (1959), pp. 143–78, and Bertram W. Korn, "Jewish 48'ers in America," *American Jewish Archives,* vol. 2, pp. 3–20.

Chapter Eight: Isaac Mayer Wise has been the subject of several biographies. The most extensive is by James G. Heller, *Isaac M. Wise: His Life, Work and Thought* (New York, 1965); it contains much material but it is a chronicle and not a history. There are also biographies by Israel Knox, *Rabbi in America: The Story of Isaac M. Wise* (Boston, 1957); and an early one by Max B. May, *Isaac Mayer Wise: The Founder of American Judaism, A Biography* (New York, 1916). Wise's orthodox opponent-to-be, Isaac Leeser, published some of his early sermons under the title *Discourses, Argumentative and Devotional, on the Subject of the Jewish Religion* (Philadelphia, 1841). See also *Selected Writings of Isaac Mayer Wise*, edited by David Philipson and Louis Grossman (New York, 1901); Guido Kisch, "A History of the Isaac M. Wise Temple of Cincinnati," *Historia Judaica*, vol. 7, pp. 205–7; and Bertram W. Korn, *Jews and Negro Slavery in the Old South, 1789–1865* (Elkins Park, Pa., 1961). The monographs most useful to this chapter, and the next, were Leon Jick *The Americanization of the Synagogue, 1820–1870* (Hanover, N.H., 1976); Betram W. Korn, *American Jewry and the Civil War* (Philadelphia, 1951); and Jeanette Baron and Salo W. Baron, "Palestinian Messengers in America, 1849–79, a Record of Four Journeys," *Jewish Social Studies*, vol. 5, pp. 115–62, 225–92.

Chapter Nine: On Reform Judaism in general, the two standard works in English are David Philipson, *The Reform Movement in Judaism* (New York, 1967), and W. Gunther Plaut, *The Growth of Reform Judaism* (New York, 1965). Three biographies were helpful: R. L. Duffus, *Lillian Wald, Neighbor and Crusader* (New York, 1938); Benny Kraut, *From Reform Judaism to Ethical Culture: The Religious Evolution of Felix Adler* (Cincinnati, 1979); and Eli N. Evans, *Judah P. Benjamin: The Jewish Confederate* (London, 1988). The most recent overview is in Marc Lee Raphael, *Profiles in America Judaism: The Reform, Conservative, Orthodox and Reconstructionist Traditions in Historical Perspective* (San Francisco, 1984).

Chapter Ten: The central argument of this chapter, that the mass emigration from Eastern Europe represented the poor, exists in far greater detail from literary and rabbinic sources, with substantial reference to statistics for the period, in a paper that I presented at The Eighth World Congress of Jewish Studies, Jerusalem, 1981. It was published in the *Proceedings of the History Section* (Jerusalem, 1984), under the title *"Treifene Medine*, Learned Opposition to Emigration to the United States." In addition to the sources cited in that article, see also H. E. Jacob, *The World of Emma Lazarus* (New York, 1949), and Mary Antin, *The Promised Land* (Princeton, 1969). On immigration as a whole, see especially John Higham, *Send These to Me: Jews and Other Immigrants in Urban America*, Revised Edition (Baltimore, 1975), and Oscar Handlin's first book on the subject, *Boston's Immigrants* (Cambridge, Mass., 1959). On nativism, see Higham, *Strangers in the Land* (New York, 1973). On the debate about the nature of immigration, see John R. Commons, *Races and Immigrants in America* (New York, 1907) and Roy Garis, *Immigration Restriction* (New York, 1927).

Chapter Eleven: The battle against limiting immigration waged by American Jews is best described in an unpublished doctoral dissertation done at the University of Wisconsin, 1969: Sheldon Morris Neuringer, "American Jewry and United States Immigration Policy, 1881–1953." The history of the American Jewish Committee was written by Naomi Cohen, *Not Free to Desist* (Philadelphia, 1972). See also John Garraty, *Henry Cabot Lodge* (New York, 1953), and a prime source, Henry Adams, *The Education of Henry Adams* (Boston, 1918). See also Louis Harap, *The Image of the Jew in American Literature: From Early Republic to Mass Immigration* (Philadelphia, 1974). Another prime source is *The Voice of America on Kishineff,* edited by Cyrus Adler (Philadelphia, 1904).

Chapter Twelve: The literature on the Jewish "Lower East Side" is vast. The most famous contemporary account is by Irving Howe, *World of Our Fathers* (New York, 1976). A somewhat earlier book, less well-known, covers the same ground in an interesting way: Ronald Sanders, *The Downtown Jews: Portrait of an Immigrant Generation* (New York, 1970). See also *The Early Jewish Labor Movement in the United States,* edited by Elias Tcherikower (New York, 1961); Jeffrey S. Gurock, *When Harlem Was Jewish, 1870–1930* (New York, 1979); Stephan F. Brumberg, *Going to America, Going to School: The Jewish Immigrant Public School Encounter in Turn-of-the Century New York City* (New York, 1986); Neal Gabler, *An Empire of Their Own: How the Jews Invented Hollywood* (New York, 1988); and Sherry Gorelick, *City College and the Jewish Poor* (New Brunswick, N.J., 1981). On crime, see Edward J. Bristow, *Prostitution and Prejudice: The Jewish Fight Against White Slavery, 1880–1939* (Oxford, 1982); and Jenna W. Joselit, *Our Gang: Jewish Crime and the New York Jewish Community, 1900–1940* (Bloomington, Ind., 1983). On the family, see Reena Sigman Friedman, "Send Me My Husband Who Is In New York City: Husband Desertion in the American Jewish Immigrant Community, 1900–1926," *Jewish Social Studies*, vol. 44, pp. 1–18.

Chapter Thirteen: All of the major actors in the dramas described in this chapter have been the subject of biographies. See: Cyrus Adler, *Jacob H. Schiff: His Life and Letters* (New York, 1922); Alpheus Thomas Mason, *Brandeis: A Free Man's Life* (New York, 1946); Allon Gal, *Brandeis of Boston* (Cambridge, Mass., 1980); Philippa Strum, *Louis D. Brandeis: Justice for the People* (Cambridge, Mass., 1984); and Norman Bentwich, *For Zion's Sake: A Biography of Judah L. Magnes* (Philadelphia, 1954). Magnes is the "hero" of the account by Arthur A. Goren, *New York Jews and the Quest for Community: The Kehillah Experiment, 1908–1922* (Philadelphia, 1970). See also the two volumes on *Cyrus Adler: Selected Letters,* edited by Ira Robinson (Philadelphia, 1985); and Morton Rosenstock, *Louis Marshall: Defender of Jewish Rights* (Detroit, 1965).

Chapter Fourteen: The discussion on the limitation of immigration in 1924 owes much to Neuringer's unpublished dissertation, mentioned above, and to the statement by Dr. Harry H. Laughlin, *Hearings before the Committee on Immigration and Naturalization, House of Representatives, March 8, 1924* (Washington, 1924). For the texture of Jewish life, see especially Deborah Dash Moore, *At Home in America: Second Generation New York Jews* (New York, 1981), and Gurock's book, mentioned above. On conflicts among the ethnic groups see Ronald H. Bayor, *Neighbors in Conflict: The Irish, Germans, Jews, and Italians of New York City, 1929–1941* (Baltimore, 1978). On the Jewish left, see especially Nathan Glazer, *The Social Basis of American Communism* (New York, 1962). On academic anti-Semitism, see the two most recent discussions, Tamar Buchsbaum, "A Note on Antisemitism in Admissions at Dartmouth," *Jewish Social Studies*, vol. 49, pp. 79–84, and Dan A. Oren, *Joining the Club: A History of Jews and Yale* (New Haven, Conn., 1985).

Chapter Fifteen: In addition to the direct citations in the text, see also *The East European Jewish Experience in America*, edited by Uri D. Herschler (Cincinnati, 1983), and *Images and Ideas in American Culture: The Functions of Criticism—Essays in Memory of Philip Rahv*, edited by Arthur Edelstein (Hanover, N.H., 1979), especially the contribution by Alan Lelchuk. Irving Howe, Sidney Hook, and Arthur Miller have written autobiographies: Irving Howe, *A Margin of Hope: An Intellectual Autobiography* (New York, 1982); Sidney Hook, *Out of Step: An Unquiet Life in the Twentieth Century* (New York, 1987); Arthur Miller, *Timebends: A Life* (New York, 1987). There is a biography of Clifford Odets, Margaret Brenman-Gibson, *Clifford Odets, American Playwright: The Years from 1906 to 1940* (New York, 1981). On religion, see the book by Marc Lee Raphael mentioned above; Moshe Davis, *The Emergence of Conservative Judaism* (Philadelphia, 1963), and Nathan Glazer, *American Judaism* (Chicago, 1957).

Chapter Sixteen: On Roosevelt and the Jews, the literature keeps growing: Henry L. Feingold, *The Politics of Rescue: The Roosevelt Administration and the Holocaust, 1938–1945* (New York, 1970); David Wyman, *The Abandonment of the Jews* (New York, 1984); Deborah E. Lipstadt, *Beyond Belief: The American Press and the Coming of the Holocaust, 1933–1945* (New York, 1986); Richard Breitman and Alan M. Kraut, *American Refugee Policy and European Jewry, 1933–1945* (Bloomington, Ind., 1987). There was even in 1984 a privately organized American Jewish Commission on the Holocaust which published a collection of studies by various hands: Seymour Maxwell Finger, editor, *American Jewry During the Holocaust* (New York, 1984). For the New Deal and Yiddish writers, see the publication by the Works Progress Administration in the City of New York in Yiddish of the Jewish Immigrants Association of New York (1938) and Jewish Families and Family Circles of New York (1939). On anti-Semitism, see the study *Jews in America*, published by *Fortune* in 1936, and Charles Herbert Stember, "The Recent History of Public Attitudes" in his *Jews in the Mind of America* (New York, 1966).

Chapter Seventeen: On Jewish-Christian relations see: Leo Pfeffer, *Creeds in Competition: A Creative Force in American Culture* (New York, 1959), and Arthur Gilbert, *A Jew in Christian America* (New York, 1966). See also Mary T. Hanna, *Catholics and American Politics*

(Cambridge, Mass., 1979). From this chapter forward, the factual account (but not the interpretations) leans heavily on the summaries year by year of public events of significance to Jews that were published in the *American Jewish Yearbook* (*AJYB*). On blacks in this period, the most important single essay was written by John Hope Franklin, "The Transformation of the Negro Intellectual." It is to be found in *Assuring Freedom to the Free: A Century of Emancipation in the U.S.A.,* edited by Arnold M. Rose (Detroit, 1964). See also, William L. Katz, *Eyewitness: The Negro in American History* (New York, 1967). On American culture, see David Riesman, *The Lonely Crowd: A Study of the Changing American Character* (New Haven, Conn., 1950). On the understanding of the changing nature of American society and American nationalism during and after the Second World War, see the article by Philip Gleason, "Pluralism and Assimilation: A Conceptual History," which is chapter 8 of John Edwards, editor, *Linguistic Minorities, Policies and Pluralism* (London, 1984), and his article "Americans All: World War II and the Shaping of American Identity," in *Review of Politics*, vol. 43, pp. 483–518.

Chapter Eighteen: On the question of "arriving," I read in a vast literature, and the books and articles mentioned here are even more selective than in earlier chapters. On interreligious and intergroup sociology, see the following: Gerhard Lenski, *The Religious Factor: A Sociological Study of Religion's Impact on Politics, Economics, and Family Life* (New York, 1963); E. Digby Baltzell, *The Protestant Establishment, Aristocracy and Caste in America* (New York, 1964); Will Herberg, *Protestant Catholic, Jew: An Essay in American Religious Sociology* (New York, 1955), and Nathan Glazer and Daniel Patrick Moynihan, *Beyond the Melting Pot: The Negroes, Puerto Ricans, Jews, Italians, and Irish of New York City* (Cambridge, Mass., 1963). On the Jews, see: Emil Lehman, "National Survey on Synagogue Leadership" (mimeographed) (New York, 1953); Alexander M. Dushkin, and Uriah Z. Engelman, "Jewish Education in the United States" (mimeographed) (New York, 1959); Marshall Sklare and Joseph Greenblum, *Jewish Identity on the Suburban Frontier: A Study of Group Survival in the Open Society* (New York, 1967), and Marshall Sklare, editor, *The Jews: Social Patterns of an American Group* (Glencoe, Ill., 1959). On economic changes, see Simon Kuznets, *Economic Structure of U.S. Jewry: Recent Trends* (Jerusalem, 1972), and Nathan Goldberg,

"Occupational Patterns of American Jews," *Jewish Review* (1945–46), pp. 3–24, 161–85, 262–90. One cannot think about the American Jewish culture of this generation without reference to two books which were "scandalous" when published, Norman Podhoretz's autobiographical *Making It* (New York, 1967), and Philip Roth's novel, *Portnoy's Complaint* (New York, 1969). On majority-minority tensions see Benjamin B. Ringer, *The Edge of Friendliness: A Study of Jewish-Gentile Relations* (New York, 1967). The "mainstream" view that Israel and American Jewry are forever united without any fundamental differences was best expressed by Melvin I. Urofsky, *We Are One! American Jewry and Israel* (New York, 1978); for a more even-handed account, see Peter Grose, *Israel in the Mind of America* (New York, 1983).

Chapter Nineteen: Most of the books mentioned in chapter 20 are relevant to this one. See also, Oscar Handlin, *Fire-Bell in the Night: The Crisis in Civil Rights* (Boston, 1964). My own views, as a participant in the "actions and passions" of the time, were collected in *Being Jewish in America* (New York, 1979).

Chapter Twenty: For the situation of the Jews in the 1960s, in addition to the survey articles in the *American Jewish Yearbook*, see Jack Nusan Porter, editor, *The Sociology of American Jews* (Washington, D.C., 1978). On the ultra-Orthodox, my account is greatly indebted to an article by Charles S. Liebman, "Orthodoxy in American Jewish Life," *AJYB*, vol. 66, pp. 21–97. See also the first book-length accounts by Solomon Poll, *The Hasidic Community of Williamsburg* (Glencoe, Ill., 1962), and George Kranzler, *Williamsburg: A Jewish Community in Transition* (New York, 1981). On black-Jewish relations, see Shlomo Katz, editor, *Negro and Jew: An Encounter in America* (New York 1967); Nat Hentoff, editor, *Black Anti-Semitism and Jewish Racism* (New York, 1969); Max Geltman, *The Confrontation: Black Power, Anti-Semitism and the Myth of Integration* (Englewood Cliffs, N.J., 1970). For the black perspective, see George Breitman, editor, *By Any Means Necessary: Speeches, Interviews, and a Letter by Malcolm X* (New York, 1970), and James Forman, *The Making of Black Revolutionaries* (New York, 1972). On the younger generation of Jewish radicals, see: Percy S. Cohen, *Jewish Radicals and Radical Jews* (London, 1980); James L. Wood, *The Sources of American Student Activism*

(Lexington, Mass., 1974); and Richard G. Braungart, *Family Status, Socialization and Student Politics* (San Diego, 1979). On the reactions to the war in Vietnam see in general Nancy Zaroulis and Gerald Sullivan, *Who Spoke Up? American Protest Against the War in Vietnam 1963–1975* (New York, 1984). Diana Winston, "Viet Nam and the Jews," pp. 189–209, in Jack Nusan Porter's book mentioned above was especially valuable. On the counter-culture within the Jewish community, see Chava Alkon Katz, "Jewish Radical Zionists in the United States, 1968–72," in the *Year Book of the Encyclopedia of Judaica*, 1975–6, pp. 115–33.

Conclusion: On the changes in American society, see, most recently, Robert C. Christopher, *Crashing the Gates: The De-Wasping of America's Power Elite* (New York, 1989). The annual declarations of the National Jewish Community Advisory Relations Council are an instructive barometer of what the Jewish "establishment" is thinking. This is a printed series of pamphlets called *Joint Program Plan*. On the neo-Conservatives, see Peter Steinfels, *The Neo-Conservatives: The Men Who Are Changing America's Politics* (New York, 1979). On the question of the nature of the "third generation," the rate of intermarriage, and the supposed stabilization of American Jewry, see Calvin Goldscheider and Alan S. Zuckerman, *The Transformation of the Jews* (Chicago, 1984); Calvin Goldscheider and Sidney Goldstein, *The Jewish Community of Rhode Island: A Social and Demographic Study, 1987* (Providence, 1988), and Egon Mayer, *Love and Tradition: Marriage Between Jews and Christians* (New York, 1985). The views of these authors were popularized by Charles E. Silberman, *A Certain People: American Jews and Their Lives Today* (New York, 1985); they were reassessed in an unpublished honors thesis in the Department of Religion, Dartmouth College: Jevin Seth Eagle, "Jewish Students at Dartmouth College: A Study of Third and Fourth Generation American Jews" (Hanover, 1988). The frequent mimeographed reports on Jewish opinion about Jews and Israel issued by the research office of the American Jewish Committee are a prime and trustworthy source. On religious stirrings among mainstream American Jews, see Jonathan Woocher, "The Civil Judaism of Communal Leaders," in *AJYB*, vol. 81, pp. 149–69, and the moving autobiography by the late Paul Cowan, *An Orphan in History: Retrieving a Jewish Legacy* (New York, 1983).

Index

INDEX